CW00459586

PUBLICATIONS
OF THE
ARMY RECORDS SOCIETY
VOL. 17

LORD ROBERTS
AND THE
WAR IN SOUTH AFRICA
1899–1902

The Army Records Society was founded in 1984 in order to publish original records describing the development, organisation, administration and activities of the British Army from early times.

Any person wishing to become a member of the Society is requested to apply to the Hon. Secretary, c/o the National Army Museum, Royal Hospital Road, London, SW3 4HT. The annual subscription entitles the member to receive a copy of each volume issued by the Society in that year, and to purchase back volumes at reduced prices. Current subscription details, whether for individuals living within the British Isles, for individuals living overseas, or for institutions, will be furnished on request.

The Council of the Army Records Society wish it to be clearly understood that they are not answerable for opinions or observations that may appear in the Society's publications. For these the responsibility rests entirely with the Editors of the several works.

The Society's website can be found at
www.armyrecordssociety.org.uk

Lord Roberts with his wife, daughter Aileen and son Freddy.
War Museum, Bloemfontein, Photo Collection, No. 11028

LORD ROBERTS
AND THE
WAR IN SOUTH AFRICA
1899–1902

Edited by
ANDRÉ WESSELS

Published by
SUTTON PUBLISHING LIMITED
for the
ARMY RECORDS SOCIETY
2000

First published in the United Kingdom in 2000 by
Sutton Publishing Limited · Phoenix Mill · Thrupp · Stroud
Gloucestershire · GL5 2BU

British Library Cataloguing in Publication Data

Lord Roberts and the War in South Africa 1899–1902
Wessels, André
(Department of History, University of the Orange Free State)

ISBN 0-7509-2555-8

Typeset in Ehrhardt.
Typesetting and origination by
Sutton Publishing Limited.
Printed and bound in England by
J.H. Haynes & Co. Ltd, Sparkford.

In memory of Theunie Steyn (1920–1998)
Allied soldier in World War II,
South African Appeal Court Judge,
grandson of M.T. Steyn
(the last president of the Orange Free State republic)

Contents

Editorial Acknowledgements

The vast bulk of the extant papers of Lord Roberts is in the National Army Museum, London. I gratefully acknowledge the kind assistance, generously given, of Dr Peter Boyden and the staff of the Reading Room of the Museum. I am grateful also to the Museum for providing access to and permission to publish documents in its possession.

I also gratefully acknowledge the generosity of the following in enabling me to consult and, where requested, to publish documents in their possession and/or copyright: Ms Pamela Clark of the Royal Archives, Windsor; Ms Kate O'Brien, Archivist of King's College, London, Ms Patricia J. Methven, as well as the other staff members of the Liddell Hart Centre for Military Archives; Mr Robert Smith of the British Library's Manuscript Room, as well as the staff members of the old Manuscript Reading Room in the British Museum building; Ms Jane Hogan of the University of Durham's Archives and Special Collections; Ms Natalie Adams of the University of Cambridge's Churchill Archives Centre; Ms Zoe Lubowiecka of the Hove Reference Library; Ms Helen Wakely of the Lambeth Palace Library, London; Brigadier K.A. Timbers of the Royal Artillery Historical Trust, Woolwich; the Bodleian Library, Oxford; the Killie Campbell Africana Library, Durban, and Ms Diana Madden of the Brenthurst Library, Johannesburg.

Documents in the Royal Archives are reproduced here by the gracious permission of Her Majesty The Queen. Material in Crown copyright is reproduced with the permission of the Controller of Her Majesty's Stationery Office. Other material is reproduced with the kind permission of the Marquis of Lansdowne and the trustees of the Bowood manuscripts; His Grace the Archbishop of Canterbury and the trustees of the Lambeth Palace Library; the Warden and Fellows of New College, Oxford; the Rt Hon the Earl Kitchener; and the trustees of the Liddell Hart Centre for Military Archives. If anyone's copyright has been inadvertently infringed, I hope my sincere apologies will be accepted.

Among other individuals – and I am sorry if I have not named them all – I am indebted to Mr John Carr and Mr James Guthrie, both of the Public Record Office, Kew; Dr Iain Smith, Department of History, University of Warwick; Colonel Frik Jacobs, Director of the War Museum, Bloemfontein; Professor M.C.E. van Schoor; Mr Johan Loock;

Dr Arnold van Dyk; Professor Kay de Villiers, and to my parents and sister for their encouragement. I owe a particular debt to Professor Ian Beckett, of the Department of History at the University of Luton and Honorary Secretary of the Society, who first raised this project with me, and for his wise guidance and all his help so generously given.

I would also like to mention the kind assistance given to me by staff members of the following archives, libraries, organisations and institutions: the Public Record Office, Kew; National Archives of South Africa, Pretoria; Free State Archives Repository, Bloemfontein; the Library of the University of the Orange Free State, Bloemfontein; the Bodleian Library and the Rhodes House Library, Oxford; Imperial War Museum, London; House of Lords Record Office, London; Lambeth Palace Library, London; Gloucestershire Record Office; Devon Record Office, Exeter; Scottish Record Office (both at the General Register House and at the West Register House), Edinburgh; Churchill Archives Centre, University of Cambridge; Royal Artillery Institution Library, Woolwich, and the Royal Commission on Historical Manuscripts, London.

Marizanne Janse van Vuuren did most of the basic transcriptions of the sometimes hardly legible documents. Without her assistance, this publication would not have been completed on schedule. The following assistants in the Department of History also assisted in one way or other: Lizette Oosthuizen, Albert Schoeman, Abrahm Sekete, Sebastiaan Biehl, Jan-Ad Stemmet and Roelof Geyser.

Mrs Christine van Zyl did an enormous amount of the typing. Typing was also done by Mrs Ansie Olivier, Mrs Miemie de Vries and Mrs Liska Engelbrecht. Eventually the final draft of the manuscript was produced with great skill and patience by Mrs Ansie Olivier.

I received a research grant from my university's Central Research Fund for which I am grateful. **Furthermore: The financial assistance of the Centre for Research Development (Human Sciences Research Council, South Africa) towards this research is hereby acknowledged. Opinions expressed and conclusions arrived at are those of the author and are not necessarily to be attributed to the Centre for Research Development.**

André Wessels
Department of History, University of the Orange Free State
Bloemfontein
Republic of South Africa
11 October 1999

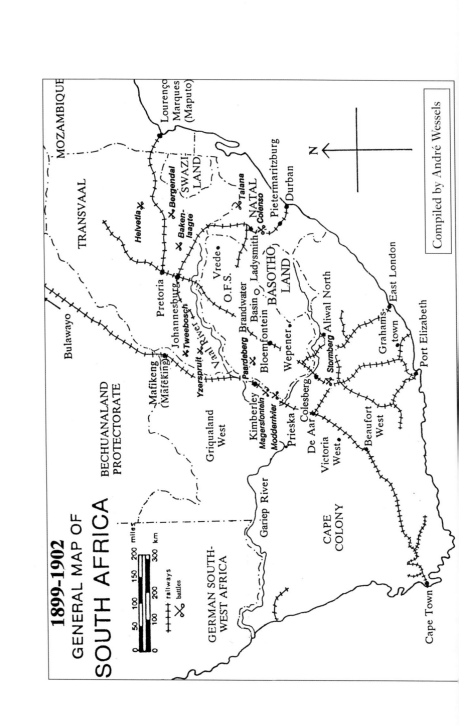

1899-1902
GENERAL MAP OF
SOUTH AFRICA

0 50 100 150 200 miles
0 100 200 300 km

┼┼┼┼ railways
✕ battles

MOZAMBIQUE

Lourenço
Marques
(Maputo)

TRANSVAAL

SWAZI-
LAND

Helvetia ✕
✕ *Bergendal*
✕ *Baken-*
laagte

✕ *Talana*
NATAL
✕ *Colenso*

Pretoria

Pietermaritzburg

Durban

Bulawayo

Johannesburg
✕ *Tweebosch*
Yzerspruit ✕

Vaal River

Vrede ●

O.F.S.

Basin Ladysmith ●

Brandwater

BASOTHO-
LAND

Mafikeng
(Mafeking)

Paardeberg ✕
✕ Bloemfontein ●

Wepener ●

Aliwal North

East London

N

BECHUANALAND
PROTECTORATE

Kimberley ●
Magersfontein ✕
✕ *Modderrivier*

Prieska

Colesberg ●
De Aar ●

Stormberg ✕

Grahams-
town

Griqualand
West

Victoria
West ●

Beaufort
West

Port Elizabeth

Gariep River

CAPE
COLONY

GERMAN SOUTH-
WEST AFRICA

Cape Town

Compiled by André Wessels

Introduction

In terms of the number of combatants, the Anglo-Boer War of 1899 to 1902 was the biggest war ever fought in Southern Africa. During the course of the war nearly half a million British and colonial soldiers and about 78,000 Boers (including Cape and Natal rebels as well as foreigners) were involved. In addition, at least 100,000 black people and coloureds, perhaps as many as 120,000, served on the side of the British, either in a combatant or non-combatant capacity. At least 10,000 blacks and coloureds were used in a supporting role by the Boers.[1] What was supposed to be a white man's war and a gentlemen's war,[2] soon degenerated into a struggle that affected all the inhabitants of the region – white, black, coloured and Asian – in some way or other and eventually left large areas destroyed, including about 30,000 Boer farm houses, more than 40 Boer towns and villages partially or totally burnt down, and nearly 28,000 Boer and at least 17,000 (probably many more) black civilians dead in British concentration camps.[3] As Iain Smith has correctly pointed out, the war was indeed not one of Britain's so-called colonial 'small wars', but the greatest of the wars which accompanied the scramble for Africa and at the same time the biggest, most expensive and most humiliating war fought by Britain between the end of the Napoleonic Wars (1815) and the outbreak of the First World War (1914).[4]

Measured against world standards, the Anglo-Boer War was not a large war; but its scale does not detract from its importance. Within the South African context, it was a war with far-reaching consequences, an instrument of cultural and social change, and a focal point in history. If all the wars, campaigns and punitive expeditions are taken into account, the Anglo-Boer War was the 226th out of 230 such conflicts in which the British Army was involved during the 64-year reign of Queen Victoria, which lasted from 1837 to 1901. In fact, not a single year of her reign passed without some conflict or other occurring.[5]

Many people on the side of both the British and Boers underestimated the other side and thought that the war would soon be over.[6] However, the Boers invaded the British colonies (Natal and the Cape Colony), albeit not always in force or with great vigour, besieged Mafikeng

(Mafeking), Kimberley and Ladysmith, and by the time General Sir Redvers Buller arrived on 31 October 1899 he deemed the situation to be so serious that he deviated from his original plan (to advance directly with his whole Army Corps into the Orange Free State – OFS) and divided his Army Corps into four parts. The forces under Lord Methuen on the Kimberley front, those under Major-General W.F. Gatacre on the Stormberg front, as well as Buller's own force in Natal, were all defeated in the course of the fateful 'Black Week' in December 1899. This led to Field Marshal Lord Roberts being sent to South Africa to replace Buller as Commander-in-Chief, and in due course he turned the tide in favour of the British.

Frederick (Fred) Sleigh Roberts was born on 30 September 1832 at Cawnpore in India, of Anglo-Irish parentage. His father was General Abraham Roberts (the son of the Rector of Waterford) and his mother was Isabella Bunbury (of Tipperary). Fred was their only son, was a sickly child and lost the sight of his right eye after an attack of brain fever. He was educated at Eton, Sandhurst, and at the East India Company's military college at Addiscombe. He was commissioned into the Bengal Artillery as a Second Lieutenant in December 1851, joined his father as an ADC at Peshawar in 1852 and became DAQMG in 1856. During the Indian Mutiny of 1857 he proved his mettle: he had several narrow escapes and fought gallantly, particularly at Khudaganji, where he captured an enemy standard and saved the life of a private, for which he was awarded the VC. By the time the Mutiny ended, Roberts had become well-known as a very promising young officer.[7]

Roberts took part in the Ambeyla Expedition of 1863, the Abyssinian Expedition of 1867–8 and the Lushai Expedition of 1871–2. On his promotion to full Colonel in January 1876, he became substantive QMG in India, and in 1878 he was promoted to Major-General. His military reputation was established beyond any doubt as a result of his famous forced march of about 500 km (300 miles) with about 10,000 men from Kabul to Kandahar in August–September 1880, at the end of the Second British-Afghan War (1878–80). He relieved the siege of Kandahar and defeated the large Afghan army which had been menacing the town. In the meantime, what is today South Africa had its own share of bloodshed, and more unrest was brewing. On 12 April 1877 Sir Theophilus Shepstone and 25 policemen annexed the Boer republic of the Transvaal without any opposition. That country had been at war with the Bapêdi tribe in 1876. In the Cape Colony, the Ninth Frontier War raged from 1877 to 1878. During the first half of 1879 the Anglo-Zulu War brought an end to the Zulu empire. In December 1880 the Boers in the Transvaal revolted, besieged British garrisons in seven towns, defeated a British force at Bronkhorstspruit (20 December 1880), as well as Major-General George Pomeroy Colley's relief force at Lang's Nek (28 January 1881), Ingogo (also known as the battle at Schuinshoogte, 8 February) and Amajuba (27 February 1881). In the latter clash Colley was killed and the British severely defeated.[8]

Roberts, at that stage on leave in England, was appointed as the new Commander-in-Chief of the British forces in South Africa, but while he was en route to Cape Town the British government decided to opt for a negotiated settlement with the Transvaal Boers. By the time Roberts reached Cape Town on 29 March 1881, peace had been concluded and the Transvaal was set on the road to regaining full autonomy. Frustrated and irritated, Roberts left Cape Town 24 hours later and returned to England. In November 1881 he took up the post of Commander-in-Chief of the Madras Army, was promoted to Lieutenant-General in 1883, and in November 1885 became Commander-in-Chief of all the British forces in India. In 1890 Roberts became a full General. At the end of his term of office he returned to England in April 1893.[9]

By the time Roberts had become a Field Marshal (25 May 1895) and had been appointed Commander-in-Chief in Ireland (October 1895), trouble was once again brewing in the Transvaal (or Zuid-Afrikaansche Republiek, ZAR, i.e. South African Republic). The discovery of rich deposits of gold on the Witwatersrand in 1886 had brought thousands of foreigners (Uitlanders) to the republic, and particularly to Johannesburg, the 'City of Gold'. President Paul Kruger's Transvaal government was averse to giving full political rights to the so-called Uitlanders, fearing that they (the Boers) would in due course be outvoted by the mainly pro-British 'foreigners'. Matters came to a head at the end of 1895 when, as part of a plot conceived by Cape prime minister Cecil John Rhodes, Dr L.S. Jameson invaded the ZAR with about 500 men on 29 December 1895. The planned uprising of Uitlanders on the Witwatersrand did not take place, and Jameson and his raiders were defeated and captured on 2 January 1896.[10]

These events put the ZAR on course for a major confrontation with Great Britain. Fearing future military intervention by the British, the Transvaal government took a number of defensive measures. Four forts were built on the outskirts of their capital, Pretoria, and another one in Johannesburg.[11] Both Boer republics imported a total of 49,810 modern Mauser rifles from Germany, to add to their total of 43,752 Martini-

Henry, 6,150 Guedes, 2,700 Lee-Metford and 100 Krag Jorgenson rifles. On the eve of the war the republican forces also had a total of 83 modern and sixteen old pieces of artillery, as well as 27 machine-guns.[12]

In an effort to avert war, a conference was held in Bloemfontein, the OFS capital, from 31 May to 5 June 1899. However, the British High Commissioner in South Africa, who was also Governor of the Cape Colony, Sir Alfred Milner, and President S.J.P. Kruger of the ZAR could not reach an agreement with regard to the granting of citizenship to the Uitlanders. With the failure of the Bloemfontein Conference, war became almost inevitable. There were, of course, many reasons for the conflict. The Anglo-Boer War should be viewed within the context of renewed European interest in Africa, especially during the last quarter of the nineteenth century, the race to secure colonies, and Britain's colonization of large parts of Africa. By the end of the nineteenth century, the question as to who was indeed in charge in South Africa was being asked with greater urgency. Two Boer republics stood in the way of British supremacy in Southern Africa.[13]

In the light of increasing pressure on the part of the British government, and more particularly the British Minister of Colonies, Joseph Chamberlain, as well as Milner – in conjunction with the fact that an increasing number of British soldiers had disembarked in the Cape and Natal and were being deployed in close proximity to the republican borders – the Transvaal government, after collaborating with President M.T. Steyn of the OFS, issued an ultimatum to the British government at 17.00 on 9 October 1899. They demanded that all British soldiers who had been deployed on the borders of the republics be withdrawn; that the troops who had disembarked since 1 June 1899 in the Cape and Natal were to be withdrawn within a reasonable time, and that soldiers who were still at sea should not be allowed to disembark. If these demands were not met within 48 hours, the ZAR would regard such inaction as a declaration of war.[14]

For obvious reasons Britain rejected the ultimatum, and at 17.00 on Wednesday 11 October 1899, the Anglo-Boer War broke out. Britain was ill-prepared for war. It should be remembered that for many years the British Army was plagued by poor administration, internal strife, an inadequate information system, tension between military and political leaders, financial problems and, therefore, also a shortage of manpower. Furthermore, it should be borne in mind that – although British politicians were indeed guiding their country, in more than one way, towards war – these signs of war had become more pronounced, especially after the failure of the Bloemfontein Conference at the beginning of June 1899. The British underestimated the Boers' abilities, and too little strategic planning was done at too late a stage. The strategy that was eventually worked out had many serious shortcomings. It was accepted that the British Army in South Africa would initially be outnumbered, and that their main objective would be, first of all, to protect the Cape and Natal against Boer incursions. An expeditionary force, consisting of an army corps of approximately 46,000 men would, therefore, be sent to South Africa as soon as possible, and be placed under the command of General Sir Redvers Buller. He would then attack the OFS from the Cape Colony, take Bloemfontein, and then advance towards Pretoria, after which the war – some British commanders claimed – would be something of the past. This improvised strategy eventually backfired heavily on the British.[15]

Like the British, the Boers also went into battle with an improvised strategy. Moreover, this strategy was not implemented decisively from the start of hostilities. The Boers were not aiming to take over British territory, and their strategy was, therefore, exclusively defensive in nature. They would eventually invade British territory, but this would only happen on a limited scale so that strategic defensive positions within the British area could be taken up, whence it was hoped that they would be able to fend off the British offensive forces. In this way – as had happened during the Transvaal War of Independence – they wanted to force the British government back to the negotiating table.

On the eve of the war, Jan Christiaan Smuts, the ZAR's State Attorney, said in a memorandum that if the Boers wanted to force a military decision, they would have to act decisively at the start of the war, while they had superior numbers, by penetrating the British colonies at various places, and on a wide front with small, fast-moving commandos, with the purpose of destroying the infrastructure. In this way, it might have been possible to prevent large numbers of British soldiers from being deployed against the Boers.[16] Smuts' ideas and warnings were to a large extent ignored. On the eve of the war, the Boers' improvised strategy was determined by their desire to safeguard their independence; the influence of the Transvaal War of Independence, 1880–1; religious motivations; the position of the Cape Colony; the size and deployment of the British forces in South Africa, and the expected British strategy. The lack of decisive strategic action on the part of the Boers during the first number of months of the war had a highly negative impact on the Boers' war effort as time progressed. The fact that the Boers' tactics were better than those of the British did not turn out to be an advantage in the end because their tactical successes were not achieved within a sound strategy.

By the end of the nineteenth century, it was theoretically possible for the British Army – if the Indian Army were included – to mobilize more than a million soldiers.[17] However, there were only 235,500 white permanent force members of all ranks, and more than half of these soldiers were stationed in other colonies of the British Empire across the globe. On the eve of the war, only 22,104 of these soldiers were inside or on their way to South Africa: 14,704 were inside, or on their way to Natal, and 7,400 were inside, or on their way to the Cape Colony.[18] Adding the number of local colonial units, for example, the Cape Mounted Riflemen, the British initially had approximately 27,000 men at their disposal in South Africa.[19]

There was simply not an adequate number of permanent force members or trained reservists who could immediately be sent to South Africa. For this reason, the armed forces who were sent to the war zone were hastily mustered.[20]

With only 27,000 soldiers available to them in the initial stages of the war in South Africa, the British were unable to protect the vast borders of 1,600 km (1,000 miles) in extent that they shared with the Boer republics. More than 10,000 men with 30 guns, under command of General Sir George White, were assembled at Ladysmith in Natal because they expected the largest Boer invasion to take place in this province. This garrison had to serve as a protective shield for the rest of Natal.[21] More than 4,000 men with eighteen guns, under the command of Major-General William Penn Symons, were stationed at Glencoe to safeguard the coal-fields in the region and to maintain a presence in Zululand. In the rest of Natal, there was a total of only 2,500 soldiers, mostly local volunteers, who were stationed at strategic keypoints such as Colenso, Acton Homes, Estcourt and Helpmekaar.[22]

In the Cape Colony, a much larger area, with longer borders to protect, there were far fewer soldiers than in Natal. Lieutenant-Colonel R.G. Kekewich was required to defend the strategic and symbolically important diamond city of Kimberley, and with 2,500 men and twelve guns at his disposal, he had to fend off an inevitable Boer offensive, while Colonel R.S.S. Baden-Powell had to defend Mafeking (present-day Mafikeng) with approximately 1,000 volunteers. Although it was unlikely that the Boers would pose a threat to Cape Town, some 1,250 soldiers were stationed in the mother city, while 400, 500 and 600 men were stationed at Orange River Station, Molteno and Noupoort respectively. At De Aar, which was rightly regarded as the most important railway junction to the British in South Africa, approximately 1,400 troops were stationed. In the rest of the vast region of the Cape Colony, a total of 700 men were stationed in various places, while the British deployed approximately 1,450 men in Bechuanaland (the current Botswana) and Rhodesia (the current Zimbabwe), in close proximity of the ZAR.[23]

In terms of a military treaty concluded between the ZAR and the OFS, the supreme commander of the republic in whose interests the war was being conducted would assume the overall command of both republics' military forces in time of military conflict against a common enemy.[24] General Petrus Jacobus (Piet) Joubert, Commandant-General of the ZAR, therefore assumed overall command of Boer forces until after the fall of Bloemfontein (13 March 1900).

When hostilities began, the largest part of the republican military force – approximately 17,500 men – was deployed on the Natal border, under the command of Joubert (ZAR) and Chief Commandant Marthinus Prinsloo (OFS). This military force had to lay siege to the mountain passes into Natal, after which they were to invade the British area so that enemy forces north of Ladysmith could be isolated and destroyed. However, there was no intention of launching a full-scale invasion with a view to taking over the entire colony. In the Western Transvaal, approximately 6,000 Transvaalers assembled under the command of General P.A. Cronjé. They were required to prevent the British force at Mafikeng from invading the ZAR. Cronjé was supported by General F.A. Grobler and 1,700 men who had been assembled on the Northern Transvaal border. In addition, there were 4,800 Free Staters who were assembled at Boshoff and Jacobsdal in the Western Free State under the command of Chief Commandant C.J. Wessels and Commandant J. Prinsloo. They were expected to keep a watchful eye on the British garrisons at Kimberley and Orange River Station. In the Eastern Transvaal, close to the Mozambique and Swaziland borders, between 1,500 and 2,000 burghers were assembled under the command of General S.W. Burger. They were expected to provide protection against possible attacks from the Portuguese and the black regions. In the Eastern OFS, the border to Basotholand was guarded by approximately 1,000 burghers, in case the latter region was used as a springboard for launching attacks against the OFS. On the Southern OFS border, there were initially only 2,500 burghers under the command of Chief Commandant E.R. Grobler (at Donkerhoek), Chief Commandant J.H.

Olivier (at Bethulie) and Commandant J.J. Swanepoel (just north of Aliwal North).[25]

The war that followed would not be over by Christmas 1899, as many British and Boers believed, but would drag on until 23.05 on 31 May 1902; i.e. for a total of 963 days, six hours and five minutes.[26] The war can be divided into four main phases.[27] The first phase involved the Boers' limited offensive (11–30 October 1899). The second phase (also known as the Buller phase) involved the first (unsuccessful) British (counter-) offensive (31 October 1899 – 10 February 1900). The third phase (also known as the Roberts phase) involved the second (relatively successful) British (counter-) offensive (11 February – 29 November 1900). The warfare during these first three main phases was of a semi-conventional nature. The fourth phase was the phase of guerrilla or movement warfare (31 March 1900 – 31 May 1902), a clearly unconventional phase during which the conflict escalated across almost the entire war zone, and ever increasing numbers of white, black and coloured civilians became involved or were affected directly or otherwise by the conflict. Since the guerrilla war had already started on 31 March 1900 (the battle at Sannaspos), the third and fourth phases overlapped to a large extent; indeed, the greater part of the third main phase may be regarded as a transitional phase.

The first two phases of the war were fought almost exclusively on British territory, the third phase partially on British and partially on republican territory, while the last and longest phase of the war was fought throughout much of the war zone. In this publication the emphasis will firstly fall on the third phase, i.e. 1900, when Roberts was Commander-in-Chief in South Africa. As far as Roberts' advance from the Kimberley front is concerned, it is possible to distinguish a further three sub-phases, namely, the advances from the Modder River to Bloemfontein, from Bloemfontein to Pretoria (see Part 1), and from Pretoria to Komatipoort (see Part 2). Roberts' role and views with regard to the war in South Africa during the fourth phase are dealt with in Part 3 of the study.

Sources and Editorial Method

Thousands of documents relating to Roberts' (and Kitchener's) conduct of the war in South Africa are preserved in repositories in the United Kingdom, with a large volume of copies in South Africa. As has been indicated by Brian Robson in the Army Records Society's Publication No. 9 (p. xxiii), the great bulk of Roberts' papers were deposited in the Army Museum's Ogilby Trust in 1955 by General Sir Euan Miller, Roberts' godson and the residuary legatee of Roberts' surviving child, Edwina. They were transferred to the National Army Museum in 1971. The papers had been used by David James for his biography *Lord Roberts* (London, 1954) in which he recorded (on p. xiv) that, by agreement with Edwina, Countess Roberts, he had destroyed those papers that were of no permanent value! According to Brian Robson there is no precise record of what was destroyed, but it would appear that much, and perhaps all, of Roberts' personal correspondence with his wife and family, together with some material of his early life, has thus disappeared. Other papers, including letters of appointment and warrants, were deposited by General Miller in the Museum in 1955.

For the purpose of this study, the Roberts Papers at the National Army Museum were of great importance and 40 of the 111 documents published here come from that invaluable source. The Lansdowne Papers, still unsorted when consulted in 1998, not long after they had been deposited at the British Library, were also of great value. Other collections of particular value for this publication were those kept by the Royal Archives, Windsor (correspondence between Lord Roberts and Queen Victoria) and the Liddell Hart Centre for Military Archives, King's College, London (correspondence between Ian Hamilton and Lord Roberts). The research has indicated that Roberts did not always make copies (or have copies made) of all his letters, and also did not keep all the letters he received.

In the 1950s the South African historian Dr W.J. de Kock copied a vast amount of documents concerning the Anglo-Boer War in British collections. The microfilms and photocopies were deposited in what is today the National Archives of South Africa in Pretoria. However, the

National Army Museum's Roberts Papers, as well as the British Library's Lansdowne Papers, are among the collections not available in South Africa.

It is not clear exactly what percentage of Anglo-Boer War documents have in fact survived. Up to 1939 the official papers in connection with the war were kept in a basement room of the War Office Library, Whitehall, London, together with documents relating to the First World War. Shortly after the outbreak of the Second World War, the military authorities requisitioned this room, and all the documents were removed to wooden huts in a small square at Arnside Street, Walworth, London. On 9 September 1940, during the Blitz, incendiary bombs struck the square, totally destroying the huts. Of more than 1,000 tons of documents, only about 250 tons, much of it damaged by water from fire engines, were saved. It is impossible to say how much Anglo-Boer War material was lost, because the lists were amongst the documents destroyed. More than half the monthly staff diaries which give details of military operations and of the movements of the various columns, could not be traced. Documents collected by the Intelligence Division are apparently also lost, as well as certain documents of Lord Roberts and Lord Kitchener.

If all the surviving documents (for example letters, telegrams, despatches, memoranda, minutes, proclamations) created by Roberts during the war, as well as all the letters that were written to him or in which there are references to him were to be published, they would fill several volumes. The correspondence between Roberts and Kitchener alone consists of nearly 900 letters. It is significant to note that in the surviving Roberts documents there are very few references to the role played by blacks and coloureds, or to the concentration camps.

For a single volume such as this, it has inevitably been necessary to make a most rigorous selection according to a number of criteria, for example, unpublished letters would receive priority; repetition of information must be avoided, and with a few exceptions, only documents written or dictated by Roberts himself, or letters directed to him personally have been included. As far as possible, documents have been included that shed light on Roberts' military strategy; on the nature and extent of his role as Commander-in-Chief in South Africa and the effect this had on the course of the war; on his relationship with Kitchener and his other senior officers; and to what extent Roberts still influenced the course of events after he returned to Britain. The reader will hopefully obtain a first-hand view of Roberts' interpretation of events.

It was decided not to automatically exclude documents merely because they have appeared in print elsewhere, because such documents sometimes fill gaps to ensure a coherent narrative (see for example documents 3 and 51). However, these were kept to a minimum. None of Roberts' despatches, proclamations or hundreds of telegrams were reproduced, but where necessary cross-references to those sources will be found in the notes.

From the outbreak of the Anglo-Boer War at 17.00 on 11 October 1899, Roberts followed the events on both the home and war fronts with particular interest. As he was not involved in the military course of the war from the outset, only a small number of documents from the period 11 October 1899 to 10 January 1900 (when he landed at Cape Town) have been included in the Prologue of the publication. Roberts' correspondence with Lord Lansdowne is of particular importance as far as this period is concerned.

Roberts' term as Commander-in-Chief in South Africa extended from 10 January to 29 November 1900, when he handed over the supreme command to his Chief of Staff, Lord Kitchener. He remained in the country for a little while after that, until he returned to Britain on 11 December 1900, arriving there on 2 January 1901. For the purposes of publication this part of his involvement in the war has been divided into two parts. Part 1 covers the period from his arrival in Cape Town up to and including the capture of Pretoria on 5 June 1900. It therefore also includes Roberts' extensive flank march, the capture of and long wait in Bloemfontein, as well as the march northwards along the railway line and the capture of Johannesburg. Part 2 deals with the events from the capture of Pretoria until shortly before Roberts' arrival back in Britain. As far as the events of 1900 are concerned, and in particular Roberts' experiences, views and interpretation of those events, his correspondence with Lansdowne and Queen Victoria are particularly important; in fact, apart from his weekly letter to Lansdowne and an occasional letter to the Queen, Roberts wrote no other letters while he was Commander-in-Chief in South Africa (see document 71). In the case of Roberts' letters to the Queen, it is particularly significant to note what he conveys (briefly) to her and what he conveniently omits.

Back in Britain Roberts held the post of Commander-in-Chief of the British Army. In this capacity he was still directly involved in the war in South Africa, and his correspondence from January 1901 to May 1902 forms the basis of Part 3. A number of his letters to his successor, Kitchener, are included. Since a separate volume on the role played by

Kitchener during the Anglo–Boer War is being planned, only two of his letters to Roberts are included in this volume.

Lieutenant-General Sir Ian Hamilton returned to South Africa in November 1901 to serve as Kitchener's Chief of Staff, and he corresponded almost weekly with Roberts. Some of his letters to Roberts are included to give the reader an idea of what happened at the front during the decisive last few months of the war. His letters also offer comments on the conduct of Kitchener and other persons in the field, and were an important source of information for Roberts, who was far removed from the war zone. Hamilton was also an important intermediary between Roberts and Kitchener. Hamilton's correspondence with Roberts is more detailed than that between Kitchener and Roberts. During the course of 1901 the correspondence between Roberts and Lansdowne dealt progressively less with the war in South Africa, and it is therefore not of much importance to Part 3.

In the Epilogue the termination of hostilities (31 May 1902) and the end of fighting are described briefly. As this volume deals primarily with the military course of the Anglo–Boer War, not much attention is paid to political questions. For this reason not much of the correspondence with Milner was included. A lack of space obviously also played a role.

The publication is neither a biography of Roberts, nor a day-to-day account of the Anglo–Boer War. The documents that were selected for inclusion will not necessarily provide a connected career narrative or refer to all the battles or events of the war, but will as far as possible illustrate the main issues and events, and perhaps provide signposts for other historians and other interested persons. The publication aims to be a military campaign study on the role played by Roberts with regard to the Anglo–Boer War, illustrated by 111 archival manuscripts, most of them never published before.

All the documents have been reproduced in full, but opening and closing salutations have been omitted. In some cases, a printed version of an original document exists, in which cases the two versions have been compared. Usually the printed version only differs with regard to minor punctuation. Where possible, the texts have been altered to conform with the original manuscripts.

Punctuation, grammar and spelling of the published documents have not been changed, although where a particularly extraordinary phrase or word appears, this has been emphasised by the addition of [sic]. Where a common mis-spelling occurs often, only the first instance thereof is, if deemed necessary, indicated to draw attention to the fault. A wide range of spellings are encountered when studying 'colonial wars'. As far as possible the philologically correct version is used in the introductions and notes, but alternative (and sometimes more familiar) versions are given in parentheses when used for the first time, for example Thukela (Tugela) River and Mafikeng (Mafeking). Where there are no full stops at the end of a sentence, two blank spaces have been left in an effort to enhance the readability of the text.

The following signs have been used in editing the text:

[ ]   indicate comment on the text
< >   indicate additions to the original text
......   indicate that it was not possible to decipher a word in the manuscript
( )   are brackets used by the authors of the original manuscripts.

The source of each document is given at the end of the document. (See also the list of abbreviations.) Within each section or part, documents run (with two exceptions) in strict chronological sequence. Nearly 350 persons are referred to in the 111 documents selected for publication, most of them on more than one occasion. Biographical information on most of them is to be found in the Biographical Notes. The following are the main sources that were used in writing the Biographical Notes: the *Dictionary of South African Biography*, *Dictionary of National Biography*, *Who Was Who*, *Standard Encyclopaedia of Southern Africa*, as well as some of the biographical notes in the Army Records Society's volumes 2, 8 and 9. Short biographical details of those mentioned only in passing, or about persons who either did not play a very important role or about whom not much biographical information could be obtained, are supplied in the Notes. Once again, the above-mentioned sources were used. The Notes also include brief annotations of the main events referred to in the documents, as well as references to sources in which some of the telegrams and other material referred to in the documents have been published.

The Bibliography includes references to the archival collections that were consulted, as well as the secondary sources used in writing the background history (introductions) to the different sections, and in writing the Notes and Biographical Notes, including some of the large number of books and theses written in Afrikaans, Dutch and German in the course of the past century. However, these sources are only a fraction of the total number of publications on the war, estimated at about 2,500 books, 2,000 journal articles, nearly 100 dissertations and theses, and nearly 1,000 smaller publications such as pamphlets.

Abbreviations

Military

AAG	Assistant Adjutant-General
ADC	Aide-de-Camp
AG	Adjutant-General
AQMG	Assistant Quartermaster-General
AG	Adjutant-General
BEF	British Expeditionary Force
CB	Companion of the Order of the Bath
CGS	Chief of the General Staff
C-in-C	Commander-in-Chief
CID	Criminal Investigation Department
CIGS	Chief of the Imperial General Staff
CIV	City [of London] Imperial Volunteers
CMG	Companion of the Order of St Michael and St George
CMP	Cape Mounted Police
CMR	Cape Mounted Riflemen
CO	Commanding Officer
CRA	Commander, Royal Artillery
CRE	Commander, Royal Engineers
DAAG	Deputy Assistant Adjutant-General
DAG	Deputy Adjutant-General
DAQMG	Deputy Assistant Quartermaster-General
DMI	Director of Military Intelligence
DMO	Director of Military Operations
DMT	District Mounted Troops
DSO	Distinguished Service Order
FM	Field Marshal
GCMG	Knight Grand Cross of the Order of St Michael and St George
GOC	General Officer Commanding
GOC-in-C	General Officer Commander-in-Chief
GSO	General Staff Officer
HMG	His (or Her) Majesty's Government

IG	Inspector General
IGS	Imperial General Staff
ILH	Imperial Light Horse
IMR	Imperial Military Railways
IY	Imperial Yeomanry
KCB	Knight Commander of the Order of the Bath
KOS	King's Own Scottish
KRR	King's Royal Rifles
MD	Military District
MI	Mounted Infantry
MS	Military Secretary
NCO(s)	Non-commissioned officer(s)
OC	Officer Commanding
PMO	Principal Medical Officer
POW	Prisoner of War
QMG	Quartermaster-General
RA	Royal Artillery
RAMC	Royal Army Medical Corps
RE	Royal Engineers
RFA	Royal Field Artillery
SAC	South African Constabulary
VC	Victoria Cross

General (official and unofficial abbreviation)

authties	authorities
BFN	Bloemfontein
Br	British
cd	could
Decbr	December
E	East
FO	Foreign Office
Garrn.	Garrison
Gov	Governor
Govnt.	Government
Hd.Qr.	headquarters
JA	Judge Advocate
Janry	January
Jany	January
milry.	military
MP	Member of Parliament

ms	manuscript
OFS	Orange Free State
ORC	Orange River Colony
Proemial	old, little used expression meaning roughly provisional
RC	Roman Catholic
SA	South Africa
sg	signed
sgd	signed
shd	should
S of S	Secretary of State
TV	Transvaal
UK	United Kingdom
W	West
wh	which
wd	would
wld	would
yr	your
Yrs	yours
ys	yours
ZAR	Zuid-Afrikaansche Republiek (i.e. South African/ Transvaal Republic)

Archives, etc.

BL MS Room	British Library Manuscript Room, London
DNB	*Dictionary of National Biography*
DSAB	*Dictionary of South African Biography*
LHCMA	Liddell Hart Centre for Military Archives, King's College, London
NAM	National Army Museum, London
PRO	Public Record Office, Kew
RA	Royal Archives, Windsor
s.a.	*sine anno* No date of publication indicated
SESA	*Standard Encyclopaedia of Southern Africa*
s.l.	*sine loco* No place of publication indicated
TAD	Transvaal Archives Depot, now part of the National Archives of South Africa, Pretoria

Glossary

berg	mountain.
Boer (boer)	literally: farmer; the Dutch-speaking armed burghers of the Transvaal and Orange Free State republics who fought against Britain.
bult	knoll; hill(ock); ridge; rising ground.
burgher	literally: citizen; male (usually of age 16–60 years) in the Transvaal and Orange Free State republics who was eligible for military service.
dorp	town; village.
drif(t)	ford; shallow fordable point in a river.
fontein	spring; literally a fountain.
modder	mud.
kaffir	mode of reference to a black person, now regarded as offensive.
kop(pie)	hill; peak; kopje.
kraal	enclosure for livestock, or cluster of black African huts.
krantz (krans)	overhanging sheer cliff-face or crag, often above a river.
laager (laer)	camp; defensive encampment of parked wagons and/or carts, but also any defensive enclosure, whether of barricades, masonry, etc.
nek	saddle or pass between two hills.
poort	gap or pass through a mountain range; literally: gate.
riet	reed.
spruit	a tributary watercourse feeding a larger stream or river, sometimes dry.
Uitlanders	foreigners; strangers, i.e. those people not of Dutch/Afrikaner origin who came to the Transvaal to seek their fortune on the gold-fields.
veld(t)	open space; open country.
vlei	hollow in which water collects; marsh.
Volksraad	Legislative Assembly of the Transvaal, the Orange Free State, and later also of the Union (1910–1961) and Republic of South Africa; literally: People's Council.

Prologue
11 October 1899 to 10 January 1900
From the Commencement of
Hostilities to Roberts' Arrival in
South Africa
Introduction

Since the Jameson Raid Lord Roberts had entertained hopes of being placed in command in South Africa, should hostilities ensue, but when the Anglo-Boer War broke out on 11 October 1899 it was General Sir Redvers Buller who was sent to South Africa as Commander-in-Chief of the British forces. The Prime Minister, Lord Salisbury, considered Roberts too old for the arduous work in South Africa.[1]

Buller left Southampton for South Africa on board the *Dunottar Castle* on 14 October 1899 and arrived in Cape Town on 31 October. In the course of the first few weeks of war, most military activities occurred on the Natal front, but the first shots were fired at Kraaipan on the Kimberley front (12 October) when a British armoured train was attacked, the locomotive derailed, and (on 13 October) about 35 of the trapped British soldiers surrendered.[2] On 14 October the siege of Mafikeng (Mafeking) started, when General P.A. Cronjé and about 6,000 burghers surrounded Colonel R.S.S. Baden-Powell's garrison of just over 1,000 men.[3]

Cronjé then sent some of his burghers to occupy the towns of Taung, Veertienstrome, Warrenton, and Vryburg, which they succeeded in doing unopposed (16–21 October). In the meantime, the Diamond City, Kimberley, was invested on 15 October with a Boer force of about 5,000 men. The defenders, under Lieutenant-Colonel R.G. Kekewich, numbered about 2,500 men. This second largest city in the Cape Colony, with its 48,000 inhabitants, was of particular strategic significance to the

1

British at that stage. It was linked by rail with all the Cape harbours, was situated on the main railway line to the north, and had the world's richest diamond mines. Moreover, Cecil John Rhodes, mining magnate and former Prime Minister of the Cape Colony, arrived in Kimberley shortly before the war broke out, and refused to leave 'his' city as long as the possibility of war and a siege was imminent. Thus, Kekewich had to defend Rhodes and Kimberley (in that order!). This was an unenviable task because Rhodes tried to influence British strategy from within the besieged city. Boer forces involved in the siege engaged in regular artillery bombardments of the city. Their artillery included a Long Tom, i.e. a 155-mm Creusot gun.[4] The Boer invasion of the North-Western Cape Colony, the siege of the two principal centres and the occupation of a number of towns, led to the outbreak of a rebellion in the area, with several hundred local Dutch (Afrikaans)-speaking inhabitants joining the Boer commandos.[5]

During the first main phase of the war, most military activities occurred on the Natal front. On 14 October, the invading Boer forces took Newcastle. General P.J. Joubert did not want to march on Ladysmith before Major-General W. Penn Symons' forces had been defeated at Dundee. The result was the battle at Talana on 20 October 1899, directly north of Dundee. General Lukas Meyer deployed approximately 1,500 of his burghers in positions on Lennox Hill and Talana Hill so that they could bombard Penn Symons' camp, where 5,000 soldiers and eighteen guns were mustered. Penn Symons led his troops in a frontal attack against the Boer positions, but he was fatally wounded and command was taken over by Major-General J.H. Yule. Gradually, the Boers abandoned their positions. There was great uncertainty about the number of casualties suffered by the two sides in most battles that were waged during the Anglo-Boer War, and in most cases, the approximate casualty figures are nothing more than estimates. At Talana, apparently 51 British soldiers were killed, 203 wounded and 246 captured, compared to the Boers' losses of at least 44 who were killed and 91 who were wounded.[6]

Meanwhile, a Boer force of approximately 800 men, equipped with two guns under the command of General J.H.M. Kock, penetrated British territory up to Elandslaagte Station. When news in this regard reached General Sir George White in Ladysmith, he immediately sent a force of approximately 3,500 men, equipped with eighteen field-guns, under the command of Major-General J.D.P. French, to eliminate the Boer force. The British attack against the Boers was successful, and the

2

latter suffered a devastating defeat. Boer casualties (including several German and Dutch volunteers) amounted to approximately 38 killed, 113 wounded (many of whom were taken prisoner), and 185 unwounded prisoners of war, while the British suffered 50 dead and 213 wounded.[7] In Britain, Lord Roberts followed all these events with great interest [1].

At Dundee, Yule did not have the courage to face another Boer onslaught, and late at night on 22 November, he quietly abandoned the town, retreating to Ladysmith. The next day, the Boers discovered to their surprise that the British had abandoned the town, and they then took control. On 26 October, Yule's entire force arrived safely in Ladysmith.[8]

In the meantime, an OFS force of 1,500 men and one gun, under the command of Combat General A.P. Cronjé, advanced from Bester Station to Rietfontein, approximately 20 km north-east of Ladysmith. White could not tolerate a Boer force so close to his base and on 24 October he personally advanced in that direction with more than 5,000 soldiers and eighteen guns. In the undecided battle that followed, the British lost approximately thirteen men killed and 100 wounded, while the Boers lost approximately eleven men killed and nineteen wounded.[9]

By 28 October, Ladysmith was almost surrounded, with a Boer force of approximately 7,500 men positioned on three sides of the town, equipped with seventeen guns and three pom-poms. White and approximately 14,500 men, who had 50 guns at their disposal, were trapped inside the town. He realized that he had to go into action as soon as possible if he wanted to break the pincer-like hold of the Boers on Ladysmith. Shortly after daybreak on 30 October, 42 British field-guns commenced firing on the Boer positions alongside the Modderspruit front. When the Boers began firing on the town with a Long Tom, great confusion ensued, the British withdrew from Lombardskop, and the Boers moved even closer to the town. Meanwhile, another British section moved northwards with a view to capturing Nicholsonsnek. Close to the latter location, they took up position on the hill Cayingubo, where an OFS force, under the command of Commandant L.P. Steenekamp and Acting Commandant C.R. de Wet, launched a charge against their positions. Most of the British soldiers were forced to surrender. Thus 'Mournful Monday' at Modderspruit (Lombardskop) and Nicholsonsnek, also referred to as the battle of Ladysmith, ended in utter defeat for the British. In total, the British lost approximately 106 men killed, 374 wounded and 1284 captured, compared to sixteen Boers killed and 75 wounded.[10]

Roberts believed that Ladysmith was not a good choice for a principal military station and advance depot and that the choice made in that regard was one of the most far-reaching mistakes of the war.[11] White preferred not to abandon Ladysmith nor to retreat in a westerly direction because he argued that the loss of the town and the munitions that would have to be left there would give the Boers a significant moral victory. Such a defeat would shake the confidence of the inhabitants of Natal and the black areas in the ability of the British to put up resistance, and could lead to the fall of the whole of Natal. Allowing the Boers to lay siege to the town, he hoped to distract the Boers' attention long enough from the rest of Natal, until reinforcements arrived. On 2 November, the siege of Ladysmith therefore commenced officially, but not before French had escaped on the last train to leave the town, to subsequently cause much annoyance to the Boers on the Colesberg front and elsewhere. Boer artillery regularly bombarded the British positions in and around Ladysmith. However, these sporadic attacks were on too small a scale and too unco-ordinated to enable the Boers to capture the town.[12]

With approximately 75 per cent of all British soldiers in Natal trapped in Ladysmith, the rest of the colony was extremely vulnerable. However, as often happened, Joubert hesitated to take forceful action. On 14 November, accompanied by General Louis Botha and 2,100 men and equipped with two guns and a pom-pom, he moved southwards – however, this move actually led to nothing more than an extensive reconnaissance operation. The next day, a heavy battle took place to the north of Frere Station on the main railway line, when a British armoured train that was out on reconnaissance was partially derailed. Four British soldiers were killed, 34 wounded and 70 captured. The latter group included the later well-known British statesman, Winston Churchill, who at that stage was the war correspondent for the *Morning Post*. Only four or five Boers sustained minor wounds.[13]

At this point the Boer force divided into two groups. Approximately 1,000 men, under the command of Assistant General D.J. Joubert, advanced eastwards via Weenen around Estcourt, while Piet Joubert and Botha advanced westwards around Estcourt. When the two forces were rejoined, they took the Brynbella Hill, west of Willow Grange Station and south of Estcourt. They were forced to abandon their positions on the stormy night of 22–23 November by a British force of 5,200 men, who were equipped with fourteen guns under the command of Major-General H.J.T. Hildyard; however, in a counter-attack, the British were forced to retreat. British casualties amounted to at least eleven dead,

60 wounded and eight captured, while on the Boer side, two were killed and two wounded. After these events, Joubert decided to retreat to the Thukela (Tugela) River, where the Boer force arrived on 27 November.[14] By the end of the first main phase of the conflict in Natal, the British found themselves in an unenviable position, but in reality they retained the strategic initiative, while the Boers did not follow up their tactical success.

Until the middle of November 1899, a phoney war situation prevailed on the North-Eastern Cape front. President M.T. Steyn of the OFS gave his assurance to W.P. Schreiner, the Cape Colony's Prime Minister, that the Boers would not invade that colony, provided that the colony was not used as a springboard for attacks against the republics.[15] However well-intentioned this promise was, Steyn's telegram to Schreiner was naïve in a strategic sense, and was to the detriment of the Boers in the long run. The handful of British soldiers in the North-Eastern Cape could certainly not successfully have defended this large area against a full-scale Boer incursion – an event that could have precipitated a large-scale rebellion.

It was only on 13 November 1899 that Boer commandos crossed the Gariep (Orange) River at various places and launched an incursion into the Cape Colony. On the very same day, Aliwal North was taken by Chief Commandant J.H. Olivier, while on the next day, Colesberg was taken by a combined OFS-ZAR force under the command of Chief Commandant E.R. Grobler and General H.J. Schoeman. On 14 November Burgersdorp was also taken, and from 18 to 23 November, the Boers occupied Jamestown, Lady Grey, Venterstad and Barkly East. Three days later, Grobler took Stormberg and disrupted the railway links joining this town to Noupoort and Molteno. The Boers were welcomed with much excitement; however, a full-scale rebellion did not occur. Fewer Cape Colonists rebelled than the Boers had anticipated.[16]

Major-General J.D.P. French's action was of decisive importance in the British handling of the Boer incursion into the North-Eastern Cape. Through continual manoeuvres and mock attacks, French created the impression that he had more soldiers at his disposal than was really the case; moreover, he also created the impression that a major attack would be launched from the North-Eastern Cape against the OFS. His show of force and sporadic attacks deceived the Boers, forcing them to refrain from exploiting the significant strategic opportunity that presented itself.[17]

Of all the fronts, the Northern Transvaal or Bechuanaland-Rhodesian front was quietest in terms of military activity. Lieutenant-Colonel

H.C.O. Plumer was the British commander in the region. He was required to frighten off the Boers through a show of force, and if possible, to launch raids into the Transvaal. General F.A. Grobler, the Boer commander, and his forces were supposed to cross the border into Rhodesia as soon as the war started, and then to advance on Bulawayo, destroying military posts as well as railway lines on their way. However, nothing came of this Boer campaign. Only sporadic clashes occurred in this war sector, for example the one at Rhodesdrif.[18]

Although on the surface, it seemed as if the Boers had achieved much success during the first phase of the conflict, this was strictly speaking not the case. Indeed, they did not follow up their successes, and preferred for the most part to besiege the passive British garrisons instead of launching incursions deeper into the Cape and Natal. For this reason, they allowed the British to consolidate their position and to land and deploy reinforcements in the country. By the beginning of November 1899 Buller had at his disposal an Army Corps of about 46,000 men with 114 guns and 47 machine-guns. By that time the strategic situation in South Africa had changed to the extent that Buller thought it advisable, in the light of new strategic demands, to re-evaluate his original strategy, and if required, to make adjustments. In the light of the apparently precarious position in which the British defenders found themselves in Kimberley, but even more so in the case of those at Ladysmith, Buller decided to deviate from his original plan, which was to advance directly with his forces via the southern OFS to Bloemfontein and Pretoria in the hope that this advance would relieve the pressure on the garrisons that were under siege and lead to the collapse of Boer resistance. Instead, he decided to divide his force into four contingents. As commander Buller would lead the largest part of the force (about 22,000 soldiers) to Natal in an attempt to relieve the siege of Ladysmith. Lord Methuen would command the second-largest force (about 15,000 soldiers) and pursue the goal of breaking through to Kimberley, while smaller forces under the command of French (about 5,000 soldiers) and Major-General W. F. Gatacre (about 4,000 soldiers) were sent to the Colesberg and Stormberg fronts in the North-Eastern Cape respectively with a view to defending the Cape Colony against further Boer incursions. As soon as the objectives on the various fronts had been achieved, Buller intended to revert back to his original strategy.[19]

On the Colesberg front, French succeeded, after his arrival on 20 November 1899, in keeping the Boers in check through mock manoeuvres. The battle activities on this front were limited to a series of skirmishes that were tactically small in scope, yet, seen as a whole, were of significant strategic importance. The Boers were kept so busy that they did not make any attempt to invade the extremely vulnerable Cape Colony, with its strategically important railway infrastructure.[20]

However, the same cannot be said of the Stormberg front. On 18 November 1899 Gatacre arrived in Queenstown to take over command. He was required to halt Boer incursions into the Cape Colony, protect the railway line from East London to the front, arm as many volunteers as possible, and consolidate the British position until Buller – as planned initially – returned to the Cape Colony. Gatacre had a hasty temperament and wanted to drive the Boers from the area as soon as possible. Unlike French on the adjacent front, he did not have the patience to play cat and mouse with the enemy – a personal trait that would soon cost him dearly. Gatacre decided to attack the Boers at Stormberg, 15 km (10 miles) north-west of Molteno, so that he could regain control of the most important railway junction in that area. The British attack force consisted of approximately 3,000 men, who were equipped with sixteen guns and five machine-guns. In the early hours of the morning of 10 December 1899, they clashed with approximately 1,000 Boers who had at least one gun at their disposal. The result was a humiliating defeat for the British – in the battle at least 25 of their soldiers were killed, approximately 100 were wounded and more than 600 were captured. Three or four of their guns were also captured. On the Boer side, at least five men were killed and sixteen wounded. However, the Boers did not follow up their success, and the British were once again allowed to consolidate their position.[21] Gatacre's defeat at Stormberg was the first of three serious setbacks suffered by the British in what became known as 'Black Week', and brought Roberts a step nearer to fulfilling his ideal of commanding the British Army in South Africa.

In the meantime Lord Methuen started his advance from Orange River Station in the direction of Kimberley on 21 November 1899 with about 10,500 men, sixteen guns and ten machine-guns. On 23 November, at Belmont, the British force's route was barred by a Boer force of about 2,000 burghers with two field-guns and a pom-pom under command of Combat General Jacobus Prinsloo. The British launched a frontal attack, and after offering some resistance, the Boers withdrew. On the side of the British about 75 were killed and 250 wounded, while the Boers lost at least fifteen killed, 30 wounded and 36 captured. The next day Methuen resumed his advance.[22]

On 25 November, between Graspan and Enslin, Methuen's line of advance was once again barred by about 2,000 Boers with three field-guns, two pom-poms and two machine-guns, this time under the command of General J.H. de la Rey. Once again the British launched a frontal attack, the Boers initially offered strong resistance, but were eventually dislodged and fell back to fight another day. On this occasion British losses amounted to at least seventeen killed and 143 wounded, and those of the Boers to at least nineteen killed, 40 wounded and 43 POWs. The next clash took place at the confluence of the Modder and Riet Rivers, where about 2,200 burghers (with five or six field-guns and four pom-poms) had taken cover in the trough of the Riet River. Methuen did not reconnoitre the terrain properly and at 08.00 on 28 November the advancing British force came up against heavy fire from the Boer positions, pinning down most of the soldiers. The battle continued throughout the day, but after nightfall the Boers withdrew because they believed that they would not be able to withstand a renewed attack. The British lost about 70 killed and 400 wounded; the Boers, at least sixteen killed and more than 50 wounded.[23]

At the insistence of De la Rey the Boers now dug trenches at the foot of Magersfontein and the adjoining hills. After resting his exhausted force at Modder River Station and receiving reinforcements, Methuen subjected the hills in the vicinity of Magersfontein on 9 and 10 December to heavy artillery fire – the heaviest bombardment since the one at Sebastopol during the Crimean War. However, since the Boers were safely dug into their positions at the foot of these hills, only three were wounded. Against Methuen's superior numbers, which had meanwhile grown to 15,000 men, who were equipped with 33 guns and sixteen machine-guns, a mere 8,200 burghers, equipped with five Krupp field-guns and five pom-poms, were deployed across the vast Boer defensive lines of approximately 7 km (5 miles). Since the British attack of 11 December was aimed primarily against the Boers' left flank, not all the Boers participated in the battle. The British soldiers came under heavy Boer fire from their trenches, and on the afternoon of 12 December, they retreated from the battlefield to their camp on the Modder River. Their casualties amounted to at least 288 dead, 700 wounded and 100 missing in action. On the Boer side, 71 were killed and 184 wounded.[24] This, the second of the so-called 'Black Week' battles, was a comprehensive tactical defeat for the British. However, the Boers again failed to follow up their success. For this reason, they squandered a strategic opportunity and gave the British the time to consolidate their position. While the Boers strengthened their defensive positions at Magersfontein and its surroundings, where even women and children found themselves in the laagers as time passed, the British amassed a large force at the Modder River.

While Methuen was licking his wounds, Buller had amassed an army of more than 21,000 men, 46 guns and eighteen machine-guns at Chieveley, just south of the Thukela River, in preparation for an onslaught against the 3,000 Boers (with four guns and one pom-pom) under General Louis Botha who had taken up position in the hills to the north of the river near Colenso, barring the way to the besieged Ladysmith. In Ireland, far away from the war zone, Roberts wrote a letter to Lansdowne in which he expressed his misgivings about Buller's ability to defeat the Boers [2]. This somewhat arrogant letter most probably played a role in Roberts' appointment soon afterwards to command in South Africa. Roberts was shocked by Britain's lack of preparations for the war [3].

The British attack at Colenso, as was the custom, was preceded by an artillery bombardment; however, not much damage was caused. At 05.30 on 15 December, British forces were deployed for the attack. Poor reconnaissance resulted in the left flank of the attack force coming up against an impenetrable part of the Thukela River, while other sections of the attack force also faltered in the attack. Buller was entirely demoralized when all the bad news was received, and at 10.00 his army was in full retreat. British losses amounted to approximately 150 dead, 750 wounded and 250 missing in action (most of whom were captured) [4]. Ten British guns were also captured. On the other hand, the Boers had lost only seven killed and 30 wounded (of whom one later died), while a burgher had also drowned. Among the British soldiers who were fatally wounded was Lieutenant Freddie Roberts, the only surviving son of Lord Roberts.[25] Roberts was shattered by the death of his son, and he and his wife and daughters received many letters of condolence [5]. Queen Victoria was deeply disturbed by the events of 'Black Week' [11]. Until her death in January 1901 she took a very personal interest in the war, and in her own way tried her best to bolster morale, even amongst the ordinary rank and file [41].

Owing to the failure of the Boers to follow up their victories, Colenso was merely a tactical defeat for the British. Nonetheless, this defeat had a devastating effect on the British Army in South Africa, as well as on the British government and public. If Buller's dividing of the army corps had led to reservations with regard to his position as Commander-in-Chief, then his defeat at Colenso and his telegram to White that pertained to possible surrender were the decisive factors. By considering surrender at Ladysmith, Buller actually shot down his own strategy, and it became clear that he was not competent to deal with the demands of his post.[26] Buller and his force were of course in an untenable position. Whoever went to South Africa first would experience serious problems, because Britain was not prepared for war; there were too few troops, and they and their officers lacked experience. At the end of the nineteenth century British military training was also not very conducive to intelligent initiative, while the Boers, in contrast, were not hampered by traditional military doctrines.

On the basis of the notorious Ladysmith telegram of 16 December 1899, Lord Lansdowne decided immediately to appoint Lord Roberts in Buller's place, and with Balfour's support, he turned to Salisbury for assistance.[27] Roberts, who had already made himself available for the post, was summoned on the same day to London. Roberts had requested Lansdowne on more than one occasion to appoint him as supreme commander in South Africa in case of a war breaking out. Lansdowne informed him that the campaign against the Boers did not justify the presence of a Field Marshal, upon which Roberts declared himself willing to relinquish his rank, and to fight as a General. However, Lansdowne was still reluctant to accede to his request. On 8 December 1899, Roberts once again repeated his request to Lansdowne, pointing out that Buller had never before taken command of a large number of soldiers, and that Britain could not afford to take risks [2]. Lansdowne showed this letter to Lord Salisbury, but the latter regarded Roberts as being too old to take command of the British Army in South Africa. Lansdowne, supported by Arthur Balfour, continued to press for a change of command in South Africa, and the events at Colenso on 15 December strengthened his hand. The British Cabinet decided to support Lansdowne, and Roberts was summond to London. On 17 December, Lansdowne offered Roberts the post on behalf of the British government, and he accepted.[28]

Objections that Roberts was too old for the post were overcome by appointing Lord Kitchener, who was then the Commander-in-Chief of the Egyptian Army, as his Chief of Staff. Roberts accepted Kitchener on the grounds of his reputation. Kitchener was at that stage, notwithstanding his success in the Sudan, only a Major-General. He asked to be given a local rank senior to that of the other officers in South Africa, but this request was not granted. In practice Kitchener was

Roberts' second-in-command rather than his Chief of Staff. The two men had radically different personalities, and Kitchener was reputed to be 'difficult', but they did not clash; as a matter of fact, their abilities complemented each other to a remarkable degree.[29]

Wolseley and Roberts, each with his own 'ring' of officers, were bitter rivals, and the defeat at Colenso evoked internal manoeuvring between the opposing military factions at the War Office. Roberts was appointed without Wolseley's knowledge, and Queen Victoria, who held Buller in high esteem, was also not consulted [6]. Wolseley had turned down attempts to replace Buller, and insisted that Buller was the best Commander-in-Chief. There was a possibility that Wolseley himself might be sent to South Africa as Commander-in-Chief, but the government claimed that they could not do without his services in Britain, and that his health was not satisfactory anyway. Wolseley denied that there was anything the matter with him.[30] Roberts' appointment meant victory to his 'ring' over the Wolseley 'ring'.

On 18 December, Buller was informed that Roberts had been appointed in his place. It was a great humiliation to him; however, he did not resign, and had already decided to make another attempt at relieving the siege of Ladysmith [8]. He could never understand that his telegram to White was the probable cause of his undoing.[31] Since he had been relieved of duties outside Natal, he would henceforth be able to devote all his attention to relieving the siege of Ladysmith – an objective that kept him busy for the ten weeks that followed.

Roberts' appointment as Commander-in-Chief [7] and his departure to South Africa on 23 December 1899 introduced a new chapter in the strategic course of the Anglo-Boer War. Provisionally, Buller would for the time being still act as Commander-in-Chief, but he had to obtain Roberts' permission before he could make any strategic moves. Owing to the Boers' lack of strategic initiative and forcefulness, the British were once again given the opportunity to recover from their errors. Out of the 'Black Week' defeats, a new British strategy was born, which soon led to a strategic turn of the tide in the war.

En route to South Africa, Roberts continually commented on the events at the war front [9]. Even before he arrived in South Africa, it had already become clear that the war also affected race relations. On the Northern Transvaal or Bechuanaland-Rhodesian front, where the second main phase of the war had otherwise not yielded much conflict, the most significant event was the attack launched on 25 November 1899 by a group of Bakgatla warriors under command of their chief, Linchwe –

11

assisted by British soldiers – on the white (Boer) community at Derdepoort. A number of white men were killed and some of the Boer women and children abducted. On 22 December 1899 Boers under Combat General Willem C. Janse van Rensburg launched a retaliatory attack at Sekwanie, in the course of which three Boers and about 150 blacks were killed.[32] When Roberts arrived in South Africa, he would, *inter alia*, have to keep the race relations in the region and the potential of civil war in mind.

1

Lord Roberts to Lord Lansdowne

17 Dover Street, London, W

[Holograph]

22nd October 1899

Private

White's telegram is most satisfactory, and his victory seems very complete. It is to be hoped that our success at Dundee on the 20th [1] and at Elandslaagte yesterday[2] will check the Boers advance, but it is ......, I think that they intend to do all the mischief they can in Natal. We have only dealt with a small number of the Boers as yet, there must be many thousands collected on the Orange Free State border, and in the North and North East of Natal watching for an opportunity to strike a blow, and I wish that White were stronger,[3] and for a time less teathered [?]. To leave Glencoe would, no doubt, have a bad effect in as much as it might put heart into the Boers, but the effect would be infinitely worse if we were forced to abandon it, or if the Boers could by any possibility advance fast enough to threaten Pietermaritzburg. That would be a very serious matter. Perhaps I ought not to offer an opinion, as I am necessarily ignorant of the whole circumstances of the case, but I know you will not mind my telling you privately what I think.

The 2nd Rifle Brigade ought to be very near Durban, and if they were landed there, if only for a time, it would help to strengthen White. Troops in great numbers will soon be arriving at Cape Town, and so far as I know, no more are intended to be sent to Natal.

The Boers ...... what they are about from the telegram Mr ...... has just sent, and their artillery seems to have been well served. I feel confident that White will have plenty to do during the next three weeks or so. I shall look out anxiously for news.

I most sincerely hope that all will go well with Buller and White personally, as well as from a public point of view, but accidents happen, and if either should be incapacitated, I hope you will send me to South Africa. My want of knowledge of the country would be made up by the many good men well acquainted with it, whom I should have to assist me.

This requires no answer.

BL MS Room, Lansdowne Papers L(5)47

2

Lord Roberts to Lord Lansdowne

The Royal Hospital,
Dublin.

[Holograph]

8th December 1899.

Private and confidential

I am much concerned to hear of the very gloomy view which Sir Redvers Buller takes of the situation in South Africa.[4] There is, of course, no disguising the fact that we are engaged in a very serious war – one that may tax our resources to the utmost, and the manner in which the difficulties, inherent to such a war, can be overcome depends almost entirely on the confidence of the commander in being able to bring it to a successful conclusion.

As I have, I think, often remarked to you, it is impossible to gauge a General's qualities until he has been tried, and it is a regrettable fact that not a single commander in South Africa has ever had an independent command in the field. It is the feeling of responsibility which weighs down most men, and it seems clear, unless I am very much mistaken, that this feeling is having its too frequent effect on Buller. He seems to be overwhelmed by the magnitude of the task imposed upon him, and I confess that the tone of some of his telegrams causes me considerable alarm. From the day he landed in Capetown[5] he seemed to take a pessimistic view of our position, and when a Commander allows himself to entertain evil forebodings, the effect is inevitably felt throughout the Army.

I feel the greatest possible hesitation and dislike to expressing my opinion thus plainly, and nothing but the gravity of the situation and the strongest sense of duty would induce me to do it, or to offer – as I now do – to place my services and my experience at the disposal of the Government.

The difficulty of making this offer is greatly increased by the fact that, if it is accepted, I must necessarily be placed in supreme command, and to those who do not know me I may lay myself open to misconception. But the country cannot afford to run any avoidable risk of failure. A serious reverse in South Africa would endanger the Empire. I might not be able to avert it, but experience of command in war ought to help to this end. Already there are signs of the rebellion being on the increase,[6] and, unless this can soon be checked, it will be scarcely possible to prevent its spreading to the surrounding Native States. The Basutos and other tribes are anxiously watching events,[7] and if we are unable at once to relieve Ladysmith, and drive the enemy away from around Kimberley, and then carry on the war vigorously into the enemy's country, we must expect to have infinitely greater difficulties to overcome than we have already experienced.

This letter would never have been written, did I not know I could depend from your knowledge of me, that I should not be misunderstood. It is for your eye alone, unless, after reading it, you think my proposal worthy of consideration, then you are welcome to show it to the Prime Minister,[8] and, if you wish, Mr. Chamberlain.

The responsibility for the successful termination of the war rests with yourself, Mr. Chamberlain, and Lord Salisbury, and, if my proposal is not accepted, I shall feel that the Government have better means than I have of knowing how affairs in South Africa are being conducted, and I shall bow to your decision.

If it be decided to accept the offer of my services, I shall hope, with God's help, to be able to end the war in a satisfactory manner.

I would ask you to do me the favour not to let any one besides those I have named read this letter, and not to mention its contents to any of the penpushers [?] at the War Office, for, impossible as it may seem, I am sorry to say I cannot help feeling they would prefer running very great risks rather than see me in command of a British Army in the field.

I do not think that Buller ought to feel aggrieved at an officer senior to him being employed. The fact that the troops now in South Africa are more than double the number it was intended to make use of when he was appointed, is surely a sufficient reason for placing a Field Marshal in command.

The force now in the field is far the largest that any British commander has ever had under him on service, and more than double what Marlborough had at any one time in Flanders or what Wellington had in the Peninsula or at Waterloo.[9]

BL MS Room, Lansdowne Papers L(5)47

3
Lord Roberts to Lieutenant-General Sir Henry Brackenbury

Dublin, 12th December, 1899.

[Printed letter]

I cannot get our conversation of yesterday out of my head. I was astonished beyond measure to hear of our utter unpreparedness, and it makes me tremble to think of what might happen if France or Russia had any idea of the wretched state we are in as regard stores, munitions of war, &c. How could this have been permitted? Or who is responsible for it? It is indeed fortunate that you have been able to gauge the depth of our shortcomings, and to put them in so clear and comprehensive a manner before the Secretary of State for War. Lord Wolseley is sure to support your recommendations, and Lord Lansdowne will, I hope, put them so forcibly before the Cabinet that there will be no question of your being given the money you have shown is so urgently needed. But, if there is any difficulty or delay, and you think I can help in any way, please let me know. When the safety of the Empire is involved there should be no hesitation or holding back, and I shall be ready to go with you to Lord Lansdowne, or Sir Michael Hicks Beach, or, if necessary, to Lord Salisbury.

The question you have raised will not admit of delay. The money required to enable the present war to be carried on in a satisfactory manner (and it may last much longer than is apparently anticipated) and to place our reserves in a condition to meet far more serious demands than are now being made upon them, must be forthcoming, and at once. On this we must insist, and you may depend upon me to give you any support that may be needed.

South African War, 1899–1900. Vol I. Home and Oversea Correspondence by Field-Marshal Lord Roberts, p. 1.

4
Lord Roberts to Lord Lansdowne

Dublin,

[Typed manuscript][10]

15th December 1899 [16. Dec. 99]

Buller's [C-in-Cs] reverse[11] makes it clear that both our strategy and tactics are at fault. We have had terrible losses without one single success, and unless some radical change is made at once our Army will be frittered away and we shall have to make an ignominous peace. [The longhand ms continues without a new paragraph] [Lord] Methuen cannot apparently force his way to Kimberley. He should, therefore, be ordered to withdraw to the Orange River without delay, otherwise his line of communication will be cut, and as he cannot have any large amount of supplies and ammunition he would have to surrender. Kimberley and Mafeking ought not to have been held after the Orange Free State declared [war] against us; and though their being left to their fate now would be deeply to be regretted it seems unavoidable. Similarly [not in longhand ms] Ladysmith also ought not to have been retained, but as White's force, especially the Artillery and Cavalry portion, could not easily be replaced, it should be relieved; and to do this effectually Warren should be sent round with every available man. Meanwhile Buller [C-in-C] should be ordered to act strictly on the defensive, until sufficiently reinforced, when Ladysmith should be approached by a turning movement. There should be no more direct attacks. All our efforts should be directed to massing troops in Cape Colony, so as to enable us to enter the enemy's country in proper [sufficient] strength. In no other way, in my opinion, can we hope for ultimate success.[12]

BL MS Room, Lansdowne Papers L(5)47

5
Mr St John Brodrick to Lord Roberts

[No address]

[Holograph]

Dec 18. 99

I hardly dare intrude on you at this moment, but I cannot resist sending you one line to say how our hearts are aching for you & L<ad>y Roberts in this terrible loss.[13] I have but one boy, but I can truly say if he were taken from us, I could wish no better for him than to be as yours. Happy is the man who is in such a care.

Some years ago you spoke to me of the S. African command in case of emergency – & it has been my one wish that you should have charge. Even at this moment, it must be some consolation to you to feel that your appointment has stayed panic & enabled the country to look forward with quiet confidence. The Press like the people are unanimous.

You will not I trust answer this.

My wife[14] I need hardly say joins with me.

NAM 7101-23-13-9

6
Sir Arthur Bigge to Lord Lansdowne

[No address]

[Holograph]

Dec. 18. 1899

On my return here last evening I informed the Queen of the decision come to by the Government on the previous afternoon to appoint Lord Roberts Commander in Chief in South Africa with Lord Kitchener Chief of the Staff – Her Majesty was naturally surprised that this important step should have been taken without reference to Her and also that the Commander in Chief[15] had not been consulted as to these appointments.

I endeavoured to explain that owing to pressure of time it had been considered necessary to at once take action upon the decision of the Defence Committee: and that there were, apparently, difficulties in discussing their nominations with Lord Wolseley –

The Queen approves of the appointments but cannot help feeling that Lord Roberts is rather old for this very responsible command and that in any case Lord Wolseley would have been preferable especially as Her Majesty gathered in course of conversation with Lord Wolseley a few days ago that if, unfortunately anything befell Sir Redvers Buller, he would like to go in Supreme Command. I must add that this remark was elicited by Her Majesty having expressed a wish that Lord Wolseley <u>was</u> <u>now</u> out in South Africa –

The Queen has decided to remain here[16] and hopes therefore that she will be kept fully informed upon all matters connected with the war – Her Majesty awaits with anxiety the answers from Sir Redvers Buller to the telegrams sent relative to the relief of Ladysmith and asks that these may be forwarded in cypher unless it is possible to send them at once by special messenger –

BL MS Room, Lansdowne Papers L(5)44

7
Lord Wolseley to Lord Roberts
War Office, London, S.W.

[Typed, signed letter]

22 December, 1899.

Her Majesty The Queen having been graciously pleased to approve of your being appointed Field Marshal Commanding in Chief the Forces in South Africa, I have to desire that you will assume the Command of the said Troops accordingly.

You are vested by Her Majesty's Warrant, addressed to your predecessor, with the usual powers of convening General Courts Martial and with limited powers as to the confirmation of the same, upon which subject I have to desire that in all cases where any person whatever may be tried by a General Court Martial and the Proceedings are reserved for confirmation by Her Majesty, you do not permit the prisoner, excepting in cases of extreme and unforseen emergency, to return to England until the Proceedings shall have been submitted to the Queen, and Her Majesty's Commands communicated to you through the proper channel.

I have to request your particular attention to the Powers granted to you by Her Majesty's Warrant, in order to prevent you from inadvertently falling into error, and by irregular action causing the whole of the Proceedings to be rendered nugatory.

With a view to preventing any misunderstanding relative to the authority of a Governor and an Officer Commanding the Troops in a Colony, and as to the mode of conducting their Military correspondence, I take this opportunity of calling your attention to Paragraphs 22 – 32 of the Queen's Regulations.

NAM 5504–64–60

8
Lord Lansdowne to General Buller
Private

[No address]

[Copy]

22. Dec.1899

Roberts' appointment must I fear have been very distasteful to you. I am sorry we had to take the step but I believe it was inevitable. I won't repeat the arguments in this note, which I am writing merely because I wish to tell you that it gave me pain to do what I knew wd. be disagre<e>able to you at a moment when you were entitled to all my sympathy and support wh. we cd. give.

I notice with pleasure that what we did has in no case been interpreted as a reflection upon you. It has been accepted I think

20

I may say universally as the natural outcome of events which had altered the whole course of the campaign, obliged us to increase our forces immensely, and compelled you to give your whole attention to Natal.

I am glad that you are going to have another try at Ladysmith – Its abandonment would have had a deplorable effect – But I fully realize that the task is one of very great difficulty – Your description of the effect of the heat on the troops is not pleasant to read and explains a great deal.

We were hard at work on mounted infantry, here and in the colonies – I don't know how many we shall get in this country but the enthusiasm among the "young bloods" is something extraordinary and an immense amount of money is flying about.

BL MS Room, Lansdowne Papers L(5)16

9
Lord Roberts to Lord Lansdowne
Near Madeira, 27th Dec: 1899.

[Holograph]
<u>Private and confidential</u>

We reached Gibraltar at 11 o'clock last night, and found Kitchener waiting for us. He had arrived at 3 in the afternoon, the hour at which Mr. Goschen calculated he would be there. Good going, close upon 18 knots an hour for 2000 miles, and only 9 hours over the week from Omdurman to Gibraltar.

Biddolph had deciphered the two telegrams you forwarded to me from Buller, and, before we left Gibraltar, I made over the enclosed reply to Biddulph to be telegraphed to you. At the time I did so, your telegram to me of yesterday had not been deciphered, and I was glad to find when I read it, that the view I had taken as to Methuen not retiring, so long as his line of communication could be protected, was in accordance with that held by the Cabinet, as telegraphed by you to Buller on the 26th, in reply to his message of the 24th instant.[17]

With regard to Buller's proposed extension of the railway to Jacobsdal, and its possible prolongation to Bloemfontein,

Kitchener agrees with me that the construction of a line, even as far as Jacobsdal, would greatly interfere with the traffic of the main line between Capetown and the Modder River, by which all the material, horses, and gangs of workers would have to be transported. It is only a single track of 3' 6" gauge. Moreover, the utility of such a line seems to me very doubtful, I thought it better, therefore, to suggest to Buller that he should consult Girouard before coming to any decision. All our railway strength will doubtless be required for repairing the many breaks that have been already, and are likely to be, made in the several lines leading from the coast to Bloemfontein and Pretoria. Moreover, I cannot believe that the route from the neighbourhood of Methuen's present camp through Jacobsdal, as advocated by Buller, is the one by which Bloemfontein can best be approached. The distance is over 100 miles. After leaving Jacobsdal water is very scarce, no forage is grown, very little fuel is obtainable, and the country is sparsely inhabited. It would take more than a month before the necessary horses for Methuen's force (increased as it would have to be by another division to bring it up to the required strength for an advance into the Orange Free State) could be collected at the starting point; [page damaged; word illegible] the front to be defended would be very extensive, upwards of 300 miles; and – a serious drawback – comparatively few troops would be available for the pacification of the Cape Colony.

I have no doubt in my own mind that we should adhere to the original intention of concentrating South of the Orange River, and working thence by the principal route to Bloemfontein. This has many advantages. In the first place it ought to go far to settle the Cape Colony. It is not much longer (only 20 miles) than the Modder river – Jacobsdal line. The front will be reduced by nearly 100 miles, and until all is ready for an advance, will be covered by a river for its entire length. The country is comparatively easy; water is plentiful; quite a little network of railways exists by which troops and stores can be moved towards the front; and, after the passage of the Orange River has been effected, the main line of railway, running through the Orange Free State will be a great help even if it should have been destroyed in places.

This is the plan I shall carry out, and as soon as I reach Capetown, I will push every available man into the district between "Orange Station" and "Arundel". Under these circumstances you might think it advisable to prevent any contract being entered into for the construction of a railway towards Jacobsdal. There is no harm in the project being talked about, but money need not be wasted on it. –

I telegraphed to you[18] yesterday the names of several officers we want from home, Egypt and India, the majority of the latter place. The transport will require constant and careful supervision, and even the number I have asked for will speedily be absorbed.

Kitchener recognizes the danger of any radical change in our ordnance arrangements during a campaign, but he is very keen to have some galloping Maxim-Nordenfelt guns,[19] provided with the latest Egyptian Army pattern carriages – Each gun to have harness for four horses, and saddles for seven men to ride. These guns have been used in Egypt and found to answer admirably. The ammunition is the same for the Lee-Metford – .303. I am writing to Brackenbury about this, and consulting him about an 18 pr. Maxim-Nordenfelt quickfiring gun.

Should more Infantry be required, on your desire to secure more Militia battalions abroad, Kitchener tells me that Cromer[20] is prepared to let us have the Seaforth and Cameron Highlanders, now at Cairo, provided they are replaced by two Militia battalions.

I am very anxious to hear whether Mr. Balfour's idea of hiring Delagoa Bay for a certain period is likely to be given effect to. The Boers would find themselves in considerable straits if they were cut off entirely from the outer world. Meanwhile would it be possible to have a few detectives at Lo<u>renço Marques to keep us informed of what stores, food, supplies, etc. are landed there?

Should it be found impossible to come to any terms with the Portuguese about hiring the Bay, would it be within the bounds of practical politics for us to land 4000 or 5000 men for the purpose of destroying some of the large bridges and viaducts which exist on the railway just beyond the Portuguese boundary. This would cause the Boers considerable inconveniance, and raise a certain amount of alarm throughout the Transvaal. Having effected their object the troops could be withdrawn. The Natal Force ought to be able to spare men enough for such an operation after Ladysmith has been relieved.

The Captain thinks we may arrive at Capetown on the 11th January.

BL MS Room, Lansdowne Papers L(5)47

10
Lord Roberts to Lord Lansdowne
Private and Confidential

[Holograph]

1109
Near Madeira, 28.12.99

After closing the letter I wrote to you yesterday, it struck me that it might be advisable to send Buller a telegram on the general situation, as a fortnight must elapse before I can get into communication with him again. I enclose a copy of the telegram in order that you may be in possession of my views. Curiously enough I was induced to write the telegram from reading the speech made by the Duke of Wellington, given on page 126. Vol. 1. of Sir Herbert Maxwell's life of that great man![21]

I suppose there is no doubt about there being sufficient money in South Africa for the wants of the army?

BL MS Room, Lansdowne Papers L(5)47

11
Arthur Bigge to Lord Lansdowne

Osborne

[Holograph]

Jany. 10.1900

The Queen is becoming most seriously concerned at the unsatisfactory position of affairs in South Africa tho, as you know,

Her Majesty has always, hitherto maintained a very cheerful and sanguine estimate of the situation.

But the heavy loss of life as compared with the slight advantages gained, the reckless way in which the troops appear to be led into impossible positions, and the almost daily occurring mishaps of a lesser or greater nature, makes Her Majesty seriously question whether we are justified in allowing matters to remain as they are –

As no doubt you are aware that the voice of the Army is beginning to be heard at home, and I fear there is no uncertainty about its declaration of no confidence in Lord Methuen. Her Majesty is unwilling to imply blame to anyone, but she feels that where the lives of hundreds of Her soldiers are concerned, we must as far as is possible guarantee that they shall be properly led –

The Queen understood that after the battle of Magersfontein,[22] the Government had decided to send Sir Charles Warren to conduct the future operations against Kimberley as the Commander in Chief felt that Lord Methuen should not be allowed to retain that responsible command – Apparently however this decision has never been carried into effect.

The Queen grieves at the newspaper reports of the panic that befell the Highland Brigade.[23]

But Her Majesty is inclined to ask before blaming those who boast of a long & glorious tradition whether any other troops in the world would have done otherwise and whether they were not led into a desperate and cruelly unfair situation.

Apart from the serious harm done to the prestige and general morale of the Army the Queen realises the ill effect which these misfortunes will have abroad where alas! the tendency is to exaggerate and almost glory in our difficulties.

The Queen knows how very busy you must be and therefore refrains from asking you to come here: but if there are any points upon which Her Majesty wishes for further information she would be glad to see Mr Wyndham.

Her Majesty is very glad to hear that Lord Roberts has arrived at Capetown.

BL MS Room, Lansdowne Papers L(5)44

Part 1
11 January to 5 June 1900
From Cape Town to Pretoria via Paardeberg and Bloemfontein
Introduction

As early as 1897 Lord Roberts had come to the conclusion that the best method of attack against the Boer republics would be to use the western (i.e. Kimberley) railway line to place the British Army in a position to undertake a flank march on Bloemfontein, the OFS capital. En route to South Africa Roberts and his staff officers had long discussions with regard to the campaign in South Africa. Colonel G.F.R. Henderson, since 1892 Professor of Military Art and History at the Staff College, Camberley, and the author of several well-known publications, was one of Roberts' confidants, and was soon to be appointed by Roberts as his Director of Military Intelligence. Henderson in particular influenced Roberts' strategic planning.[1]

It was nearly twenty years since Roberts had last commanded an army in the field (i.e. during the Second British–Afghan War, 1878–80). Since then the bullet had superseded the bayonet, the invention of smokeless gunpowder had made battles more complex, along with the fact that the range of both guns and rifles had increased enormously. As in Afghanistan, Roberts' first strategic aim was to position his force in such a way that the enemy would have to fight at a disadvantage. But Roberts' first challenge after his arrival in Cape Town on 10 January 1900 was to maintain the existing British positions on all the fronts until the logistical and other preparations for his offensive had been completed [12]. These preparations not only entailed matters of organization such as centralizing the complex transport arrangements (to enable him to march across the OFS without the support of a railway line) and forming more detachments of mounted infantry (although the scarcity of horses hampered those efforts), but also ensuring that his officers understood the lessons learnt from the 'Black Week' and other events. Roberts advocated good scouting, the better use of cover, and flank movements instead of frontal attacks against well-entrenched Boer positions. He also authorized the formation of a Colonial Division. On 6 February Roberts left Cape Town for the operational base on the Modder River, where he arrived on 9 February 1900 [16].[2]

Roberts' appreciation of conditions in South Africa, particularly his observation that only along the western railway line (i.e. De Aar-Kimberley) did the British have possession of a bridge across the Gariep (Orange) River, confirmed his opinion that this strategy was preferable to the earlier British plan of an advance along the central (i.e. Colesberg-Bloemfontein) railway. Subsequently he slightly modified his initial plan, but not even the opposition expressed by the British High Commissioner in South Africa, Sir Alfred Milner, on the grounds that it would leave the Cape Colony dangerously vulnerable to invasion and rebellion, or the further setbacks suffered by Buller in Natal at Spioenkop on 24 January 1900 and Vaalkrans on 5–7 February 1900, caused him to abandon his basic idea of a flank march.[3]

After his defeat at Colenso (15 December 1899), Buller moved the bulk of his force to the Upper Thukela in an effort to break through the Boer line of defence. He selected Springfield as his new operational headquarters, and from 10 to 16 January he re-deployed 24,000 soldiers, 58 guns and approximately 650 wagons from Frere to the Upper Thukela – the wagons and columns of soldiers spanned a distance of 24 km (15 miles), and took thirteen hours to move past a given point! The differences of opinion that obtained between Buller and his new second-in-command, Lieutenant-General Sir Charles Warren, were not a good omen for the British campaign on the Upper Thukela, especially when Buller placed Warren in command of the operation, while Buller himself retreated to Springfield.[4]

Next the British tried unsuccessfully on three occasions to break through on the Upper Thukela. At the battle of iNtabamnyama (20–23 January 1900) they succeeded in forcing back the Boers in certain battle sectors; however, large losses eventually forced the British to retreat. There is some uncertainty about the exact losses; however, British killed and wounded amounted to approximately 600, while the Boers apparently suffered fewer than a hundred casualties. In certain respects, the undecided battle at iNtabamnyama was the prelude to Spioenkop, the second-bloodiest battle of the war. Major-General E.R.P. Woodgate took

1,700 British soldiers up against the steep slopes of Spioenkop to the top of the hill where in the early hours of 24 January they forced approximately 200 Boers to retreat. The British tried to take up sound defensive positions on the plateau – but these were prepared in the wrong place. At daybreak, the Boers led a charge on the British positions, Amajuba style. Moreover, they did so under cover of artillery fire, which effectively trapped the entirely vulnerable British force on top of Spioenkop. Woodgate was fatally wounded, while scores of British soldiers surrendered to the advancing Boers; however, the arrival of reinforcements allowed the British to keep the Boers at bay. After sunset, the British decided to withdraw, and it was only on the next morning that the Boers could again occupy Spioenkop. Apart from the battle at Paardeberg (18 February 1900), this was the bloodiest day in the war: approximately 225 British soldiers had died, 550 were wounded and 300 were either taken POW or were missing in action; 58 Boers were dead and 140 wounded.[5] Roberts was shocked by the events and by Buller's despondency [15].

The day after the Spioenkop fiasco, Buller personally took direct charge of the British Army on the Upper Thukela. He was sent reinforcements and by 5 February he had amassed at least 24,500 men, 72 guns and nineteen machine-guns on the Upper Thukela. Facing this superior force were a mere 3,600 Boers, ten guns and two pom-poms, deployed over an area of 30 km (20 miles). Under cover of artillery fire, the infantry crossed the Thukela River on a pontoon bridge (5 February) and then embarked upon a charge of the Boer positions in the vicinity of Vaalkrans. Although the British attacks were fended off time and again, a part of the republican force did indeed succumb, and retreated to Groenkop; however, at this point, Buller's courage failed him and he did not launch follow-up attacks. The battle continued at a low level of intensity for another two days until Buller decided to withdraw his force from Vaalkrans and the Upper Thukela. Casualties on both sides for this three-day battle were reasonably light: at least 25 British soldiers had been killed and approximately 350 were wounded; 38 Boers were dead and 45 wounded.[6]

Buller's campaign on the Upper Thukela exacted more than 2,000 British casualties compared to approximately 400 on the Boer side. Although the campaign unsettled the Boers and left them exhausted, it was nonetheless a complete failure for the British. By the end of the second main phase in Natal, Buller was back at Frere, and not much closer to Ladysmith at all. For this reason, he tried next to break through on the Lower Thukela.

Superficially it appears as if by the end of the second main phase (i.e. after four months of military activity) the British showed no military-strategic progress, and that as a result the balance had swung strongly in favour of the Boers. Three British garrisons were still held under siege by the Boers, almost all Boer forces found themselves within British territory, and to top everything the republican forces had achieved three sound tactical victories in the so-called 'Black Week', as well as other victories along the Upper Thukela and elsewhere. By 10 February 1900, however, British forces in South Africa numbered about 120,000 soldiers and were more formidable than ever before in the conflict, and the morale of the soldiers was high, while the Boers' morale had been undermined by idleness (Kimberley front), persistent battles (Natal) and nerve-racking deceptive manoeuvres by French (Colesberg front). As a result of the Boers' laxity and lack of forceful action and strategic initiative, the strategic initiative was firmly in the hands of the British by 10 February.[7]

Roberts was on the verge of outwitting the Boers. Thus, Buller had indeed created the climate for Roberts to implement his strategy with positive consequences. In this sense, therefore, the British were strategically successful up to the end of the Buller phase. However, they were very fortunate in that they were repeatedly offered the opportunity to correct their errors. If the British wanted to defeat the Boers decisively, it would be necessary to do so within three or four months from the outbreak of hostilities. They failed in this objective, and the repercussions would haunt them until 31 May 1902, when peace was eventually agreed to.

To determine the strategic meaning of the battles that occurred until 10 February 1900, it should not only be noted to what extent the British moved closer to their political and military objectives, but also the extent to which the Boers still could or wanted to proceed with the war. Superficially, it appeared that the armed forces of the Boers were still almost unaffected. At that stage, they had suffered only about 480 dead, 1,180 wounded and 350 captured; moreover, more than 10,000 Cape rebels had joined them since the invasion of the Cape Colony. On the other hand, the British had lost approximately 1,600 killed in action, 5,400 wounded and 3,000 captured.[8] The most important difference was, however, that by the start of January 1900, the Boers had deployed the highest number of men ever employed by them in the war – approximately 47,000 – in the field and would henceforth be able only partially to compensate for their losses, while the British already had approximately 120,000 soldiers in South Africa by 10 February 1900. Almost daily, new reinforcements arrived.

Buller's sustained attacks on the Natal front had exhausted the Boers by 10 February 1900, and precipitated a feeling of despair among the Boers, which would also set in on the other fronts. The Boers expected a massive attack, but did not know for sure where and when Roberts would attack. It is nonetheless interesting to note that both Kruger and Steyn argued correctly that Roberts would attack on the Kimberley front.[9] The weeks that preceded 11 February were therefore characterized by the transfer of commandos; for example, burghers were moved from Natal to the Kimberley front,[10] but eventually this could not prevent Roberts from achieving a strategic breakthrough. By 10 February the Boers were psychologically exhausted on all fronts, and their morale was probably at its lowest point ever at that stage. Apparently, the Boers realized that they would not easily force the British into a situation similar to the one in 1881. On the other hand, it was clear that the British, in spite of serious losses, were determined to persist until they achieved victory.

Since the Boers apparently did not realize by 10 February 1900 how large the British force was that had been assembled against them, there was, in the midst of problems with their morale and discipline, still a feeling that they would once again at least be able to ward off the British attacks. Meanwhile, the Boers had nothing more than a strategy of hiding. The way had been prepared for Roberts' short-term strategic success even before the end of the Buller phase.

While on his journey to Cape Town, Roberts – in collaboration with his staff officers – decided to move the strategic point of gravity of the war to the Kimberley front with a view to implementing an extensive indirect strategy so that the Boers' positions at Magersfontein and its vicinity could be surrounded, Kimberley relieved, the Boers thrown off balance and hopefully defeated in quick time, while providing some relief of the pressure on Buller in Natal. The Modder River was then to be followed more or less as the line of a forced march to Bloemfontein, on the model of Roberts' epic march from Kabul to Kandahar in 1880.[11]

On 11 February 1900, exactly four months after the start of the war, Roberts began his advance from the Modder River. He had at least 49,500 soldiers and 110 guns under his direct command. As part of his deception plan, Roberts first took his force southwards to Enslin Station, then eastwards via Ramdam to Watervalsdrif and De Kielsdrif on the Riet River, and then northwards to Rondawelsdrif and Klipdrif on the Modder River. When Cronjé realised that he was being surrounded, he gave the order that his force of more than 4,000 men, plus a number of women and children, as well as all his wagons, were to move eastwards, along the Modder River, in an effort to escape. Meanwhile, French and his cavalry advanced from Rondawelsdrif in a northerly direction and then in a north-westerly direction, and were able to lift the Boer siege of Kimberley on 15 February 1900.[12] That same day Roberts' huge supply convoy at Watervalsdrif was captured by the Boers [17].

Forced to move at a very slow pace, Cronjé's wagon laager was cornered, and surrounded on 17 February in the vicinity of Vendusiedrif, close to Paardeberg [18]. There the Boer forces dug themselves in on both banks of the Modder River. The next morning, Kitchener – in the absence of Roberts who was ill – tried to overrun the Boer positions through unimaginative frontal attacks. His tactics failed, and at least 303 British soldiers were killed, 906 were wounded and 61 taken prisoner – the largest number of soldiers killed and wounded that the British Army would suffer in one day during the entire war. On the Boer side there were not more than 70 casualties. Several Boer commandos were sent to Cronjé's assistance, including that of General Christiaan de Wet, who nearly broke the British investment. De Wet took Oskoppies on 18 February in an attempt to create an opportunity for Cronjé to break out, but on 21 February British forces recaptured Oskoppies (also known as Kitchener's Kopje). After Roberts took over command again at Paardeberg on 19 February from his Chief of Staff, Kitchener, the Boer laager was bombarded incessantly with artillery fire. This bombardment did not result in serious loss of life, but nonetheless had an extremely demoralising effect on the Boer defenders. By this time British soldiers had come as close as 90 metres to the laager, and Cronjé and his entire force then surrendered on 27 February 1900 (Amajuba Day) [19]. Through his great flank march, Roberts surprised the Boers and dislocated them both physically and psychologically. Their surrender had a very negative effect on the morale of the republican forces on all fronts and they never fully recovered.[13]

In due course the Boers would, in desperation, resort to guerrilla warfare, but after their defeat at Paardeberg they could hardly win the war any longer – they could merely try to prolong it. Ironically, however, the events at Paardeberg soon also affected the British soldiers negatively, because, as shall shortly be pointed out, thousands of them became ill from drinking contaminated water at the battlefield. The question can in fact be asked whether Roberts' strategy should be judged by his success at Paardeberg, or by the fact that eventually he was forced to halt for seven weeks in Bloemfontein, thereby affording the Boers the opportunity to rethink their strategy and regroup (for guerrilla warfare).

In the meantime, in Natal, by the middle of February 1900, Buller was ready to advance with more than 25,000 soldiers and 70 guns towards Ladysmith via the Lower Thukela. Opposing the British, there were approximately 3,000 Boers at Colenso and on the Lower Thukela, with at least two guns and two pom-poms. This campaign led to a number of battles. Major-General N.G. Lyttelton advanced eastward in the direction of Moordkraal, and forced the Boers on 16 February to take up position around the strategically situated hill of Cingolo. On 17 February the British took Cingolo without any difficulty. Only four British soldiers were killed and 32 wounded, while on the Boer side one was killed and eight wounded. The British continued to bombard the Boer positions and captured Monte Cristo, Groenkop and Hlangwane (18–19 February 1900). Buller succeeded in driving away the Boers to the north of the Thukela River, and in this process he apparently lost only 25 men who were killed, 276 wounded, and four missing in action, while fifteen were killed and 71 wounded on the Boer side.[14]

After Warren had tried without success on 21 February to take the Boer positions in the vicinity of Rooikop, the British forces' 11th Brigade, under command of Major-General A.S. Wynne, launched a full-scale attack on Hedge Hill (soon to be known as Wynne's Hill), as well as the adjacent Horseshoe Hill. The battle continued next day, but the British were unable to take any of their targets. However, the Boers did not follow up their success and did not try to drive back the British across the Thukela River. The British attack against Terrace (also referred to as Hart's) Hill (23–24 February 1900) followed on the battle at Hedge Hill, and was aimed at relieving the pressure on the British troops who were positioned on the latter slopes. Major-General A.F. Hart's 5th Irish Brigade formed the largest part of this attack force. The British attack, which was preceded by a heavy artillery bombardment, started at 17.00 on 23 February and lasted throughout the night until the next day. By 23.00 on the evening of 24 February, however, Terrace Hill was still in Boer hands. In their attacks against Hedge Hill and Terrace Hill, the British lost at least 196 men who were killed, 912 wounded and 74 taken prisoner, while on the Boer side at least 22 were killed and 80 wounded. On the morning of 27 February – Amajuba Day for the Boers – British soldiers built a pontoon bridge, starting at the foot of Naval Hill, across the Thukela River, while a heavy artillery bombardment was directed at the Boer positions. Shortly before the British infantry began to move across the pontoon bridge, they received news of Cronjé's surrender at Paardeberg – news which made the British even more determined to defeat the Boer forces. Attacks were launched at Hart's Hill, Spoorwegkop and Pietershoogte, and after heavy fighting, the Boers retreated. Then the Boers left their positions on the rest of the Thukela line, as well as their positions around Ladysmith and retreated northwards in the direction of the Biggar's Mountains. On 27 February the British lost at least 87 men who were killed and 400 wounded, while on the Boer side, at least 34 were killed or died of their wounds, 115 were wounded and removed from the battlefield by the Boers, and 83 – including some wounded soldiers – were taken prisoner. On the evening of 28 February, Ladysmith was officially relieved of the Boer siege.[15]

Glad to hear that White had at last been relieved, Roberts advanced eastwards from Paardeberg in the direction of Bloemfontein. At Modder River Pass, in the vicinity of Poplar Grove Drift, De Wet and 5,000 men, with seven guns, took up positions over a wide front. On 7 March 1900, British forces launched an attack. When French's cavalry began to surround the Boer positions, they abandoned their positions and fled. On the British side, eight soldiers were killed and 49 wounded, while on the Boer side at least one burgher was killed and one wounded. Three days later, British forces engaged in battle with the Boers, who were under the command of De Wet and De la Rey, in the vicinity of Abrahamskraal and Driefontein. At that stage, De Wet had at his disposal at best 3,000 men and approximately twelve guns and pom-poms. The Boers generally put up greater resistance than at Poplar Grove. Nonetheless, the British were the superior force, and they compelled the Boers to flee eastwards; but the British lost an opportunity to strike a decisive blow. On the British side, at least 60 were killed and 361 wounded, while the Boers lost 32 killed, nineteen taken prisoner (including some wounded), as well as about 40 others wounded.[16]

On 13 March 1900 Roberts entered Bloemfontein without any opposition, delighted with the success he had achieved since 11 February [20], and praised the role played by the war correspondents [21]. He knew how to deal with the press; knew how important it was to have a good press; used the press for publicity and, to promote the careers of those he wanted to use later, treated the war correspondents in a polite and liberal manner. He had his own way of 'managing' the news; for example he made sure that no telegrams about operations were sent before his own despatches had been sent, well knowing that if his despatches were comprehensive enough, they would dominate the newspapers and would satisfy the general reader. More than 200 correspondents were in South Africa during the war, but by July 1900 most of them had left again.[17]

Roberts' great flank march can be compared with his epic march from Kabul to Kandahar in 1880. Within the space of four weeks, Roberts had dramatically changed the entire strategic situation in South Africa, and had placed the Boers in a position from which they never fully recovered. Soon, however, the success that he had so far achieved would be overshadowed by the supply and other problems he and his army faced in Bloemfontein, far away from the Cape ports [22].

By this time Roberts had also lost the services of his Director of Military Intelligence, Colonel Henderson, whose health failed owing to malaria and exhaustion, and who had to return home just before Cronjé's surrender. This was a grievous blow. Henderson helped in shaping the course of the war, emphasizing that the Boers were to be thoroughly defeated in the field, and that the capture of their capitals as such would not end this particular war. With him back in England, this insight was lost, with detrimental effects for the British Army in South Africa.[18]

Meanwhile Major-General R.A.P. Clements was performing well under the circumstances prevailing on the Colesberg front. The Boers were indeed able to force him back to Rensburg (13 February 1900) and then to Arundel (14 February), but he was able to resist long enough, without risking his communication lines, to provide Roberts with an opportunity to begin his indirect advance on 11 February. British successes on the Kimberley front forced the Boers on the Colesberg front to retreat to OFS territory. On 15 March, Clements himself crossed the Gariep (Orange) River and participated in British attempts to subject the Southern OFS to British authority. He pursued the retreating Boer commandos into the OFS, and on 21 March he continued his advance from the Gariep River in the direction of Bloemfontein: Philippolis, Jagersfontein, Fauresmith, Koffiefontein and Petrusburg were taken, proclamations were distributed and the burghers' surrender accepted. On 11 March, further east, the Colonial Division, under command of Brigadier-General E.Y. Brabant, took Aliwal North. For three days, the British had to defend the bridgehead against General J.H. Olivier's burghers; however, on 15 March this Boer force was also compelled to retreat northwards. Subsequently, the Colonial Division pursued the Boers into the Eastern OFS. Although the Southern OFS was almost never entirely free of Boer activities, Clements, Gatacre and Brabant succeeded in creating conditions that allowed Roberts to consolidate his position in Bloemfontein.[19]

With Bloemfontein (now also jestingly referred to as 'Bobsfontein', in honour of Lord Roberts) in British hands, the OFS government had temporarily moved to Kroonstad – which was declared the temporary capital. In the meantime, De Wet gave the OFS burghers the opportunity to return to their farms. Those who wanted to continue with the war had to assemble at the Sand River railway bridge on 25 March 1900. At a war council meeting held at Kroonstad on 17 March 1900, where both President S.J.P. Kruger of Transvaal and President M.T. Steyn of the OFS were present, it was decided, among other things, that the Boers would change their tactics, and instead of trying to halt the British advance through taking up defensive positions, they would in future concentrate on destroying enemy communication lines; moreover, they decided also that Boer forces had to be organised into smaller units and had to abandon the use of wagon laagers.[20] It is ironic that it took a serious defeat at Paardeberg, and the loss of Bloemfontein, to force the Boers to exploit what was in all probability their strongest weapon against a conventionally-trained foe, namely their mobility.

In some ways this meeting was a watershed with regard to Boer strategy during the war, although some commandos continued for several months to resist British forces in semi-conventional ways. The Kroonstad decisions may be regarded as the theoretical starting point of the guerrilla war or fourth main phase of the Anglo-Boer War, although this phase commenced, in practice, with the battle at Sannaspos (31 March 1900) where De Wet and approximately 1,500 of his men dealt a heavy defeat to a British force of approximately 1,800 men, under command of Brigadier-General R.G. Broadwood. British casualties included at least eighteen men killed, 134 wounded and 426 taken prisoner, while seven guns and more than 100 wagons and carts were captured by the Boers. On the Boer side, at least three men had been killed and five wounded.[21] Roberts did not know how strong De Wet's force was or what exactly was behind the attack at Sannaspos, but had he (Roberts) taken a calculated gamble and sent out a large mobile force, De Wet might have been defeated and the war taken a different course.

De Wet followed up this success when he launched an attack against a British force stationed at Mostertshoek, east of Reddersburg, under command of Captain W.J. McWhinnie, and after a brief siege, forced them to surrender (3–4 April 1900). Ten British soldiers were killed, while the rest of the British force (581 officers and soldiers) were taken prisoner, including 35 wounded. It appears that only three Boers were killed and three wounded [23]. De Wet was subsequently unsuccessful in laying siege to a British garrison at Jammerbergdrif, approximately 5 km north-west of Wepener. Casualties during the siege were as follows: 34 British soldiers killed, 146 wounded; ten or eleven Boers killed, 25 wounded.[22] As a result of their drinking contaminated water from the Modder River in the vicinity of Paardeberg, coupled with the gross neglect of elementary sanitary precautions in the military camps, several thousand British soldiers went down with typhoid (then called enteric fever), and more than a thousand of them died in Bloemfontein alone. The lack of water in Bloemfontein complicated matters, made worse by the British defeat at Sannaspos. Bloemfontein's water supply was only restored on 23 April 1900. Roberts was forced to remain in the OFS capital for seven weeks to give his soldiers time to recover, to refine his war strategy and to clear the Southern OFS of Boer commandos. By this time Roberts had also already realised that he had to acquire more mounted troops if he wanted to defeat the elusive Boers.[23]

On 3 May 1900, Roberts and more than 20,000 soldiers, with 80 guns and 49 machine-guns, resumed their advance from Bloemfontein, this time all along the main railway line in the direction of the ZAR. The railway became the central source of supply to the British Army, and consequently the Army became to a large extent bound to it. The Boers would henceforth try their best to destroy the railway, with the result that repairing the railway as quickly as possible was the biggest challenge facing the Royal Engineers – something they did with great skill and speed. This advance was co-ordinated with that of Buller from Natal; Methuen's advance which had to follow the route from south of the Vaal River over Boshof, Hoopstad and Bothaville in a northerly direction; that of Lieutenant-General Archibald Hunter who had to cross the Vaal River and advance on a route including Christiana, Bloemhof, Klerksdorp and Potchefstroom; and that of Lieutenant-General Ian Hamilton who had to advance east of, but parallel to the main railway line in a northerly direction – an enormous sweeping action in which a total of 150,000 soldiers, with approximately 300 guns, would participate, and who were supposed to drive all Boer commandos systematically ahead of them [24, 25]. Against Roberts' formidable main force, the Boers were initially only able to deploy approximately 1,700 men along the main railway line, although this force grew in size as time passed. It was no wonder, therefore, that the Boers did not achieve much success in their attempts to halt Roberts' advance. At Brandfort (3 May 1900), the Vet River (5 May) and the Sand River (7 and 10 May), the Boers tried in vain to stop the British advance, and on 12 May Kroonstad was captured by the

British [29]. Here the British force had to stay for ten days in an effort to rest, wait for supplies and more horses, and try to shake off the typhoid that had once again taken its toll. On 28 May they reached the Vaal River, whereupon Roberts formally annexed the OFS [31]. The annexation was made retrospective in force from 24 May so that it would coincide with Queen Victoria's birthday.[24] In London Lansdowne was very pleased with Roberts' success [27]. Roberts had to thank, *inter alia*, Lieutenant-Colonel E.P.C. Girouard, his Director of Military Railways, for his progress [29]. He hoped to keep up the pace, notwithstanding the ever increasing length of his lines of communication [30]. Even as Roberts was still advancing through the OFS, Milner was already writing to Roberts about the administration of the Transvaal [26], and Roberts shared some of his own views in that regard with the High Commissioner [28].

Although his Natal Army was not as badly plagued by illness as was Roberts' force in Bloemfontein, Buller did not, after the relief of Ladysmith, pursue the retreating Boer forces; indeed, he remained in Ladysmith for two months, after which – as part of Roberts' wide-ranging strategy – he first advanced eastwards to Helpmekaar, and then marched northwards to Dundee which was taken on 15 May. On the way, a number of skirmishes took place. On 18 May, Buller entered Newcastle, but his northward route of advance was blocked by Boer forces who had dug themselves in at Lang's Nek. Buller remained in Newcastle until the beginning of June to consolidate his position.[25]

Meanwhile, on the western front, the siege of Mafikeng took its slow course. The Boers maintained their siege half-heartedly, while Baden-Powell, through inspiring leadership, succeeded in keeping his small garrison's morale high. Baden-Powell sent Roberts a message which stated that the garrison could not last longer than 22 May 1900. This message compelled Roberts to order Lieutenant-General A. Hunter to mobilize a relief force. This force, under command of Colonel B.T. Mahon, consisted of approximately 1,150 men, with four guns and two machine-guns. On 4 May they advanced from Barkly West in a northerly direction and on 15 May, this force combined with Colonel H.C.O. Plumer's southward moving force at the Molopo River, approximately 30 km (20 miles) west of Mafikeng. Meanwhile, Commandant S.J. Eloff, a grandson of President Kruger, attempted on 12 May to take the town through a direct frontal assault. After a battle that lasted for the entire day, Eloff and 97 other Boers were captured. Apparently ten Boers were killed. After a number of men from the relief force had arrived in the town on the evening of 16 May, Mahon officially lifted the siege of the town the next day [30].[26]

Roberts hoped in vain that the various British units' advance over a broad front would drive all the Boer commandos ahead of them. Instead a few mishaps occurred. Lieutenant-General H.M.L. Rundle attacked a Boer force on 29 May 1900 at Biddulphsberg, near Senekal, and failed. British casualties were more or less 180, and those of the Boers approximately 40. Meanwhile, on 27 May, Colonel B. Spragge and his 13th Yeomanry Battalion were surrounded by a Boer force about 3 km north-west of Lindley. As more Boers and guns arrived, the British force's position deteriorated, and on 31 May they surrendered: 443 officers and men, including 55 wounded (25 were killed). Boer casualties were apparently more or less 70.[27]

Roberts continued his advance in the direction of Johannesburg [32]. After a battle that lasted for longer than a day at Klipriviersberg and its surroundings, south of Johannesburg (28–29 May 1900), British forces entered the city on 31 May, without experiencing any resistance. However, the Boers were allowed to withdraw northwards. This was a serious strategic mistake by Roberts. On the Sesmylspruit, just south of Pretoria, the Boers once again tried to halt the British advance, but they were repelled, and the capital of the ZAR was taken on 5 June, once again without any Boer resistance. The Transvaal government and president fled eastwards.[28] According to Roberts, the war was now almost over [33]. In reality, however, the war was far from over; as a matter of fact, it would in due course escalate all over the war zone, and would once again include the Cape Colony. The capture of both the republican capitals did not have the envisaged psychological effect on the Boers, and Roberts erred in not dealing decisively with the commandos of De Wet and others who were allowed to operate behind the main British line of advance. Roberts was so anxious to end the war as quickly as possible that he made a serious strategic mistake.

Up to the capture of Pretoria, Roberts had lived up to his reputation as a commander who combined a very real concern for the welfare of his soldiers with the determination and will to drive them hard and continuously if necessary. Superficially it also seemed as if he had been very successful from a strategic point of view. However, since the battle at Abrahamskraal-Driefontein (10 March) Roberts had not been able to bring a relatively large Boer force to battle; the Boers had since then suffered very few casualties, and the commandos had been dispersed rather than defeated. So far Roberts' proclamations also did not have any significant effect.

12
Lord Roberts to Lord Lansdowne
Government House,
Cape Town.

[Holograph]

15th January 1900.

Private and confidential

I trust that, before this letter has to be despatched on the 17th instant, satisfactory news will have been received from Natal. The movement for the relief of Ladysmith must be going on now, for, with the limited amount of supplies Buller has in hand, every movement [moment?] is precious. It is an intensely anxious time, for our own position throughout South Africa, and the future conduct of the campaign depend on the result of the present operation.[1] If it is as successful, as I think it will be, I should hope that the war will henceforth be practically confined to the Orange Free State and the Transvaal.

My cipher telegram, No. 7 of the 12th instant, will have placed you in possession of my views of the situation as it existed on my arrival.[2] You would have learnt from it that, if all goes well in Natal, my hope is that it will not be necessary to draw upon England for more troops than those named by you in your cipher telegram No. 80 of the 9th instant,[3] except possibly a few battalions of Militia Infantry. Large bodies of Mounted Infantry are what are chiefly required. Those that are coming from the colonies and from England, as well as the Imperial Yeomanry, will be most useful, and I am doing all I can to raise more in this country. Men are being enrolled and horses purchased daily, and I am to interview presently four gentlemen of note (recommended to me by Sir Alfred Milner) who, it is believed, will be able to collect a number of useful men from outlying districts – men who know the country and can talk the language. It will, of course, take time to

39

organise these several bodies, but that will not, I trust, interfere with the movement of troops into the Orange Free State as there are a certain number of local troops now in the field.

I intend to abide by the plan I sketched out before I left England and with which, I am glad to find, Kitchener entirely agrees. It is briefly to mass troops at Naaupo<o>rt and in the neighbourhood of Colesberg, in order to let the Boers believe that we intend to force our way across the Orange River at Norval's Pont and Bethulie, where the advantages would be all on their side, owing to their being already in possession of the bridges (which is reported they have mined), and to the nature of the ground which is higher on the north than the south bank. –

I trust that, in this way, I shall be able to draw the enemy's attention off the Orange River Station, where, when the time comes, a force will be collected as rapidly as circumstances will admit, and strong enough to advance towards Fauresmith, and attack the rear of their positions on the Orange River.

It will be February before anything can be in readiness for this move. Meanwhile I am working up an Intelligence Department.[4] I felt sure this would be needed, and in a letter I received this morning from Buller he alluded to it as "our great want". With Milner's assistance I have succeeded in getting hold of some likely men, and I shall be disappointed if we are not able ere long to obtain reliable information of the enemy's numbers, movements, etc.

I have gone carefully into the important question of supplies and transport. In the matter of food and forage there would seem to be no cause of anxiety, as sufficient arrangements have apparently been made to meet the heavy demand which 150,000 men and some 60,000 animals will make on the Commissariat Department.

I am a little doubtful, however, about a few important items, such as boots etc, and regarding these I am communicating by telegraph with Brackenbury.

It is not so easy to get a thorough grasp of the state of the transport, on account of the animals being necessarily a good deal scattered. But, as well as I am able to judge, there is a sufficient amount now in the country, or on the way here, provided we are fortunate enough to escape an outbreak of the terrible sickness from which horses and mules so often suffer in South Africa.[5]

What is not so satisfactory is the system under which the transport has hitherto been organized. This is known as the Regimental system. Kitchener and I have had considerable experience in the matter of transport, and we are both agreed that, however suitable the Regimental system may be for manoeuvres, where every unit is required to make a march for a week or ten days in succession, it is not adapted for war, where the movement of regiments is so uncertain, some being constantly marched about, while others may be more or less stationary. At the present moment Methuen has more than 4000 mules which have been doing nothing for upwards of a month, and which might have been usefully employed elsewhere. The change from Regimental to Departmental charge can be made without interfering with Army Service Corps arrangements. The officers of that corps seem to have been doing very well, and will, I feel sure, recognize the advantage of having the entire control of the transport in their own hands.

Sir William MacCormack[6] has sent me a copy of the letter he has written to the Director, Army Medical Department, in which he expresses his entire approval of the manner in which the medical arrangements have been worked. I have inspected the three large hospitals near this, and can endorse for Sir William's as to their having all that could be desired. The camps are pitched on high, dry ground. The water supply is good and plentiful. The rations are in all respects satisfactory. There is ample space for the number of officers and men likely to require accommodation, and the surroundings are very attractive. I shall be surprised if the sick and wounded soldiers invalided home do not speak well of the way in which they have been looked after.

16th January. I am unable to send you any news of Ladysmith having been relieved, as I hoped <to> have done today, but I find from a telegram received from Buller last night that Warren had not apparently crossed the Tugela. I sincerely trust there will be no delay on the road, for the success of such an operation depends on rapidity of action – a halt of even a few hours on the river bank might enable a mobile enemy like the Boers to construct such formidable works as

41

would render the passage of the river a very difficult business. This is a most critical time, and it will be a relief to me to hear that Buller has been able to effect White's relief in a satisfactory manner.

As Kelly Kenny's troops at Naaupoort are more than sufficient to act as a support to French, I have directed him to turn his attention to the section of Railway which runs from Rosmead towards Stormberg. Some of the culverts have been destroyed, but no great damage has been done and it is an important piece of Railway to have in our hands as it connects the Midland and Eastern lines, and a movement in that direction will, I hope, draw off the enemy's attention from the western Railway.

17th January. No news yet from Buller. The move towards Ladysmith must, however, I think, have taken place, as this is the third day since he reported the concentration would be effected on the Tugela north of Springfield.[7]

I enclose yesterday's Intelligence report. It is, I believe, fairly reliable. You will notice that the number said to be in arms against us is about 61,000.[8]

BL MS Room, Lansdowne Papers L(5)47

13
Sir Ralph Knox[9] to Lord Roberts

War Office,
London, S.W.

[Typed letter]

16th January, 1900.

I am directed by the Secretary of State for War to acquaint you that it has been decided that your Staff Pay as Field Marshal Commanding in Chief in South Africa shall be at the rate of £19. (Nineteen pounds) a day, and Messrs Cox & Co. have been instructed to make the issues at that rate from the 23rd December 1899 inclusive. I am to add that the allowances of the post will be at the highest rate of allowances provided for in the regulations, viz., those of a General Officer.

NAM 5504–64–61

14
Lord Roberts to Queen Victoria

Capetown, 21st January 1900.

[Holograph]

When taking leave of Your Majesty at Windsor, I felt highly honoured at the suggestion that I might write to Your Majesty from time to time, and now that I have had a few days to look about me, and see how matters stand in South Africa I gladly avail myself of the valued privilege accorded to me. Your Majesty's gracious telegram reached me the day after I landed, and I replied expressing my grateful thanks and informing your Majesty that we had had a most successful passage.

The state of affairs here is, I regret to say, far from satisfactory, and I fear no change for the better can take place until peace is restored, and the several factions into which South Africa is divided, realize that it is our unalterable determination to maintain British Supremacy from Capetown to the Zambesi. Party feeling seems very high and as intermarriage between the Dutch and other settlers in the several Colonies has been the custom for many years past, relations are divided against relations, and, friends of long standing have become bitter enemies.

Some few of the Dutch are staunch loyalists, but the sympathy of the great majority is with the Boers, and owing to the idea (which was widely spread about by the Transvaal Government) that we would not continue the struggle, and to the successes which the Boers met with at the commencement of the war, many waverers joined against us. Others are watching events, and the general opinion seems to be that if we get well through the next month or six weeks, the Boers will not be able to obtain many more recruits from districts south of the Orange river.

The importance of encouraging the loyal subjects of the Crown is fully appreciated by the civil as well as the military in South Africa. During the short time Sir Redvers Buller was here he ordered some local corps to be raised, and with Sir Alfred Milner's assistance, I am now arranging that these should be considerably strengthened. Colonel Brabant, a gentleman possessing considerable influence in the Colony, is increasing the number of men in his regiment to over 8000, and his promotion to the rank of Brigadier General has, I understand, given the greatest satisfaction to all your Majesty's loyal subjects in South Africa.

It will, I am sure, interest Your Majesty to learn that the hospitals I have been able to visit are well managed and in excellent order. So high an authority as the eminent surgeon Sir William MacCormack has expressed himself well satisfied with them, and with the medical arrangements generally. The nursing sisters are indefatigable in their care of and attention to the sick and wounded officers and men, and their labours are well seconded by the many ladies who have come forward to help in the hospitals, and whose presence in the wards, coupled with their gifts of flowers, books, and newspapers goes far towards brightening the somewhat sad scenes amidst which they work.

I had a curious experience a day or two ago. I entered a ward some paces ahead of the hospital staff and enquired from the first patient I came across to what regiment he belonged. As I asked the question, I thought it odd that so old and so well bearded man could be serving in the ranks. The explanation was afforded when I heard that the ward was full of wounded Boers. They were most respectful in their manners and bore themselves with great dignity. All were unanimous in their thanks for the kind and skilful treatment they have received.

24th January. I have kept this open until today in the hope that I might be able to give Your Majesty good news about Sir Redvers Buller's force, but a telegram received last evening[10] shows that the advance portion of it under General Warren, has still some distance to go before it can reach Ladysmith. It is a very anxious time, for so much depends on the result of Sir Redvers Buller's operations.

I am distressed at not being able to afford some assistance by threatening Bloemfontein, but the want of a properly organized transport precludes my taking the field at present. This, however is gradually being remedied and I sincerely trust that, by the time this letter reaches England, some of Your Majesty's troops will have entered the Orange Free State.

RA VIC/P5/150

15
Lord Roberts to Lord Lansdowne

Capetown. S.Africa.

[Holograph]

January – 29th 1900.

It was a great shock to me to learn that Buller had been compelled to relinquish his second attempt to reach Ladysmith,[11] and I can understand how deeply the news must have been felt in England. Buller's despondent telegrams from the very first made me fear the worst, and it is difficult to believe from the reports that the enemy would not have given way if he had continued to press them – The mere fact of their having allowed him to carry out his retirement practically unopposed shows they had not much heart left in them, or they would undoubtedly have taken advantage of the retrograde movement of our troops to seriously harass the retirement. The despondent tone of Buller's telegram regarding the possible result of a third attempt to relieve Ladysmith makes me think it had better not be attempted until we have seen the result of my operations in the Orange Free State – my telegram of the 28th will enable me to learn what his intentions are, and unless I consider them sound and likely to be carried through I shall direct him to remain on the defensive.[12]

I sent you a copy of a telegram I have sent to White which will, I hope, strenghten him in holding on to Ladysmith[13] – Any attempt he might make at present to break out from there would probably be disastrous, and might result in his force having to capitulate while striving to reach the Tugela river – Even if he were successful in doing so, the moral effect of relinquishing a post he has so long held, and of abandoning as he would necessarily have to do his sick and wounded and materiel, would be most damaging to our prestige.

The copies of my recent telegrams to Buller, which have been sent on to you, will have kept you informed of my views on the general situation as it now presents itself to me – After a very careful consideration of the various ways by which the difficult problem before me can be solved, I have come to the conclusion that my best course is to relieve Kimberley – For this operation, by taking almost every available man from the West of the line held by Gatacre, I shall have quite a strong column, especially in artillery, and by making proper use of my guns I earnestly hope we may be able to effect the relief without any very serious loss – Whether this will be so or not you will probably have learnt by telegram before this letter can reach you – Even should we fail to capture the enemy's guns and inflict on them heavy loss, which I shall strive to do, the result of relieving Kimberley should have an immediate and important political effect throughout South Africa, and I shall be disappointed if it does not also, to a certain extent, relieve the pressure in Natal. This should be still more the case when we approach Bloemfontein.

My first idea was to move there and leave the relief of Kimberley for later on, but the plan I now propose will have the special advantage that I shall not be leaving in my rear a hostile force of some strength, which might have caused me some anxiety had I moved fast towards Bloemfontein – You will remember that I told you I would not ask for more troops unless it were unavoidable, and so long as all went well in Natal I believed we could do without them, but it must be remembered that the longer White remains in Ladysmith the more unfit will his troops become for future operations, and also that this recent reverse will necessarily add to the feeling of unrest in the Colony and raise the hopes of the Boers – under these circumstances I have therefore, with very great reluctance, asked that the eighth division of Infantry and a brigade of Cavalry may be sent here from England as soon as possible.

Apart from the general question of Buller's recent withdrawal to the South of the Tugela river I was much concerned to read what he states regarding "mutual recriminations" – I will enquire into this later, but I fear it means that Warren's disagreeable transfer unfits him for holding an important position in the field – My recent telegram would have replied to your enquiry[14] about Methuen – When I reach Modder river, if I find matters to be as bad as described, it will be a matter for consideration whether Methuen should not be advised to vacate his present command. In any case I am resolved that he shall not be entrusted with any independent command in the future – At present it is difficult for me to decide what commanders I can rely on for work in the front.

Kelly Kenny seems to me to be nervous and over cautious – Tucker I have recently met for the first time and he impressed me unfavo<u>rably – He struck me as being of the old fashioned hard swearing type of regimental officer, without much personality or initiative – French has hitherto done well and I hope he will justify his position as Commandant of all the Cavalry – I propose to take in with me in the field Marshall,[15] in command of the large force of artillery which will be available for our future operations – Events will prove later whether any good commanders among the younger men come to the front.

I replied to your queries about Sir W. MacCormack's opinion on the medical arrangements here and the number of nurses we require, and I enclose two letters I have received from him – You will see from the class of Civil Surgeons he considers should be sent out if more are required – Although he telegraphed that he thought we had a sufficient number of lady nurses in the country, I gather from his letters that he is not averse to more being employed. The Surgeon General in the force is not very responsible or sympathetic in the question of securing an ample supply of lady nurses, but I think you will not be far wrong if you send us out 40 to 50 instead of the 20 we asked for.

It is difficult to reply about the Chaplains – The head Chaplain of the Church of England here, the Rev. E. Goodwin [?], says he considers there are enough chaplains of his denomination in South Africa, but there is no head of the Roman Catholics, Presbyterians, or Wesleyans here to whom to refer such a question – I think therefore that if any of those chaplains you mention who have offered their services voluntarily could be sent here, with no other expense to the Government but the cost of their passage, it would be as well to send a few of each local denomination. On hearing that they are coming I will see that they are posted where required.

I send you a letter about Kerry[16] which I have received from his Commanding Officer. I hope you will consider it is satisfactorily [sic] – At present he is with Sir Alfred Milner whose staff was

47

somewhat weak, so I let him go to the Governor as I had no immediate need of his services, and he can rejoin me later on when I move up country –

I forward for your information some "Notes for guidance in South African warfare" which have been issued to all concerned.

I am very grateful to you for the kind message contained in your telegram of the 28th, which is most gratifying and encouraging. I have found it necessary, in order to complete the concentration of my force, to postpone my departure from here for a few days, so I shall probably leave here a week later than I had previously intended.

BL MS Room, Lansdowne Papers L(5)47

16
Lord Roberts to Lord Lansdowne
Cape Town, 6th February, 1900.

[Printed letter]

My arrangements are now all ready for me to proceed to the relief of Kimberley.

I would gladly have postponed the operation, if by doing so I could have got a stronger force together, or if it were possible for Kimberley to hold out longer, but after the wire from Kekewich, which I forwarded to you under my No. 79, cipher, of 31st January,[17] it is evident they will shortly come to the end of their food resources and must therefore be relieved without delay. A move into the Orange Free State at this period has the further advantage that, while the enemy are briskly engaged in besieging Ladysmith and in defending their position north of the Tugela river against Buller, they cannot spare any considerable reinforcements to add to their forces in the Orange Free State.

I am sending you with this letter a return showing the strength and distribution of the troops in South Africa, an epitome of which you will have received by cablegram.[18] This differs, as you will see, very materially, from the statement which Reuter reports Wyndham to have made in the House, to the effect that we have some 180,000 troops in South Africa. It is only within the last few days that I have been able to ascertain, approximately, the actual number of the troops, and I confess I am somewhat concerned to find that we have only about 79,000 Infantry and Cavalry. If we add the Royal Artillery, the Royal Engineers, the Army Service Corps, and the Royal Army Medical Corps, we find the total number of Regular troops to be about 86,503 with 270 guns.

Besides these we have about 11,195 Colonial troops. Ere long we shall be stronger in Artillery, as 12 field batteries, 3 howitzer batteries, 2 companies of Garrison Artillery, and some Colonial Artillery will be here before the end of the month. The Yeomanry, which is, I see, reported to be some 4,000 strong will arrive in due course, as will the remainder of the City of London Volunteers, which the Lord Mayor informs me is 1,600 strong.

So far as I know these are all the reinforcements we can expect in addition to the 6 battalions of Militia, which you recently informed me will leave England about the 15th instant. The numbers which I give of troops in Natal are necessarily only approximate, for I have no returns from Buller, nor is it possible to say what White's strength is, but I think you will be as surprised as I am to learn how numerically weak our force is to operate in a country of great natural strength, and against an enemy who can put a force in the field almost equal in strength to our own.[19]

If the results of the impending operations do not bring the Boers of the Free State to terms, and if Buller fails in his third attempt to relieve Ladysmith, you must be prepared to send us out very considerable reinforcements at no distant date. The battalions now in the country must be kept up to strength and the drain on them, especially in Officers, must be replenished. I find that the average number of men in the Infantry and Cavalry regiments which will operate in the Orange Free State are as follows:–

Infantry, per battalion, 820.
Cavalry, per regiment, 480.[20]

Out of these it is obvious that a considerable number of casualties will occur. Fortunately for us the climate in this country is extraordinarily healthy. There is little sickness and wounds heal wonderfully quickly.

As regards the impending operations, one of the greatest difficulties in this country is the absence of water, which practically confines our operations to the rivers, the banks of which are often hilly and thus in the enemy's favour. This difficulty of water applies specially to a large force. Smaller parties can obtain a limited quantity from the wells of the farmhouses which lie scattered about the Free State, in many cases at a great distance from each other. In the detour which I propose to make to reach Kimberley, a distance of some 60 miles, I shall have to cross the Riet and Modder rivers, on which the main portion of my force will have in a large measure to depend for its water supply.

As you will have heard by telegram[21] I leave here to-day, and as soon as I reach the Modder river operations will commence.

The enclosed copy of telegrams which have passed about the case of Commandant Pretorius may interest you. I sent an Officer of my Staff to tell him he would be released, and he spoke in very appreciative terms of the kindness which has been shown to him here.

I also send you a copy of a telegram I have received from the Presidents of the Orange Free State and the South African Republic,[22] and my reply to it, which was prepared in consultation with Milner.

South African War, 1899–1900. Vol. I. Home and Oversea Correspondence by Field-Marshal Lord Roberts, pp. 29–30.[23]

17
Lord Roberts to Lord Lansdowne

H.Q. Camp. Jacobsdal

[Holograph]

Febr. 16th 1900.

Events have moved rapidly since I despatched my last letter to you from Modder river.[24] We left that camp on Monday the 12th instant and the force marched across country to Ramdam. It was necessary to make this long detour as Ramdam is the only place in that neighbourhood where a sufficiency of water is obtainable for the passage of a large force – I had formed the Mounted Infantry into two Brigades, each consisting of four regiments – one under Colonel Hannay,[25] the other under Colonel Ridley – Colonel Hannay's force moving up to join the Cavalry division from Orange river had an engagement with a party of Boers near Wolveskraal,[26] and the morning of our arrival at Ramdam French had seized the De Kiel's drift on the Riet river after a slight resistance, but which resulted, I regret to say, in the death of Captain Majendie[27] a very promising young officer in the Rifle Brigade – The 6th and 7th Divisions followed French and the work of getting the transport and heavy guns across the drifts of the river was very arduous – As soon as the 7th Division had joined French at De Kiel's drift, I ordered him on at once to seize a passage on the Modder river which was most successfully performed – The heat was very exhausting and a dust storm raged through the latter part of the day, but he pushed on and gained his objective before nightfall. I sent the 6th Division at once to reinforce him, and I followed with the 7th and 9th Divisions – Yesterday, as I wired to you French got through to Kimberley and found the garrison cheery and well[28] – I was sorry that a force of Boers was able to harass yesterday a convoy of provisions at Watervals drift,[29] on which we greatly depended for food, and before I could send back reinforcements to the escort, they had so damaged the oxen and carts with their guns, that they could not be removed without a risk of the force becoming involved in an attempt to dislodge the Boers from the strong position they had taken up which would probably have resulted in an unnecessary loss of life – I therefore ordered the officer commanding to leave the convoy and withdraw his force during the night, which he did not unopposed. This loss of provisions and transport has of course been very inconvenient, but we have been able to replace deficiencies by having opened up direct communication with Modder river.

It is unfortunate that Clements has been obliged to retire from Rensburg in order to protect Naauwpoort, but I half expected this might happen, as the only force I could leave at Rensburg after the withdrawal of French with the Cavalry left Clements somewhat weak –[30]

The slight advantage which the enemy has gained at Colesberg has, I have no doubt, been fully compensated for by the manner in which Kimberley has been relieved – It is satisfactory to learn that the occupation of Kimberley has broken up the Boer army to which Methuen has been opposed for so long, and that the heavily entrenched position north of the Modder river has been abandoned – As I write, [Kelly-] Kenny's division is engaging what is believed to be the rear guard of Cronjes main army about 5000 strong, with guns, which is heading for Bloemfontein – I have wired the news to French, who is a long way off, but his force is so mobile that perhaps he may be able to come up with Cronjes column and inflict heavy loss on it – I must confess that I did not expect such a complete collapse of the Boer army, without a determined effort on their part to prevent us from relieving Kimberley, but their leaders are evidently disconcerted to find how mobile we are – The results of the last few days work are in the highest degree creditable to the troops – The heat has been exceptionally trying and all ranks have suffered from the fatigue and want of sleep – Each evening the hospitals have been crowded by officers and men suffering from exhaustion caused by the sun, and the dust storms have added to the general discomfort – The only water for drinking purposes has been drawn from the Riet river – this of the colour and consistency of the water in a dirty village in England, but all hardships have been cheerfully endured, and after hard and long days marching in the sun, working parties have toiled at night to drag the guns and vehicles through the heavy sand and up the steep banks of the "drifts" –

I shall probably make some slight difference in the constitution of some of the brigades. By posting Colvile to the 9th Division I have been able to give Pole Carew the brigade of Guards, a happy appointment to all concerned. My idea is to when I reorganize the force to leave Methuen with a brigade, some Militia, and Canadian artillery in charge of our western line from Orange River northwards, with Kimberley as his head quarters, whence he could work up towards Mafeking – I shall give Colvile command of the division of Guards and the Highland Brigade, but I shall take an early opportunity of finding some more suitable appointment for him as I do not think he is quite the man to command the two finest brigades in the British army.

I considered it was essential to send Kitchener on ahead with French and Kenny, as he alone was thoroughly conversant with my plans – We have been in constant communication with each other by telegraph, either by cable cart or a light aerial wire and it has been of the greatest advantage to me to have him with our advanced force – I feel that, in some instances, I have taken somewhat drastic measures as regards the position of some of the senior officers, but I have had to consider national and not private interests.

I have telegraphed to you about the German ambulance here – The surgeons whose names I mentioned have been most kind to our wounded and I hope our Government will suitably acknowledge their services –

I forwarded to you a copy of the telegrams recently sent to Kekewich which I was glad to find resulted in satisfactory replies from the mayor of Kimberley[31] and Mr. Rhodes – Kekewich has had a very arduous task to perform, and he deserves the greatest credit for the way in which he has faced all difficulties and has kept up the national prestige.

The enclosed translation of a private letter found in the Post Office here yesterday may interest you[32] – It shows that our troops have been behaving in a conciliatory manner towards the inhabitants of the Orange Free State.

The latest phase of the situation is that I pushed the 9th Division across last night to the support of Kelly Kenny, who has been instructed to do everything in his power to harass Cronje during his retreat. French will I hope join Kenny tomorrow, and I am hopeful that we may capture Cronje's guns and break up his force.

In view of the complete disorganization of the Boer forces in this quarter, it seems to me essential we should push on to Bloemfontein without delay, but any decision on this point must necessarily depend on the news I shall receive about the pursuit of Cronjes force.

BL MS Room, Lansdowne Papers L(5) 48

18
Lord Roberts to Lord Lansdowne

Camp. Paardeberg – Feby. 22nd 1900

[Holograph]
<u>Private</u>

My telegrams will have kept you informed of what has occurred during the last few days[33] – As soon as I heard from Kitchener that our force was harassing Cronje during his retreat from Magersfontein, I wired to French to move down from Kimberley and head him, which was done most efficiently. I was detained at Jacobsdal to make arrangements connected with supply and transport,[34] but as I understood from Kitchener's report on the evening of the 18th instant, that it was apparently only a question of hours when Cronje's force would either be driven out of the place where he had made a stand, or that he would have to surrender, I decided to push on here, a distance of about 30 miles in one long march. I found Cronje in a peculiar position in the bed of the Modder river, which at first sight would appear to be untenable for any length of time, but which owing to the peculiarities of the ground has proved to be an extremely strong position and not at all easy to be searched, even by howitzers. The river which winds about is deep and is from 30 to 40 yards broad – It has steep banks fringed with bushes and trees, and the banks are much broken up by steep ravines. All this provides excellent natural cover which the Boers have rapidly improved – A few determined men can bar an advance along the banks of the stream, and on each side of the river the ground is an absolutely bare plain which can be swept with rifle fire from the Boer entrenchments – I found on my arrival here on the 19th instant that Cronje had asked for an armistice of 24 hours to bury his dead. He knew, as we knew, that reinforcements is hastening to his assistance[35] so I refused his request, for it was obviously only an expedient to gain time, and he can bury his dead at night as we did. Two days later on learning that some women and children are in the laager[36] I sent Cronje a letter under a flag of truce – I told how distressed I was to hear that they had, without my knowledge, been exposed to our fire, and I said I would pass them through our lines if they wished to leave – I also offered to send him doctors and medicines for his wounded. He declined to send the women away and accepted the services of our doctors, provided it was clearly understood they were not to leave his laager after they had entered it until, as he expressed it, "my laager is removed" – I replied to him that I could not spare the services of my doctors for such an indefinite period – He then made a further proposal that I should establish a hospital for his wounded about 1,000 yards west of his laager, to which he would allow free entry for my medical officers – I refused this for the reasons that it would give Cronje a thousand yards more cover along the river bank, and also because I have no means of establishing a hospital for the Boer wounded – We have come here with such light equipment that it has been most difficult to arrange for our own wounded, most of whom have had to lie out in the open in great discomfort – I am sorry for Cronje for he must be in a desperate plight – He told me in his letter that he has no doctors[37] and no medicine for his wounded – His laager is crowded with dead animals, which are also lying about in the bed of the river, and I hear the stench in his camp is indescribable – In one way he is better off than we are, for the bulk of our troops are about a mile and a half down stream, and it is sickening to see dead cattle and horses floating down in our only water supply, and to realize the dangerous pollution which is taking place above us – Yet there is no remedy for it,[38] and all ranks are as cheerful as if they were undergoing no discomforts – It was suggested to me that we should assault Cronje's position at daybreak yesterday. As I wired to you, the personal inspection which I made of the position convinced me that such a course would result in a loss of life which I consider unjustifiable under the circumstances, and which I am loth to incur after our heavy losses of the 18th instant[39] – moreover Cronje is so crippled and shaken that the morale of his force must have suffered, and the place he holds is of no strategical importance –

We are experiencing extreme difficulty about supplies – None are obtainable locally, and owing to the drought water is rarely found except in the rivers – In most places there is little or no grazing for the animals and it is impossible to carry forage for them – Another point which affects military operations nowadays is the long range of modern weapons, which necessitates such a large area of ground to be taken up, that troops are exhausted before they reach a point where a supreme effort is required of them, and this is accentuated here by the great heat, and the impossibility of providing an ample supply of drinking water to troops on the march – We had learnt from spies and other sources that reinforements are being rapidly pushed into the Orange Free State from Natal, and as, by an oversight arrangements had not been made on the arrival of the force here to hold a kopje, which some Boer reinforcements had seized and which somewhat threatened our right flank, I decided yesterday to dislodge the enemy from it – The Cavalry and Horse Artillery moved round to the rear of the position by both flanks while it was shelled in front – The result was that the Boers numbering some 2000 hastily evacuated the kopje, with a loss to us of only 2 officers and 4 men wounded – About 100 of the enemy were killed and wounded[40] – They were thoroughly discomfited [sic] and their hasty retreat should have an excellent effect on the surrounding country – We took 80 or 90 prisoners from one of whom we learnt some interesting details about the fight at Spionkop – I enclose a report of his statement[41] which will show you how probable it is that, if our troops had persevered, the Boers would have retired from there – All the information we receive points to the fact that strenuous efforts are being made to prevent us from reaching Bloemfontein – It is impossible to predict as yet by what road we shall get there but, if practicable, I shall leave the river route, as I hear that halfway between here and Bloemfontein a position on the river of great natural strength is being strongly entrenched. The main question at issue is, will the supply of water available permit of my leaving the river route, and this I am enquiring into by sending the Cavalry and Horse Artillery on to Petrusburg. It will be a very anxious time during the next few days until we reach the railway, when I shall probably cut the railway line – Girouard with a battalion of railway Pioneers will be with us to repair the railway, and while I shall endeavour to force my way in to Bloemfontein from the South I shall do all that is possible to repair the line to Cape Colony, probably via Bethulie, but for a few days we shall be in the position of having a troublesome enemy in our front while cut off from communication with our rear –

I must again impress on you the constant and severe drain on the army in horses, in men, and especially in officers. I strongly urge the necessity for more horses for Cavalry and Horse artillery being speedily sent to us, and also that endeavours should be made to send us periodically officers and drafts of men to replace casualties.

I am very hopeful that Buller may succeed this time in relieving Ladysmith – It seems clear that several thousand men have been withdrawn from there and from the Tugela to oppose my advance, as I expected would be the case, and I shall be bitterly disappointed if we do not hear of White being relieved within the next few days – Sir Alfred Milner is very anxious about the state of affairs in Cape Colony and continues to press me to send troops in various directions, especially to the North West and West of the main line of railway[42] – I am doing all I can to help him, but I feel that the one thing which will put an end to the war is to advance in strength in the Orange Free State, and that everything must be sacrificed to that end.

Our wounded, to the number of 700 or 800, left here last night in waggons for Modder river, whence they will be moved down country in the ambulance train. They have suffered great discomfort poor fellows, which has been unavoidable, but they have borne their sufferings without a complaint or a murmur in a most admirable manner.

As soon as I received your telegram conveying the sanction of Her Majesty's Government to issue the proclamation to the Burghers of the Orange Free State, I sent copies of it into the districts,[43] and I have managed to get some copies into Cronjes laager – Deserters say that the Orange Free State men are much discouraged by our advance and weary of the war, but that the Transvaalers are determined to continue their opposition.

I must close this letter now as the post goes very shortly, but I will continue to keep you informed by telegram of all that goes on.

BL MS Room, Lansdowne Papers L(5)48

19
Lord Roberts to Lord Lansdowne

[Holograph]

Hd. Qr. Camp. Paardeberg Camp.

Febr. 28th 1900.

It was a great pleasure to me to receive your letter of the 2nd instant.

You remark regarding hospitals that "the number of beds is far below what it ought to be" – my telegrams No. 120 of the 6th and 127 of the 8th instant, together with my letter of the 9th February[44] will have told you what my views are on the subject, and I have not the least doubt that, although our medical arrangements at the base are in a very satisfactory condition, they are inadequate with the army in the field. As regards nurses I have almost always found medical officers averse to employing them, and I have thought that one reason for this may be that they resent their presence, as they know the nurses keep a vigilant watch over their patients and detect at once any carelessness or want of attention on the part of the doctors –

I note what you say about the complaints made by Moberly Bell.[45] At my request Stanley has written to him fully and explained all the regulations in force here which, so far as I can learn, meet with the complete approval of all the Press Correspondents with this portion of the army. I see them constantly and never hear a complaint of any kind – I believe this is mainly due to the fact that Stanley is carrying on his duties with unusual tact, discretion, and intelligence.

My telegrams and letters will have told you of our urgent need for horses, and I am much reassured to learn from you that almost any number of horses can be supplied from England. I am confident that the only means of bringing this war to a speedy and satisfactory conclusion is for our force to be more mobile than that of the Boers – We should have pushed on from here ere this had it not been that our Artillery and Cavalry horses are quite unequal to any prolonged effort without rest and an opportunity of grazing. I would gladly have advanced, for the effect would have been excellent, following on Cronjes surrender,[46] but I feel it is useless attempting to move 70 miles across a country in which neither food or forage can be obtained, until I can make sure of doing it in a thoroughly satisfactory manner –

Wyndham's speech was excellent, and I am glad he did not attempt to defend whatever shortcomings have come to light or the regrettable accidents which have occurred of late, but that he promised the public every advantage should be taken of the experience gained in this war to make the Army of the future thoroughly practical and serviceable –

I visited the Boer position yesterday and from what I saw I am very thankful I did not allow myself to be persuaded to be committed to an assualt, at any rate until we had advanced our trenches sufficiently to make it extremely awkward for the Boers in theirs – we were gaining ground with our trenches each night, but meanwhile dissension among the Boer troops, scarcity of food, and loss of morale caused by our bombardment and by a want of confidence in their Commander, were bringing about the result I ardently hoped for. I confess it was a great relief to me when I was able to despatch a telegram to you yesterday morning saying that Cronje and his troops had surrendered unconditionally.[47]

They had constructed their entrenchments in an extraordinarily skilful manner – Deep narrow trenches, with each side well hollowed out, in which they got complete shelter from shellfire, and if their food could have lasted, they might have defied this large force for some time to come –

Three officers and nine of our men were prisoners in the hands of the enemy – They were treated with great consideration by the Boers, who did their best to secure them from being injured by our fire – These officers tell me that after personally witnessing the effect of lyddite, they are unanimous in considering it is of little or no value against purely field entrenchments. This opinion was corroborated by Major Albrecht, the commander of the Orange Free State artillery and other Boer officers, who gave their opinion very frankly on the subject – It seems to me it is worthy of serious [and?] of early consideration whether we should not take steps at once to provide some other kind of shells for use in our heavy howitzer batteries –

It is satisfactory to find among the prisoners are some of the leading men of the Orange Free State and South African Republic[48] – They were evidently nervous when they first reached our camp as to the reception they might meet with, but after they had been fed and spoken to kindly they soon became reassured, and talked quite openly with our officers about recent events. The principal topic was the unpopularity of Cronje in his force, and they resented his having declined my offer to give safe conduct to the women and children and to afford medical assistance to the wounded – Some of the latter are in a deplorable state – Cronje informed me he had only about 70 wounded, but over 170 have been found lying about in the trenches, uncared for, their wounds festering, and they say the only treatment they have had has been applications of tobacco and vinegar –

Cronje is a short, strongly built man of about 60, with a determined, coarse, cruel face. He compares unfavourably with Chief Commandant Wolmarans of the Transvaal Army, who is a fine looking old fellow, rather like a Scotch shepherd, whose only request to me was that he might not be deprived of a favo<u>rite old horse, which of course I gladly complied with.

Mrs. Cronje and one or two other officers' wives, with several women and children were in the laager all the time we were bombarding it, and I feel very strongly about Cronjes cruelty in subjecting them unnecessarily to such an ordeal. Mrs. Cronje will accompany her husband to his destination and the others will be sent to their homes as soon as it can be arranged –

Tomorrow I ride into Kimberley, returning here the following day – I earnestly hope that ere very long we may be gladdened by hearing of the relief of Ladysmith – The telegram from Buller which I have just wired on to you makes me hope that he will certainly attain his object this time.

Kimberley, 1st March. This is glorious news about Dundonald being in Ladysmith.[49] I am so delighted. I came over here this morning to see Mr. Rhodes and Methuen about Mafeking, and return to camp tomorrow. The relief of Mafeking is troublesome on account of the great distance it is off – 215 miles from this.

Methuen wants to start off at once, but I don't think he quite realizes all the difficulties.

Very many thanks for your very kind telegram of congratulations on the relief of Ladysmith – and please thank Lady Lansdowne[50] for her nice postscript to it.

BL MS Room, Lansdowne Papers L(5)48

20
Lord Roberts to Queen Victoria

Army Head Quarters,

[Printed letter]

Bloemfontein, 15th March 1900.

I am quite distressed to think that nearly two months should have elapsed since I had the honour of writing to your Majesty. I appreciate so highly the privilege of being permitted to address your Majesty direct, and I have so many kind and gracious acts to thank Your Majesty for that I would not have allowed a mail to pass without writing to express my gratitude, had it been possible to do so, but we have been so constantly on the move since we left Cape Town that I have been obliged to confine my correspondence to telegrams. I trust, therefore, that your Majesty will be pleased to forgive a silence that may have appeared as carelessness or forgetfulness on my part.

In the first place let me offer my most grateful thanks for your Majesty's most gracious letter of the 16th February, and telegram of congratulations on the occupation of Bloemfontein,[51] both of which reached me to-day. The telegram will be published in Army Orders[52] to-day, and will afford the greatest gratification to all the troops.

I have endeavoured, by daily telegrams to the Secretary of State for War to keep the country informed of what has happened since I left Cape Town on the 6th February, and it is a great satisfaction to me and the Army in South Africa to learn that the operations in which we have been engaged have met with the approval of your Majesty and the British Nation.

It is impossible for me to describe to your Majesty how admirably the troops have behaved. They have been tried greatly during the past few weeks. Want of transport prevented tents being carried. The heat during the day was great, and the extreme dryness of the air caused an almost intolerable thirst which it was difficult to quench on account of the scarcity of water, and such water as was to be had was scarcely drinkable. Officers and men had frequently to bivouac under a drenching rain, and more than once they had to be satisfied with half rations owing to the supply wagons being unable to keep up with the column. But nothing damped their spirits, and they cheerfully responded to any call that was made upon them. The day we arrived here the Guards Brigade, under Major-General Pole-Carew, marched 40 miles almost without a halt in their desire to take part in the entry into Bloemfontein.

It would amuse your Majesty to see the officers in their new costume. They wear belts with pouches and carry rifles slung over their shoulders, and, but for the gallant way in which they come to the front whenever the danger is greatest, it must puzzle the Boers to distinguish them from the men.

I took the opportunity of being encamped within 30 miles of Kimberley to ride in there for one day[53] to consult with Lord Methuen as to the best means of effecting the relief of Mafeking. The inhabitants gave me, Lord Kitchener, and our Staff, a very cordial reception, and it delighted me to witness the outburst of loyal feeling. Flags were flying all over the town, and "God save the Queen" was sung both at the beginning and ending of the ceremony that was held in the Town Hall in our honour. I enclose a copy of the address[54] presented to me, as I told the inhabitants of Kimberley I would not fail to bring their expressions of loyalty to your Majesty's notice.

We had for some days previous to my visit been sending our sick and wounded to Kimberley, and it was gratifying to find how well they had been looked after. All the public buildings had been turned into hospitals, and the people seemed to think they could not do enough for our soldiers. Once in hospital the wounded want for nothing, but the poor fellows often suffer much before they are picked up by the ambulances. The extent of a modern battlefield is so considerable that troops become greatly scattered, and it often takes a long time for the Doctors with the stretcher bearers to go to the assistance of the wounded. The behaviour of the men under such circumstances is beyond all praise. Not a murmur or complaint is ever uttered. All are most patient, and when help comes to them their anxiety is that those of their comrades who are more seriously injured than themselves should be attended to first. Your Majesty's soldiers are indeed grand fellows.

It will, I think, interest your Majesty to read the enclosed account[55] given by a trooper of Kitchener's Horse, of the time he spent as prisoner in Cronje's laager. It gives an insight into Boer life, and shows that no ill feeling exists between the people of the two Republics and our soldiers.

The Orange Free State south of this and the whole of the Cape Colony, except on the extreme west, is rapidly settling down. The Proclamations I have issued are having the desired effect, and men are daily laying down their arms and returning to their usual occupations.[56] It seems unlikely that this State will give much more trouble. The Transvaalers will probably hold out, but their numbers must be greatly reduced, and I trust it will not be very long before the war will have been brought to a satisfactory conclusion.

We are obliged to rest here for a short time to let men and animals recover, and provide the former with new boots and clothes.

With my most respectful duty.

South African War, 1899–1900. Vol. I. Home and Oversea Correspondence by Field-Marshal Lord Roberts, pp. 71–3.[57]

21
Speech by Lord Roberts
At a Dinner given by the War Correspondents.[58]
Bloemfontein, 28th March 1900
[Typed copy in a bound volume]

I can assure you I most fully appreciate your kindness in inviting me to dine with you to-night, and I value highly the very cordial manner in which you have responded to the toast of my health, proposed as it has been in such complimentary and flattering terms by Mr. H.A. Gwynne.

Gentlemen, the position of the Commander of an Army in the field with regard to War Correspondents, whose duty it is to describe to the British public the manner in which a campaign is being conducted, is no doubt a peculiar one. Indeed, I have heard it compared to that of a prisoner in the dock, awaiting the reply of the foreman to the question put to the jury – "Guilty or not guilty?" I confess I never have had occasion to feel myself in such a predicament. I may say, moreover, that if I were permitted to select a jury to pronounce a verdict on the operations entrusted to my charge by Her Majesty's Government, or to express an opinion on the efficiency, the fortitude, and the discipline of the splendid troops it is my good fortune to command, I would ask for no more impartial, and certainly no more competent, judges than the brilliant band of War Correspondents who accompany this Army.

No one, gentlemen, recognizes more clearly than I do the benefits which are conferred by War Correspondents on the millions who anxiously look for news from the seat of war, especially when that news is collected and communicated to them by experts who do not hesitate to run any risk to procure it, and who seem insensible to fatigue in the performance of their duty.

I read with the deepest interest the War Correspondents' contributions to the principal newspapers, and at times I find myself at a loss which to admire most, the vivid pictures they give of what has occurred during long and anxious days, when the rapidly changing incidents make it difficult for even the best informed to know what has really taken place, or the determination and tenacity of purpose which enable such scenes to be recorded in the bivouac long after the camp has sunk to rest, and then transported for perhaps over a hundred miles, as was recently the case, to a telegraph station whence the news could be flashed all over the world.

Gentlemen, the best years of your lives are spent among soldiers, you share their hardships and their dangers, and as comrades you must allow me to greet you to-night. There is one among you who has a special claim on the hearts of soldiers, my friend Rudyard Kipling.[59] I can assure him that of all those who watched anxiously for good news during his recent severe illness, none were more interested than the soldiers, amongst whom his name is a household word.

Gentlemen, I must not trespass longer on your time; for however much I might wish to do so, I could not overlook the fact that, in our midst, there is a stern official, who relentlessly limits the number of words which may be telegraphed, written, or even uttered, and in his presence I feel that I must content myself by expressing to you again my thanks for your kind hospitality. I shall ever remember with pleasure the evening I have spent in your company in the Railway Station refreshment rooms at Bloemfontein.

NAM 7101–23–126–3

22
Lord Roberts to Queen Victoria

Army Head Quarters

[Printed letter]

Bloemfontein, 15th April 1900

I had the great honour to receive last mail Your Majesty's gracious letter of the 16th March for which I beg to tender my most respectful thanks.

I did not think when I wrote to Your Majesty on the 15th March that my next letter would also be dated from Bloemfontein – but the delay here has been unavoidable.

We are dependent upon a base 750 miles away for the main portion of our supplies, and as the railway is only a single line, the transport of goods is necessarily slow – a great trial to one's patience when everyone wants everything at the same time. The Cavalry and Horse Artillery have had to be almost remounted, their horses were so done up by hard work and getting very little food.

The transport animals were in much the same plight. Then the soldiers required a fresh kit, for many of them were in rags. Ammunition and stores of all kinds had to be replaced, and large supplies of food had to be collected. A great deal has been done during the past month, and in another ten days the Army will, I trust, be ready to take the field again.

Meanwhile the enemy have not failed to take advantage of our enforced idleness. They have spread over the country in small parties, threatening our long line of communication,[60] frightening, in some instances indeed ill-treating, the Burghers who had laid down their arms and returned to their farms under the conditions of my Proclamation. Not being able to give these people proper protection has caused me considerable concern, and I am glad to think that this state of affairs will not last much longer.

In Bloemfontein itself there has been no trouble. The inhabitants were, naturally perhaps, anxious when we first arrived lest the soldiers should prove inconvenient neighbours, but after a very few days the shops were all opened, and business was carried on as usual. Soldiers walk about in the most orderly manner, and not a single instance of their being rude or rough has been brought to my notice. The people are quite surprised that such a large number of troops, especially during a time of war could be so orderly and well-behaved. I know what pleasure it will give Your Majesty to hear this.

The health of the men too is very good. There are some 2,000 in hospital, but this is only at the rate of 4 per cent., a very small proportion during a campaign – mainly owing, no doubt, to the absence of malaria, from which the Orange Free State is remarkably free.

The climate now is quite perfect, and I hope that Lady Roberts and my daughters will be able to come here ere long. They will find it an agreeable change after Cape Town.[61]

I understand that Your Majesty does not approve of ladies coming out to South Africa from mere curiosity. I am forbidding any to enter the Orange Free State except those who may have a son or husband in hospital, or whose husband is likely to be quartered in Bloemfontein for some time.

We were all delighted to hear of the splendid reception Your Majesty met with in Dublin.[62] I know how very pleased the Irish people are at Your Majesty honouring their country with a visit. Their hearts were won by Irish soldiers being permitted to wear shamrock on St. Patrick's Day, and I am sure that the formation of an Irish regiment of the Guards will be thoroughly appreciated. –

We were all greatly shocked to hear of the attempt to assassinate the Prince of Wales,[63] and we rejoice that His Royal Highness's life was so mercifully spared. It is terrible to think what might have happened.

I wish I could have been present when Your Majesty so kindly reviewed 30,000 children. How pleased and proud they must all have been. I am sure that the boys of the Royal Hibernian Military School did not pass by Your Majesty unobserved.

South African War, 1899–1900. Vol. I. Home and Oversea Correspondence by Field-Marshal Lord Roberts, pp. 98–9.[64]

23
Lord Roberts to Lord Lansdowne
Bloemfontein, 29th April 1900.

[Holograph]

I had the pleasure yesterday to receive your letter of the 6th April.[65] Many thanks for your kind expressions and cheering words about the mishaps at the Waterworks[66] and at Reddersburg.[67] I trust we shall have no more similar troubles, and that any encouragement the capture of our guns and men may have given the enemy has been more than counterbalanced by their inability to take Wepener,[68] and by their force in front of Dewetsdorp having had to retire after the labours they had expended in making it as they considered impregnable.[69]

Dewetsdorp will now be permanently garrisoned, and an officer has gone there as District Commissioner, whose duties will be to make himself acquainted with the people, to encourage those who are for us, and to punish those who have behaved treacherously after having taken their oaths to abide by the conditions of my proclamations. It is absolutely necessary, I find, to carry out disarmament in the most thorough manner, and to requisition all riding horses and ponies. Even the most anti-English Boers will be of no use as a fighting unit if he has no rifle to shoot with, and no horse to ride on.

The lenient way in which the Boers have been treated has, no doubt, had a good effect generally, but it is necessary to let them see that they cannot be friends with us one day and enemies another. A few have been made examples of in the way of imprisonment and confiscation of property, and nothing more will I hope, be required.

I send with this a copy of the Volksraad proceedings held at Kroonstad on the 3rd and 4th April, from which you will see that Mr. Steyn accuses us of violating the Red Cross and white flags, and that a Mr. Beukes stated "that when the English came into the country they devastated everything".[70]

I need not say there is not a word of truth in either of these statements. The first little town we visited in the Orange Free State was Jacobsdal. Not a house was injured, not an inhabitant ill treated.[71] I was there myself for the first two days, and when I left Major-General Wavell took charge. On his departure he reported to me that not a single complaint had been made against a soldier and the people thanked him for the way in which order had been maintained.

During the march we came across very few homes; those which were occupied remained uninjured. Those from which the owners had fled had been gutted by Boers or Kaffirs before our arrival.

As regards the violation of the White and Red Cross flags, I feel sure that the Boers will not be able to prove our soldiers guilty on any occasion.

I enclose also an account given by a Mr. Williams who resides near this, and who was, I believe, Commissary General in the Boer Army during the early part of the war. It is interesting as showing the numbers opposed to us now and six months ago. There may be 3,000 or 4,000 more than Mr. Williams estimates, but I expect he is not far wrong in giving the present strength of the Boer force at about 30,000 –

One would think there ought to be no difficulty in bringing this number to terms with our large force, and there probably would not be if we could only come across them, but they slip away in the most extraordinary manner. At the same time I think we might have done better on more than one occasion if our Cavalry had been judiciously handled. French will never be a great Cavalry leader, he is wanting in initiative and has no idea how to take care of his horses. He carried out the relief of Kimberley in a satisfactory manner because he acted exactly in accordance with the instructions I gave him. But the following day, instead of giving his horses a much needed rest, he worked them from daylight till dark without any injury to the enemy or advantage to ourselves. I have never been able to get a complete return of the horse casualties on that occasion, but a large number of men had to be left at Kimberley as they had no horses to ride.

At Poplar Grove[72] French started late and allowed himself to be beguiled by the enemy into fighting a series of rear guard actions, instead of giving them a wide berth and placing himself on the Boer's line of retreat. They were thus enabled to carry off their guns, and Kruger and Steyn effected their escape!

It was much the same at Driefontein,[73] and at Dewetsdorp[74] a day or two ago the enemy ought to have caught it if our Cavalry had shown a little intelligent activity.

Our Mounted Infantry has much improved of late, and I intend to see whether their employment in large bodies will not bring about more satisfactory results.

We make a move tomorrow,[75] and I trust that by the time you receive this we shall be well on our way towards Kroonstadt.

The arrangements for the Relief of Mafeking are well advanced, and Hunter telegraphs that he hopes to be able to start on the 3rd May. The main difficulty will be forcing the passage of the Vaal River, but once that has been effected, I trust the Flying Column will proceed without meeting with any serious opposition.[76]

I am endeavouring to carry out the second of Lord Salisbury's wishes, viz: The destruction of the railway somewhere to the west of Komaiti [sic] Po<o>rt.[77] A Mr Forbes, the gentleman who offered to conduct a small force for the purpose when I was in Capetown, is now returning there. The scheme fell through then because Buller said he could give no assistance. I now propose to make over to Mr. Forbes as many of Strathcona's Horse[78] as he desires, and a young Engineer officer with a few Sappers, and I shall be delighted if the business is carried out successfully.

BL MS Room, Lansdowne Papers L(5)48

24
Lord Roberts to Lieutenant-General Leslie Rundle
Brandfort 4 May 1900

[Manuscript copy]
Strictly confidential

Before I move further[79] I think it is desirable to place you in possession of my general intentions for our advance north.

It seems clear, from what has happened in the past, that if the enemy gets an opportunity, they will again at once invade the South Eastern portion of the Orange Free State. By doing so, they would strategically speaking, have the best chance of injuring us, and should they succeed in getting a footing there, our lines of communications would be materially threatened. It would cause great consternation in Cape Colony, and it would be necessary for me to send back troops from the front, which would materially interfere with my plan of campaign.

Under these circumstances I look to you to take such measures as you may consider necessary to prevent any large body of the enemy being able once more to invest Wepener, or to move towards Smithfield through the Dewetsdorp–Wepener gap.

As soon as it can be arranged, Chermside with the Head Quarters of the 3rd Division, will proceed to Bloemfontein, and he will have under his especial charge the line of railway from Bethulie and Norval's Pont up to this point.

It will be your duty to exercise a vigilant control to the east of the railway, and prevent the enemy from gaining a footing there.

My belief is that, as we move north, the Boers will find it necessary to withdraw the whole of their troops now in front of Thabanchu, and also the small bodies now roving about the country south of Dewetsdorp.

As soon as you are satisfied that they have withdrawn in the manner I anticipate, you should move such a portion of your force as you think necessary to Ladybrand.

With Thabanchu and Ladybrand occupied in sufficient strength, with Dewetsdorp, Wepener, and Smithfield properly garrisoned, with the people disarmed, and their horses taken from them – a measure which is now being thoroughly carried out – the Boers will be quite unable to move down South, and even if they do get there, they will find no armed and mounted burghers to assist them.

I regret to hear that Hamilton has taken on one of your Field Batteries, but if it can be possibly arranged, the Battery shall be returned to you, either before we reach Kroonstadt or immediately afterwards.

We are now working north on two lines. Hamilton on the east is moving direct to Winburg. He has with him the following forces:–

Broadwood's Brigade of Cavalry
2nd Brigade of Mounted Infantry
19th Brigade of the 9th Division
and the 21st Brigade.

Following him, and sufficiently near to support him, if necessary, is Colvile with the Highland Brigade.

I have with me the 1st Brigade of Mounted Infantry, and the 7th & 11th Divisions, and hope later on to be joined by French and his Cavalry.

To morrow [sic] we shall reach the Vet river, and on Sunday Smaldeel Junction, at the same time that Hamilton reaches Winburg. Both forces will then move north towards Kroonstadt. I hope no time will be lost in getting there, but I fear that our progress will necessarily be slow as we must repair the railway as we move along to replenish our supplies.

Please keep me fully informed of what goes on. You have a most important task to perform, and I feel sure I may rely upon you to carry out with energy, and ability the responsible duty I have assigned to you.

Please acknowledge the receipt of this letter.

The Sudan Archive, University of Durham: Wingate Papers, 231/1/53[80]

25
Lord Roberts to Lord Lansdowne

Brandfort, 4th May 1900

[Holograph]

I am afraid we shall have left Brandfort before the mail of the 14th April arrives, in which case I shall have to wait until next week to reply to any letter you may have sent me by the mail of that date.

We are on the move again I am thankful to say, and, if I may judge by the very half-hearted manner in which the Boers fought yesterday, we are not likely to meet with any determined opposition between this and Kroonstad.[81] Advancing as we are now doing in two columns prevents the enemy from meeting both columns in great strength while we are near enough to support each other should there be reason to do so.

The railway up to this has not been seriously impaired and the telegraph line hardly so at all, but, as we advance further north, we shall have trouble no doubt in repairing the bridges over the Vet and Zand, but as the rivers are low at this season, there will probably be no difficulty in making diversions fairly quickly. These will answer all practical purposes, and I trust that, as you receive this, we shall be at Kroonstad.

There is no other place north of that where Steyn can form a so-called government,[82] and when we get there I presume the time will have arrived to announce the annexation of the Orange Free State by Great Britain. I am in communication with Sir A. Milner about this.

The Boers have remained in certain numbers in front of Thabanchu in the hope of being able to make a second raid on the South-East portion of the State, but with Rundle's division at Thabanchu, and with Dewetsdorp, Wepener, and Smithfield occupied, it will be scarcely possible for the enemy to give us serious trouble again in that direction and I expect to hear that all who intend to prolong the war will soon be moving off towards the Transvaal.

It is too late now for Buller to afford me any assistance by operating through the passes of the Drakensburg,[83] and as the enemy cannot act against him from that direction in any force, and are almost certain to withdraw numbers of their men from the Biggarsburg as we advance north, I have suggested to Buller that he should work up the line of the railway, and endeavour to help us when we enter the Transvaal. I fear, however, from his reply (which I enclose)[84] that we shall have to depend mainly on ourselves.

Amongst the prisoners taken here yesterday is a man named Maurice belonging to the Irish Contingent. He and his compatriots marched through Brandfort in the morning with their green flags flying, and took up a position immediately above the little town. But they scuttled off in hot haste, headed by their Commandant Blake, as the Guards Brigade approached within rifle shot.[85]

A Mrs. Richard Chamberlain[86] has given great trouble by her persistence in visiting the hospitals at Capetown at all hours without leave or licence. Neither Forestier Walker nor the P.M.O. seemed able to cope with her, but fortunately one of the patients complained indirectly to me of the inconvenience caused by the lady's unwelcome visits, and this enabled me to prohibit Mrs. Chamberlain being admitted to any of the hospitals in future.

This episode aptly illustrates the remarks about the interference of busy bodies in our hospitals, which Reuter reports Mrs. Treeves to have made on a recent ...... in London.

I am very sorry you should have thought it necessary to suggest the omission of that part of my Despatch of the 26th March which refers to the working of the Transport Service. I have entered so fully into the matter in the telegraphic reply which I have just despatched that I will not trouble you with any further explanation – except to say that nothing was further from my thoughts, when I wrote the despatch, than to make any reflection on Buller or anyone else, I merely wished to point out for future guidance the defects of a system which had for the first time been tried in a great war, and which, if left unchanged, might lead to some serious disaster in the future.[87]

I hear that the Boers object to our following their example, and helping ourselves to what we require for man and beast. We have acted in this way lately when treachery has been brought home to the owners, and the Resident Commissioner in Basutoland[88] impress me it is having the best possible effect. The farmers are beginning to think that it will be better for them to stay quietly at home and look after property instead of fighting against us.

I wish we could punish the Boers severely in some fight, but they are too quick for us, and always manage to carry off their guns and property.

You and Lady Lansdowne will, I know, be glad to hear that Charlie[89] will join us shortly.

BL MS Room, Lansdowne Papers L(5)48

26
Sir Alfred Milner to Lord Roberts[90]

Government House,
Cape Town.

[Typed copy]

10.5.1900.

Confidential.

I have just received your telegram, announcing that the enemy are in full retreat beyond the Zand River. So far the advance has been more rapid than anybody could have expected. People are already beginning to talk as if we should be in Pretoria tomorrow. I am more modest in my ideas and should be perfectly satisfied, and think it very good business, if we get Johannesburg in two months. I have always maintained that the war would last till August.

At the same time my thoughts are much occupied just now with what ought to be done, when we do arrive, as an immense deal may depend, for the future, on our making a proper start.

The moment you reach the Rand,[91] there will be an immense pressure put upon us to get back. This will have to be resisted, as for some time the single line will have its work cut out for it in supplying the army and the people already there. And this will give us an opportunity of getting in the right people first – a matter of great importance – and keeping the undesirables back to the last.

I was very glad to get your telegram about the Criminal Investigation Department and fully agree as I shall wire to you tomorrow with the idea of getting out a man from England. And I take this opportunity of telling you what I have been thinking about the question of the policing of Johannesburg generally.

It does not seem to me it would be a good plan to mix up the Detective business (which will be very heavy and complicated in this case) with ordinary police business. They ought to be separate departments, though to prevent friction there ought to be one officer over both to whom the Chief of the Detective Department and the Chief of the Constabulary, being co-ordinate with one another, should both report.

The policing of Johannesburg will be a very peculiar business, quite distinct from that of the rest of the country, which should be entrusted to mounted marksmen of the C.M.R. or C.M.P. type.[92]

Indeed I should like to see <u>one</u> body of Police of this kind (at least 2,000 strong) take over the whole of the country work in the Transvaal and O.F.S.

But apart from these, and totally different in character, as their work will be totally different, we must have a <u>Rand Police</u> to look after not only Johannesburg but the whole mining district of which it is the centre. This Police, including both a detective department and an ordinary Constabulary, will ultimately, no doubt, be under the future municipality. But we shall have to create it and I have no doubt we shall be able to create, and in time to hand over to the future municipality, a much better Police than they could, at starting, frame for themselves.

My idea as to its composition (except the detective Branch which must be separately recruited) would be as follows: As soon as we get hold of the Rand to <u>disband entirely all</u> existing forces (consisting largely of the greatest scoundrels unhung, and altogether of our enemies) and to entrust the policing of the town to the irregular Corps, recruited mainly from the Rand, such as the Imperial Light Horse, the 1st Regiment of the South African Light Horse, Thorneycroft's and Bethune's or a selected portion of them. Their local knowledge would be valuable and under a strong Commander like Wools Sampson I believe they would keep perfect order. Of course this would only be a temporary arrangement, but the advantages of it would be (1) it would be instantly adopted, the material being to hand (2) it would not lead to any embarrassing claims, as the great bulk of these forces, though they might in their own interest be willing to do police duty for a few weeks or months would want to get back to their several employments and would certainly not stick to Police work, but (3) a certain number will probably remain and supply a nucleus (especially of officers) for the new force, which could then be filled up by enlistment throughout South Africa. By that time the war would be over and many Reservists Yeomen, &c., with previous police experience, would be available. I think we ought thus to get one of the best police forces in the world – as certainly it will have one of the toughest jobs in dealing with the international scoundrelism which is at present establishing itself on the Rand.

I should be glad, at your leisure (if you ever have any; perhaps you may pass a day or two at Kroonstad) to know your views about this.

Meanwhile our C.I.D. man will be coming from England.

There are a lot more things to be settled beforehand in regard to our new occupation. But perhaps this will suffice for today.

I am anxious that the Revd. Mr Darragh (an Irish R.C. Priest but very loyal) who has only just left Johannesburg, should be attached to your advancing force. He has been 13 years in the place, and not only would his local knowledge (he is known to the Intelligence Department) be of use to you in getting in, but he would be a great help to the new Government at its first establishment because of his intimate acquaintance with different classes of the population.

TAD, FK Milner Papers 115–1204 (original in Bodleian Library)

27
Lord Lansdowne to Lord Roberts

12th May 1900

[Copy]

Thanks for your letter of 15/4, which throws an interesting light upon what is now happening. It is very pleasant to watch your steady onward movement which has been brilliantly successful, and has made an excellent impression here and abroad. I fear you may have a stiff fight before you at Kroonstadt – and I don't quite like the presence of an apparently considerable force in the Thaba Nchu region; but Rundle should be strong enough to control it.

We kept the Mafeking column a dead secret on this side – I trust all may go well with it.

The moment too should come when Buller ought to be able to assert himself. I wonder that he has not been 'demonstrating' ere now.

By the way I thought it best to let Wolseley and some of my colleagues see the telegrams which passed between you and him. I think it more than probable that unauthentic accounts of these communications may be coming home, and it is desirable that Wolseley should know exactly what happened. I have circulated your recent Despatches to the cabinet and we shall decide next week whether to publish them or not – After our Spion Kop experience, there is an inclination to give the public as little as possible.[93]

The cabinet yesterday agreed readily to your proposal that you should proclaim the annexation of the O.F.S. as soon as you are in possession of Kroonstadt. To do so sooner would I think have been premature.

The new C. in C. India has not yet been selected. I don't think I [G?] Hamilton would take Palmer for his Council, but he is holding his hand pending further consid<eratio>n of the other appointments.

My attention had already been called to the refusal of armament pay to the garrison artillery officers, and I have put the matter right. I share your view that it would have been a hardship to deny them this privilege.

I enclose a memo as to horses and mules supplied or to be supplied   I hope we are keeping pace with your requirements, and that the quality of the animals is fairly good.

I had a most interesting talk with Henderson,[94] & hope to see him again. He gave me a good report of you which I was glad to hear, and he seemed to think that on the whole the S. African Force had been well provided for.

I am so glad Marlborough is doing well. I repeated your commendation of him to Lady Blandford[95] who was hugely pleased.

Elphinstone will, I am sure make himself useful.

BL MS Room, Lansdowne Papers L(5)48

28
Lord Roberts to Sir Alfred Milner

Kroonstad, 16th May 1900,

[Typed letter]

I have to acknowledge your letter of the 10th instant[96] in which you discuss the question of what police arrangements will be necessary after we reach the Transvaal, both as regards the rural police, and also the special corps of Rand police.

I am quite in accordance with your views as to the necessity of keeping undesirable people out of Johannesburg and the Transvaal generally, until such time as we may consider necessary; and this can easily be arranged by refusing to grant permits to enter the country by rail, both from Natal and also from Cape Colony.

Irrespective of whether it is advisable to have a large influx of people into the Transvaal before the country has quite settled down, and military precautions can be relaxed, I foresee quite enough difficulties in supplying the troops by means of the single line of railway from Cape Colony without desiring to have them added to by having to feed a large civil population, which cannot be arranged until the line to Natal is repaired.

I agree with you that the rural police should be men of the type now serving in the various Colonial corps, and I anticipate no difficulty in getting a sufficient number for the work. They should, as you say, be picked mounted men, and their duty will be to keep order throughout the outlying districts.

The general administration of the force might be on the lines of the Irish Constabulary.

I also concur in your view as to the necessity for a <u>Rand Police</u>, and that such a body must be entirely distinct from the District Constabulary. The first step, as you suggest, must be to disband all existing forces of the kind, and it may be necessary to deport a certain number of them. I consider your proposal an excellent one, to entrust the policing of the town and the Rand generally as soon as we reach Jonannesburg, to men who have been enlisted from that district, until arrangements can be made for organizing the body of men that will eventually form the Rand police.

From all I have heard of Wools Sampson, I imagine he would do admirably as head of such a body, and the selection would be a very appropriate one in view of the position he originally held in the Reform Committee,[97] and his subsequent detention in prison after the Jameson Raid.[98] Am I right in understanding that you would propose him as the head of the Rand Police, to whom the Chief of the Constabulary department and the Chief of the Detective department would be subordinate?

For such a post I consider a strong man of special administrative ability and soldierlike instincts is indispensable, so unless Major Wools Sampson is, in your opinion, fitted for the work, we must look for someone else.

Brigadier General Settle is well spoken of, and he has shown energy and administrative ability on the line of communications. Colonel Benson A.A.G. in the 6th Division seems a likely candidate, but the man who would, I believe, be in all respects best fitted is a Colonel Hill in the Indian Staff Corps. He would make an excellent Commissioner of Police.

As regards the detective department, the Chief of it will, as you say, be shortly coming out from England, and he must by degrees select his own men. As a temporary measure we could lend him some detectives from the Metropolitan police, now serving in the Guards, and I have no doubt the old members of the Reform Committee could tell us of some reliable men for such a service.

As we both agree on the general principles to be followed I would suggest you should have a scheme for the Rand Police drawn up at once, to be put into operation as soon as we reach Johannesburg.

I shall be glad to have the Rev. Mr. Darragh in my force, so I hope he will join us as soon as practicable. The enclosed permit will enable him to travel up country.

TAD, FK Milner Papers 115–1204 (original in Bodleian Library)

29
Lord Roberts to Lord Lansdowne
Army Head Quarters, Kroonstad,

[Holograph]

17th May 1900

I did not write to you last mail, but I kept you informed as well as I could by telegraph of what was going on. We have been moving pretty rapidly since my letter of the 4th instant from Brandfort, although the enemy have done their best to delay us by destroying the railway. The bridges over the Vet and Zand rivers will take months to repair, but luckily this is the dry season and the diversions are not likely to be much damaged before October by rain, and long before that time I sincerely trust that the war will be over. Lt. Colonel Girouard, the Director of Railways, is full of resource and understands his business thoroughly; It is really wonderful how quickly he gets trains over broad rivers and deep spruits.

The short time it took us to traverse the distance between Bloemfontein and this (124 miles) has done much to disconcert the Boer's plans. They hoped to have been able to stop us for at least a week at the Vet and the same time at the Zand.[99] They are greatly disheartened in consequence, and I doubt the Free Staters giving us much more trouble although Steyn and the other officials with them are doing their best to keep them in the field by telling them that large contingents of French, Germans, and Russians are coming to their assistance and that America and the

Continental nations are sure to intervene if they will only hold out long enough.[100]

I was a little anxious when I left Bloemfontein lest the enemy should endeavour to make another raid into the South-Eastern portion of the State. They had a large force in front of Thabanchu, and I should have liked to have driven it off before moving north, but I thought it better not to delay the advance as it was so desirable to attract the enemy's attention from the neighbourhood of Kimberley and the little Flying Column destined for the relief of Mafeking. Moreover, I am a firm believer in the maxim that the surest way to disconcert and discourage an enemy is to go straight to their Head Quarters. Sir Philip Lagden, the Resident in Basutoland telegraphs from Maseru that "your rapid advance northwards has staggered and paralized the Boers in these parts". It has had the effect of clearing off the large force that was around Thabanchu and I hope in a few days time, when Rundle has occupied the Winburg-Ladybrand line, all fear of further disturbance in the South East will have ceased. Disarmament and deprivation of riding animals are being carried on in a very satisfactory manner. Boers are giving up their arms voluntarily in various places, notwithstanding that Steyn has been telling them that their choice lay between continuing the war or being sent to St. Helena.[101] They are beginning to find out that all who have not taken a prominent part against us are allowed to return to their houses and live in peace.

I am glad to hear from Milner that the Cabinet approve of my proposal to announce the annexation of the Orange Free State. It will, I feel sure, do more than anything to settle the country. I shall have to remain here a few days longer until the repaired railway has reached this far, and shall then push on to the Vaal river where there will necessarily be another short delay. Meanwhile I am sending Columns about the country to disperse the marauders and encourage the well disposed.

Ian Hamilton's compact little force has gone to Lindley which Steyn has made the new seat of his so called Government. From there it will proceed to Heilbron and then take part in the advance to the Vaal river.

Methuen started on the 14th for this place via Hoopstad. He has a sufficient number of troops to overcome any opposition he is likely to meet with, and I trust he will not get into trouble.

Hunter is preparing to drive the enemy out of Christiana for so long as they hold that place the railway northwards from Kimberley will always be liable to be attacked.

Buller has at last made a move, and I fancy he will find his task much easier than he has been calculating upon. There cannot be any large number of the enemy in the Natal direction. It is important he should push on as Natal must be my base for supplies when we reach Johannesburg. I have advised him to avoid Lang's Nek and to move from Newcastle to Vrede and then on to Standerton. If he could be on the Vaal by the end of this month it would help me greatly.

I will be very pleased to see Major Crompton[102] and hear what he has to urge in favour of traction engines.[103] I pronounced against them for line of march purposes as they can only go a certain distance without a renewal of fuel, but for station work or for victualling outposts they are very valuable. We are using some in this way both at Kimberley and Bloemfontein.

I have been asked to bring to your notice the Bishop of Stepney as a successor to Edghill.[104] He did good work as head of the Oxford Mission in the East End of London, and I remember thinking him an able, practical man. "Padre" Adams begged me to mention his name to you, but he would never do for such a position as Chaplain General. A man of note, like Winnington-Ingram,[105] would I believe be acceptable to the Army Chaplains generally. A really good man at the head of that Department is very necessary.

You will see from the enclosed telegram[106] that the project for destroying a portion of the railway between Delagoa Bay and Pretoria is well advanced. It is, however, a very risky business, and I shall not be surprised if it does not succeed. I am sending a man to try and cut the railway between Pretoria and Elandsfontein, the junction of the three lines from Klerksdorp, Vereeniging and Natal. The enemy have hitherto succeeded in carrying off all the rolling stock, but if the line can be cut at the junction within the next ten days, we ought to be able to secure some.

I hope that Charlie would have been here ere this.

3 p.m. 17th May. Charlie has just arrived, looking very well but a trifle thin.

BL MS Room, Lansdowne Papers L(5)48

30
Lord Roberts to Queen Victoria

Army Head Quarters

[Holograph]

Kroonstad, 17th May 1900.

I have had the great honour and pleasure to receive your Majesty's letter of the 13th April, for which I beg to offer my most respectful thanks. The medallion Your Majesty was so kind as to enclose in the letter is most interesting. I feel very proud at being associated with your Majesty in such a way, and I shall always prize the little gift as one of my treasures.

We have got on well so far on our way towards Pretoria, and I hope that by the time Your Majesty receives this letter we shall have entered the Transvaal. The country is said to be fairly open to the north of Kroonstad, and there is only one more river of importance – the Vaal – to be crossed.

The rivers have delayed us greatly, for, although there is very little water in them at this season, they are broad with high steep banks, and as the enemy invariably blow up the bridges, diversions have to be made for the railway, and the roadways improved for the ox and mule wagons. These take time and we must wait until they are completed for we are almost entirely dependent upon the railway for our supplies. It is a long way from Capetown, which is our chief depot, to Kroonstad, over 870 miles, and, with the exception of meat and a little forage, everything required for men and animals has to be brought all that way.

I trust, Madam, that so far as the Orange Free State is concerned the war will soon be over. The people are thoroughly tired of it, they see they have no chance against us now, and they are beginning to realize how disgracefully they have been deceived by their Rulers, who, in order to induce them to continue fighting, have published false reports of the reception given to the peace delegates by the Continental Powers,[107] and have even gone so far as to state that many thousands of French, German, and Russian soldiers have landed at Delagoa Bay and are on their way to join the Boer Army. Anyhow it is improbable that many Free Staters will cross the Vaal, and it remains to be seen whether the South African Republic will be able to carry on the war if left to its own resources.

I am now looking out anxiously for news from Mafeking. The Flying Column which left the neighbourhood of Kimberley on the 4th May ought, if all has gone well, to be very close to the beleaguered garrison by this time. It would be sad indeed if Mafeking could not be relieved after the magnificent defence it has made.[108]

Colonel Baden Powell's pluck and resource are quite wonderful. He has been the life and soul of the place, and during the two hundred odd days Mafeking has been invested he has trained peaceful citizens to become valuable soldiers. In his latest report, dated the 1st May, he says that they are making excellent brawn out of horses heads!

I trust, Madam, you were pleased with the reception Your Majesty met with in Ireland, and that the visit was in all respects satisfactory. I am sure that my fellow country men and women are intensely gratified at the great honour paid them, and I shall be much disappointed if your Majesty's long stay in Dublin has not the happiest results throughout the country. I could not help thinking how agreeable it must have been to Your Majesty to have the Duke of Connaught as the Commander-in-Chief in Ireland on the occasion. His Royal Highness is sure to be popular wherever he goes, and no where more so than in the country from which he takes his title.

I had the honour yesterday to receive Your Majesty's gracious telegram of congratulations. It afforded the greatest gratification to the whole force.

Trusting that this letter will find you, Madam, in the best of health. With my most respectful duty,

RA VIC/ P9/91

31
Lord Roberts to Lord Lansdowne

Rhenoster River Camp,

[Holograph]

23rd May 1900.

We are not very far from the extreme northern limit of the Orange Free State, or, as it will be called "The Orange River Colony". Satisfactory in one way, but it is disappointing to think that the war is likely to end, so far as this state is concerned without our having given the Boers a beating since Dreifontein.[109] They will not give us a chance. Each time we get near them, they make elaborate arrangements to oppose us, but their hearts fail them at the last moment and off they go with their guns. They must have worked hard here at their entrenchments, and up till yesterday they apparently intended to give us a fight, but as soon as they heard that Heilbron was occupied,[110] and that our Cavalry had crossed the river a few miles lower down, they went off as fast as they could.

It is impossible to say whether they will oppose us on the Vaal — some think they may do so as the Transvaallers are most anxious to prevent our entering their country. If they do not make a stand there we ought to be at Johannesburg early in June.

24th. The annexation Proclamation will be dated this day,[111] and will be issued as soon as I can get printed copies from Capetown. The administration of "The Orange River Colony", will not, I trust, be a very difficult matter but I am afraid that "The South African Republic", especially Johannesburg, will give a great deal of trouble.

Then I am puzzled to know who to appoint as Governor. The one or two senior officers who would be suitable cannot be spared, and I am thinking of selecting Colin Mackenzie.[112] You will perhaps remember him at Simla as my A.D.C. – and afterwards as the officer who did so well in Hunza-Nagar when Durand was wounded. He is very determined and is unusually intelligent with a good deal of common sense. We had to leave Charlie at Kroonstad – He got a chill while sleeping on the Veldt, and the

Doctors thought it would be wise for him to remain in a house for a day or two. I daresay he will tell you himself how he is getting on.

Kerry looks wonderfully well.

BL MS Room, Lansdowne Papers L(5)48

32
Lord Roberts to Lord Lansdowne

Germiston, 30th May 1900.

[Holograph]

I hoped to have dated this letter from Johannesburg, but, as I have informed you in my daily bulletin, the town was too full of armed Boers to warrant our entering it today. The present Commandant is a Dr. Krause – an intelligent, sensible man – who had a long conversation with me today. He was in low spirits at the idea of having to surrender the town, but he admitted that the Boers could no longer hold out against us – I told him I would guarantee that our troops would make no disturbance in the town, and that I must have his assurance the Boers would not offer any resistance, or I should refuse to enter it and would arrange to bring them to terms in my own way. He then begged me to give him 24 hours to arrange matters. This I agreed to, and I hope before I finish this to be able to telegraph to you that the British flag is waving over the town which brought about the war. Our casualties are exceedingly small considering the difficult nature of the hills by which Johannesburg is surrounded – Under 150 I hope. The heaviest losses occurred in Ian Hamilton's column, and chiefly in the Gordons – a grand regiment and no mistake.[113]

Dr. Krause told me that Kruger and his officials had all left Pretoria, they only got away just in time before we broke up a bit of the railway. Our rapid advance took them all by surprise. I pushed on in the hope of being able to secure some rolling stock for our railway resources were nearly at an end. It is a long way from Capetown – 1014 miles, and we have had the greatest difficulty in bringing up a sufficiency of supplies – a difficulty considerably increased by the methodical way in which the railroad has been destroyed. Every bridge and large culvert has been blown up, and in many places the rails have been sent flying – but thanks to Lt. Colonel Girouard and his assistants repairs have been rapidly executed. On this side of the Vaal, the Netherlands Railway Company[114] had sufficient influence to prevent their line from being injured, a great mercy for us – and especially for me, for I have often had the greatest anxiety as to whether there would be eno' food for the troops. We had only one day's supplies in hand when we arrived here! Fortunately some wagons came up in time, but Hamilton's force being off the main road has, I fear, fared badly. In his report which reached me late yesterday he says: – "No biscuit or groceries left and the men have nothing for breakfast. I am trying to borrow from French who is five miles off." It is impossible to describe the anxiety which the feeding of this large army has caused me. I hope that the Boers who are still in arms in the Orange Free State will now experience some difficulty about food. They are cut off from the Ladybrand district which was their main source of supply, as we have now got the Transvaal Railway communication in our hands, we can prevent them drawing on this country.

Rundle has incurred a heavy loss for no purpose. His attack on the Boers near Senekal on the 28th instant was unnecessary, and can only give them encouragement.[115] I was pretty sure from the way he acted at Dewetsdorp that he is not a commander to be trusted, and I have warned him now that we cannot afford to have 45 men killed and 135 wounded when there is no object to be gained.

Hunter is, I think, a good man. He has got his wits about him and does his work thoroughly.

Buller will, I hope, now be able to move forward. He persisted in thinking that our advance only increased the numbers against him, while we had certain information that trains full of Boers were hurrying up from Natal to the Transvaal. He still imagines that he is opposed by large numbers, though I am glad to see from his last telegram he admits they are disorganized, and are not likely, therefore, to give him serious trouble.

The men are quite splendid. They march 20 miles during the day and sleep without any covering but their cloaks and blankets without a murmur, although it is very cold at night now – several degrees of frost, and very often, poor fellows, they have not had too much to eat.

I have consulted Milner over the administration of Johannesburg which is a very different place from Bloemfontein, and I am now waiting for a letter from him which he despatched by a special messenger more than a week ago. The population is very heterogeneous and contains many disturbing elements, and the officials, I believe, with scarcely an exception, are most untrustworthy. I propose to leave a Brigade in the town and to appoint Colin Mackenzie to be military Governor as a temporary arrangement.

Mr Robinson's house was nearly blown up the night we arrived, and was only saved by Dr. Krause hearing of the scheme in time to arrest the ringleader. He also put a stop to the arrangements which were in progress for blowing up some of the principal buildings after our entry into Johannesburg.[116]

BL MS Room, Lansdowne Papers L(5)48

Part 2
6 June 1900 to 1 January 1901 'Mopping-up Operations' and Roberts' Return to England
Introduction

By the time he reached Pretoria, Lord Roberts was a very tired man. After four months in command of a huge army in the field, the strain of overwork and old age was beginning to take its toll.[1] Maybe that is why he wanted to believe that the war was over. Impatience, however, was perhaps Roberts' greatest defect as a military commander. Immediately after the capture of Johannesburg and Pretoria, Roberts introduced military government in the two towns, and in due course in the rest of the new colony. His Military Governors were Lieutenant-Colonel Colin Mackenzie (Johannesburg) and Major-General Sir John Grenfell Maxwell (Pretoria), with G.V. Fiddes as his Political Secretary (and advisor). In his administrative arrangements Roberts willingly allowed himself to be guided by Sir Alfred Milner, for in due course civil government would have to be built on the foundations laid by the military [34], a civil government led by Milner [36]. Roberts tried unsuccessfully to pacify the inhabitants of the Transvaal, which led to the implementation of the scorched earth policy in that region.[2]

Roberts initially believed that with the fall of their capitals, Boer resistance would crumble [33]. He was mistaken. The Boer armies did not come in to surrender. As a matter of fact, on 7 June 1900, General Christiaan de Wet launched simultaneous attacks against British units at Vredefort Road, Renoster River Bridge and Roodewal. De Wet himself attacked the latter station, forced the British soldiers to surrender and captured large quantities of arms, ammunition and provisions worth at least £100,000.[3]

Until the end of the Buller phase, the British followed a direct strategy. In itself, this was not incorrect, but it would have been better if the line of advance had gone through the OFS from the start. In turn, Roberts saw how Buller's direct strategy – with its limited strategic objectives – had failed; therefore, an indirect strategy was followed. Initially, Roberts achieved great success with his flank advance, but after the fall of Pretoria (5 June 1900), his strategy lost momentum. He lost sight of the dangers of a guerrilla war. In due course Kitchener therefore deemed it necessary to add a further dimension to the indirect strategy. By destroying their property and sending families to the concentration camps, he attempted to overcome the Boers through indirect means.

Roberts did not learn his 'lessons' very well because his strategy too was directed at occupying the capitals, and not so much at destroying the Boers' military strength in the field. As Thomas Pakenham pointed out, Roberts was neither a fool nor a genius, but a successful general with tactical (and one would like to add strategic) and diplomatic skills on the one hand, and on the other hand certain limitations.[4] While Buller therefore established the foundation for a protracted war, Roberts contributed to a situation where a counter-guerrilla war would have to be waged by the British. If Roberts had ensured that all the areas in the rear of his advancing forces were properly under British military control, and therefore truly protected areas, the later need for drives, farm-burning and concentration camps would have been eliminated. Roberts realized that after the war Boer and Briton would have to work together in South Africa, and that throughout the campaign he had to exercise sound military and political judgement, but his velvet glove and mailed fist approach to the war was not always successful.

When it became clear that the fall of the republican capitals was not the end of organized resistance on the part of the Boers [35], Roberts was compelled to prepare for a large-scale advance and campaign in the Eastern Transvaal. General Louis Botha deployed some 6,000 men and 23 guns from Doornfontein in the north, via Donkerhoek and Diamond Hill, all the way to Kleinzonderhout in the south on both sides of the Delagoa Bay railway line, over a distance of approximately 40 km (25 miles). On 11 June 1900, Roberts attacked these positions at various places, employing a force of approximately 14,000 men with 70 guns. The British forces were unable, on either 11 or 12 June, to outflank the Boer positions; however, their superior numbers and fire-power took their toll, and on the night of 12–13 June, the Boers left their positions and retreated eastwards. British casualties amounted to at least 28 dead and 145 wounded. It is unknown how many casualties occurred on the

Boer side.[5] The Boers were driven from the battlefield, but they were not really defeated, and would soon regroup to fight again.

After Roberts had consolidated his position in and around Pretoria, Major-General J.D.P. French was tasked to lead the British advance eastwards, along the Delagoa Bay railway line to Komatipoort. This advance was co-ordinated with Buller's advance from Ladysmith. After Buller captured Botha's Pass on 8 June 1900, he advanced to Allemansnek on Transvaal territory where he defeated a Boer force on 11 June. The next day the Boers evacuated their positions at Lang's Nek (the scene of one of their victories over the British in 1881), and that same day Buller's force marched into Volksrust. Buller continued his advance slowly northwards, entering Standerton on 22 June [37]. He then continued northwards along the Natal-Transvaal railway line [39].[6] On 4 July 1900 Queen Victoria gave Roberts the authorization to annexe the Transvaal [38], something that was eventually done on 1 September 1900.

In the meantime, guerrilla activities (or 'unrest' as Roberts sometimes euphemistically preferred to call them) increased. Although the British succeeded in suppressing the rebellion in the North-Western Cape, De Wet and others continued their successful guerrilla action in the OFS. This kind of warfare was also being implemented with success in the Transvaal [40]. On 11 July 1900, the guerrilla phase was started in the Transvaal when four attacks were launched on British units, including De la Rey's attack at Silkaatsnek when Colonel H.R. C-Roberts was defeated and forced to surrender. The British lost at least 23 men who were killed and 189 taken prisoner (including 45 wounded). There is uncertainty about Boer casualties. Several other battles followed.[7]

In an effort to curb the guerrilla activities, Roberts resorted to stern measures. On 16 June 1900 he issued his controversial Proclamation No. 5 of 1900 (and three days later an even harsher Proclamation, No. 6 of 1900) warning the Boers that when they destroyed railway bridges and culverts, the houses in the vicinity would be burnt.[8] The aim was strictly military, i.e. to make an example of certain culprits in an effort to deter others from aiding the guerrillas. Roberts realised that it would be very difficult for his forces to corner and destroy all the mobile Boer commandos in the field. Some of the British officers applied the proclamations with discretion; others did not, and consequently many farms were burnt unnecessarily. By taking stern measures against the civilian population, Roberts hoped to dislocate the Boers psychologically and undermine their will to continue the struggle. These tactics were similar to those which he had employed in Afghanistan and India. In South Africa, however, the measures in due course backfired. To some extent they motivated the Boers to invade the Cape Colony (with the aim of taking the war to the British areas and population, while relieving the pressure on the former Boer republics), and later led to much bitterness.

In the Eastern ORC the Boers suffered a major setback. After Roberts took over Pretoria, he had to take urgent action to eliminate Boer forces operating to the rear of his forces. While some British units were advancing in a northerly direction along the Basotholand border, other British forces advanced from the north-west in the direction of the Brandwater Basin with Fouriesburg as the centre. By the middle of 1900, large portions of the OFS commandos were trapped in this basin. While the Boer officers argued about the overall leadership of the Boer forces in the basin, the British captured one pass after another. Chief Commandant Marthinus Prinsloo engaged in negotiations with Lieutenant-General Archibald Hunter, and after the Boers agreed on 29 July 1900 to submit to the British demand for surrender, Prinsloo formally surrendered the next day. Although some Boer commanders did not heed the surrender and escaped with their burghers, 4,314 burghers, as well as three generals and nine commandants had lain down their arms by 9 August. The British also captured three guns, approximately 2,800 head of cattle, 4,000 sheep, 5,500 horses and approximately two million rounds of rifle ammunition. Already on 15 July, De Wet, along with President Steyn and approximately 2,000 men and five guns, escaped from the British forces' lines across Slabbertsnek. They were pursued by various British columns as far as behind the Magaliesberg in what became known as the first De Wet hunt [41]. Thence, De Wet returned to the ORC to continue the guerrilla war with even more vigour.[9]

Meanwhile, French led the British advance further eastwards from Pretoria – an advance which was co-ordinated with Buller's from Natal. On 27 July 1900, French took Middelburg, but he was subsequently required to remain in the region for about a month so that Buller could be given the opportunity to advance further. When the British advance was resumed, Botha and 5,000 Boers blocked the British forces' advance at Bergendal and in its vicinity, to the north-west of Dalmanutha Station. From 21 August, British forces under the command of Buller attacked the Boer positions. During the main attack on 27 August, British forces succeeded in driving the Boers eastwards. British casualties in this battle came to about thirteen dead and 103 wounded, while on the Boer side there were at least fifty casualties. Five days later, on 1 September 1900,

Roberts annexed the Transvaal.[10] By that time Roberts knew for sure that the character of the war had changed [42], and that, at his rear, De Wet and Steyn were the heart and soul of the Boer resistance [45]. At home in Pretoria, Roberts had to contend with a plot to kidnap or kill him [43], as well as criticism levelled against the presence of Lady Roberts [43, 44]. Roberts' views of some of his senior officers make interesting reading [46], as do his letters concerning the way in which returning soldiers should be treated in Britain [51, 52].

In the meantime Buller captured Amersfoort on 7 August, then took part in the battle of Bergendal (which has already been referred to), and subsequently operated in the vicinity of Lydenburg. On 6 October 1900 his army was disbanded and he returned to England, where he received a hero's welcome. In January 1901 he took command at Aldershot, but was soon embroiled in the controversy with regard to the publication (in April 1901) of his Spioenkop despatches, which reflected negatively on his role in Natal. Buller's infamous telegram of 16 December 1899 in which he suggested that under certain circumstances General Sir George White should consider surrendering, was not published, but the content was an open secret. At a luncheon with the Queen's Westminster Volunteers on 10 October 1901 Buller, embarrassed and irritated by all the rumours and allegations, disclosed and tried to explain and justify the content of the controversial telegram [84]. This was deemed a violation of the King's Regulations. Buller was relieved of his command on 23 October 1901, retired on half-pay, and withdrew to his estate.[11]

Although Botha and the Boer commanders persisted with their attempts to check the British advance, the British reached Komatipoort on 24 September. Before approximately 2,500 Boers crossed the border into Mozambique, with two guns, a pom-pom and two machine-guns, the Boers destroyed large quantities of provisions, and in the preceding weeks they had destroyed most of their remaining artillery. The semi-conventional phase of the war was definitely something of the past. Meanwhile President Kruger arrived in Lourenço Marques (the present-day Maputo) on 11 September, whence he departed for Europe on the Dutch cruiser *De Gelderland* on 19 October [48].[12] In the last week of September 1900 Roberts was offered the post of Commander-in-Chief of the British Army in succession to Lord Wolseley [50].

With organized Boer resistance at an end, Roberts was, once again, of the opinion that the war was over for all practical purposes [49, 56] and that only 'mopping-up operations' had to be performed. It is clear that he neither fully appreciated the nature of the Boer resistance, nor what remained to be done by the British in order to win the war. On 29 November 1900 he handed over supreme command to Lord Kitchener. Meanwhile, however, it was already clear that although the Boers could no longer win the war, the struggle was far from over. The death of Prince Christian Victor, beloved grandson of Queen Victoria, cast a shadow over the last few weeks of Roberts' tenure as Commander-in-Chief in South Africa [45, 53, 54].

The serious illness of Roberts' eldest daughter, Aileen (who nearly died of typhoid) and his fall from a horse delayed his departure from South Africa until 11 December 1900. The day before he left to take up his new post at the War Office, Roberts was honoured by the mayor and people of Cape Town [56]. Under Roberts' leadership a radical change in Britain's military fortunes in South Africa was brought about. However, it must be kept in mind that Roberts had much more support and more resources than Buller ever had, and that he also had the opportunity to learn from Buller's mistakes. After Cronjé's surrender at Paardeberg and the occupation of their capitals, the Boers could no longer realistically hope to maintain their independence. From the end of February to the end of November 1900 (when Roberts handed over the supreme command to Kitchener), almost all the fighting took place on republican soil. However, Roberts did not complete his task and left a legacy of many complex, unsolved problems to his successor. This can be primarily attributed to misconception and his under-estimation of the Boer character, love of liberty, tenacious nationalism, and resolve to resist the numerically far superior British force. Other factors were the undue importance which Roberts attached to the capture of the republican capitals and his strange reluctance to relieve Buller of his command, although he had no hesitation in dismissing lesser men like Major-General Sir William Gatacre and Major-General Sir Henry Colvile (both of them not part of his 'ring'). His annexation of the republics before the complete subjugation of the Boer forces in the field constituted a total disregard of the accepted practices of international law. In addition, of course, Roberts also had to take responsibility for many of the administrative blunders, including the problems with the transport system and the red tape of the hospitals. For obvious reasons the annexations did not force the Boer commanders to surrender, and in desperation Roberts resorted to a scorched earth policy. This was in effect an admission of his failure to find a clear-cut military solution to the problem posed by continued Boer resistance. Ironically, this probably prolonged the war, because the guerrilla war escalated.[13]

Roberts outmanoeuvred the Boers strategically, but did not defeat them tactically. By the end of Roberts' command the British controlled almost all the towns and villages, but in the vast expanses of the South African veldt the Boers to a large extent roamed freely, threatening the British lines of communication. In what appeared to be their moment of victory, the British in fact (at least temporarily) lost the military initiative.

As Roberts was preparing to leave South Africa, the guerrilla war was about to escalate geographically [55, 57]. De Wet's escape from the Brandwater Basin, and the subsequent hot-pursuit operations aimed at capturing him, have already been mentioned. While the rest of his commando were resting north of the Magaliesberg, De Wet and approximately 230 of his men moved south. After he had taken part in the unsuccessful siege of the British force under the command of Major-General Geoffry Barton at Frederikstad (20–25 October 1900), De Wet once again returned to the ORC, and in consultation with Steyn decided to invade the Cape Colony. However, this attempt was almost nipped in the bud when, on 6 November 1900, his commando was surprised by a British force at Doornkraal, near Bothaville. De Wet succeeded in escaping, but at least nine burghers were killed and more than 100 (including several wounded) were captured, as well as six guns. On the British side at least thirteen soldiers were killed and 33 wounded. Next, De Wet regrouped his commando and broke through a British blockhouse line at Sprinkaansnek, then besieged a British force at Dewetsdorp and defeated them (21–23 November). However, the Gariep River was in flood, so that he was forced to retreat northwards, pursued by Major-General C.E. Knox, in what became known as the second De Wet hunt.[14]

In the Transvaal, Major-General R.A.P. Clements was dealt a heavy blow at Nooitgedacht on 13 December 1900,[15] but Kitchener's main concern was the Cape Colony. While the British occupied larger and larger parts of the ORC and the Transvaal and restricted the movements of commandos – but not entirely so – Boer commanders such as De Wet considered the option of engaging in incursions into the Cape Colony with a view to enlarging the size of the operational area, so that the pressure on the Boer commandos could be relieved – as was done during the first two main phases of the war – and the struggle be taken into British territory. For this reason a series of incursions took place from the middle of December 1900. On the night of 15–16 December 1900 General J.B.M. Hertzog crossed the Gariep River at Sanddrif, between Norvalspont and Petrusville, with about 1,200 burghers. His force occupied Philipstown on 17 December and Britstown on 22 December. The Boers then moved as far south-west as Vanrhynsdorp (19 January 1901). Some of the burghers went on to Lambert's Bay on the Atlantic coast, where they fired on the British cruiser HMS *Sybille*, which retaliated with a few gunshots. The bulk of Hertzog's force eventually returned to the ORC at the end of February 1901 in the company of De Wet (whose second invasion attempt on 10 February 1901 was successful). Another invasion force of about 300 men, under Commandant P.H. Kritzinger, also crossed into the Cape Colony on the night of 15–16 December 1900. Kritzinger returned to the ORC in April 1901 (only to launch two further invasions at a later stage), but portions of his force, under the command of Commandant Gideon Scheepers and Commandant W.D. Fouché, reinforced by Cape rebels, continued to operate over a wide area in the Colony.[16] From the War Office Roberts would in due course have to advise Kitchener on these and other developments on more than one occasion.

33
Lord Roberts to Lord Lansdowne

Pretoria, 7th June 1900.

[Holograph]

I am glad to think that I can date this letter from Pretoria, and trust that our having gained possession of the capital of the South African Republic will enable the war to be brought to a rapid conclusion.[1] The Transvaalers are now working separately from the Orange River Colony burghers so that we are not likely to have any large force to deal with in the future. On the other hand a kind of guerilla warfare has been commenced which will give us trouble for a short time. The railway is being threatened, the telegraph line is being cut, and convoys are being attacked. I quite expected this would happen, and it was a risk I had to run, for it was impossible to spare enough troops to make our long line of communication secure without unduly weakening my fighting force. I felt that all my efforts should be directed to the occupation of Pretoria, and I shall be greatly disappointed if our being here does not result in the war being soon brought to a conclusion ere long. Meanwhile I am despatching troops from this to strengthen the posts in the rear, and Kitchener starts off today to see that they are properly disposed.

It was fortunate for us that the enemy were in a demoralized condition before we came to Pretoria, for if it had been properly defended, we must have lost heavily. Johannesburg is a strong position, but this is infinitely stronger, the strongest indeed that I have seen in the country.[2] Pretoria is a beautiful little town, and will in time become a most desirable place of residence.

Botha tried to delay us when he found that we were not to be denied, and, after I had turned in on the night of the 4th June, he sent me a letter, under a flag of truce proposing that he should meet me the next day and discuss the terms under which the town should be surrendered. I told his messenger that I would be very pleased to meet the Commandant General, but that I could not consent to any Armistice as he desired, that my troops had orders to move on the town as soon as it was daylight, and that if he had any further communication to make, it must reach me before that time. Just before dawn I received Botha's reply informing me that he "had decided not to defend the town, and that he trusted the women, children, and private property would be protected".

On reaching the railway station, which is on the outskirts of the town, I was met by the chief civil officials who expressed their willingness to make the place over to me. It was settled that the official entrance should be made at 2 o'clock in the afternoon. Meanwhile the most persistant [sic] stories were being circulated that treachery was intended, and that as soon as we were well inside the town, we should be attacked. I did not pay much heed to these reports as I had heard that the place was full of women and children and that Mrs. Kruger and Mrs. Botha were living in their own houses in Pretoria. All proper precautions were of course taken. The forts and neighbouring heights were all held by our troops, and guards marched into the town, and I was agreeably surprised at the reception we met with. Here and there a sullen face could be seen, but on the whole it was far better than expected. The Grenadier Guards lined the principal square. As soon as I had taken my place in the centre, Pole Carew gave the word "Royal Salute", Neshminster [?] and Kerry hoisted the Union Jack on the main building, and taking off my helmet, I called out "Three cheers for the Queen". The troops then marched past – a two hours business – and between 4 and 5 pm, I found myself in the British Residency not sorry to get a cup of tea.

It was well that I did not agree to an Armistice or the whole of the British prisoners would have been carried off. About 900 were hurried into trains during the 4th June, and the officers were awoke<n> during the night and told to make their way to the Railway station. They all refused as they knew we were close by – so close indeed were we that had there been an hour's more daylight, we should have captured the town on the 4th June!

It was most unlucky the poor Irish Yeomanry being captured.[3] They were to have joined the Highland Brigade, which was badly off for Mounted Infantry, at Ventersburg, but, owing to delays which occurred on the march from Bloemfontein, the Highlanders had passed Ventersburg before the Yeomanry could arrive there. The Yeomanry then went on to Kroonstad between which place and Lindley there is unfortunately no telegraph line, and from there they marched to Lindley. The Highlanders had left that place two days before the Yeomanry arrived there for Heilbron which was their destination, soon reaching Lindley   Spragge (who commanded the Irish Yeomanry) found it occupied by Boers. Spragge was a soldier, and is a smart fellow, and he at once retired to a position about three miles west of Lindley and sent a messenger to Kroonstad for assistance. As soon as the news of Spragge's situation reached me I ordered Methuen to hurry towards Lindley. Methuen had under previous arrangements, been directed to cross the Vaal and threaten Potchefstroom, or else to support French and Ian Hamilton, but it struck me that we were strong enough for any opposition we were likely to meet with in the Transvaal, and as I was anxious about our communications I had ordered Methuen to make for Kroonstad. On hearing of Spragge's danger Methuen pushed on. He marched with his mounted troops 44 miles in 25 hours, only to find, when nearing Lindley, that Spragge had been obliged to surrender. At first he was opposed by a small body of Boers, but the numbers increased and on the 31st May he was surrounded by 2000 or 3000 with ...... guns. Methuen arrived on the scene early on the 1st June, engaged with the enemy, drove them before him and reoccupied Lindley.[4] Methuen did very well and he reports that he cannot speak in "too strong terms" of the Militia battalions with him. The auxiliary troops are doing wonderfully well, and with more experienced officers would be even more valuable. No battalion looked better or marched past on the 5th June in a more soldierly manner than the C.I.V. Every one on the ground remarked them.

I sent you a long telegram in reply to your message about our hospital arrangements. I felt sure that Burdett-Coutts was the author of the private reports as my Military Secretary had had a letter from him on the subject. No one could have been more distressed than I was at the poor sick soldiers having to suffer, and I did all that was possible for them during the short time we were at Kroonstad. Kroonstad is quite a small place, the church, hotels (such as they are), and every available building were occupied – scarcely any beds were procurable, and with great difficulty – a few mattresses were got hold of from private houses. I appointed the only civilian Doctor in the place to assist our medical officers. Cows cannot be taken about with an army in the field, and for the first day or two after we reached Kroonstad tinned milk had to be given to the majority of the patients, but before I left, and I was only ten days there,[5] several cows had been collected for hospital use.

I was quite surprised at the unusual number of men who fell sick on the road to, and at, Kroonstad. I attributed it in a great measure to the sickly condition of Bloemfontein, where the seeds of enteric were doubtless laid, and also to the desire of men to join in the march to Pretoria although they were physically unfit for the great exertion and exposure which such a march entailed. Since Kroonstad, comparatively few men have fallen out, and enteric I am thankful to say has ceased. Before leaving Bloemfontein I had No. 3 General Hospital capable of accommodating 500 patients prepared ready for despatch by rail, but as I have reported, every bridge and almost every culvert on the line were blown up. Trains could not therefore run until the line had been repaired. This necessarily took some days – and for the same reason horses could not be sent to Kroonstad, but as soon as trains could travel and a sufficiency (a very bare sufficiency) of supplies had been brought to the front, the hospital and nurses were sent to Kroonstad. I tell you this long story as Burdett-Coutts' account is sure to attract attention, and it is well you should know the whole state of the case.

I am almost afraid that you will not receive this letter until the first week in July as the railway has been interfered with again between the Vaal river and Kroonstad.

BL MS Room, Lansdowne Papers L(5)48

34
Sir Alfred Milner to Lord Roberts

[Typed copy]

Government House
Capetown.
5.6.1900.

There has been no time yet to receive an answer from you to my long letter sent down by Davenport. Since writing it, I have exchanged telegrams with the Secretary of State, which I enclose.

They are purely private & personal, of course, & I have no right to show them to anybody, or knowledge, whether the arrangement contemplated by the Secretary of State will be carried out. But I thought it right that you should see them, as they will explain the direction in which I am trying to work. One must have some principle to guide one trying to deal with such a chaos as the overthrow of the Republics leaves us in, & what I am trying to think out at present is the form & the personnel, of a strong Crown Colony Govnt after the military Govnt & martial law are withdrawn.

Why I am so anxious to place Fiddes at your disposal just now is because I think he understands well, what kind of arrangements will be required under the new system, and will, therefore, be helpful to you in all questions of a non military character wh will arise and the manner of dealing with which will necessarily affect the future administration. He is the man, whom, as at present advised, I should propose <to> the Home Govnt as Colonial Secretary of the new Govnt, if I were to be its head. I should therefore like him to have the opportunity of becoming acquainted with all questions affecting the future civil Govnt, even where they would in the first place, come before others (as for finan<cial> questions, for instance, would come before Evans) & being enabled to make his observations about them. He perfectly understands that his present position is a purely advisory one & that he forms part of the present administration, which is a strictly military one with all authority vested in the C in Chief. Fiddes still remains on my staff as High Commissioner, and is, so to speak, lent by me to you as long as you require his services for the purpose which I have indicated.

I will not trouble you with the long despatches wh I have sent to the S of S, containing suggestions as to the form of the future Government. They are merely sketches, much of wh may never be adopted by the Home authorities & part of wh I might myself desire to modify from time to time <from> a wider experience. But if there are any points as to future administration, on wh you wd like to know my view, Fiddes will be able to tell you what it is, provided the matter is one about <which> I have been able to form an opinion.

I cannot close this letter, written as it is within a few hours of the taking of Pretoria, without repeating the congratulation, wh I have already had the honour to send you by wire, on this splendid termination to the military operations wh we have all followed here with such intense interest & admiration.

Bodleian Library, MS Milner dep. 15 ff. 150–3

35
Lord Roberts to Queen Victoria

Pretoria, 21st June 1900.

[Holograph]

I have had the great honour to receive the most gracious telegrams and a letter dated the 10th May from Your Majesty since I reached Pretoria. I beg to offer my most respectful thanks for the same, and to assure Your Majesty that the telegrams, which were published in Army orders, gave the liveliest satisfaction to all the troops in South Africa.

Everything is, I trust, going on well here. The war still hangs on and will continue to do so until we have been able to bring the whole of the Orange Free State to terms.

Contrary to all expectations, the inhabitants in the North East portion of that Colony have proved themselves more difficult to deal with than the Transvaalers. The latter would, I have reason to believe, give in if they had only themselves to consider. With us in occupation of Pretoria and Johannesburg, they feel that it is hopeless for them to resist any longer. President Kruger is living in a railway carriage[6] in constant terror of being captured and sent to St. Helena. He is distressed at being separated from his wife, whom he left here, and it is said he feels that he acted in a manner unworthy of the Ruler of a Province, in having carried off all the gold he could lay hands on, leaving the state officials to be paid their salaries by means of notes which no Bank, under existing circumstances, will cash. But the two states made a compact that there could be no peace overtures without the consent of both parties, and as Mr. Steyn is still able to hold out, Kruger has to live in his railway carriage, ready to move off at a moment's notice in the event of our troops appearing anywhere near him.

The country is of great extent, and hitherto I have had to be satisfied with limiting operations to that portion through which the main line of railway runs. It was necessary in the first instance to gain possession of the principal towns, for so long as they were occupied by the enemy no one believed that we were getting the upper hand.

We are now firmly established at Bloemfontein, Kroonstad, Johannesburg, and Pretoria, and the only places where the enemy exists in any numbers are in the neighbourhood of the Vaal River to the East of Johannesburg and Kroonstad. Strong columns are moving in that direction and if all goes well, by the time Your Majesty receives this letter, the enemy ought to have been driven into a very small corner, a measure which will, I trust, result in a general submission.

Pretoria has the makings of a beautiful place, it is picturesquely situated and well watered. Everything seems to grow here. Flowers and fruit of both Europe and Asia flourish here, and the climate at this season is quite perfection. In summer the days are hot, but the nights are always cool.

The people are naturally somewhat sullen in their manner, but they are gradually becoming less so on finding how considerately they are being treated, how orderly and well behaved the troops are, and how liberally we pay for all the necessaries of life.

I have had two visits from Mrs. Botha, the wife of the Commandant General who succeeded Joubert. She is a very nice person – Colonial born not Dutch, and is evidently most anxious for peace to be made. On the second occasion of her coming here she brought Mrs. Lucas Meyer,[7] the wife of another Boer General, who wanted some little help which I was able to give.

Major General Baden Powell has been in Pretoria the last day or two. It was most interesting hearing all about the siege of Mafeking from him. I was glad to find him in famous health and spirits.

I am thankful to say that sickness is gradually decreasing. Enteric still exists, but the type is milder and the deaths fewer. There was great difficulty about hospital arrangements when we first arrived at Kroonstad, which is quite a small place, the Dutch church[8] being the only fairly large building. No tents could be sent up from Bloemfontein in time as the enemy had destroyed all the railway bridges and culverts, so that for a few days the poor patients were very uncomfortable. Matters were set to rights as soon as possible, and Kroonstad has long since been well provided with medical officers, nurses, &c. –

Here we are well off. There are several large buildings which have been turned into hospitals – one quite an ideal place, intended for a Law Court, but which had never been used as such.[9]

I enclose a few papers[10] which will, I think, interest Your Majesty.

In the fervent hope that this will find your Majesty in the best of health, and with my most respectful duty.

RA VIC/P10/101

36
Sir Alfred Milner to Lord Roberts
Confidential

Government House
Capetown.
21 6 1900.

[Typed copy]

Hanbury Williams will take down this letter.

I have so many things I want to say – and yet I do not wish to waste your time unnecessarily. So I will confine myself to certain matters which are not likely to be disposed of by telegraph before this letter reaches you, and with regard to which Fiddes would not be able to act as my interpreter.

These questions are mainly personal. In the first I note that as I always expected you are desirous of leaving as soon as the big military task is over & our main army withdrawn.

I suppose even now the Govnt at home is consulting you as to the number of men, who should be left as a garrison for the next year or two, and the places where they are to be stationed.

These are military problems, on which I do not feel justified in expressing opinion. But they have also a political side, on which I may be allowed to put in a word.

I have a strong feeling in favour of keeping our main SA garrison in the Colony, and preferably in the North of the Colony. It must of course be at some convenient point or points on the railway line, for purposes of supply and also for purposes of quick movement in case of need.

The reason why I advocate the Colony is that I believe this will shortly be the only disaffected part of S A. Natal & Rhodesia are allright now, the Transvaal is bound to become so, if we do not make a too awful muddle of its Govnt. The immigration of a large industrial & commercial population will surely result in that. The O R C, though Dutch, will not I think be very unfriendly especially if as I hope we seize the unrivalled opportunity it affords for horsebreeding for military purpose. But in the Cape Colony the party of sedition will carry on the struggle until they see it is absolutely hopeless. A large force in Cape Colony will have the double effect of overawing disaffection, where it is likely to be most serious, and of slowly modifying the composition of the population. In the sense of every large occupying army in a Colony fit for Europeans to live in a certain proportion take their discharge in the Country and stay there. Nothing could be better for us in this Colony than a greater admixture of men, or the descendants of men, who have served the Queen. It is very remarkable in the present struggle how many of our best Colonial loyalists have been the descendants of old officers or soldiers, or have been in the Army themselves long ago.

105

Is it necessary that if we have for some time to come to keep a considerable army in the Colony, is it necessary that it should be an idle army, a mere garrison? Are not many places – on the line – especially in the North East of the Colony, ideal places for camps of exercise? I am thinking of such neighbourhoods as those of Naauwpoort Colesberg Aliwal Stormberg or even De Aar (though De Aar is perhaps too arid). In most of these there is a good grass country with any amount of room and a great diversity of country – ideal ground, in its expanse, variety and naturalness, for training troops especially mounted infantry – at least so it appears to my lay mind. And the horses would be there in quantities too if we used our present opportunities hand and cheap. And the climate is good and developing Boys would be made into men faster than elsewhere, to judge from what I have seen myself, And there it is central for an Empire, wh is hardly likely to engage in European wars but who may at any time have to reinforce its regular garrison in India or the further East. If the Suez Canal were ever blocked it might make a great difference to us to be able to send 10,000 men quickly to India.

It has always been an idea of mine that we shd be killing 2 birds with a stone if we did some of our Army training in South Africa. Overcrowded England is becoming more & more impossible while Cape Colony with an Aldershot or a Curragh in it would in another generation be as loyal as any Colony. We have after all only a small European population & the British element is already 2/5ths. With such a gradual leavening as the constant presence of a field army would cause the scale would soon be turned in their favour. While on the military question there is another delicate question which I cant wholly pass over   S A will for years to come be a big command. It is all important that we should have a real good man at the head of it.

Here again it would be easier to get him if he was training troops & not merely looking after an idle garrison. But in any case I hope we shall keep one of our really good men not simply some senior who has yet to have a post found for him. Buller is too big and would not be the right man. [Forestier-] Walker <u>is too weak</u> and besides as he has told me himself he does not want to stay. It would be a grand thing for us if we could keep one of the men who has made & not impaire<d> a reputation during the war. The mere fact of his having prestige would mean much especially in the difficult years immediately ahead of us.

There is another post wh will need a very good man though not quite of the same rank   I mean the command of the Military Police, on wh as far as the TV & ORC are concerned, I should be disposed to rely very much even for military protection. This will be a work requiring energy   organisation   a knowledge of the country and a power of getting on with its people.

Baden Powell is the sort of man, who naturally occurs to one. I think the large & fine force wh I have in my mind – would not be beneath the dignity of a Major General at any rate to create, especially if he has the whole of the local defensive forces – such as volunteers under him.

If as seems increasingly probable though by no means certain, I am ordered by H M's Govnt to transfer myself from Capetown to Pretoria in order to take over the Govnt of the 2 ex Republics (with a Lt Governor in the O R C) I should feel it a very great personal assistance, and indeed it would make all the difference to have a strong man in charge of the Local Forces. He would be a member of the Government and in that capacity would have a share in a most interesting piece of political construction.

As regards myself I am getting rather anxious to learn what the decision is. Not that I want to stay in S A. I shd much prefer to leave it and rest any claim to credit in connection with it on the fact that I precipitated a crisis wh was inevitable before it was altogether too late. It is not a very agreeable and in many eyes not a very creditable piece of business to have been largely instrumental in bringing about a big war. Still I think in the distant future people will say it was better than burying my head in the sand as I might easily have done.

But I am wandering from the point. All I mean to convey is that I am not keen to stay but if I must stay I should vastly prefer to make Pretoria and not Capetown the head qrs of Br policy. But supposing that I am to be at Pretoria keeping an eye also on Bloemfontein I shd be glad to know it soon for I shd be in a far better position to advise and prepare than I am now, when I don't know whether it is or is not to be my business.

Speaking for the moment as if I were to be entrusted with creating a civil Govnt in the 2 Republics, my first difficulty wld be to find a man for BFN.

It wld be a biggish post for even if nominally under me the Lt Gov of the O R C wld have to run his own show very much in his own way, There is no idea of merging the 2 administrations.

I do not suppose that Pretyman wld care for such a position. In any case I think he is not quite the man for it. A younger man and one of many civilians and if possible S A experience wld be best. But I shd like to know your view about this & also to know whether you have any idea as to P's wishes.

It would not be fair to him to let him settle down as for a permanency if he has any such idea supposing that it was decided to appoint someone else very shortly & barring some unexpected turn in the war I suppose the introduction of Civil Govnt in the O R C is not very far off.

There are still some points in which I should like to have touched out of consideration for you and also because I am rather short of time to explain myself fully I will abstain from raising them today.

With renewed & very hearty cong<ratulation>s on your cont<inue>d successes I am yrs very tr<u>ly A Milner

Bodleian Library, MS. Milner dep. 15 ff. 161–9

37
Lord Roberts to Lord Lansdowne

Pretoria, 28th June 1900.

[Holograph]

I had the pleasure yesterday to receive your letter of the 1st June. You had then heard of our entry into Johannesburg, but the report of Pretoria being in our possession (founded on Rosslyn's foolish telegram) was somewhat premature.

We have been here now just three weeks, and it is satisfactory to see the way in which the town is settling down. The market place yesterday was crammed with farmers eager to sell their produce – the best sign of confidence, so far as this class is concerned, is becoming restored. It is the officials and foreigners who keep up the excitement in the districts, and this will continue until we are able to deal effectively with the forces which Botha and Steyn manage to keep together. Botha thought he had got a chance when I sent Ian Hamilton's column towards Heidelberg, but I waited to despatch it until some of Hunter's troops were close by. I quite expect that Botha will make some sort of attack during the next few days. He has managed to get a fair number of men together, and the temporary success gained by the capture of some of our convoys in the Orange Free State,[11] added to the difficulties which have suddenly cropped up in China,[12] are putting heart into the Boers, but beyond cutting the telegraph wire and destroying a culvert here and there, I doubt their being able to do us much harm. The several columns I told you of in my last letter are now on the move, and ought in a few days to commence harassing the bodies of the enemy which keep worrying us in the neighbourhood of Heilbron, Lindley, and Kroonstad. Ian Hamilton has unfortunately broken his collar bone which will temporarily disable him, meanwhile his column will be commanded by Hunter.

By forming small columns I have been able to avoid employing Colvile, who has not proved himself a satisfactory commander.[13]

I am glad to hear you consider my telegram of the 25th (No. 765) helpful as regards throwing light on some of the difficulties with which the R.A.M.C. have had to grapple. I have no wish to shield two officers of that department – Many of them are most inefficient, but some of the shortcomings to which, I understand, Burdett-Coutts wishes to attract public attention are inseparable from war, especially in a country like this, where an Army has to depend almost entirely on its own resources for the care of the sick and the wounded.

Neither Wilson nor Stevenson (the latter has been P.M.O. with the force in the field)[14] are big enough men for the job. I have usually had to double the number of Civil Surgeons and nurses they applied for, and generally to keep them up to the mark.

Mrs. Chamberlain will probably give trouble in regard to hospital management. The enclosed correspondence will explain what happened with regard to that lady.

Please tell Lord Strathcona that I hope to get his Horse here ere long. The regiment would have joined me when it first landed, but the horses had fared so badly during the voyage that some 90 per cent were unfit for work when they reached Capetown. By the time the horses had recovered, a mounted corps was required for the party told off to destroy a bridge on the Delagoa Bay Railway, and Strathcona's Horse was the only one available at the time. When that little plan fell through, Strathcona's Horse was sent to Durban instead of East London, and was at once seized upon by Buller. It is not very far off now and I will not forget about it.

It is a great matter Buller having reached Standerton,[15] and I hope I shall be able ere long to get him to move forward some of his large force. He has a strange fancy for augmenting the numbers likely to oppose him.

I have replied to your telegram about clasps for the medal to be given for the war. Buller was consulted as regards the conditions to govern the Ladysmith Clasps.

The Foreign Officers left us yesterday.[16] They have given very little trouble, which I attribute in a great measure to the tactful way in which Downe[17] managed them. He goes home by the mail which takes this, and I should like you to read the letter I have written to the War Office about him.

I don't think you need be anxious about the Colonials wanting to remain after peace has been signed. They would be off now if I would let them, indeed I have considerable difficulty in keeping them. They think the war is over now that we are at Pretoria, and four fifths of them want to join the Police or any local force that may be raised. The Yeomanry are much the same. I have allowed a certain number of each to leave, as it is necessary for the towns we occupy to be properly policed.

The Australians and New Zealanders are greatly taken with this part of South Africa, and many of them will try and settle here. At this season the weather is quite perfection.

As soon as I have a little leisure I will prepare a scheme showing how I would propose to garrison South Africa. The Government will then be able to judge what troops will be released. I imagine the Guards should be among the first to be sent home.

I have heard from Milner about this matter, and also about the best man to take my place. He is desirous to have some one who has added to his reputation during the war. Ian Hamilton is by far the most promising Commander I have seen, and he would be a persona grata to Milner, but he does not care to stay in this country, and I would strongly advise his being allowed to go home. He may be required elsewhere. Neville Lyttelton would also be agreeable to Milner, and I think he would do very well. He is not brilliant, but he is a gentleman, and tactful. Next in succession I would name Pole-Carew. The officers I have omitted are Buller, Warren, Clery, Tucker, Kelly Kenny, Rundle, Hunter, Hildyard, Chermside, Colvile, Methuen, and French. Of these Hunter is the best soldier in the field, and Kelly Kenny is the most painstaking, careful Commander, but neither of them would, I think, suit as well as one of the three I first named.

I shall enquire about the Sisters of Nazareth[18] and let you know how they have done.

The correspondence about Mrs. Chamberlain will be sent next mail.

BL MS Room, Lansdowne Papers L(5)48

38
COMMISSION empowering
Field Marshal the Right Honourable
LORD ROBERTS OF KANDAHAR, P.C., K.P, G.C.B., G.C.S.I., G.C.I.E., V.C., to annex the South African Republic to Her Majesty's dominions, and to make provision for the temporary Government thereof.

[Typed, signed document]

VICTORIA, by the Grace of God of the United Kingdom of Great Britain and Ireland Queen, Defender of the Faith, Empress of India: To Our Right Trusty and well-beloved Councillor Frederick Sleigh, Baron Roberts of Kandahar, Field Marshal of Our Forces, Knight of Our Most Illustrious Order of Saint

Patrick, Knight Grand Cross of Our Most Honourable Order of the Bath, Knight Grand Commander of Our Most Exalted Order of the Star of India, Knight Grand Commander of Our Most Eminent Order of the Indian Empire, upon whom We have conferred the Decoration of the Victoria Cross.

GREETING:

Whereas, the territories in South Africa, heretofore known as the South African Republic, have been conquered by Our forces, And Whereas it is expedient that such territories should be annexed to, and should henceforth form part of Our dominions.

Now Know You that We reposing especial trust and confidence in you, the said Frederick Sleigh, Baron Roberts of Kandahar, do hereby authorize and empower you, in Our name, to annex the said territories, and to declare that the said territories shall henceforth form part of Our dominions.

And We do hereby constitute and appoint you to be thereupon Administrator of the said territories provisionally and until Our pleasure is more fully known; And We do authorise and empower you as such Administrator to take all such measures and to make and enforce such laws as you may deem necessary for the peace, order, and good government of the said territories.

And We do strictly charge and command all Our Officers, civil and military, and all other Our faithful subjects, that in their several places, and according to their respective opportunities, they do aid and assist you in the execution of this Our Commission and for so doing this shall be your Warrant.

Given at Our Court at Saint James's this Fourth Day of July One thousand nine hundred, in the Sixty-Fourth Year of Our Reign.

BY HER MAJESTY'S COMMAND.

NAM 8310–156[19]

39
Lord Roberts to Queen Victoria

Pretoria, 5th July 1900

[Holograph]

I had the honour to receive Your Majesty's gracious letter of the 8th June a few days ago, for which and for the telegram of the 5th June congratulating me and the Army under my command on the occupation of Pretoria, I beg to tender my most grateful thanks. The telegram was published in Army orders and gave the liveliest satisfaction to Your Majesty's soldiers.

It was unfortunate that the Boers were able to carry off some 900 of our prisoners just before we reached Pretoria – they intended to take them all away and would have done so had we been a few hours later in entering the town. I trust, however, that it will not be very long now before we shall be able to effect the release of all the prisoners now in the enemy's hands.[20] It was necessary to halt at Pretoria for a while to get up supplies and generally to refit, but we are now nearly ready for another advance. Sir Redvers Buller is gradually coming nearer, and in a few days I hope that railway communication with Natal will have been restored. This will be of great assistance in the matter of supplies as the distance to Durban is only 511 miles against 1040 miles to Capetown. We are still having trouble in the North-Eastern portion of the Orange River Colony but I am hopeful that the four movable Columns now working in that part of the country will be able to drive the enemy into a corner. The Boers, however, are so mobile and so intimately acquainted with every inch of the country that they are not easy to catch. They keep clear of anything like a large force and look out for convoys, small detachments, &c – At first it was difficult to spare enough men for our Railway line, but that is, I think, now securely guarded.

I hear that a great outcry is being made about the management of hospitals in South Africa. There may, no doubt, be room for improvement in the system, but I can state from personal knowledge that medical officers and nurses have been most devoted, and that no suffering which could have been prevented with the means at our disposal, has been allowed. I hear too it is the opinion of those, who have taken part in wars in other countries, that they have never known a campaign in which so much has been done for the sick and wounded.

We have established some very comfortable hospitals here, and have a large proportion of nurses. Enteric still continues, I grieve to say, but it is of a milder type than formerly.

I wish I could tell Your Majesty that the war was likely to end soon, but at present the Boers seem inclined to hold out. I trust, however, it will not be very long before peace is made.

RA VIC/P11/39

40
Lord Roberts to Lord Lansdowne

Pretoria, 19th July 1900.

[Holograph]

Another week has passed since I wrote to you a few lines and I am still here, whereas I hoped to have been well on my way to Middleburg.[21] The delay has been caused by various circumstances which could scarcely have been guarded against. The transfer of Methuen's column from Kroonstad to Krugersdorp took no less than 22 trains, in the collection of which there was considerable difficulty, and one of the trains was delayed 17 hours en route owing to the men in charge of one of the water supply places being drunk. Then Ian Hamilton found the country north of this not so easy as was expected. And French reported that one or two more days were needed for the collection of sufficient supplies to admit of his making the long turning movement required to place his Cavalry well in rear of Botha's present position.

Buller too telegraphed that the force he had promised to send to Bethal to assist in our operations could not arrive there until the 20th, twenty four hours after the date he had named. In other respects we are ready to advance, and I hope to be off in a day or two.

I despatched to Commandant General Botha's camp this morning, greatly to his annoyance, several families we have been supporting in Pretoria for some weeks past while their male relations have been fighting against us. I gave him warning of my intention in order that he might make suitable arrangements for their reception. His reply is a vehement protest against what he calls the "inhuman removal" of the families! The families were only too glad to go, they were singing and seemed as happy as possible at the idea of getting to their husbands and brothers. Only those in good health were sent. I have told Botha in answer to his protest that he cannot expect me to let my soldiers starve in order to feed people who have no claim on us, while he and his army are doing their best to prevent our getting up supplies by destroying our railways.[22]

If he protests again I shall remind him of the 500 Natives who were driven into Sir George White's camp at Ladysmith in order to add to the garrison's difficulties about food during the siege.

You will have been informed by my telegrams that 1,500 Boers managed to break through Hunter's cordon two or three days ago.[23] They are being followed by Broadwood's Cavalry and Ridley's Mounted Infantry, and also by the 3rd Cavalry Brigade, for thinking that something of the sort might happen, I had fortunately ordered it to march towards Winburg, and it should have been near the line taken by the Boers when the news of their escape reached me. This Brigade is temporarily commanded by Lt. Colonel Little of the 9th Lancers, as I had to transfer Gordon to the 1st Brigade vice Porter disabled in consequence of having broken a collarbone.

Porter's brigade is unfortunate as its commanding officers. The "Scots Greys" are commanded by Lt. Colonel Alexander[24] of whose fitness for the position you will be able to judge when you receive the proceedings of the Court of Inquiry on the loss of the Uitval's Nek's post, which I am sending home by this mail.[25]

The Inniskillings are commanded by Lt. Colonel Page Henderson, who I gather will shortly be placed on halfpay, and the Carabineers by Major Sprot, a very ordinary officer.

Little is an untried man as a Brigade Commander, but he has done well at the head of his regiment.

I trust that the Boers will not be allowed to escape, especially as Steyn is reported to be of the party. He is probably trying to make his way to the Transvaal and join Kruger.

The remainder of the Orange Free Staters are still in the hilly country between Bethlehem and Ficksburg. Hunter and Rundle are busy reconnoitring them, and will, I hope, soon attack them. It will be most disappointing if the Boers escape us this time, they ought not to do <so> as all possible precautions seem to have been taken to prevent this.

I have placed Smith Dorrien temporarily in command of one of Methuen's brigades. He will help to prevent any unnecessary delay in clearing the country between Krugersdorp and Rustenburg, for I am most anxious that Baden Powell should be released in order that he may be able to guard the country round Pretoria when I move on. At present Rustenburg is practically cut off from communication with the outer world.

I wonder what will be the result of my telegram of yesterday about Kitchener. Although he did not say so, I gathered he thought he ought to be made Commander-in-Chief in India, and not have to wait for five years before being appointed. He admitted that no previous experience of the Indian Army was a drawback, and if there were anyone with that experience who had Kitchener's other good qualities, I would not say a word in favour of the latter being appointed, but I know no one. Kitchener is not the hard man I thought he was, and there are few officers in our Army who have seen so much of war as he has.

Colonel Roberts[26] will, I suppose, be removed of the command of his regiment when the proceedings of the Court of Enquiry are received. Had he not been made a prisoner I would have suspended him pending instructions from home.

Lt. Colonel Alexander has served his four years in command, and might be allowed to disappear. He is evidently wanting in military instinct.

BL MS Room, Lansdowne Papers L(5)48

41
Lord Roberts to Queen Victoria
Pretoria, 8th August 1900.

[Printed letter]

I had the great honour to receive a few days ago Your Majesty's gracious letter of the 6th July, for which I beg to offer my most respectful thanks.

The war which Your Majesty trusted was drawing to a conclusion on the date when the letter was despatched, is not yet at an end, but I trust that the events which have occurred during the last fortnight will help considerably to bring it to a satisfactory conclusion ere very long. The surrender of over 4,000 Boers to Sir Archibald Hunter near Bethlehem, and the move of Commandant De Wet with Ex-President Steyn into the Transvaal, practically closes the war so far as the Orange River Colony is concerned.[27] We are now doing all we can to cut off De Wet's force and prevent their joining Commandant-General Botha, an intensely interesting and exciting operation, rendered more so by the great size of the country, and the extraordinary mobility of the Boers, who manage to slip away in the most marvellous manner.

Lord Kitchener is in temporary command of the troops who are following up De Wet, and General Ian Hamilton has a column in readiness to move in any direction that may be required.

Your Majesty will, I daresay, remember sending four scarves made by Your Majesty to be given to four Colonial Private soldiers. There was the greatest competition to become the fortunate possessors of these scarves, and it took a long time to get the required information, which would enable me to decide as to the merits of those eligible for such a coveted reward, on account of the troops being very widely scattered and so constantly on the move. It was finally settled that the following men were in all respects the most deserving of the great honour, viz.:–

Canadians. Private R.R. Thompson.
New South Wales. Private Duprayer [Dufrayer].
New Zealand. Private H.D. Coutts.
Cape Colony. Trooper L. Chadwick.

117

It turns out, as Your Majesty will see from the enclosed correspondence, that the Colonial recipient is an American. He is evidently a grand fellow, and as he is fighting for us, and was unanimously elected by his comrades in Roberts's Horse as the man most worthy in all respects to receive the scarf, I decided that the question of his nationality need not be considered a deterrence. I hope that this will meet with Your Majesty's approval.

I am thankful to say that sickness is decreasing fast, both as regards numbers and virulence; even Mr. Burdett-Coutts could scarcely find fault with our hospitals at present. There were some grains of truth in his strictures at the time he wrote his letters to "The Times", but his statements were in all cases grossly exaggerated, and in some instances quite untrue, as I hope will be proved to the satisfaction of the Commission now on their way to South Africa to enquire into the matter.[28]

As I telegraphed to Sir Arthur Bigge, the Army in this country sympathizes deeply with Your Majesty on the death of the Duke of Coburg.[29] I am so very sorry that Your Majesty should have this great sorrow at a time when there are so many important and serious questions to occupy Your Majesty's attention.

The assassination of the King of Italy, too, is a terribly sad thing, and demonstrates in a deplorable manner how strong is the spirit of anarchy in some countries.[30]

South African War, 1900. Vol. II. Home and Oversea Correspondence by Field-Marshal Lord Roberts, pp. 54–5.[31]

42
Lord Roberts to Lord Lansdowne

Pretoria, 16th August 1900.

[Holograph]

I hope, as no letter came from you by the mail of the 21st July, that you were able to take a short holiday to Bowood, and I much wish I could think of you now as being at Durreen [?], but I am afraid you would scarcely be able to go so far away from London. You will regret this, but what a relief it must be to have done with

Parliament for a time. I have often thought how irritating it must have been for you, and even more for Wyndham to have to reply to the many ridiculous questions people are so fond of asking.

I deeply regret to say that De Wet and Steyn managed to elude their pursuers. Up to Ventersdorp Methuen and Kitchener were close upon them. Then they lost touch with them, owing I suspect to their breaking up into small parties, but of this I have no certain information. It is very unfortunate for I firmly believe that the capture of De Wet would have put an end to the war. Now he will in all probability be able to join Botha, and put fresh heart into the Transvaalers, the majority of whom, I am informed, would be glad to give in and return to their farms. I shall be better able to judge of the truth of this report in a few day's time, when I hope to find myself at Machadodorp. Buller's arrival at Carolina with a division of Infantry, a brigade of Cavalry, and several guns will be a great help, and enable us to shut up Botha and his army in the Lydenburg hills if they do not surrender.

I am in hopes that the Eland's River garrison will be rescued after all. Hore was holding out on the 10th, and Kitchener was within a few miles of the post last evening. Carrington did not apparently show much interest in his endeavour to reach Hore, who seems to have been doing extremely well.[32]

I gather from Reuters' telegrams which have reached me during the last few days that I am considered to be treating the Boers too leniently. When we first entered the Orange River Colony I did not wish to do anything that would be likely to engender a feeling of race hatred, and the satisfactory manner in which that Colony has accepted the change of [late?] proves, I think, that I was not wrong. South of Bloemfontein we have scarcely any troops, and Policemen are few and far between. The people give very little trouble and there is scarcely any crime.

Matters are somewhat different here. The war has gradually assumed a gueril<l>a character, and the irreconcilables from the Orange River Colony and the Transvaal, some rebels from Cape Colony, and a good many foreigners whose living depends on the Governments of the two states not falling into our hands, have to be dealt with. I have recognized this change in the condition of affairs for some time past, and have taken much more severe measures than formerly. The people are beginning to understand this war, and the raids on the railway, cutting the telegraph wire etc, are not nearly as frequent as they were.

The ringleader of the badly planned plot to carry me off is being tried by Court Martial today. He will probably be sentenced to death, a sentence I am prepared to confirm, though I confess I wish that the offence had been committed against some one else than myself.[33]

Colonel Helyar, whose death I reported a day or two ago, was certainly murdered.[34] The man who fired the fatal shot is fighting against us, but two Boers who were accessories to the death have been brought in as prisoners.

I have replied to your telegram received today about Buller's despatch, saying that I have no objection to the publication of all the telegrams which have passed between him and me. I only referred, in the Appendix to my covering letter, to such telegrams as seemed to me to bear on the subject. But it is better, perhaps, that the whole pile should be published.[35]

My despatch giving an account of our operations up to the occupation of Pretoria goes by this mail.[36] I wish I could have sent it sooner, but the interruptions are so incessant it is scarcely possible to write more than a few lines at a time.

I hope we shall soon hear that our troops have reached Pekin in time to save the legations.[37] Count Waldersee is, I think, a good selection for the command of the combined forces. I met him on two occasions at German manoeuvres, and he struck me as being an able man, and he is friendly disposed to the British.

BL MS Room, Lansdowne Papers L(5)48

43
Lord Lansdowne to Lord Roberts

17.8.1900

[Copy]

First let me congratulate you on the miscarriage of the plot. It may have been a clumsy affair, but if it had not been discovered as it was the consequences might have been serious. I trust that the conspir<ator>s will be summarily & severely dealt with. Public opinion here will support you in any strong measures you may deem necessary to adopt – The complaint generally made is that we have been too lenient. I believe yr leniency will have a good effect in the long run, & that when the war is over it will be gratefully remembered & help to restore confidence & goodwill; but we must make it clear that the men who have exper<ien>ced that leniency & have taken advantage of it in order to resume hostilities against us will be dealt with severely. I wish there were some means of identifying them readily – The Berlillon system would I fear be too elaborate & difficult to apply.

Yr letter of 19/7 told me much that I wanted to know – I fear we have any number <of> duffers in command of units   In theory I don't think our system of promotion has much the matters with it, but in practice the milry. authties. have been too tenderhearted. Moller's[38] was a leading case. I will keep an eye on the action taken in regard to Peter[39] and Alex<ande>r.[40]

Yr action in sending the Boer families to Botha's camp was much to be commended   By the way Crowe's[41] report as to the state of things there makes me hopeful that Botha will not hold out long.

On the other hand de Wet is apparently able to elude any number of generals & Methuen has I am afraid been obliged to direct his attention to the relief of Hore's force, instead of helping to catch de Wet. The story of the Elands river Garrn. is difficult to understand particularly Carrington's action in abandoning the attempt. The newspapers say that he burned the stores at Zeerust & relied upon Mafeking! from which you have I gather called him back.[42]

You will I hope not have been annoyed by my telegram repeating what the Queen said to me about Lady R. I have told her that in my opinion Lady R's presence at Pretoria was clearly desirable & I do not suppose that you would in any cir<cumstanc>es have taken her with you during your advance on Machadodorp.

I am to see the Q. next week at Osborne & will talk to her about this. The Q. has strong views about ladies at the front & I have no doubt that she thought that Lady R's action might be quoted as a precedent – I do not however admit that what is done by the C in C's need be regarded as establishing for other people –

I was glad to receive yr let<ter> of 16th as to the public<ation> of the tel<egra>ms which passed between you & Buller – some of wh. were attached to yr despatch of July 3rd 43 – To tell you the truth I am not quite sure whether it was worth yr while to take up Buller's challenge. He suggests it is true that the whole of the delay which took place was the result of yr instructions that he shd remain on the defensive – this was certainly not the case, and I understand yr desire not to leave the statement uncontrovented.

On the other hand it is very difficult to disentangle the true story from this involved series of tel<egra>ms – Buller shews considerable ingenuity in his way of putting the case, &, mainly no doubt from yr desire to meet him so far as you cd, you did not insist as strongly as you wd perhaps have been justified in insisting on his following your instructions.

For these reasons I should in yr place have been inclined not to enter into this controversy with an opponent who is not over scrupulous & whose backers will readily seize an opportunity of fighting his side of the case against yrs.

But this is really for you to decide. I don't think the despatch will be published before this letter reaches you, & if you think there is anything in my argument you will have time to instruct us by tel<egra>m. –

I am sure however that if any of the tel<egra>ms. are to be published, you cannot be too careful to omit nothing which has has [sic] any bearing on the ...... Attention would at once have been called to the fact that the collection was not complete & every sort of motive wd have been attributed to those responsible for leaving out the missing documents. I shall therefore if we publish, publish all.

Can you do anything for poor Lord Romney whose letters I enclose? I cd hardly refuse to send on his request. Nor cd I refuse to ask you to forward a private tel<egra>m from the Maxse [?] family to M. of the Transvaal Constab<ular>y – The matter a legal one   is I believe of very great importance to them.

Nothing is yet settled about India much to my annoyance, I will telegraph to you as soon as I can obtain a dicision – (re Lord C.F.).

* * *

I trust that the next few days will bring us good news both from the E & W sides of the theatre of war.

BL MS Room, Lansdowne Papers L(5)48

44
Sir Arthur Bigge to Lord Lansdowne

Osborne

[Holograph]

Aug: 18.1900

Private

The Queen desires me to thank you for so promptly acting on her suggestion, and telegraphing to Lord Roberts about Lady Roberts' presence at the front. Her Majesty thinks your telegram is very kind and will do admirably –

As you know the Queen has a great admiration for Lord Roberts and it is really for his own sake and reputation that H M wishes that he should be put on his guard. Endless stories, probably many of which are untrue, reach The Queen respecting Lady Roberts' interference and her influence even exerted on the careers of officers in high command in South Africa – If half of these reports were true The Queen feels that the confidence of the Army would be shaken in the man to whom popular opinion seems to point as the future Commander in Chief – Her Majesty cannot help regretting that Lady Roberts ever went even to Bloemfontein let alone Pretoria.[44]

If she was not at Head Quarters there could be no possible ground for the accusations which are but too common against her –

I fear de Wet has got away: but Kitchener seems to have done fine work in reaching the beleaguered force at Elands River.

123

The enclosed,[45] in my humble opinion, admirable letter from Grierson I send to you with the same confidence that I showed you some of his previous ones, tho' of course they were not written for the eye of the S of S!

Lord Wolseley seems to have endorsed his views as to want of military training of the Militia if the newspaper reports of the C in C's comments at Aldershot are true. I do hope that we shall in the future make our Militia up to strength: improve its officers & NCOs and by degrees produce a well trained disciplined force: and in spite of landlords & game preservers insist upon big manoeuvres – Why not make Ireland the great training ground of our Army: there must be vast tracts of land some of which resembles in character the country of N. Natal.

Transport the Army there for the summer. It would bring a lot of money into Ireland and might even politically do good –

Forgive this long letter. You can bring G's [?] letter when you come Thursday.

Just heard officially Peking being taken 15th & ...... safe[46]

BL MS Room, Lansdowne Papers L(5)44

45
Lord Roberts to Queen Victoria

Pretoria, 21st August 1900.

[Printed letter]

I had the great honour this morning to receive Your Majesty's gracious letter of the 27th July, for which I beg to offer my most respectful and earnest thanks.

I much wish that, in this my reply, I could give some certain news as to the war being near its end. It still drags on, and in its guerilla form is most difficult to deal with. So long as the Boers kept in fairly compact bodies, we knew what to do with them, but now that they have broken up into small parties, with an intimate knowledge of the country and of the whereabouts of all our troops, and with everyone ready to assist them (an enormous help), the advantage is all on their side. Every farm they pass is a depôt of supplies and an arsenal from which they can replenish their ammunition. They can get food for man and beast where our troops would starve, and notwithstanding all the precautions we take, I believe they come and go pretty freely amongst us. One of their most enterprising leaders, Commandant De Wet, boasted to a British Officer, who was with him as a prisoner, that the daily paper was regularly brought to him from Kroonstad when he was in that neighbourhood. The Boers dress up in our clothes, and having so many Colonials and Afrikanders in our service,[47] it is impossible for our sentries sometimes to tell enemies from friends.

This same De Wet has given our troops a long chase, more than 300 miles from Bethlehem to just north of Pretoria. He was yesterday within 15 miles of this place, and is being followed by Generals Ian Hamilton, Paget and Baden Powell. They are still on his track, and I am anxiously waiting for their reports.[48] If they succeed in capturing De Wet, the war will practically be over, for I am told that the Transvaal Commandant General, Botha, would give in, but he considers it a point of honour not to do so, so long an any Free Stater General holds out.

I was greatly distressed to hear that Your Majesty had been caused the slightest uneasiness as to the impression which might be made by Lady Roberts's presence in Pretoria, and I trust that the answer I sent to Lord Lansdowne's telegram will have satisfied Your Majesty. I asked my wife to come here for two reasons. One, that she had been subject to such a heavy strain for 10 weeks at Bloemfontein, where she and my daughters were through all the worst time of the typhoid epidemic (five out of her small establishment were attacked by the disease), added to the constant anxiety she had had on account of the war, that I did not consider it right to leave her longer there. The other, that I greatly needed her assistance in establishing hospitals here. I have very little time for going into such matters myself, and at Bloemfontein she was the greatest possible help to me in bringing to my notice what needed improvement, without interfering in the slightest degree with doctors or nurses (who do not hesitate to appeal to her for help). She can discover a great deal more than I can in my periodical visits of inspection.

I think the Commission will find every hospital at Bloemfontein and here in good order, due in a great measure to Lady Roberts's exertions.

Pretoria itself is now so perfectly settled, there is no reason why English ladies, whose husbands are here, should not come up, and I think their presence has a quieting effect on the residents. The difficulty is to get here, the line of rail being so blocked with supply, troops, remounts, and ambulance trains, that passenger trains cannot come up.

I am very pleased to be able to inform Your Majesty that Prince Christian Victor joined me a day or two ago. He is looking in robust health, and I am glad to think he will be with me in what, I hope, may be my last advance.

The health of the troops is excellent, and the climate just now quite perfection.

South African War, 1900. Vol. II. Home and Oversea Correspondence by Field-Marshal Lord Roberts, pp. 63–4.[49]

46
Colonel Neville Chamberlain to Lord Lansdowne

Camberley. August 28th 1900.

[Typed copy]
Private.

Lord Roberts asked me to send you, for your personal information, the enclosed brief notes on some of the senior officers now serving under him in South Africa, which he dictated to me before I left Pretoria.

Lord Kitchener.

I cannot describe what an assistance he has been to me.

From his antecedents it might have been expected that he would hold strong opinions of his own, and that if we differed in our views he might have been difficult to work with. I can only say that I have never been served more loyally or more efficiently than by Kitchener, and on no single occasion has there been the slightest friction between us, or anything but the most complete harmony. After giving me his opinion fully and frankly on all points he has accepted at once whatever decision I arrived at, and carried it out as energetically as if it were his own line of policy.

He is untiring in the performance of his duty, and the services he has rendered during the war have been most exceptional and distinguished. It has been a real pleasure and of the greatest advantage to me personally to have had him with me during the anxieties and difficulties of the Campaign.

<u>Wood – Marshall.</u>
Neither men of any note.

The former is a man of very ordinary capacity, scarcely fitted to be C.R.E. of a division, let alone of a large army.

The latter, an officer who might have done better if he had had experience other than regimental experience – but all his life he has been in a subordinate position with no special responsibilities devolving on him, and he has quite failed to rise to the position of the C.R.A. of a large army.

As regards the Brigadiers – I should put Smith-Dorrien at the head of the list – Macdonald also is good – So is Bruce Hamilton.

I would mention especially two other good men, Maxwell and Colin Mackenzie, who are Military Governors at Pretoria and Johannesburg respectively – They are both fit for any employment.

<u>Doctors.</u>
With scarcely an exception are a very inefficient lot and have given me more trouble than I can describe. I have had to do their work for them throughout the Campaign and the department must be thoroughly reorganized. They are insufferably conceited and are inefficient as surgeons   as physicians, and as administrators.

<u>Ward</u>
Quite excellent in arranging for our supplies and has done invaluable service for the Country. The man who preceded him at my Hd.Qrs., Richardson, nearly broke my heart – I had to do his work as well as my own and the strain tried me more than I can

describe until Richardson's health broke down – He returned to Capetown, and Ward joined me.

Lord Methuen.

I did not relieve him of his Command on my arrival, for I felt that, whatever he had done, had taken place before I assumed Command in South Africa. I think he was given a force insufficient to carry out the task before him, especially as regards his mounted men, but after seeing him at Modder and talking over matters with him, I came to the conclusion that he did not appreciate he had made any mistakes, and I determined not to give him any Command involving responsibility in the future.

He has certain good qualities – He is very careful about his men and about his transport, and since I have been in this country he has carried out satisfactorily the minor operations which have been entrusted to him.

Sir H. Rundle.

He was never tried as a Commander in Egypt – He was Chief of the Staff to Kitchener, and Chief of the Staff to a man like Kitchener with a comparatively small force had probably but little to do. He has failed twice in this Country as a Divisional Commander. He failed to fight at Dewetsdorp when he ought to have fought,[50] and he went out of his way to fight on the Senekal-Bethlehem road when he ought not to have fought[51] – He went out of his way to engage the enemy – his losses were extremely heavy, and at the end of the engagement he had to retire because there was no object in his going on.

Kelly-Kenny.

On the whole he has done very well. He had very responsible work to carry out both at Paardeberg and on the engagement of the 10th March.[52] He is careful, painstaking, and showed coolness, steadiness, and resource, when our line of railway was cut early in June.[53] He looks after his men and his sick and wounded, and knows all that is going on in his Command. He is probably not a brilliant Commander, but can, I believe, be trusted to carry out whatever he is told to do.

Sir H. Chermside.

I have had very little opportunity of trying him. My impression is that he is a man of mediocre abilities. He is theoretical and talkative, but I doubt his being a man of action. I have, in consequence, purposely not entrusted any responsible operations to him.

Sir A. Hunter.

He did excellent work in the despatch of Mahon's force towards Mafeking and, as far as I have had opportunities of judging until now, he is a reliable General. I shall be able to speak more confidently about his abilities when the present operations he is conducting in the Orange River Colony are brought to a conclusion.[54]

Tucker.

The ordinary type of regimental officer – Active habits, and fairly intelligent, but I doubt if he has ever studied his profession, or if he appreciates the responsibilities of a General in Command. He is not a man I would trust with any independent operation.

Pole-Carew.

Has done very well in Command of his Division[55] – He takes a great interest in his work – He is active, intelligent and looks carefully after his men. He is indefatigable in trying to get information about the enemy's movements, but he is not always very correct in the way he sifts the information he gets, so he is apt at times to magnify the enemy's numbers. His charming manner makes him most popular with all ranks serving under him, and with more experience as a Commander I think he will do extremely well.

Ian Hamilton.

Is quite the most brilliant Commander I have serving under me. He shares with Pole-Carew the love and admiration of all his force. He takes infinite trouble in matters of detail and knows his work thoroughly. He is most careful to assure himself exactly what he is required to do. He is very intelligent, untiring in the performance of his duty and he has that military instinct which would enable him to appreciate when a risk should be run in order to achieve some given object. I would select him before all others to carry out any difficult operation.

French.

I think he has improved immensely during the past few months, and although he has the great defect in a Cavalry Commander of not understanding how to take care of his horses, he is the only man except Broadwood whom I could trust to use a body of Cavalry with dash and intelligence. He is a man of iron nerves who has learnt how to cope with boer tactics. He has been unfortunate in two of his Brigadiers, Dickson[56] & Porter, who are men of very ordinary ability. Gordon, the third Brigadier, is better than the other two, as he ought to be for he is younger than they are, but he has not come up to my expectations of him. The 4th Brigadier, Broadwood, is undoubtedly good, and he would be better still if he were more intelligent – but he is a brave, resolute, active man, and the troops he commands believe in him.

Hutton.

Is a man I feel confidence in and he has managed several difficult affairs[57] with considerable skill. I believe his troops do not like him, but they trust him as a Commander. He is inordinately conceited and talks too much, but still is a valuable officer.

NAM 7101–23–188; BL MS Room, Lansdowne Papers L(5)48

47
Lord Roberts to General Louis Botha

Army Head Quarters, South Africa.

[Typed letter, signed]

2nd September 1900.

I have the honour to address your Honour regarding the operations of those comparatively small bands of armed Boers who conceal themselves on farms in the neighbourhood of our lines of communication and thence endeavour to damage the railway, thus endangering the lives of passengers travelling by train who may or may not be combatants.

2.   My reason for again referring to this subject is that, except in the districts occupied by the Army under the personal command of your Honour, there is now no formed body of Boer troops in the Transvaal or Orange River Colony, and that the war is degenerating into operations carried on by irregular and irresponsible guerillas. This would be so ruinous to the country and so deplorable from every point of view that I feel bound to do everything in my power to prevent it.

3.   The orders I have at present issued, to give effect to these views, are that the farm nearest the scene of any attempt to injure the line or wreck a train is to be burnt, and that all farms within a radius of 10 miles are to be completely cleared of all their stock, supplies, etc.

4.   In connection with the foregoing the time has now come when I must refer again to my C. in C./670 of the 5th August 1900, to which letter your Honour replied on the 15th August. I feel that when once the war has entered into the stage of irregular or guerilla fighting, I should not be doing my duty towards the national interests if I continued to permit the families of those who are fighting against us to remain in towns guarded by us. This is not now a question of supply so much as one of policy, and of securing ourselves against the transmission of intelligence to our enemies. I should esteem it a favour, therefore, if your Honour would warn all Burghers on Commando, who have their families living in districts under the control of our troops, to make early preparations for their reception and accommodation. The removal of these families will commence in a few days, those at Pretoria being first sent. They will proceed by rail to the British outpost and there be made over to any one your Honour may depute to receive them. I will keep your Honour informed of the number to expect day by day, and I would take this opportunity of informing you that, as nearly all the passenger vehicles belonging to the Netherlands Railway Company have been removed eastward, the families must, I regret to say, travel in trucks, for the most part open ones. I will

endeavour to provide Mrs Kruger, Mrs Botha, and as many other ladies as possible with closed carriages, but as I am not sure that I shall succeed in finding any I would suggest that your Honour should send suitable accommodation for them. I need not say how distasteful this measure is to me, but it is forced upon me by the apparent determination of you and your Burghers to continue the war after all doubt as to its ultimate issue has ceased.

Killie Campbell Africana Library, Campbell Collections of the University of Natal

48
Lord Lansdowne to Lord Roberts

13.9.1900

[Holograph]

Thanks for your letter of Aug. 16th

You refer to comments which have been made upon your lenient treatment of the enemy – So far as I am able to judge public opinion was extremely in favour of the generous policy which you at first adopted in dealing with the men who had fought us fairly in the field – I believe it had good results at the time, & that its remoter effects will be advantageous. But the constant violations of the oath of neutrality, and the treacherous attacks made upon us along the lines of Railway, no doubt created a feeling that the time had come for abandoning a 'kid gloved' policy, & resorting to sterner measures – This is what you have done, & the new departure has been welcomed.

Events are now moving rapidly, & Kruger's flight,[58] altho' it may not much effect the military situation, will convince the waverers that the game is up –

I am afraid you were disappointed at the Foreign office decision not to interfere with the importation of ordinary food stuff (i.e. foodstuff not prima facie of such a nature as to make it clear that they were destined for the use of an army in the field.) Lord Salisbury's absence has made the discussion [?] of all such questions very difficult & I will speak to him again about this matter as soon as he returns – But all such interferences with trade are likely to get us into trouble with neutral forces, and are consequently as a rule deprecated by the F.O. – I cannot help hoping that you will be able to get hold of the junction at Komati Po<o>rt before long and once there to stop all movement of supplies towards the Transvaal –

I have sent you a telegram as to the Portuguese offer of permission to use their country[59] – This too is a matter with regard to which we must move warily, and we shall have to take the F.O. with us.

I foresee considerable difficulty in dealing promptly with your recommendations for honours – They must ...... be very numerous – Are you likely to send in a great many names in addition to those which we have already received from you? You may probably think it worth while to send me a few lines by telegram as to this – It is desirable that these rewards should be bestowed as promptly as possible.

I know you will lose no time in ...... me whenever you can see your way to letting go any of the troops now serving in S. Africa – I have told my colleagues that you wanted every man of whom you could dispose at the front, & that you had indeed been obliged to call in your garrisons in the Zeerust Rustenburg district, because you wanted the troops for offensive purposes ...... – That is a conclusive engagement. But have you not a great number of men in Cape Colony some of whom might be spared? Our distribution returns are always struggling, and may be misleading, but I see that they show <u>as on Cape Colony lines of communic<atio>n under Forestier Walker</u>

Return of   7/7 c. 14.000
              30/7 c. 19.000
              31/8 c. 24.000 + 82 guns

I suspect these figures include a certain number of men who are mostly passing through F-Walker's command, but the increase in the total is curious – There seems to be a considerable quantity of artillery of one kind or another, and perhaps some of this will soon be available for withdrawal.

14.9[.1900]

Since I wrote the above I have read your telegram 1161 of yesterday – My no. 236[60] was intended as a hint that we were not in my opinion free to take immediate action on the strength of the Portuguese ...... to make use of their territory. You will probably have gathered before you read this letter what the nature of the difficulty is – I hope to see Lord Salisbury (who has just arrived) very shortly, & I shall then be able to find out how far we can go – I can well understand that you should have wished to jump at such an opportunity.

Your proclamation has just come in[61] – I like it very much, and trust it will do good – We have I suppose no ...... of the ignorance in which the common [?] ...... of the Boers exists.

All these events are I am sure bringing us near to the moment when you will be able to turn your back on the country in which you have achieved so much for us. What a pleasure it will be to see you again when the time comes.

The issue of the general election will be in no doubt when this reaches you – We shall I fancy keep the greater part of our majority but it is dangerous to prophesy –

I have just seen your evidence before Romer's [Hospital] commission – The summary given by the Times reads very well.

NAM 7101–23–34–406

49
Lord Roberts to Queen Victoria
Army Head Qrs, South Africa.

[Holograph]

Machadodorp, 17th Sept. 1900

I venture to send the enclosed letter[62] as I think it will please Your Majesty to know how greatly the scarf knitted by Your Majesty is appreciated by the Private of the New Zealand Mounted Rifles, to whom the most acceptable gift was unanimously awarded by the officers and men of his regiment. I have not heard from the other three fortunate recipients, but

I feel sure that they consider themselves as much honoured as does H.D. Coutts, No. 96 –[63]

My last letter to Your Majesty was despatched from Pretoria on the 21st August and I then almost hoped that when next I had privilege of writing to Your Majesty, I might be able to announce that the war was over and peace made.

Practically speaking the war is over, but after such a convulsion as has been taking place, it cannot be expected that the country will settle down with any great rapidity. For some little time outbreaks will, I fear, occur, but these will become fewer and fewer as the people learn that we bear them no animosity, and find that they are being treated justly and kindly.

The flight of the Ex-President, Kruger, and the resignation (if true) of the Commandant General Botha[64] will induce many Boers to return to their farms, as they will feel that two of their principal advisers have given up the cause as hopeless. The numbers against us in the field are week by week becoming fewer.

I telegraphed direct to Your Majesty the release of the prisoners at No<o>itgedacht near Barberton, as I knew how gratifying the news would be. Very few of our men are now in the Boers' hands, not more than twenty I think, while we have nearly 15 000 of their people as prisoners of war. When the terms of peace come to be settled these prisoners will be useful as hostages for the delivering up of all the guns still in the Boers' hands.

Princess Christian's Hospital train[65] is here, and returns to Pretoria tonight with sick and wounded men. It is most complete in all respects. The medical officer in charge seem<s> a capable intelligent man, and there are two nice bright Lady nurses. Princess Christian will, I am sure, be glad to hear how much the soldiers appreciate her Royal Highness's most comfortable train.

I trust Madam, that Your Majesty is continuing in good health, and enjoying Balmoral.

Prince Christian Victor is in the best of health, and making himself extremely useful.

RA VIC/P13/67

50
Lord Roberts to Queen Victoria

Pretoria, 4th Oct: 1900.

[Holograph]

I had the great honour to receive by the last mail Your Majesty's gracious letter of the 7th September, for which I beg to tender my most respectful thanks.

On the very day the letter reached me I heard from Lord Lansdowne that Your Majesty had been graciously pleased to select me for the high and important position of Commander-in Chief.[66] I need not say how proud and grateful I am for this mark of Your Majesty's appreciation of my services. I earnestly trust I may be able to carry out the difficult duties connected with the office to Your Majesty's satisfaction and to the benefit of the Army.

I have not been able yet to reply to that part of Lord Lansdowne's telegram in which he asked when I thought I could take up the appointment, but I trust it will not be long before I can fix a date. Troubles continue in different places, and the ubiquitous General De Wet is still at large, but there are signs that the Burghers are getting tired of the war, and beginning to realize what a frightful calamity it is for their country.

In many parts of the Orange River Colony and the Transvaal the distress amongst the women and children must be very great. I pointed this out to Commandant General Botha just a month ago in a letter, a copy of which I enclose for Your Majesty's perusal.[67]

I am today sending copies of it to ex-president Steyn and General De Wet by the hand of an influential Burgher, who surrendered at Barberton and offered his services in view to explaining the hopelessness of the situation to the Boer leaders. If Mr. van der Post's mission is successful it will be very satisfactory, under any circumstances I trust that affairs will have been settled sufficiently to admit of my leaving South Africa early in November. The majority of the Transvaalers are anxious to give in, but they think they are in honour bound to carry on the war so long as any of the Orange Free Staters hold out.

The City Imperial Volunteers left this yesterday en route for London looking thoroughly efficient and workmanlike. It is really wonderful the way in which they have adapted themselves to the rough life of a soldier in the field. They have had to draw their own water, cut their own wood, and cook their own food – often under considerable difficulties, but no one has ever heard a word of complaint from them. The country owes the C.I.V. a deep debt of gratitude, if only for showing what admirable material for our army we possess in the Volunteer Force.

It will I think gratify Your Majesty to know that in a telegram I received from New Zealand congratulating me on my new appointment, the Premier, Mr. Seddon,[68] says: – "our earnest desire is that ere long you may be not only Comander-in-Chief of the British Army, but also of all military forces of the Empire." A grand feeling of loyalty pervades the Colonials, and they certainly make most excellent soldiers.

P.S. I have no intention of sending away any of the ladies alluded to in the penultimate paragraph of the enclosed letter. Prince Christian Victor is very well.

RA VIC/P14/10

51
Lord Roberts to the Archbishop of Canterbury[69]

Army Head Qrs., South Africa,

[Holograph]

Pretoria, 9th October, 1900.

As it will, I hope, be possible for some portion of the Army in South Africa to return home ere long, I have written, as you were good enough to suggest,[70] a letter expressing my hope that the soldiers will be welcomed in a manner worthy of men who have done good service for their Queen and Country. I am sending a copy of the letter to all the principal Newspapers in the United Kingdom, and I beg to enclose two copies with these few lines.

Lambeth Palace Library: F. Temple Papers, Official Letters. 1900. Foreign C.1 – S.8. Vol. 41, ff. 420–421.

52
Lord Roberts to the Editors of London Daily Newspapers
Head-quarters of the Army in South Africa,

[Printed letter]

Pretoria, 30th September, 1900.
(Despatched 17th October.)

Will you kindly allow me, through the medium of your paper, to make an appeal to my countrymen and women upon a subject I have very much at heart, and which has been occupying my thoughts for some time past.

All classes in the United Kingdom have shown such a keen interest in the Army serving in South Africa, and have been so munificent in their efforts to supply every need of that Army, that I feel sure they must be eagerly looking forward to its return, and to giving our brave soldiers and sailors the hearty welcome they so well deserve when they get back to their native land.

It is about the character of this welcome, and the effect it may have on the reputations of the troops whom I have been so proud to command, that I am anxious, and that I venture to express an opinion. My sincere hope is that the welcome may not take the form of "treating" the men to stimulants in public houses or in the streets, and thus lead them into excesses which must tend to degrade those whom the nation delights to honour, and to lower the "Soldier of the Queen" in the eyes of the world – that world which has watched with undisguised admiration the grand work they have performed for their Sovereign and their country.

From the very kindness of their hearts, their innate politeness, and their gratitude for the welcome accorded them, it will be difficult for the men to refuse what is offered to them by their too generous friends.

I, therefore, beg earnestly that the British public will refrain from tempting my gallant comrades, but will rather aid them to uphold the splendid reputation they have won for the Imperial Army.

I am very proud that I am able to record, with the most absolute truth, that the conduct of this Army from first to last has been exemplary. Not one single case of serious crime has been brought to my notice – indeed, nothing that deserves the name of crime. There has been no necessity for appeals or orders to the men to behave properly. I have trusted implicitly to their own soldierly feeling and good sense, and I have not trusted in vain. They bore themselves like heroes on the battlefield, and like gentlemen on all other occasions.

Most malicious falsehoods were spread abroad by the authorities in the Orange Free State and the Transvaal as to the brutality of Great Britain's soldiers, and as to the manner in which the women and children might expect to be treated. We found, on first entering towns and villages, doors closed and shops shut up, while only English born people were to be seen in the streets. But very shortly all this was changed. Doors were left open, shutters were taken down, and people of all nationalities moved freely about, in the full assurance that they had nothing to fear from "the man in khaki," no matter how battered and war-stained his appearance.

This testimony will, I feel sure, be very gratifying to the people of Great Britain, and of that Greater Britain whose sons have shared to the fullest extent in the suffering as well as the glory of the war, and who have helped so materially to bring it to a successful close.

I know how keen my fellow-subjects will be to show their appreciation of the upright and honourable bearing as well as the gallantry of our sailors and soldiers, and I would entreat them, in return for all these grand men have done for them, to abstain from any action that might bring the smallest discredit upon those who have so worthily upheld the credit of their country.

I am induced to make this appeal from having read, with great regret, that when our troops were leaving England, and passing through the streets of London, their injudicious friends pressed liquor upon them and shoved them bottles of spirits into their hands and pockets – a mode of "speeding the parting" friend which resulted in some very distressing and discreditable scenes. I fervently hope there may be no such scenes to mar the brightness of the Welcome Home.

South African War, 1900–1901. Vol. III. Home and Overseas Correspondence by Field-Marshal Lord Roberts, pp. 27–8.

53
Lord Roberts to Queen Victoria

Army Head Qrs, South Africa.

[Holograph]

Pretoria, 26th October 1900.

I have had the honour to receive Your Majesty's gracious letter of the 28th September, for which I beg to offer my most respectful thanks. –

It distressed me greatly to have to telegraph that Prince Christian Victor was laid up with enteric fever, for I know how terribly anxious it would make Your Majesty and Princess Christian. So far all has gone well, and, as I was able to telegraph yesterday, there are no complications and His Highness's strength keeps up. Today's report is even better, and I am very hopeful that the attack will pass off without any bad results. The Prince will not, of course, be able to accompany us to England for which we are all extremely sorry. I trust, however, he will not be long after us. I will arrange for His Highness being sent in a hospital train to Capetown, as soon as he is fit to travel, and I daresay I shall be able to manage for Dr. Washbourne[71] to take charge of him during the voyage.

The Annexation parade passed off most successfully.[72] The buildings which surround the main square were crowded with spectators, many of them Dutch. The impressive ceremony must, I think, have satisfied the most firm believer in Boer predominance that our hold over this country is of a permanent nature. Your Majesty's troops looked quite magnificent.

RA VIC/P14/44

54
Lord Roberts to Queen Victoria

Army Head Qrs, South Africa.

[Holograph]

Pretoria, 1st November 1900

I little thought when I mentioned in my letter last week, that Prince Christian Victor was laid up with enteric, that I should so soon have to give your Majesty the sad details of His Highness's death. Everything then seemed so hopeful and there were no complications up till the time the mail left Pretoria on the 26th October. That evening the pulse and respiration became quicker. The next morning, as I telegraphed, the Prince was decidedly worse, and by evening His Highness was dangerously ill. On the morning of the 28th (Sunday) the symptoms were rather more favourable but the report early on the 29th was so bad that I sent the telegram which I thought would prepare Your Majesty and the poor mother for the sad news I feared I should have to send a few hours later.

Lady Roberts, Lord Stanley and I drove to the Yeomanry Hospital on receipt of the first telegram that morning. Lord Stanley and I went up to the Prince's room, and arrived there just as the Chaplain was about to administer the Sacrament. The Prince seemed to recognize me when I got to his bedside, and I am pretty certain he was conscious when receiving the Holy Sacrament. The nurse who was in the room at the time is quite positive about this. Towards the end he became unconscious, and when I left the room I felt he had a very short time to live. There was no suffering, and but for the difficulty in breathing, one could not have known that the end was so near.

I was told by Surgeon Major-General Wilson that it was the desire of Your Majesty and Princess Christian that if anything happened to the Prince during the campaign, the body was to be embalmed and sent home. The necessary arrangements were accordingly made, and all was ready for the removal of the remains to Capetown. Sir Arthur Bigge's telegram came in time to stop this, and Your Majesty's Grandson now lies in the Pretoria Cemetery amongst the many other soldiers who had been buried there during the past five months.[73]

As I have just telegraphed to Your Majesty the ceremony was most impressive. Everything was carried out as I think Your Majesty and Princess Christian would have wished. The following officers of the 60th Rifles were present, Lt. Col. Campbell,[74] Major Pakenham,[75] Captain Blore,[76] Captain Cumberland,[77] Captain Lord Robert Manners,[78] Lieutenants Blundell,[79] Wake,[80] Martin[81] and Kennedy.[82]

I will not take up Your Majesty's time by writing more today, but I must mention that I have had the great privilege to receive Your Majesty's letter of the 5th October on the subject of the position of the Commander-in-Chief. I entirely share Your Majesty's views, and I have more than once ventured to explain to Lord Lansdowne that it seemed to me an impossible position for any officer to fill with credit to himself or with benefit to the nation.

I trust I shall be able to make this clear to whomever may be Lord Lansdowne's successor at the War Office and it will be of the greatest possible help to me to know that I shall thus be acting in accordance with Your Majesty's wishes on this very important matter.

RA VIC/P14/55

55
Lord Kitchener to Lord Roberts

Bloemfontein

[Holograph]

9th Decber [1900]

<u>Private</u>

De Wet has been giving us a good deal of trouble but I think we have fairly prevented his very determined attempt to get into the Colony and I hope we may bring him to book though with such a slippery customer it is no easy matter —[83]

I have just heard from Stephenson that Barberton is being pressed[84] and boers very active all round   Whenever they get left alone for a short time they become aggressive   I have wired Lyttelton to arrange a column   he is strong out ...... & his mounted troops have recently been reinforced –

Cape   When [Forestier-] Walker goes I think Settle might do for it with local rank of M<ajor> G<eneral>. He knows all the ropes and would I feel sure greatly prevent scares in the Colony – Wynne is doing so well at Standerton and it is such an important point in our line for supplies that I do not like the idea of moving him –

Pretyman might then go to Kimberley and would look after a district from Orange River through Koffiefontein, including Boshof, Hoopstad and Christiana and as far north as Methuen's command and as far west as he likes – Would you wire me if you think this arrangement satisfactory – Pretyman says he would be glad to accept this arrangement

I hear Kennedy C.O. of the Camerons would be better in some other employment   He has lost his nerve – I am having him sent down here for the present –

Proemial has approved of officers being tried if posts are surrendered   I fear Dewetsdorp was not a good business at all.[85] I am having a statement of what took place drawn up by each of the wounded officers who are now here – I expect the prisoners have gone in to Smithfield as we have not yet heard of them –

Chamberlain's plan for the future of this country seems to leave the present state of hostilities completely out of his calculations I am afraid the boers will tear up his scheme

Some Regiments out here are getting very weak for want of drafts and also for want of officers –

I have sent the Coldstreams from Potchefstroom to Orange River line   The Scots Guards to Albert Junction – The Connaughts and Suffolks to Aliwal North – Parsons now in charge of Settle's column which is now going to Reddersburg to drive out more boers there   he is then available for West –

Rundles column will be at Senekal on the 12th – De Lisle at Kro<o>nstadt on the 10th – Bruce Hamilton looks at Heilbron and west of line to Botha   A new column is being formed of the Bulawayo Yeomanry at Kimberley under Grove, who did so well at Frankfort [?] to look after all that district as far as Hoopstad – I hope you will have a pleasant voyage home.

P.S. As I think you know the boers employ natives to pick up the cartridges dropped by our men. We have given repeated orders for the greatest care to be taken of cartridges but I am afraid with little effect. Yesterday I tried an experiment of loading one of our cartridges with dynamite   when fired it burst the rifle – Do you think there would be any harm in scattering a few of these cartridges where boers come   they would even give up using our rifles – Personally it does not seem to me much difference [different] to using mines, but I should like your opinion   would you wire what you think of it.

NAM 7101–23–33–5

56
Speech by Lord Roberts
Reply to the Addresses presented by the people of Capetown
and the Mayor[86] and Councillors of that City
Capetown, 10th December 1900.
[Typed copy in a bound volume]

I am deeply sensible of the great distinction conferred upon me by the people of Capetown in preparing for me this magnificent welcome, and to you, Mr. Mayor, and the Councillors of this historic town for presenting me with a "Sword of Honour," which I shall always look upon as one of my most valued possessions. The pleasure to me of receiving these most gratifying marks of your approval is greatly enhanced by the cordiality with which I have been greeted by this representative company, and by the kind and appreciative terms in which the Mayor and Town Clerk have referred to the service it has been my privilege to render to this country.

The war, which I thank God is now practically over (irrespective of its magnitude and its being the first war in which every Colony and Dependency of Great Britain has taken part), has a peculiar interest for me, inasmuch as it has given me the opportunity of carrying to what I hope will prove a satisfactory conclusion, the work entrusted to me nearly twenty years ago. That work, as I understand it, was to dispel, by force of arms if necessary, the aspirations of the Boers to make themselves independent of British control. Scarcely, however, had I started on my mission before "a change came o'er the spirit" of the Ministry of those days, and the first thing I heard, as we dropped anchor outside Capetown, was that peace had been made, and my services were not required.[87]

What "might have been" is proverbially an unprofitable subject for reflection, nevertheless one cannot entirely prevent oneself from thinking over, and deeply regretting, the grievous sacrifice of life and waste of property which might have been spared had wiser counsels prevailed and a less timorous policy been favoured by our rulers at that time.

But, Ladies and Gentlemen, "The wisdom of this world is foolishness with God". The guiding hand of Omnipotence can bring good out of what, to our finite understanding, appears most evil – most deplorable. And in preventing the war of 1881 being brought to what we then thought should have been its legitimate conclusion, that Guiding Hand can now, in the light of recent events, be clearly discerned; for we must all recognize that the war of 1881 could not have had the far reaching results that this war has had, the benefits of which to South Africa will, I believe, be felt to be greater and greater as time goes on. It could not have welded the whole British Empire firmly together as this war has done, for the war of 1881 would have been fought entirely by our regular troops, whereas this war has been brought to its successful termination, not by our regular army alone, but by the aid of the Militia, the Yeomanry, and the Volunteers of Great Britain, as well as by the help of the admirable and workmanlike contingents furnished by South Africa, Canada, Australia, New Zealand, India, and Ceylon, all fighting as brothers in arms under the dear old flag of the Mother Country, in the service of their Empress Queen.

In this respect, Ladies and Gentlemen, I hold a unique position for a Field-Marshal of the United Kingdom, for I am the first to have had the privilege to command an Imperial Army formed of representatives from all parts of Her Majesty's Dominions, bound together by one common aim and object – to uphold the honour of the Mother Country, and to die if need be for her interests.

Mr. Mayor, Ladies and Gentlemen, the effects of this spontaneous and unanimous outburst of patriotism will not be, I am convinced, of an ephemeral nature. Every Council Chamber throughout the world will have noted and will remember how England, isolated as she may be from other nations so far as treaties and alliances are concerned, had but to give the signal and, from all quarters of the globe, forthwith flocked men of her own stock to do battle for her honour and prestige. Never has the truth of the old saying "Blood is thicker than water" been better exemplified. Never has a mother had more reason to be proud of her valiant sons than England has to-day.

And so we stand, and please God shall continue to stand, a united, world-wide Empire, bound together by ties of blood, of friendship, and an equal love of justice and truth, ready now, henceforth, and for ever to fulfil the glorious destiny of our race. And God in his wisdom and mercy has blessed the combined efforts of England and her Dependencies in this war, and given success to her arms. He has brought us out of what, in the dark days of December, appeared to us as the valley of the shadow of death, and we are now able to look back upon those dark days of tribulation with deep gratitude for the victories vouchsafed to Her Majesty's forces.

For myself I shall ever remember with the utmost pride and pleasure my association with the grand men I have had the privilege to command. I thank them from the bottom of my heart for their bravery, their devotion, their fortitude, and their unexampled discipline. I am deeply sensible of what all ranks have done for the cause of liberty and justice, and for what they have done for me personally I am more grateful than words can express.

Speaking in the Capital of Cape Colony, it will not, I think, be inappropriate if I dwell for a moment more particularly on the work performed by the South African Colonials during the campaign. At the first outbreak of hostilities and within a few days of their being raised, nearly all of them were engaged with the enemy, and then, as on all subsequent occasions, they behaved with the greatest gallantry and in the most soldierlike manner. At Ladysmith, Mafeking, Kimberley, and Wepener[88] the South African Colonial soldiers especially distinguished themselves. And there are other South African Colonials who, though not called upon to take up arms, deserve the thanks of their fellow subjects throughout the Empire for their steadfast attitude during the past most trying year. These loyal people have never wavered in their allegiance, in spite of the hardships which many of them have experienced and the sacrifices they have been called upon to make for their Queen and Country.

Mr. Mayor, Ladies and Gentlemen, the war, as I have already said, has now come virtually to an end, and my work is finished. The soil has been prepared for the good seed which it will be the task of others to sow, and from which, I trust, and do not doubt, you will all reap plentiful harvests in years to come. But my interest in South Africa will not cease when I leave these shores. I shall watch with the utmost eagerness the settlement of the country, its development, and its unification, and on this head I would crave permission to say a few words.

The prosperity and the well-being of South Africa do not depend upon the action, the ability, or the governing power of any one man, so much as upon the cordial co-operation in their efforts for the good government of the Transvaal and the Orange River Colony.

We must forgive and try to forget all that would encourage bitterness of feeling or tend to transmit to succeeding generations the idea that anything remains to be atoned for on either side. But, at the same time, we must remember the lessons that the war has taught us. God has given into our hands a great heritage, for which we have been called upon to pay a heavy price in the blood of our dearest and our best. We must not, in the future be negligent of our trust as we have been in the past. We must strive to be able – when called upon to do so – to give a good account of our stewardship. We must be watchful, "strong and of a good courage," and we must try to think, not so much of the glory of conquest, as of the many responsibilities conquest imposes upon the conquerors, lest we forget that which alone makes war justifiable and conquest laudable – the good of the many, the better government of the conquered country, and the establishment within its borders of justice, mercy, liberty and truth.

Three years ago, when England's Sons from over the seas were gathered together in London to rejoice with those at home over our beloved Queen's Jubilee, and we were all glorying in the manifestation of our world-wide Dominion, that Imperial-minded poet, Rudyard Kipling, called upon us to remember that there were other duties besides that of natural [sic] glorification; and, in words breathing forth all that is best in Patriotism and Imperialism, he sounded a solemn note of warning which I cannot, I think, do better than recall to your memory, and thus conclude what I am afraid you will consider an all too lengthy speech –

God of our Fathers, known of old!
Lord of our far-spread battle line!
Beneath whose awful hand we hold
Dominion over palm and pine.
Lord God of Hosts, be with us yet,
Lest we forget – Lest we forget.

NAM 7101–23–126–3

57
Lord Kitchener to Lord Roberts

Pretoria

[Holograph]

28th Decbr 00.

I have put off writing till the last moment in hopes of receiving good news from the Colony – The operations there drag on and it seems as if our troops could not catch the very mobile parties of boers now out in the Colony[89] – It was no doubt a great coup that we were able to drive de Wet north as the commandos that crossed the Orange River have been in consequence all thrown out and are no doubt waiting for him, but I am much disappointed at our troops not having yet been able to clear the enemy to the north of the Orange River, and greatly fear de Wet will one day soon give us the slip and dash south to join them – I went down to Na<a>uwpoort and D'Aar and arranged all I could – I had to hurry back as my absence might have given cause for exaggerated reports here of how affairs were going in Cape Colony   very few people knew I had been away –

Settle has been doing very well   He has a good head. Hunter has also been a great assistance to me – I have not had much help from Chowder [?]

Broadwood, Douglas, & Talbot Coke are going home by this mail – Knox of the 18th Hussars takes Broadwood's place & I think will do well.

The boers have lost a good many men during the last week   they have certainly fought everywhere with great determination up to a point considerably beyond their usual rule, but then they bolt and so we never get a real bag –

I have worked up a Burgher Peace Committee[90] here to try and induce boers now out on commando to come in   I hope it will be successful but one must not expect too much from this sort of thing – Douglas will tell you what has been done –

We are short of good leaders and officers in battalions   I hope you will be able to send some out –

I have sent in another report about Phillips[91] of the Norfolks   he is evidently no use whatever   also Curran[92] of the Manchesters and Gosset[93] of the Derbyshire   the latter is believed to be slightly mad and has resigned his commission.

Fresh troops will be a great boon and I hope enable me to give a much needed rest to some out here –

I hope you will approve of an order I have issued releasing all soldiers who are undergoing certain sentences at the commencement of the new century –

I have decided to try one officer for putting up the white flags at Dewetsdorp without authority; also some men who did not behave well – The C.O. Massey RA[94] did not do badly but he will be asked certain questions regarding his conduct at the critical time when the white flag was put up without his authority

Clements will I think require change before long. He has been a good deal shaken by recent events –

As long as de Wet is out I can see no end to the war   if we could only manage to catch him   I believe all the others are heartily sick of it but it is not an easy matter in this country to catch such a slippery customer as de Wet – I am sending his brother Piet to Kro<o>nstadt to see what can be done –

With kind regards to Lady Roberts and Miss Roberts

NAM 7101–23–33–8

Part 3
2 January 1901 to 30 May 1902
Roberts at the War Office and the
War in South Africa
Introduction

Lord Roberts arrived back in England on board HM Hospital Ship *Canada* on 2 January 1901, landed at Cowes on the Isle of Wight where he received a rousing welcome, was presented with an address, and delivered the first of many speeches [58], often praising the assistance he received from Lord Kitchener. He immediately went to Osborne to be received in special audience by Queen Victoria. He was awarded an earldom and created a Knight of the Garter. This was one of the Queen's last acts, as she passed away on 22 January 1901 [59]. On 3 January Roberts received a hero's welcome on arrival in London and was driven through the city, where 14,000 troops lined the streets and spectators stood six or more deep along the route. Parliament voted to give him a grant of £100,000 in recognition of his services.[1]

In the South African war zone, Roberts' successor as Commander-in-Chief had to contend with an escalating guerrilla conflict. It was almost as if the war had started all over again. General De Wet was determined to embark on an incursion into the Cape Colony in spite of his failed attempt of December 1900. On 10 February 1901, he entered the Cape Colony at Sanddrif with at least two thousand men. From the start, his commando was pursued and attacked by some twelve British columns. On 16 February, Kitchener himself took command of the operation to capture De Wet. The Boers moved westwards across the De Aar-Kimberley railway line, but on 19 February they came up against the Brak River, approximately 16 km (10 miles) east of Prieska, where they found that the river was in flood. The closest British column was only 15 km behind them. De Wet realised that there was no other meaningful

150

alternative than to abandon the incursion and to return to the ORC. Under cover of darkness, De Wet and his commando sidestepped the British pursuers and retreated in a north-easterly direction. After Hertzog joined him on 27 February, De Wet led the commandos back across the Gariep River into ORC territory. The third, or great De Wet hunt was over [63]. On his return to the ORC, De Wet divided the area into seven military districts, each under the command of an Assistant Chief Commandant. A small portion of De Wet's commando, under Commandant Wynand Malan – cut off from the main force on 12 February – stayed behind in the Cape Colony, mainly operating in the Midlands. In April 1901, one of Malan's officers, Manie Maritz, was sent to the North-Western Cape Colony where he organized and commanded a commando of rebels.[2] Roberts regarded the safeguarding of the Cape Colony as being of great importance [72, 80]. In this regard martial law played an important role [83].

On 28 February 1901 Kitchener and General Louis Botha, Commandant-General of the Transvaal, met for peace negotiations at Middelburg (Transvaal). This meeting was preceded by telegraphic and other correspondence between Kitchener and Roberts regarding the terms that should be offered [61]. Each commander put forward his government's conditions for the cessation of hostilities. Kitchener was in favour of a negotiated peace settlement, but was adamant that republican independence was out of the question and would not be discussed, but, using the talks as a basis, he drafted the proposed terms of settlement. These terms were modified by Sir Alfred Milner and by the British government, and subsequently rejected by Botha on 16 March 1901. Kitchener criticized Milner for the refusal to grant an amnesty to the Cape rebels (which he regarded as the main reason for the breakdown of the talks), but it seems that even if that condition had been granted, it was highly unlikely that the Boers would at that stage have opted for a peace settlement.[3]

With the failure of the Middelburg talks, hope of a relatively early end to the guerrilla war faded, and Kitchener, urged on by Roberts [73, 75], had no other choice but to invest a great amount of time and money, as well as many men, in the designing and implementation of an elaborate anti-guerrilla strategy. In the final analysis, it became a war against space [77], with a large number of British troops, backed up by an elaborate blockhouse system, striving desperately to find, corner and destroy mobile die-hard Boers [74]. Sterner measures were contemplated and sometimes taken against British officers who failed in action [64], but those who performed well were duly given the necessary honours and awards [65, 67, 68].

From the War Office Roberts followed events in South Africa with great interest. He expressed his views freely in his weekly letters to Kitchener, and through his letters and telegrams still exerted an influence on the course of events. When it was clear that Kitchener was despairing, he offered words of encouragement [76, 81, 84]. The British were forced to take drastic action in order to ensure victory over the guerrilla units of the Boers in the field. As a result, many conventionally-organized British units were transformed, in the course of time, into mounted (anti-commando) columns in an attempt to take on the Boers on their own terrain. An extensive blockhouse system was developed which eventually consisted of approximately 8,000 blockhouses, across a distance of about 6,000 km (3,750 miles), that criss-crossed over large parts of the war zone. The blockhouses were manned by a total of about 60,000 white soldiers and 25,000 blacks and coloureds. The cost involved in erecting the blockhouses amounted to some £1,000,000. The aim of this blockhouse network was, among others, to safeguard strategic railway lines, bridges and other key points. Furthermore, the blockhouse lines were intended to limit the Boer commandos' freedom of movement and prevent them from launching incursions into vast areas such as the Cape Colony. During the various occasions on which hot-pursuit operations were conducted by the mobile columns against the commandos, it was presumed that the commandos would be trapped within the blockhouse lines. The British blockhouse system was an expensive, yet essential emergency measure adopted in order to sway the geographically escalating guerrilla war in favour of the British. Eventually, the system played a significant strategic and tactical role, and although the system did not restrict the Boers entirely, it did nonetheless hamper their freedom of movement to a greater or lesser extent [90].[4]

The longer the war lasted and spread over ever-enlarging parts of the country, the greater the manpower demands were on the British Army. As a result, more and more black and coloured inhabitants were employed, for example, as blockhouse guards and as guides for the mobile columns. There were also cases where entire columns were made up of, for example, coloured soldiers, in most instances under command of white officers. Generally the Boers displayed a ruthless attitude towards blacks and coloureds who were armed, and several of them, once taken prisoner, were executed on the spot – actions that may indeed be regarded as war crimes. Furthermore, there were also other controversial incidents that jeopardized race relations, for example, the actions that led to Abraham Esau's death, and the events at Leliefontein in Namaqualand.[5] In addition, the execution of the Cape rebels resulted in great bitterness,[6] while the fact that approximately 5,500 burghers and officers, after they had surrendered, had taken up arms against their former comrades, resulted in much division during and after the war.[7]

As time passed, the British military strategy affected ever-increasing numbers of ordinary citizens – white as well as black. For example, to prevent the roving commandos from obtaining food and information, eventually as many as 30,000 farm houses and more than 40 towns were partially or entirely destroyed. Roberts inaugurated the scorched-earth policy, but Kitchener extended and applied it more rigorously. Soon this policy, which started as a military necessity and as part of the overall military strategy, got out of hand. In most cases, the civilian victims of this scorched-earth policy were transported to camps. These camps were not merely refuges for Boers who were homeless or who had surrendered voluntarily and had their black or coloured servants with them, but were concentration camps where recalcitrant Boer men, but especially women and children who had been removed from their destroyed farms were housed – as part of an elaborate anti-commando military strategy. Of the at least 160,000 whites and 130,000 blacks who were held in camps across the war zone, close to 28,000 whites and more than 17,000 blacks died (although the latter number is most probably much higher in reality). The British simply could not cope with the stream of refugees.[8] While Roberts on the one hand gave advice with regard to the military operations, he also commented on the re-introduction of civilian control in the former Boer republics [79]; and, as long as the war lasted, he continually enquired about the performance of individual officers [81, 107].

Kitchener had always set his sights on the post of Commander-in-Chief in India, but first had to bring the war in South Africa to a successful conclusion [78]. Towards the end of 1901 this still seemed to be a long way off. In September 1901 the British had to cope with a new invasion in the Cape Colony. Former Transvaal State Attorney, Jan Smuts, left the Western Transvaal on 1 August 1901 in what became, in due course, an epic trek through large areas of the war zone. He moved through the ORC, and in the early hours of 4 September 1901 crossed the Gariep River in the Herschel district with a commando of about 250 men. He moved southwards, then westwards and eventually northwards, recruiting rebels along the way, finally reaching the Vanrhynsdorp area in November 1901 after several clashes with British columns. In the North-

Western Cape Colony he took over the command of all the Boer forces and re-organized them. Smuts planned to infiltrate further southwards, but after suffering a defeat on the farm Windhoek (25 February 1902), he decided to concentrate on the mining towns of Namaqualand. Nababeep, Springbok and Concordia were occupied, but the British garrison in Okiep gallantly resisted the Boer siege. At the end of April 1902, Smuts left this operational area to take part in the peace negotiations.[9]

Since Buller had driven the Boers out of Natal in June 1900, there had been no military operations in that colony. In September 1901 this tranquillity was threatened when General Louis Botha left the Eastern Transvaal on 7 September with a commando of about 1,000 men and moved southwards in the direction of the Natal border. At Blood River Poort he defeated a British force of 1,200 soldiers commanded by Lieutenant-Colonel H. de la P. Gough (17 September 1901) and then divided his commando into two. One section attacked a British post at Itala (25–26 September), just inside the Natal border, south of Babanango, while the other section launched an attack against Fort Prospect (26 September), east of Itala. Both attacks were unsuccessful, and Botha retreated to the Eastern Transvaal. There, on 30 October 1901, he dealt the column of Lieutenant-Colonel G.E. Benson a shattering blow at Bakenlaagte.[10] In an effort to bring the war to a close, more soldiers were sent to South Africa [86].

On 29 November 1901 Lieutenant-General Ian Hamilton arrived in South Africa to take up his new post as Lord Kitchener's Chief of Staff. Hamilton had previously rendered extensive service during the war. He accompanied General Sir George White as AAG to Natal in September 1899, fought with distinction at Elandslaagte (21 October 1899), Rietfontein (24 November 1899) and Lombardskop (30 October 1899), and was besieged in Ladysmith. After the relief he went to Cape Town, but Roberts summoned him to Bloemfontein. Once again he tendered sterling service, taking part in several clashes in the OFS and Transvaal. On 11 December 1900 he left South Africa in the company of Roberts, to serve as the latter's Military Secretary. When it became clear that Kitchener needed assistance, Roberts sent Hamilton back to South Africa [85, 87]. Hamilton sincerely hoped that he would be able to lighten the Commander-in-Chief's burdens [88], but Kitchener's temperament made it difficult for him to use Hamilton's services to the full. Consequently Hamilton was never more than a nominal Chief of Staff, and on 6 April 1902 he was given the command of all British forces in the Western Transvaal. In the second week of May 1902, i.e. just before the peace negotiations started at Vereeniging, Hamilton organized a successful drive in the area which led to the capture of 367 Boers.[11]

Almost every week Hamilton wrote a fairly long letter to Roberts, and vice versa. Hamilton's letters are of particular importance because they were the most comprehensive private letters written to Roberts from the war zone, and gave the Commander-in-Chief at the War Office an excellent idea of what was happening in South Africa during the last crucial six months of war [89, 91, 92, 93, 94, 96, 97, 98, 101, 106, 108, 109]. His commentary on the role of other senior officers is also of value [96, 97], because at the War Office Roberts was keen to know how these officers performed under operational conditions.

President M.T. Steyn and General C.R. de Wet were the most important obstacles in the way of a British military victory in South Africa. Steyn, whose health deteriorated towards the end of the war, usually accompanied De Wet's commando. On Christmas Day 1901, De Wet surprised and defeated a British force at Groenkop in the Eastern ORC [92, 93]. During February and March 1902, Kitchener launched his so-called New Model Drives against De Wet in that area, utilizing the blockhouse lines as an integral part of his tactics to drive on and corner the Boer commandos, but although several hundred burghers were captured [98], De Wet always succeeded in evading the traps [97, 99].[12]

In the meantime, in the Western Transvaal, shortly before Ian Hamilton turned the tables, the Boers under General Koos de la Rey inflicted severe losses on British columns at Yzerspruit (25 February 1902) [98] and De Klipdrift/Tweebosch (7 March 1902), wounding and capturing Lord Methuen in the latter clash, but magnanimously setting him free almost immediately to ensure that he received the best possible medical treatment [100]. These defeats once again led to debates regarding the steps to be taken, if any, against officers who failed in the field [106]. At Boschbult (31 March 1902) two British columns beat off a determined Boer attack, and at Rooiwal (11 April 1902) one of General J.C.G. Kemp's commandos was severely battered when it launched a suicidal attack against two British columns [106].[13]

By this time members of the Transvaal and OFS governments had already gathered at Klerksdorp (9–11 April) to discuss the possibility of entering into peace negotiations with the British [102]. This meeting was made possible by the mediation of the Dutch Minister-President, Dr Abraham Kuyper, who contacted Lord Lansdowne, who in turn contacted Lord Kitchener, who then gave the Boer governments safe conduct to enable them to hold the meeting. Those present gave a review of the circumstances under which the commandos were fighting and of whether it was possible to continue with the struggle. It was decided to negotiate for peace under the following conditions: some retention of republican independence; the Uitlander franchise question had to be settled; the Boers must be prepared to demolish their forts; future disputes were to be settled by arbitration; Dutch and English were to receive equal status in schools, and there had to be bilateral amnesty. These proposals were presented on 12 April to Kitchener in Pretoria [104, 105], who declined to negotiate on the basis of the republics retaining their independence. Lansdowne also rejected the proposals, but authorised Kitchener and Milner to request new proposals from the Boers. The Boer leaders rejected Roberts' annexation proclamations of 1900 as invalid, regarded themselves as the legitimate governments of the republics, and argued that they did not have the constitutional right to negotiate for peace on the basis of losing their independence without having consulted the republican electorate.[14]

It was impractical to test the republican voters on the above-mentioned question, and consequently it was decided that the commandos would elect 30 delegates each for the Transvaal and the OFS, who would then meet at Vereeniging on 15 May 1902 to discuss the basis of the peace negotiations. After two days of discussions, a Boer commission of five members (Smuts, Botha, De la Rey, De Wet and Hertzog) left for Pretoria on 17 May, where from 19 to 28 May the 'acts of peace' were hammered out in tough negotiations with Milner and Kitchener [107, 108]. From 29 May the Boer commission was back at Vereeniging where the conditions of surrender were presented to the other delegates, and discussed in heated debates. Die-hards such as Steyn and De Wet resisted the idea of a peace settlement without the retention of independence, but Botha, Smuts, and even De la Rey were in due course successful in convincing the greater majority of delegates that it was in the interest of the Afrikaner nation to accept the British peace terms. Of crucial importance were arguments with regard to the dwindling number of Boers in the field; their lack of horses, arms, and ammunition; the overwhelming British military manpower resources; the fact that European powers were definitely not going to intervene on behalf of the Boers; the increasing number of blacks and coloureds who were taking part on the side of the British; the plight of the Boer women and children in the concentration camps, and the fact that it was in the interest of the Boers to accept reasonably advantageous proposals while they were still in a position to do so and the British were still prepared to make certain concessions, even though the republics would lose their independence.[15]

58
Speech by Lord Roberts
Reply to an Address presented by the Mayor of Cowes
Her Royal Highness Princess Beatrice being present.
[Typed copy in a bound volume]

Cowes, 2nd January 1901.

Your Royal Highness, Mr. Mayor, Ladies and Gentlemen,
I respectfully thank your Royal Highness for your welcome to me, and the Mayor of Cowes for the kind Address with which he has, on behalf of his town, received me on my first setting foot in England after more than a year's absence.

Would that I could think that my own return was the immediate precursor of the return of all the troops, amongst whom, doubtless, many of those I see have dear ones fighting for their Queen and country – including, I think, your Member for Parliament, Captain Seeley.

It was one of the bitterest disappointments to me that I was forced to leave South Africa before the war was finished, but I felt that much as I should have wished to have seen peace proclaimed, my duty called me elsewhere.

All resistance by large organised forces may be at an end, but guerilla war of a serious type still exists – and will exist – and the people of this country must understand its danger.

I, myself, should never have left South Africa if I had not had the most implicit confidence in my successor Lord Kitchener, whose task is a great one, and one that I am very anxious should not be in any way under-estimated by the people of this country – but it is one which I have no doubt he will ere long overcome, though you will all be called upon to show patience, and a determination that, whatever the cost, you will not allow the fruits of this last year's trials to be lost.

I cannot resist taking this opportunity, as I shall every other that occurs, to testify to the loyalty, devotion and bravery of my comrades in arms from the highest to the lowest, and thanking them for past services rendered to me when Commander in Chief in South Africa.

The gallantry of the private soldier has, I firmly believe, won for himself a very different position in the eyes of the people from what he has hitherto had, and I trust that his example in devoting himself to the service of his Queen and Country without any hope of reward, except the consciousness of having done his duty, will inspire others who have hitherto held aloof to at all events (if not in the regular army) at least in the Militia, Volunteers, or that gallant force, the Yeomanry, fit themselves for the defence of their country whether it be Great Britain that be attacked, or the Greater Britain beyond the seas. If they do not do so it is not a very agreeable prospect for this country, but I have confidence that they will, and that, in the event of our being attacked, our foes will find that we, taking an example from our present opponents, will meet them not only with an army, but with a nation in arms in which all will have fitted themselves voluntarily to play their part, and which will be composed of men from Great Britain, India, Australia, Canada and other Colonies, all united under a common flag and owing allegiance to a common Sovereign.

Once more Mr. Mayor I thank you for your kind and flattering Address.

NAM 7101–23–126–3

59
Lord Roberts to Lord Kitchener

War Office 25th Janry 1901

[Manuscript copy]
Private

The weeks fly by in an astonishing way, but it is time for a letter to you – Many thanks for yours of the [no date] Dec from Pretoria[1] – I can well understand what an anxiety this incursion into Cape Colony must be to you for altho' the Boers do not appear to be in great numbers they are formidable from the fact that the majority of the inhabitants are on their side and against us, whatever may be their professions of loyalty[2] – It is most fortunate that De Wet was prevented from getting south of the Orange River, but he is pretty sure to make another attempt, and his presence in the Cape Colony would have a very serious effect –

The 5000 Yeomanry are coming on well, and I hope we shall be able to despatch the first lot 'ere long – I am forming them into companies instead of sending them out as drafts – This will, I think, make them much more serviceable – And, as you wish, they will be landed at Durban as will the 5000 Mounted Infantry – These latter, however, will take a little longer to get ready – I have not heard yet how many companies of volunteers have come forward, but I hope that each district will furnish enough to enable the companies now in South Africa to come home. It is very desireable in the interests of volunteering generally they should not be kept longer from their homes –

After some difficulty I got the Cabinet to agree to relieve the militia now in South Africa by eight battalions at a time – under the distinct promise that the eight relieved battalions would be sent home without delay – I will keep you informed by telegraph when the first eight will be likely to reach Cape Town, and you can then decide which eight battalions had best be sent home – Colonel Dixon will, I believe, start by tomorrows mail   and if you agree to Mildmay Wilson being sent he shall go next week –

I saw Broadwood a day or two ago, he says he will be quite ready to return to South Africa in two or three weeks time –

On receipt of this please sent [sic] me a telegram to say whether it would suit you to have Command of an Army Corps in England, should it not be possible for you to be appointed to India – Palmer seems to be giving satisfaction and there is a feeling both here and there that he should not be displaced. We are going to divide the home Army into six Army Corps, and I will keep the Salisbury Plain for you if you like – Always supposing India is an impossibility –

We are all very sad about the Queen's death – I was at Osborne on the 14th inst. exactly one week before Her Majesty died[3] – She was greatly changed from what she was in December 1899, but she appeared fairly well, and talked for nearly half an hour about the Army and the war – and did not seem weary – indeed when I offered to leave, she made me stay on – There is a Capt. Sladen[4] in the K.O.S. Borderers who is well fitted for Mounted Infantry – I think Cowan[5] gave his name to Hamilton – I long to hear of you being able to bring the war to an end – Kind regards from us all –

NAM 7101–23–122–1–6

60
Lord Roberts to Lord Kitchener

17 Dover Street. London. W.

[Manuscript copy]

22nd February. 1901.

I was very glad to receive your letter with an account of the various arrangements you were making for carrying on operations in Transvaal and Cape Colony. I had read in the papers that plans were being prepared and I was wondering how you would manage the supply question. You seem to have met this difficult matter by bringing convoys from the Vrede direction to Standerton and that French was thus enabled to follow Botha close up to the Swaziland border. Smith-Dorrien seems to have done well and moved down from the north in time to help French. But for the past three or four days we here had no news from either French or Smith-Dorrien and we want much to learn how it has fared with them.[6]

From Cape Colony the news is satisfactory, and I hope to hear that Plumer has captured De Wet. Anyhow the latter's attempted invasion of the Colony has not been successful, and that was the last card he had to play.[7]

You will have heard from Brodrick by telegram long ere you receive this that the question of the Indian command had to be settled. I fear you will be disappointed at not getting it as soon as the war in South Africa is over but you will not have to wait very long for Palmer is only to hold it until the date that Lockhart would have vacated it, something less than three years I think. The main reason for coming to a decision about the command was the fact that two other appointments depended upon it: the Military Member of Council in India, which will be vacant in a couple of months, and the vacancy in the India Council here caused by Sir Donald Stewart's death nearly a year ago.[8] The wish to see you Commander-in-Chief in India is I believe very general and you may depend on being Palmer's succesor.

A good many changes are in contemplation at the War Office. Your request for a financial advisor resulted in Fleetwood Wilson[9] being sent. This suited Brodrick as he had decided not to appoint him to succeed Ralph Knox but to give the Permanent Under Secretaryship to a soldier. Ward has been selected for it.

Then I hope that the Cabinet have agreed to my request to place the A.G. in a lower position than he has hitherto held at the War Office and to make the Commander-in-Chief practically the head of the military element. Work has gone on smoothly enough since I joined, but it is not carried on as I think it should be, and the change I have asked for will improve matters considerably.

Over 10,000 Yeomanry have now been enlisted, and the Cabinet have agreed to the number being increased to 15,000. Three companies of Mounted Infantry have sailed, and seven more will be ready by the 15th March. We will go on with other companies, and I hope you will not again be so badly off for mounted troops as you have been the last few weeks.

Seven Militia battalions are under orders and will be despatched so as not to interfere with the Yeomanry. Fetherstonhaugh seems to have been forgotten. He will now be sent out.

The Court of Inquiry on the Nooitgedacht affair shows clearly that Clements was mainly responsible.[10] He will not be included for any reward in the first Gazette and what he may receive eventually will depend on the report you may make of him.

How disappointing officers are. Lyttelton promised well but from what you say he must have lost his nerve like so many others have during the war. The fact is it is impossible to say what a man is fit for until he has been tried in some impossible position. Many men will do well enough so long as they have someone else to lean upon, but when they have to depend on themselves, they break down –

The Adjutant-Generalship in India has to be filled and will probably be offered to Smith-Dorrien. I had thought of bringing him to the War Office and will probably give him the choice of two appointments.

I have spoken to Grove about the want of regimental officers – you are to have the nomination of 250 and I will see that vacancies are rapidly filled up from this.

NAM 7101–23–122–1–17

61

Note [by Lord Roberts] on certain proposals by Lord Kitchener in the event of Commandant General Botha enquiring what terms would be conceded should the Boers desire to make peace

London, 24th February 1901.
[Manuscript copy]

The questions mooted in Lord Kitchener's telegram of the 22nd February[11] and 25th January should, I think, be referred to Sir Alfred Milner.

My own views are that for the present the laws in force in the Orange Free State might be maintained.

The compensation for damage to private property would have to be very carefully gone into. A great number of the farms we came across in the early part of the war were destroyed by (it was said) the kaffirs – every farm indeed deserted by the owners was more or less in ruins.

Later on some farms were destroyed by us on account of their being used as depots for arms and ammunition – or as places where Boers assembled before raiding the railway, or from which our troops had been fired at when the white flag was flying over them.[12]

And some have been destroyed by the Boers, in Natal for the sake of plunder – and in the Transvaal and Orange River Colony on account of the owners having joined us[13] – For all these compensation should certainly be paid, but with regard to the others A & B careful enquiry should be made.

I don't think Cape rebels should be included in a general amnesty – nor should men with De Wet, Kruger, Steyn and a few other men who have taken a prominent part in the war. On this point I am under the impression Sir Alfred Milner has a strong opinion. I do not allude so much to men who have been fighting against us, but to those who formed the Governments of the Transvaal and Orange River Colony, and are mainly responsible for the war.

With regard to the future Government of South Africa I think the Boers may be safely informed that they will not be ruled by Capitalists.

24.2.01

added to above.

All Boers' guns and rifles should be accounted for and until the country is thoroughly settled and the people have shown that they intend to behave loyally, I would not allow anyone to possess a rifle except by license.

25.2.01

NAM 7101–23–122–1–18

62
Lord Roberts to Lord Kitchener

17 Dover Street. London. W.

[Manuscript copy]

9th March 1901.

Private

I am very hopeful that, before you receive this letter, peace will have been made, for I doubt if Botha would have agreed to meet you, had he not felt that further resistance was useless.[14] I long to be able to send you a congratulatory telegram and to arrange for the return home of a portion of the Army now in South Africa. The Volunteers, Militia and Guards should be first despatched, and the rest in such order as you may think desirable. This will take some weeks, if not months, to carry out but it will still give you time for a holiday before you have to start for India.

The arrangement arrived at about the Indian command will I hope, be agreeable to you. Palmer is to remain for one year more. He took over from Lockhart in March 1900, and, as you could not relieve him before the coming hot weather, it was decided to allow him to complete his two years in the command. When you come home you can either take leave or we will find some berth for you at the War Office where your presence would be of the greatest use to me.

The papers will keep you informed of the Debates in the House of Lords on the Duke of Bedford's motion about the Order in Council of 1895,[15] which defines the relative positions of the Com'-in-Chief and the other officers at Army Headquarters. The Duke stated the case fairly enough, but Wolseley did himself harm by overstating his part of the story. The Debates will do no harm, probably good, but, as Brodrick said in the House of Commons last evening, the Government had decided to reconsider the Order in Council, and were only waiting for the Estimates to be made public and for me to have time to look about me, to decide what changes would be reasonable. When I was first offered the Com'-in-Chiefship, I telegraphed to Lord Lansdowne that it was not practicable for the work of the Army to be properly carried out under the existing system, and I wrote to Brodrick in the same sense on my way home. It was about the first subject about which the Queen spoke to me when I landed at Cowes, and the King has alluded to it more than once during the last two months. The one thing I have insisted on is that the A.G. must be under the direct control of the Com'-in-Chief, & this will be done. Indeed I am satisfied that the provisions of the Order in Council will be changed as I think necessary.

This information is for yourself alone, please, and Lord Salisbury is anxious that the arrangement about your succeeding Palmer a year hence should not be made public just at present.

I am in communication with Brodrick about Clements & Yatman.[16] I agree with the opinion expressed in your Private Confidential telegram of the 7th instant & hope that the Court Martial will not take place, but Brodrick considers himself bound in the promise he unfortunately made to the House of Commons on the 25th February; to the effect that officers who surrendered posts or are responsible for their being surrendered would be tried by Court Martial.

I have pointed out to Brodrick the danger to the Army of allowing the House of Commons to deal with questions regarding the conduct of officers.

NAM 7101–23–122–1–22

63
Lord Roberts to Lord Kitchener

17 Dover Street. London W

[Manuscript copy]

16th March 1901

Private

The weeks go by in the most marvellous manner, it seems like yesterday since I wrote to you, and now it is time for another letter. Yours of the 16th Feb. reached me in due course. You were then at De Aar and De Wet was still in Cape Colony. I wish he would have been caught while there but he is a very slippery fellow and though he managed to elude all our Columns, he must be pretty well discredited by his abortive attempt to raise the Cape Colony. I see he is now making for the North East of the Orange River Colony through Senekal which looks as if he had not heard of French's successes and expected to join hands with Botha in that direction. I was against Clements being tried but Brodrick thought he was committed to a Court Martial after the sort of promise he made in the House of Commons.

After the receipt of your telegram I again pointed out to B. that I doubted the expediency of bringing Clements to trial.[17] Since then both Brodricks time and mine has been pretty well taken up with Debates in the two Houses, but I will endeavour to get him to give a decided opinion tomorrow.

The Colville [sic] affair has damaged no one but Colville. I trust it has ended but his ill-advised friends seem inclined to ask more questions.

Wolseley has done himself no good by his motion in the Lords. It is clear from his own showing that he allowed Ladysmith to be held against his own judgement and that he did nothing to have it protected. The whole truth is that neither he nor any one at the War Office had the slightest idea of the fighting power of the Boers. They all thought that it would be a simple affair if we went to war, and they decided to operate through Natal.[18] A most curious proceeding seeing the Orange Free State cut in on our line of communication on the left, and the Transvaalers on it on the right.

NAM 7101–23–122–1

64
Note [by Lord Roberts] on Mr. Brodrick's proposal to try certain officers by Court Martial[19]

War Office 23rd March 1901.

[Manuscript copy]

Secretary of State

I have again carefully considered the several serious cases alluded to in your note of the 20th instant and which you seem to think are not unlikely to be brought before Parliament in connection with the war in South Africa

By far the most important of these is the case to which you give precedence, viz:– that of Nicholson's Nek[20]

As regards Captain Duncan,[21] I am more convinced than ever that he has been made a scapegoat and that, from the point of view of justice as well as expediency, he should be reinstated in the service.

At the same time I quite understand your hesitating to take my opinion without its being supported by some independent authority, seeing that it is opposed to the views expressed by the late Commander-in-Chief and accepted by the late Secretary of State for War.

To get over this difficulty I would propose to place the case before a specially constituted Court of Enquiry with orders to record their opinion.

The three other officers mentioned by you in regard to Nicholsons Nek, viz:– Lt Colonel Carleton,[22] Major Adye and Captain Fyffe[23] are in a different category. They were arraigned before a Court of Enquiry by whom they were acquitted[24] and for several months past they have been carrying on their military duties.

I feel very strongly that they ought not to be subjected to a fresh trial, and the conclusion I have come to is that if they were tried it would not be possible to avoid trying Sir George White.

The first error, and the principle one, was sending a comparatively small force by night into the immediate neighbourhood of the Enemy's main position. For this Sir George White was solely responsible. Then Lt Colonel Carleton has been blamed for not having retired when the mules stampeded with the mountain guns and the spare ammunition. I have no knowledge as to whether Lt Colonel Carleton could, or could not, have retired but I know it is not as easy, indeed it is a very difficult matter to change the direction of a body of troops moving over an unknown Country during the darkness of night – a difficulty which would be very considerably increased owing to the panic caused by the mules stampeding. It must be remembered too that Lt Colonel Carletons force was taking part in a combined movement, which he very probably thought might be jeopardized if he retraced his steps.

I am informed that Sir George White and his staff were aware before daylight the following morning that something serious happened to Colonel Carleton's Column and it was then open to Sir George to send it assistance, or to modify the plan of operations in which it was taking part.

I mention this not with any wish to criticize Sir George White's action (for it is easy to be wise after the event) but to explain that it would be impossible to try Colonel Carleton and the other officers; and not to try Sir George White

The Nooitgedacht affair comes next in importance.[25] On this occasion Major-General Clements committed errors of judgement for which he has been heavily punished by being deprived of his Command in the field and will be still further punished by his being deprived of any rewards he might otherwise have received for his previous service during the campaign – which were of considerable merit.

The Commander in Chief in South Africa who pointed out the faults committed by General Clements deprecates his being tried by Court Martial and in this view I concur. If on such questions as we are now considering the opinion of Commander-in-Chief on the spot, supported by that of the Commander-in-Chief of the Army, both of whom are intimately acquainted with the officer concerned, with the nature of the country in which operations were carried on is not to be accepted, I must say I view the future of the Army with grave apprehension. The difficulty in war is to find officers who will accept responsibility – a difficulty which will be immeasurably increased if they think they will be tried by Court Martial should they happen to be unsuccessful owing to the chances of war, or to dispositions which may be shown (after the event) to have been imperfect

Officers who fail on Service are heavily punished. Their military career is practically ended and they are marked men for the rest of their lives if they have behaved in a disgraceful manner by surrendering a post unnecessarily, or by showing want of courage, I would have no mercy on them, but for mere errors of judgement, I will not condemn them before the whole world.

It would I am satisfied do an infinite amount of harm and no good.

The Lindley affair[26] is much on a par with the Nicholsons Nek case. I consider that Captain Robin[27] has been unjustly treated, and as my views differ from those of the late Commander in Chief I would suggest that his case should also be brought before a specially constituted court of enquiry.

On Colonel Dickson's, Lt Colonel Frewen's[28] and Captain Skipwiths[29] case I have written short Notes which will be found with their respective files.

NAM 7101–23–122–1–34

65
Lord Roberts to King Edward VII

Dingley, Market-Harborough.

[Holograph]

8th April 1901.

I have had the honour and pleasure to receive Your Majesty's gracious letter of the 6th instant, and am glad to learn from it that Colonel Paget does not intend to leave the Army. I asked him to call upon me at the War Office on Wednesday next, but I am glad that Your Majesty advised him to go to Cannes in the first instance and see his mother.

It is true, Sir, that the 10th Hussars have been almost incessantly engaged with the enemy since they arrived in South Africa,[30] but nearly every corps has been similarly situated. Indeed, I doubt if in any former war the marching, fighting, exposure, and hard work have been so absolutely continuous as in this one. There has been no rest whatever. Fortunately the climate is superb, or the number of our casualties would have been very much increased.

I think Your Majesty will find that Colonel Fisher's[31] name is in the list of recommendations for the C.B. – I entered it myself as I considered that he well deserved the reward. I believe Colonel Fisher was a little injudicious in the early part of the campaign in his criticisms on the management of the Cavalry, and some kind friend repeated his remarks to General French. This I have been given to understand was the cause of Colonel Fisher not getting an extension of his command; the matter was settled at the War Office without any reference to me – an unusual proceeding I think.

I shall be greatly gratified if some special reward could be given to the Colonials. Sir Alfred Milner and I both strongly urged that a new Colonial Order should be created, as it seemed to us scarcely possible to meet the claims of the (civilians as well as soldiers), who have done good service during the war, with the Orders of the Bath and St. Michael and St. George alone; but for some reason or other our recommendation was not accepted.

RA W60/124[32]

66
Lord Roberts to Lord Kitchener

17. Dover Street – London.

[Manuscript copy]

12th April 1901.

Many thanks for your letter of 15th March – Yours to Brodrick of the same date, with Enclosures showing the formation &c of the several Columns recently formed, I have seen also – I really do not know what more you could tell the Secretary of State, he seems to be kept very well informed of all that is going on – I have telegraphed to you to send Clarke[33] home on account of his bad health, and to tell you that Hobbs shall be relieved by Butcher,[34] as soon as the latter can be spared. This will enable you to have Barrett as your Chief Ordnance Officer[35] – The Photograph of you and Botha with your respective staffs is most interesting, and I am much obliged to you for sending me a copy of it.

Writing on 15th March to Ian Hamilton, Rawlinson said you were anxious about the commissions which had been long promised. There was some unaccountable delay, but I find that on the following day, the 16th, a telegram was despatched to you on the ...... It is very wonderful that work ever gets on, for I have never come across so badly managed an office – I hope that it will be possible to effect some improvement in this respect – The question as to what extent the Order in Council of 1895 is to be changed is still unsettled, except that the A.G. is no longer to be independent of the Commander-in-Chief – That officials pay will be reduced and will be directly under the Chiefs control – I am pressing to get the LMG's department resuscitated, and for the L.M.G. to be given his proper duties at Head Quarters – If I succeed, it will be necessary to have a new arrangement under a kind of Director of Supplies to deal with subjects which do not properly belong to the L.M.G. but are now under him –

Nicholson takes over from Ardagh on the 1st May and under my plan he will become L.M.G. The Military Intelligence Officer and Nicholson's own room will I hope be in the War Office – Where Ardagh is seldom or ever seen. Hamilton becomes Military

Secretary on the 6th May, and I expect it will not be long before these changes are made – What a pity Gorringe had the wounded Boer shot without a trial – It is just the sort of thing to cause trouble in the House of Commons – We are waiting to hear the result of the Court of Enquiry before telling you what to do with him –[36]

As I telegraphed to you the batch of rewards will be published next week –

It has been a troublesome business, and will I fear give disappointment to many – I had put Hamilton down for an unattached Lieutenant Colonelcy before receiving your request – You can recommend him for a Colonelcy at the close of the war if you wish.

I hope you have managed to get rid of Wools Sampson – I gather from what Rawlinson writes that you wished for more help from me in the matter than I gave – This I did not understand, and trust you have not been troubled in consequence.

People are ever asking when I think the war will be over – It is not easy to say, that I feel pretty sure that Botha would never have proposed a meeting with you had he not felt that it was useless to continue this struggle – Plumers occupation of Pietersburg will have a good effect[37] – Where do the Boers get their ammunitions from? I am glad that Milner is taking leave;[38] the rest will do him good, and it is better for you to have civil as well as military control while the war continues –

When you can spare him, please send home Major G.D. Baker R.A.[39] who is required for some app<oinmen>t at home. There is no great urgency about it –

I am glad to hear you have been able to make a start at opening the Johannesburg Mines, a Capital saver [?] –

Your telegram S.325 has just arrived and given me great pleasure to hear that the prisoner taken by Gorringe was legally tried before he was shot –

I hope you will think that the rewards have been fairly & wisely distributed & please let me know whether in your opinion deserving officers have been left out or insufficiently recognized –

The rewards will to a certain extent rest with you, but I should be glad to do all I can to remedy matters in the mean while.

P.S. The manager of the Times has brought to our notice that letters posted in Bloemfontein and addressed to London have been "opened under Martial Law" & in one case a sentence was erazed & a marginal note added by a certain H.P.Y.[40] – I gave strict orders that no letters were to be opened, unless there was good proof that they were from Boers, and there is reason to believe that H.P.Y. knew perfectly well by whom the letter to which I allude was written – I would suggest your getting rid of H.P.Young, he is not the sort of man to be employed by us as a censor or in any other capacity.

NAM 7101–23–122–1–43

67
Lord Roberts to Lord Kitchener

17 Dover Street 19th April 1901

[Manuscript copy]

<u>Private</u>

Brodrick's telegram about the G.C.M.G. will have informed you that the first part of the Gazette with honours and rewards is published, many no doubt will be pleased, and many, I daresay will be disappointed – It is not easy to deal with such a mass of recommendations as have being received during the last 15 months, but I hope that, on the whole, the honours have been fairly distributed – You will let me know where you think this is not the case, and you will be able to remedy any shortcomings when you send in your own recommendations – The rewards now Gazetted are only for services performed up to the time of our leaving South Africa, and it will be for you to consider what should be done for those who have brought themselves to notice since then. Lyttleton [sic] has been made a Lieut General, he was down for it and the list has been submitted to the King before I telegraphed to you, and as he will in all probability succeed you, I let it stand – I telegraphed to you because it seemed to me that Lyttleton had not been altogether a success since he was moved to the Orange River locality.

Your being given the "G" instead of the "K" before the C.M.G. is only a forerunner of further rewards –

Rawlinson gets the C.B. I see you have given him a Column, he is sure to command it well, and he can be given his Colonelcy at the close of the Campaign. That is the rank he wants; there is a feeling against him at the War Office, but I am sure he is an officer well worth pushing on – I am advising him not to go to India, where I think it is likely you may wish to take him first, because I would like to have him at the War Office to help me to resuscitate the Quarter Master Generals Department, and secondly because his wife is very delicate and I doubt her standing the Indian climate –

There will be an outcry at Buller's being given so small a reward, but I had great difficulty in getting him even that, and I confess after visiting the scenes of his operations before the relief of Ladysmith, I don't think he deserves much consideration. The difficulty about Buller prevented White being given a higher honour, but, in my opinion, he and Buller are in quite a different category –

The officials have condemned White, but any trouble he got into was their doing not his – He had to deal with things as he found them and though he made mistakes, he showed considerable pluck and resolution and it was in the latter quality Buller so signally failed.

I have only seen an epitome of Milner's report[41] as yet, but I gather from it that he takes exception to our having pushed on to Johannesburg and Pretoria before pacifying the Orange River Colony. He does not apparently appreciate that the Transvaal was the Boers stronghold, that so long as Johannesburg and Pretoria were in their hands and they were in direct communication with Lo<u>renço Marques they could get all the gold they required, as much ammunition and as many guns and rifles as they needed, and if they had been able to show that they could hold the Transvaal against us, numbers of foreigners would certainly have joined them, and, it is within the bounds of possibility, that they or one or other of the foreign nations, might have interfered on their behalf – I have no doubt in my own mind that we did the right thing – I never expected that the Orange River Colony would settle down, or that there would not be disturbances in Cape Colony as we advanced further north – It would have required an army at least twice the size of ours to have prevented such things occurring –

Brodrick will no doubt write to you today about the Cabinet meeting yesterday at which the Peace proposals were discussed – I agree with Chamberlain that the disloyal Cape colonists could not be allowed to go unpunished, – but it would perhaps suffice to prohibit their returning to their own houses for a period of years instead of putting them in prison – I got Brodrick to slightly alter the telegram that was sent to you last evening in this sense.

NAM 7101–23–122–1–44

68
Lord Roberts to King Edward VII

17 Dover Street, London. W.

[Manuscript copy]

25th April 1901.

I beg to acknowledge with respectful thanks the receipt of Your Majesty's gracious letter of the 23rd instant, regarding the rewards given to Lieut. General Kelly-Kenny and Colonel Metcalfe.

It was thought in each case that a Brevet would be more valuable than a decoration. General Kelly Kenny will be 62 next February, and if he were not promoted or given an appointment carrying with it the rank of Lieut. General he would then be retired.

Colonel Metcalfe in ordinary course would not have got his Colonelcy until December 1902, and, as he has given promise of being a good commanding officer, it seemed that promotion would be a more suitable reward than the C.B. and would prevent his being superseded by a large number of officers.

Very few officers were recommended to your Majesty for a double honour, only those who had had the responsibility of important commands; or who had borne the brunt of the fighting, as did most of the officers commanding Mounted Infantry Regiments; or who would have been entitled to a slip in rank regimentally within a short time of the Gazette being published. Colonel Metcalfe did not come within any of these conditions. He commanded his regiment gallantly and with credit, but not more so I think than several other officers in the same position.

General Kelly Kenny's case is somewhat different and I regret that his name was not included in the list of K.C.B.'s for Your Majesty's approval. He did good service by the judicious way in which he commanded in the Orange River Colony after we crossed the Vaal, and by the steady front he showed at a time when the line of communication behind the main Army was cut, and affairs looked somewhat serious. I will mention to the Secretary of State what Your Majesty's wishes are about the K.C.B. being given to General Kelly Kenny and I hope that his name will be submitted for that honour in the next list of names for rewards.

NAM 7101–23–122–1–46

69
Lord Roberts to Lord Kitchener
17 Dover St. London. W.
4th May. 1901.

Your letter of the 12th April[42] reached me yesterday giving me on the whole very satisfactory accounts of affairs in S. Africa, & since its despatch things seem to have been going on well. The Boers having found it necessary to destroy their last "Long Tom" shows that they have no ammunition for it,[43] & not much heart for fighting left.

As Milner is to leave Cape Town, I see, on the 8th instant, you must have your hands pretty full – It is as well, I think, that he should come home for a rest & change before peace is made, for he has a difficult task before him. The settlement of the country will be no easy matter. The food supply alone will be very troublesome; I am glad that it has not fallen to my lot to settle S. Africa.

I will put S. Africa out of bounds to officers on leave, as you suggest, meanwhile you should order all those who trouble you to leave it.

I believe Blood was thought of as Military Member of Council, but it was considered that he would be the man for a command in the field in the event of trouble in the Afghanistan direction. Elles,[44] who has been appointed to succeed Collen,[45] is a clever fellow, & will, I think, do well – better certainly than in an important command. He showed a want of initiative to go, when troubles broke out in Afridiland, & I have always put down the subsequent Tirah expedition to his hesitating action on that occasion. I am very anxious to hear your opinion of Blood, Elliot & Beatson and hope they will prove themselves worthy of their Indian training.

I gather from the Babington-Shekleton papers you sent me the former is not the sort of man to gain the confidence of his troops. The fact is he has not confidence in himself, & this was the cause of his coming to grief in the early part of the campaign.[46] At the same time, Shekleton's letter to Babington is a very improper one, & he showed a want of appreciation of the present state of the Boer, in halting his whole force to look after the convoy, when 300 or 400 men would have sufficed.

It is curious that Baden Powell should not be acting with more vigour. He certainly showed himself to have resource while defending Mafeking, but he disappointed me afterwards, & I gather that those who were with him at Mafeking, do not look upon him as a great commander. So much stir was made in the country about the defence of Mafeking that some people thought that B.P. should have been knighted, but promotion to Maj-General's rank and the C.B. seem to me quite sufficient reward.

Archibald Hunter has been given the Scotch command – It will be a disappointment to Forestier Walker, who was practically promised it by my predecessor, but nice gentlemanly fellow as the latter is he has not the necessary qualifications for a command & would not have been able to work up the Militia and Volunteers in Scotland as I hope Hunter will.

Brodricks army scheme is to be brought before Parliament in a few days. Winston Churchill somewhat officiously proposed an amendment to the effect that the Army Reform question might be advantageously postponed. Campbell Bannerman has now taken the matter up & intends his motion as a vote of censure upon the Government. No harm will be done, I think. I tell Brodrick it will be necessary to increase the soldiers' pay not by much at first perhaps but after say three years' service for all men who have made themselves efficient & whom it is desirable to retain in the service.

I have telegraphed to you to send Herbert[47] home – He ought not ever have been given the 17th Lancers. Haig has been selected to succeed him, & though you would I daresay like to help him with a column, it is desirable he should take over the command of the 17th for if Ricardo[48] is left in the command on service it will be asked why he was not given it permanently. I would have appointed Lawrence as you suggested, but Haig seems to be the most capable & distinguished of all the young cavalry soldiers – & then Lawrence left S.A. during the war.

We must push Plumer on. He is evidently a good man.

Hart's farewell order is a wonderful production.

NAM 7101–23–122–1–52

70
Lord Roberts to Lord Curzon
War Office, London, S.W.

[Manuscript copy]

27th May 1901.

I have been intending to write to you for some months past, for I have more than one kind communication to thank you for, but, though long delayed, this letter will, I think, be more welcome than any I could have written on an earlier date, as I am now able to tell you of my having had the great pleasure of seeing Lady Curzon.[49] She is looking remarkably well, and it delights me to find how much she knows of, and how deeply interested she is in India.

I am very pleased too to hear that your health keeps good, notwithstanding the marvellous amount of work you manage to get through. I always think that the Viceroy of India is the hardest worker of all Government Officials. He never gets a days rest, and it is very satisfactory to learn that you are so well able to stand the heavy strains.

The India Office have been a long time replying to your proposal about "The Grant of Commissions in His Majesty's Service to Indians of noble birth," but their despatch is likely to reach you soon for I have just seen the draft, which I hope you will consider satisfactory. I shall watch your scheme with considerable interest and trust that it will meet with the success you anticipate.

The question is an extremely difficult one, and I might not perhaps have been quite so strongly opposed to the admission of Native Gentlemen with the Commissioned ranks of our Army (British or Indian) had I not seen how seldom any of them turn out well when they have been much associated with Europeans, and I can hardly bring myself to believe that they would prove an acquisition to our Army from the soldierly point of view. Even in the days of the Mahrattas and Sikhs, when war was the profession of almost every Indian of note, the best of them were only too glad to lean upon the commonest European adventurer whom they happened to come across. And the long years of peace that have intervened since then cannot have tended to foster any soldierlike qualities they may have possessed. At the same time I can see nothing to object to in your proposal, but I have expressed a hope that it will be possible to find extra regimental employment for all the young nobles you may select.

I must thank you for the great assistance afforded by India in carrying on the war in South Africa. I regret that I did not make this publicly known in my last despatch, but I have still one more to submit and in that I hope to make it clear how much we are indebted to India. The rapidity and completeness with which the Contingent was despatched to Natal enabled Sir George White to prevent the Province being overrun by the Boers, and I do not know what we should have done without the excellent remounts and establishment of Native Farriers which reached Capetown a couple of months later.

I was most unwilling to ask you to let us have more officers after all you had done for us, but there were so many casualties in the senior ranks, from one cause or another, about the time I was making the command over to Kitchener, that I could not resist begging that Bindon Blood, Elliott and Beatson might be sent to South Africa. Kitchener is very pleased with them, and I hope that the experience they are gaining will be of use to them in their future careers.

Smith-Dorrien will, I think, do well as Adjutant General. He has proved himself to be a good commander in the field, and it will be an advantage having him available in India should there be any serious trouble in the Afghanistan direction during the next few years.

I am glad that Smith-Dorrien is coming to England on his way to take up his appointment, as I am anxious to impress upon him the necessity for encouraging musketry throughout the Army in India. Government is very liberal in allowing ammunition for musketry practice to be purchased at reduced prices, and until the last year or two, most regiments were so keen to shoot well, that they bought all they could get and often asked for more! Now, I understand, that in many instances the ordinary regulation allowance of ammunition more than suffices. The fact is that the older generation of Cavalry Officers cannot be made to understand that, under the present conditions of war, it is as essential for mounted, as for Infantry, men to be skilful in the use of their rifles, and it is unfortunate that both the Commander-in-Chief in India and the General Officer Commanding the Bengal Army Corps (in whose Province the great Rifle Meetings have always been held) rose in the Cavalry. So long as Palmer & Luck[50] are at the head of affairs, I fear there will be no improvement, a great misfortune for the Army in India.

I need not say how rejoiced I was at you separating the trans Indus districts from the Panjab Lieutenant-Governorship. It has taken 24 years to bring about that very desirable measure. It was lucky, perhaps, for me that it was not carried when proposed by Lord Lytton,[51] I was greatly disappointed at the time, but how little one knows what the future may bring forth.

With kind regards, and every good wish that your reign in India may end as successfully as it has begun.

NAM 7101–23–122–1–64

71
Lord Roberts to the Earl of Minto
War Office 28th May 1901.

[Manuscript copy]
Private.

I really do not know what you must think of me for not having long ere this thanked you for the many kind letters and telegrams you have sent me during the past 12 or 14 months. Over and over again, I have been wishing to write to you, and for many weeks I have had a .... to your dying before me! It has been very difficult for me to do anything in the writing line. I never attempted it in South Africa beyond the weekly letter to the Secretary of State and an occasional one to the Queen; and since I came home, there has been an incessant racket. The Whitsuntide holiday has taken me out of London for two or three days, and the quiet of Dingley, where we are staying with the Downes, enables me to have the pleasure of writing you a few lines.

I need hardly say how much I appreciated all your friendly congratulations, and how glad I should have been to have had you with me, as in the Afghanistan days. I was fortunate in having a good many old friends to help me – Neville Chamberlain, Pretyman, and Cowan you would remember; others like Ian Hamilton and Nicholson are of a later date, and I am not sure whether you ever met them –

It is just a year ago since we crossed the Vaal. I little thought then that the war would drag on so long, and even now the end does not appear in sight. Kitchener, however, writes hopefully. The Boers have scarcely a gun left, & where they get their ammunition from is a mystery to me – I hoped, when we reached Komati Poort, and got control of the Lo<u>renzo Marques Railway, their munitions of war would soon come to an end, but they seem to have had an endless supply, cunningly distributed in various out-of-the-way places, and they have managed to hold out longer than any one expected –

The Canadian troops did extremely well, and I was pleased with the Artillery, about the efficiency of which, you were, I think a little doubtful – the Batteries had some long marches over difficult country, but they were always well to the front, and we were very sorry when their time as well as that of the rest of the contingent came to an end –

I greatly regret there was a mistake about Lt Colonel Lessard being given the C.M.G. instead of the C.B. It was remedied as soon as your telegram reached me; and I trust he understands that it was quite un-intentional

I have noted what you write about Lt Colonel Cartwright, and will see if his name cannot be included in the next list of honours.

I am very sorry that Dr. Borden is disappointed at his sons name not being mentioned in my final despatch,[52] and also at his not being given the V.C. – the instance of his swimming the Vet river, you mention, was never brought to my notice. I was most anxious to recognise good work done by the Colonials, for I strongly appreciated their coming forward at a time of Englands difficulty, and I should have been delighted to have recommended young Borden for the V.C.   he was, I know, a most gallant fellow, and I wrote a few lines to the father at the time the son was killed, telling him how much we mourned his early death – Borden was, I think, mentioned in one of the earlier despatches, and perhaps you would kindly explain to his father, that it is not customary, indeed it would be scarcely possible, to name, in the final report all who have done well, and have lost their lives during the war –

Lord William Seymour's case has come before me recently – It is an unfortunate affair, but as is very likely, it may occur again if an officer of his rank is placed in charge of the Imperial troops (a very limited number) while a much junior officer commands the local forces, it would seem better to make the rank and position of the Imperial Commander more commensurate with the extent of his command. A colonel on the Staff with one staff officer would probably suffice – He could not be always hankering to command and inspect the Dominion Troops as well as ours, and it would be no reflection on him or on his position for the Government not to devolve on him in the absence of the Governor General – Please let me know if you approve of this arrangement.

29th May. I have just received your letter of the 16th instant about the Hon. Sydney Fisher   I will make a point of seeing him and discussing the remount question. I am entirely in favour of thoroughbred stallions and avoiding Hackneys. It took me a long time in India to convince the Government of the mistake they were making in breeding from Hackneys

NAM 7101–23–122–1–65

72
Lord Roberts to Mr St John Brodrick
47 Portland Place. W. June 2nd 1901.

[Holograph]

Nicholson showed me yesterday the paper he had drawn up at the request of Mr Chamberlain explaining how in his opinion certain areas of the theatre of war could be occupied if the army in South Africa were reduced to a strength of 150,000 men. Nicholsons proposed disposition seems to me allright so far as I can judge but I trust that if the reduction is to be made, it will be left to Kitchener to dispose of the troops as he may think best. At the same time I would venture to point out that any withdrawal of troops now, would, in my opinion, result in a considerable addition to the numbers of the Boers against us, and inevitably make the war last longer. Any such measure could not fail to give encouragement to the Boers; waverers would turn against us; and, even those loyally inclined, would lose heart.

My advice is to tell Kitchener that he must in the first place clear Cape Colony of the several bands,[53] now giving trouble in that front of South Africa, and make the line of the Orange River strong enough to prevent any further invasion possible. He should then turn his attention to one particular commando, deal with that and when he had succeeded in breaking it up, take another commando in hand.

Nicholson explains the desirability of this in the latter part of his paper, and I trust this view will be accepted, for I cannot conceive anything more fatal to our future in South Africa than to let the Boers think we consider the struggle hopeless – They are gradually dwindling in numbers and in their power to oppose us – It is a slow and expensive operation I grant; but any attempt to change our tactics now, would, I feel confidently be slower and more expensive –

NAM 7101–23–122–1–77

73
Lord Roberts to Lord Kitchener

29th June 1901

[Manuscript copy]

47 Portland Place.

I had a long meeting yesterday with Arthur Balfour, Chamberlain and Brodrick in continuation of the meeting I told you of in my letter of the 15th instant,[54] about the possibility of changing our tactics when the winter is over in South Africa, if by that time the war should not have been brought to a conclusion.

In the course of the day I will despatch a long telegram to you, explaining, as well as I can, what the Cabinet wish to be done.[55] They are influenced by a feeling that the ...... will resent the present heavy expenditure when it is brought home to them in the shape of fresh taxation, and when they realize that the Boers fighting against us do not now number more than 16.000 or 18.000 –

The idea of the Cabinet is, now that you have so completely devastated the country, that during September a beginning should be made to reduce our troops very considerably, and confine ourselves to holding the several lines of railway, and the principal towns – and in addition to organize a sufficient number of small but sufficient mounted columns under carefully selected officers, and in positions from which they would be able to act against any body the enemy might bring together.

The first thing that seems to me essential is to clear the Boers out of Cape Colony, as this I hope French will succeed in doing. Their presence in the Colony must cause considerable unrest, give them hope of being able to raise the people against us, put heart into the waverers, and discourage those who may be loyally disposed.

Besides, I imagine that the Boers can get food fairly easily, and possibly ammunition in the Colony. Anyhow, no reduction of our force would seem possible until the whole of the country South of the Orange River is in our hands, and I am sure you will agree with me that all our efforts should now be directed towards that end.

You can of course Judge best on the spot what troops can be spared for this purpose but, as after the end of August, the Government will insist on our practically vacating all the district<s> not immediately on the line of rail, it seems to me that perhaps Rundle's and Elliots columns might be moved South of the Orange River. Harrismith must be held, but between that place and Kroonstad we can have no troops, nor between Harrismith and Standerton to the north and Ladybrand to the South.

The South African Constabulary, which you mention in your letter of the 31st May[56] as gradually getting into order, will, I hope, be able to pacify the country between Jacobsdaal [sic] & Ladybrand. South of the line we shall not be able to hold much at first perhaps, but we must have strong posts all along the Orange River to prevent another invasion of the Cape Colony. That I look upon as the most important part of the programme.

In reply to the telegram I hope to send you today, and to this letter, and any subsequent communications on the same subject, telegraph to me direct, and as fully as you think necessary. Let me know what troops and commanders you will send home first and whether there is any one now in this country you would wish ordered out.

I have warned Neville Lyttelton to be ready, as his health has been quite restored. Settle can go back, and so can Arthur Paget. He would do well in some place where he would be more or less independent.

I will endeavour to arrange with the Indian Government to relieve the troops they sent to South Africa at the beginning of the war. This would give you five new regiments of Cavalry, 10 or 12 battalions of Infantry, and three Field Batteries.

The relief would be carried out in October, or earlier if necessary, but it is inadvisable to move troops in India until after the hot season on account of their liability to being attacked by Cholera.

I can understand its being a disappointment to you not being able to end the war in a steady & satisfactory manner, for I know what I felt, but we must have patience –

With kindest regards from us all

NAM 7101–23–122–1

74
Lord Roberts to Lord Kitchener

47. Portland Place, London. W.

[Manuscript copy]

6th July 1901.

I am afraid you will think I am rather bombarding you with long cipher telegrams the last few days, but, as I daresay you will have derived, my 441 of the 2nd Inst. and my [blank space] of yesterday[57] were intended to convey to you the views of the Cabinet on the present state of affairs in South Africa – As I think I mentioned in a former letter, they are getting alarmed at our spending a million and a quarter a week, and at the possible outcry when the British public realize that we require between two and three hundred thousand men to cope with the eighteen or twenty thousand men now left in the field against us without giving thought to the enormous area over which this comparatively small body are scattered

I agreed at the meeting of the Defence Committee of the Cabinet to send you the telegram of the 2nd instant, because I thought you would not object to a change of tactics if you were not able to bring the Boers to terms during the next two months, and that it would satisfy you to have a force large enough to hold the several lines of railway and the principle places in their

185

vicinity. I think you are quite right to keep possession of Heilbron & Winburg   Indeed, I think I promised the last time we occupied Heilbron that our troops would not be again withdrawn from it. Pietersburg too it seems advisable to hold, it covers Pretoria and prevents communication between the North-East and North-West portions of the Transvaal.

The idea of Corps d'elite is Chamberlain's   I told him you might not find it possible to carry it out but I was sure you would do your best. You have not mentioned Plumer recently but if he is still in good form he would probably make such a corps a success.

I cannot get any information as to the answer sent by Kruger to Botha's telegram.[58] The Government are willing to pay handsomely but up to the present no due has been obtained

The clasps question is a difficulty. I enquired what could be done when your letter of the 7th June reached me, and found that no alteration in the conditions would be made until the 15th of July, the date fixed for the preparation of medal rolls. A new order will soon be issued but some men I fear, will wear clasps that have been very cheaply earned.

I have told Forestier-Walker that his command in South Africa is at an end, as you do not wish Wynne to be disturbed.

Walker must return to the Cape to dispose of his property, but he will not resume his appointment there.

Brackenbury is sending out the Martini Henry rifles you require – It is a prudent measure, I think, to arm the Town Guards[59] with them instead of Lee Metfords.

Thanks for yours of the 4th June[60] received yesterday. I am afraid the government would never consent to prisoners of war being despatched for a French settlement. It would be a capital way to get rid of a number of troublesome men and women, but any such proposal would cause a great row.

I have been hoping you would be calling out for drafts to keep the Imperial Yeomanry up to strength. You will certainly need some if the war lasts, and men sent out hurriedly raised and without even a short training are not much use. I proposed to begin recruiting on the 1st July, in sufficient numbers to enable between 300 and 400 men to be despatched monthly from the 1st Sept. But the government decided to wait a bit. Brodrick, I think, gathered from your letter that you had enough mounted men, but considerable wastage must be going on, and on the strength of your telegram S.480[61] in which you say "The new yeomanry owing to want of riding and general inexperience will be very little use for the most of two months" I am again urging that recruiting be recommenced.

You mention in your letter to Brodrick that you could spare Hart, Barton, W. Knox and Mildmay Wilson. The change of tactics, if carried out, will enable you to dispense with their services and there is no use in keeping Generals for whom you cannot find suitable employment.

We are still struggling with the list of Honours and Rewards, it is a terribly long one, but I hope we shall get through it by the end of this month.

With our united kindest regards,

NAM 7101–23–122–1–81

75
Lord Roberts to Lord Kitchener

47 Portland Place, W.

[Manuscript copy]

13 July. 1901.

Since writing to you this morning I have come to the War Office and found your letter of 21 June,[62] I will reply to it more fully next mail, meanwhile I would like to assure you that, however much disappointed the Government may be at the war lasting so long, every member of it has full confidence in you, and knows that you are doing all that is possible to bring it to an end – I never cease pointing out the difficult nature and vast area of the country over which you are operating, and how impossible it is to inflict any severe punishment on an enemy who will never stand to fight –

I have (as I have already told you) urged that something should be done in the way of confiscation, and I will recommend that every Boer, who comes into your hands, should be sent out of S. Africa – Let me say from myself how satisfied I am with all you have done & how much I feel for your disappointment in not having been able to achieve greater success. I, at any rate, can appreciate the great difficulties with which you have to contend.

NAM 7101–23–122–1–85

76
Lord Roberts to Lord Kitchener

[Manuscript copy]

47 Portland Place. London. W.

20th July 1901.

This has been an interesting week, first of all the de-ciphering of the Botha & Kruger telegrams[63] and then the capture of Steyn's papers.[64] The telegram ...... was really well done, & the accuracy of the de-ciphering is proved by Reitz's[65] letter to Steyn. On receipt of your letter telling us about Botha having been permitted to telegraph to Kruger, I pressed Lord Lansdowne to get hold of the telegram & Kruger's reply, as I thought it very likely it could be de-ciphered. Nicholson managed to find someone in Ireland who had given much time and thought to such peculiar kind of work, & that man & the assistant librarian at the Intelligence Office managed to do what was wanted. The telegram was in French and dictionaries were used. The telegrams & Steyn's papers show clearly the straits the Boers are in, & that it is Steyn alone who prevents them coming to terms – What a splendid thing it would have been if Broadwood had caught Steyn at Reitz, but I daresay the capture of his brother,[66] young Fraser,[67] & the state papers will have a disheartening effect.

I have ?not seen Brodrick since the receipt of your telegram S.609 of yesterday,[68] so do not know whether the government will agree to your proposal to tell Botha, Steyn & Delarey that they will be severely dealt with if hostilities do not cease on a certain date. I may hear the decision before I close this, I trust it will be in accordance with your views, for I quite believe in what you say about "serious danger in Cape Colony". I impressed upon the Cabinet that nothing could be done in the way of reducing troops until the Cape Colony had been cleared of rebels. It is a difficult job, but our fellows must know the country better now than they did some months ago. Without assistance from the Cape Colony it seems impossible for the war to be continued, that is why I long for a telegram from you announcing that French has succeeded in driving the several rebel bands to the north of the Orange River. It is weary work, & I feel much for you but you must not be down-hearted. The Cabinet are well aware of the tremendous difficulties you have to contend with, that you have done all that is possible to bring the war to a close.

So Baden-Powell is coming home. Should he return, do you think to South Africa, or is there anyone you can name who would do better at the head of the Constabulary?[69] I gather from your reports that you are not altogether satisfied with B.P., & as you will remember, he greatly disappointed me when he was given an independent action. He certainly is not a General, but I thought he would prove to be a good organizer.

When you have leisure, I wish you would place the first twenty officers now with you in the order you think they should stand for commands & higher staff employment. Your opinion of them will be a great help to me.[70]

We have nearly finished the list of Honours & Rewards for regimental officers. It has been a big business, & I think that the result will be considered satisfactory. Chesham approves of the Yeomanry selections. He tells me he proposes to return in September, I hoped to have appointed him Inspector General of Imperial Yeomanry, & must try & keep the berth open for him. He knows what Yeomanry have to do on service, and they believe in him.

I troubled you with a telegram about sending out money instead of comforts. It seemed to me a ridiculous proposal, but Mrs. Wynne wrote to say that her husband was in favour of it.

I also troubled you about Brand with a telegram. I doubt his serving much longer, but he will be very useful getting the Shropshire Yeomanry into order. When you can spare him, I shall like Dawnay, also of the 10th Hussars, to be sent home for a Yeomanry appointment.

Goodbye for to-day; keep up your spirits. You have done splendidly.

NAM 7107–23–122–1–86

77
Lord Roberts to Mr Joseph Chamberlain

4th August 1901.

[Manuscript copy]

The State of Affairs at Johannesburg, as depicted by Sir Wlm. Marriott in his letter to you of the 11th July is certainly far from satisfactory. I trust, however, they are not quite so bad as he makes out.

I can quite understand officers with Columns being disappointed at not catching many Boers, after a long weary trek, but I would not condemn Kitchener's plan from complaints such as Sir Wm. Marriott describes.

The fact is the Boers are spread over such a vast extent of country, it is difficult to catch any of them, – and officers are not always reasonable, especially when they get stale, as most of those who have been long in South Africa have become –

You will see from the enclosed letter from Kitchener that he is preparing to carry out the plan sketched for him at the meeting of the Cabinet which I attended some weeks ago, and when this has got a fair start and Milner is on the spot to reassure civilians, I trust things will go on more smoothly than seems to be the case at present – I do not lay any great stress on the grumbles of the Colonials – When I was in South Africa they gave one considerable trouble – At the beginning of the war they fought and behaved well, but as soon as the Corps to which they belonged got near Johannesburg, they thought they ought to be given their discharge – It is evidently much the same now – I feel quite certain that the Colonials have misrepresented the conditions of their enlistment to Sir William Marriott – Kitchener knows the difficulty the Colonials placed me in last October and November by claiming their discharge at a time when their services were most urgently needed – I had then to send them back to the coast for their discharge, and it is unlikely that Kitchener would have offered them any terms which could result in similar troubles –

Then as regards permits, I can quite understand the necessity for great caution – Johannesburg is inhabited by a great mixture of people – Some of them very dangerous. I hear Boers can come and go much as they please – A very difficult thing to prevent in a long straggling town, and it is essentially necessary to keep them from wandering about the town at night. That Sir William Marriott was offered a free pass shows, I think, that the authorities have not been strict except with people whose loyalty is doubtful –

Considerable changes have, I think, been made in the administration of Johannesburg since I left, and what its form is now I do not know – Whatever that form may be there is no excuse for soldiers giving themselves airs, and I trust that Sir Wm. Marriott has somewhat exaggerated matters – I will, however, bring the subject to Kitcheners notice at once by telegraph – Also about Kaffirs being armed, and the action of the censor in stopping the publication of telegrams which cannot possibly do harm – It will probably I think be found that the armed Kaffirs are employed as Police, possibly over some of the mines –[71]

I leave London this afternoon for Aldershot and tomorrow after Lady Hilda Brodrick's funeral I go to Dingley Market Harborough – to which place perhaps you will kindly send me Kitchener's letters – I propose to return to London for the day as soon as I know that Brodrick will be at the War Office, and if you would wish to see me about Sir William Marriott's letter, I will with pleasure wait upon you at the Colonial Office.

NAM 7101–23–122–1–93

78
Lord Roberts to Lord Milner
4th August 1901

[Manuscript copy]

I send you an extract from a letter I wrote to Kitchener yesterday,[72] giving him the gist of our Conversation the other day – You will observe I have not said anything about his giving up the command so long as the war last<s>, for I do not think it would be desirable for him to do so, unless a great change for the better takes place when our troops are concentrated within the areas comprising the railway lines and the more important towns – So long as Columns have to take the field, it would, I am sure, be a mistake to make a change in the Chief Command, the officers (ii) and (iii) divisions should, I think, be allowed to communicate freely with the Governor of Cape Colony, but it is necessary to have our head of the Army who should be with you, and that head must, I think, be Kitchener until it is possible to dispense with the services of French, Methuen, and all officers senior in rank to Neville Lyttleton [sic] – I hope you will agree with this arrangement, although it is not I fear exactly what you would wish carried out. I leave London today and am not likely to return before you start for Cape Town.

I need not say I wish you every possible success in your most arduous undertaking –

No one can perhaps appreciate the difficulties before you, so well as myself, and no one can be more confident than I am that you will overcome them –

NAM 7101–23–122–1

79
Lord Roberts to Lord Kitchener

Aug 1901

[Typed manuscript]

I have had a long talk too with Milner on the future of South Africa. His idea is that at the stage we have now reached, civil considerations, and especially all that is connected with the return of the people, the resumption of industrial and agricultural pursuits, and the gradual establishment of orderly government in the settled districts are, if not paramount, of at least equal importance with the work of subduing the districts which are still infested by the enemy. He urges that, throughout the whole country, constant communication between the High Commissioner and the several Generals Commanding are essential to a satisfactory result. In order to give effect to this policy, he thinks the army should be separated into three distinct commands.

(i) the first to include the bulk of the Transvaal, the Orange River Colony (except some of the most western districts – and Natal. (ii) the second to comprise the western Districts of the Transvaal (Waterberg, Rustenburg, Marico, Lightenburg,[73] and Bloemhof); Rhodesia and the Protectorate;[74] the western portion of the Orange River Colony (Jacobsdal &c.); and the Cape Colony north of the Orange River. (iii) the third, all the Cape Colony south of the Orange River. The General in command of (iii) as well as the General in command of (ii), in so far as that the division falls within the borders of Cape Colony, should be in communication with the Governor of that Colony on matters directly affecting that Colony, and that both these Generals, as well as the one in command (i) should be in free and direct communication with him as the High Commissioner, and that he should have the right to call upon every General in South Africa to furnish him with any information he may require. I have explained to Milner that his plan might work well enough when peace has been proclaimed and martial law no longer exists, but, until then, that you, as the Commander-in-Chief, can be the only one in direct communication with the High Commissioner. I added, I was sure you would give the Officers Commanding (ii) and (iii) as free a hand as possible, and allow them to communicate direct with the Governor of Cape Colony. I have told Milner also that you are as anxious as he is to see Civil Government established, and that, as soon as the troops have been concentrated within the areas we can give protection to the inhabitants, you would be only too glad to let the civilians undertake the administration. Indeed, I gather from the papers that a beginning has already been made at Johannesburg and Bloemfontein. Lyttelton, as I have telegraphed to you, returns with Milner who would like him to be given a command at or near Pretoria, in order that he might see all that is going on, and be ready to take your place when the war is over. I have told Milner you would probably be able to manage this, but that Lyttelton could not be placed in command of the whole of (i) while officers senior to him are employed in South Africa.

Bodleian Library, MS. Milner dep. 16, ff. 96–7

80
Lord Roberts to Lieutenant-General J.D.P. French

War Office.

[Manuscript copy]

16th August: 1901.

I have told the A.G. to call upon you and all officers concerned for an opinion as to whether the front rank of Dragoon Guards and Dragoon regiments should be armed with the sword or lance. Please ascertain their wish as soon as you can and forward them through Lord Kitchener with an expression of your own opinion. It is quite clear, I think, that Cavalry men only require the one besides the rifle, should that be the lance or the sword, should there be some of one kind & some of the other. It has been said that we cannot take our South African experience as a guide for what would be required in a war with an European nation. No doubt there is some truth in this, in as much as the Boers have no cavalry but on the other hand they have shown us more than once that the way to keep Cavalry off is by dismounting and opening fire with the rifle. This they did effectually at Elandslaagte siding when you tried with Gordon's Brigade to turn their right flank. Shock actions may be possible in the future, but my belief is the side which demounts and opens fire with their magazine rifles will prevent the other from coming near them. However your experience is unrivalled, and I am more anxious to get your views on this subject, and on other important matters connected with Cavalry equipment. I was very pleased when I heard that you had been given the command in Cape Colony, and I am watching your movements with intense interest, for I can't help thinking that the war would end, if we could only drive the Boers out of that part of the country. Their being there raises the hopes of the disloyal Colonists, and I presume enables them to get a certain amount of food, clothes and ammunition.

When you reply to this, which please do without waiting for the official letter from the A.G. I wish you would put down the officers who have been commanding Columns and regiments under you in the order you estimate their qualities as soldiers. I want this for my own information.

194

You will have a warm welcome when you return to England, which I sincerely trust will be ere many months are over.

NAM 7101–23–122–2

81
Lord Roberts to Lord Kitchener

Wyteham Abbey. Yorkshire.

[Manuscript copy]

6th September. 1901.

Best thanks for yours of the 9th August. I sent it to Brodrick to read as you said you were not writing to him. Poor fellow. He is greatly cut up, and I am afraid he has been a good deal worried of late. The list of promotions and rewards have given a deal of bother. The former, I hope will be published on Tuesday next, the latter will be a few days later, as it has to go to the King for approval and, as His Majesty is abroad, any references he may make will take some time to answer.

I cannot tell you how much I feel for you having to report regrettable incidents for I know how much they troubled me. Some people at once jump at the conclusion that the war is going against us and things are being mismanaged, and the radical papers seem to delight in crowing over our misfortunes. But on the whole the public behave well and you must try and not mind what effect the reports of derailing trains &c will produce.

It was most unfortunate Vandeleur[75] being killed. He was a very promising officer and is a great loss.

I see in your list of Cavalry Commanders you place Broadwood first and Gilbert Hamilton[76] second. I want to find men for brigades at home after the war is over and feel inclined to select men like Haig, Rimington, Allenby, Scobell, Bethune, &c. rather than older men nearly all of whom have failed lamentably. Even Gordon, a comparatively young man, proved to be of little use. I watched him carefully when we were nearing Bloemfontein and again the day before Pretoria. He had no go, no better it seemed to me than the men we had cast in the hope that he would show what a Cavalry commander should be. I would gladly give Broadwood a command, but I am under the impression he could not afford to live at home. Have you thought of him for a Cavalry Brigade in South Africa when the force is reduced? He might perhaps be the Cavalry Commander? We have heard nothing about Gilbert Hamilton since he got a Brigade. Has he really done well?

I am very anxious to know exactly what you think about all the Senior Officers, so that only those that could be trusted in war, may be placed in high Commands. I want a first rate General for the Quetta District. The man, who was appointed to succeed Hunter, has held it for two years; he begged me to give him the command for the full time but I have refused. He[77] is a brother of Hart now with you and is a fair sort of fellow, but not the man I would place at Quetta, for if we have trouble in Afghanistan, the Quetta commander will have to move at once to Kandahar. What would you think of Plumer for such a place? or should we give him a Brigade at home first? Failing him, who would you recommend? The Amir is said to be very far from well. He has ceased dyeing his beard and has taken to praying – a sure sign of a villainous, cruel Mahommedan such as Abdul Rahman is, that he feels his end approaching, and wants to make his peace with Allah.

I send you a cutting from some illustrated paper which was forwarded to me by an anonymous correspondent. I confess I agree with his remarks, and think it somewhat incongruous for officers to be playing polo while the enemy are close up to their position. Polo is all very well at proper times but during war officers might be much more profitably employed. You are most welcome to let this be known as my opinion.

The people in this country are all hoping that important surrenders will take place before the 15th instant.[78] I tell them not to be too sanguine, and I am impressing upon the authorities not to expect any reduction in your force, until you have cleared the Boers out of Cape Colony. You may perhaps be able to send away some Artillery but I would not even do that if it is likely to give the slightest encouragement to the Boers and the disloyal Colonials. We have got to finish the war in a satisfactory manner and it is no use now groaning over the cost. The money must be found. Any attempt to curtail necessary expenses would probably increase expenditure in the end.

I am very glad and the King is greatly pleased that you have been able to give Tullibardine[79] a local Lieut Colonelcy.

If you accept the offer of Sir James Willcock's[80] services, you might send home Bar Campbell.[81]

I have decided to have Clarke's and Hobbs' actions in South Africa enquired into by a committee – Fleetwood Wilson speaks so badly of them that for their own sakes it is better the whole matter should be sifted.

Goodbye. Kindest regards from us all

With reference to your telegram S 555 of the 18th August[82] the 5000 Yeomanry you propose to keep should be over and above the 140,000 men allowed for South Africa. I would have telegraphed this, but it seemed to me very improbable you would come down to 140,000 for some time to come. Many thanks for sending Dawnay home.

NAM 7101–23–122–2–118

82
Minute [by Lord Roberts] on the necessity for having a loyal Government and a dependable body of police in Cape Colony

Dingley Market Harborough

[Manuscript]

19th September 1901.

S. of S.

You should read the enclosed. To put an end to the war it seems to me essential to establish Martial Law throughout Cape Colony and to take over the government of the country. The object of the Cape Ministry is, as it was when I was in South Africa, to exaggerate the effect of Martial Law and to put all possible difficulties in the way of its being carried out. I tried in vain to get Cape Town and the other parts placed under Martial Law, and the result of the refusal to take this absolutely necessary step is that the war lingers on, and will continue to do so until the government of Cape Colony is taken out of the hands of a thoroughly disloyal set of ministers.[83]

I do not see how anything else can be expected so long as there is any inlet for arms, ammunition and foreigners with Boer sympathies. Indeed, after the letter I found at Bloemfontein from the then Prime Minister, Schreiner, to the Orange Free State Government, apologising for having unwillingly allowed a battery of our Artillery to be sent up to Kimberley a few weeks before the war broke out,[84] it is difficult to understand how any faith can be placed in the loyalty of any set of Cape Colony ministers.

The cry to have the police and the loyal troops placed under their control is plainly [?] to ensure their being made ineffective for our purposes, and to prevent the country becoming settled. The police and loyal troops are useful to us to get information and to act as guides &c, so long as we have control over them, but alone they would be of no value and in the hands of the ministry would be an increased danger.

"Blood is thicker than water" and the police and local troops are in many instances near relations of the very men against whom we are fighting.

Lord Kitchener and the officers serving under him are doing all that is possible of soldiers to do to bring into order a country inhabited for the most part by people intensely hostile to us. But, as I have more than once pointed out, the work before us is now not one with which soldiers can effectively deal – it is work for police, but the police must be a thoroughly dependable body of men, acting under the orders of a strong and loyal not a disloyal, Government.

19.9.01

NAM 7101–23–122–2

83
Lord Roberts to Mr St John Brodrick

Dingley. Market-Harborough.

[Manuscript copy]

20th September. 1901.

I have just been reading Kitcheners telegram (no. 603. cipler) of the 18th Sept:,[85] in which he again strongly urges Cape Town being placed under Martial Law. I most sincerely trust this will be insisted on, even if the ministry resign – their resignation, indeed, might result in the Government of Cape Colony being taken over for a time by the Crown. This, I believe, would have the best possible effect. It would give heart to all who are loyal, many whom must be having their allegiance sorely tried, and it would do more than anything to convince the rebels that we are determined to take the most severe measures in order to prevent the war dragging on through another year.

As regards any reduction of the force now in South Africa we need not trouble ourselves. I consider that an impossibility, until peace has been established throughout Cape Colony, and a reliable Police Force has been raised. Kitchener may be able to send away a few batteries of Artillery, but nothing else and I trust that the Cabinet will realize and arrange accordingly. "The Times" of today takes the view, which I feel pretty sure is generally held throughout the country, and it is for us at the War Office to see that everything is done to keep the Army in South Africa in a thoroughly efficient state.

I am telling Grant that it will be his duty to see any Yeomanry sent from this country, and I will make a point of inspecting the regiments before they are despatched. The regiments should go as complete units.

Are we wise, do you think, to let Sir George Clarke[86] go out of the country? I don't know him personally, but he is undoubtedly an able man, and with the possibility of the Director General of Ordnance and President of the Ordnance Committee having to be replaced, can Clarke be spared?

NAM 7101–23–122–2

84
Lord Roberts to Lord Kitchener

47 Portland Place. W.

[Manuscript copy]

25th Oct 1901

I am glad you approve of Oliphant's being sent out. I telegraphed about him because I found he was senior to Hildyard as a Major-General, and although the latter will be given the temporary rank of Lieut-General I thought Oliphant would prefer not to serve under him – The King begged me to ask you to give Oliphant a chance if you could, and not to place him on the line of communication.

You will read all about Buller's affair in the newspapers – It is most unfortunate, but I am sure you will agree with me that there was no alternative but to relieve him of his command and place him on halfpay – What could have possessed him to give himself away so completely? He really must, I think, have been mad at the time   he made his marvellous speech to a body of volunteer officers – The press, except the extreme Radical section, condemn him entirely, but there are a certain number of people who try to defend him[87] – However, we may well be satisfied with the report we have received –

The question about sending you more troops is to be considered by the Cabinet Council on Monday next – The majority of the members agree with Brodrick and me, indeed all do, except possibly Hicks-Beach – I have proposed to send the 2nd D<ra>g<oo>n G<uar>ds and the 7th Hussars – They are both in good order (and especially 7th Hrs) well commanded – I have not yet seen the C<ourt> Martial on Major Cotton,[88] but if you have approved the sentence, I shall have no difficulty in recommending the King to confirm it.

I am anxious to hear how Martial Law in Cape Colony acts and whether you find the control it gives over the Ports is sufficient –

I have to make an early start in the morning and, as I may not be able to write more, I will end now –

Your difficulties are, I can assure you most thoroughly appreciated by all who know South Africa, and by none more than by

NAM 7101–23–122–2–162

85
Lord Roberts to Mr St John Brodrick
47 Portland Place, London W.

[Manuscript copy]

2nd November 1901.

It seems clear to me from reading the enclosed letter that Kitchener is overworked and I blame myself for not having proposed long ere this to give him the assistance of a General Chief of Staff – I found Kitchener himself most useful in that capacity and I should like to give him similar help.

Ian Hamilton is quite the best man I can think of for such a position, and if you approve, I will ascertain from Kitchener whether Hamilton's appointment would be agreeable to him.

Hamilton would be a great loss to me, but I daresay I could find someone to take his place temporarily.

I know you are averse to having more transport, but I am sure it would be wise to return some of the tired out regiments and I suggest that we ask Curzon to send a Cavalry Corps from India to take the place of the 9th Lancers or 5th Dragoon Guards and as soon as one of these regiments return to India, to send a second Cavalry regiment from there to South Africa.

NAM 7101–23–122–2–168

86
Memorandum by Lord Roberts
War Office.

4th November 1901

Memorandum for Cabinet.

With a view to strengthening the army in South Africa, I recommend that a certain number of fresh troops be sent there, and would suggest that India be asked to arrange that the 5th Dragoon Guards and 9th Lancers may return from South Africa to India, on being relieved by the fresh Cavalry regiments from that country, and that, in addition, India should also send four Infantry battalions to South Africa in relief of the 1st Battalion Devon

Regiment, and the 2nd Battalion Gordon Highlanders (who originally went from India to South Africa) and two other battalions, to be selected by the War Office from those now in South Africa, who would then go to India.

I would also suggest that the 4th Battalion King's Own Rifle Corps and the 4th Battalion Rifle Brigade, both now in Ireland, should be sent to South Africa to relieve two battalions of their own regiments now there.

These changes, with the troops already under orders from home to South Africa, i.e. the 2nd Dragoon Guard, 7th Hussars and new 800 Cavalry drafts, will materially stiffen the force now in South Africa.

The question of militia reliefs will take some little time as the men of each unit have to be consulted.

NAM 7101–23–122–2–169

87
Lieutenant-General Ian Hamilton to Lord Roberts

S.S. Briton,

[Typescript copy]

Madeira, Nov. 13th/01

I am going to give Victor Brooke[89] and his typewriter a preliminary canter this morning by writing you a letter in which I shall try to give you a few of the ideas with which I am starting out on this adventure.

(1). My first, my most important, and fortunately my most easy business will be to cheer up Lord K. and make him understand that he continues to be thoroughly well appreciated by all his old backers at home.

(2). Next, and not so easy, I shall have to try and persuade Lord K. to let me initiate a system of decentralization, which shall commence in his own office, and go down through the Districts, especially in such matters as command, supply, remount depots and transport.

I cannot help feeling that the success or failure <of> my mission will depend almost entirely on whether I can get

202

Lord K. to let me really share his burden, and free his mind to think of the higher military problems, and his body to run about to the different commands on inspection.

(3). I have had a great idea growing on me lately, which I have not communicated to you – owing to want of leisure – concerning what I may call the politico-military part of the situation. This idea is that we should endeavour on some pretext or another, to arrange for a month's armistice in the Transvaal and Orange River Colonies. My conviction is that if we could do this, and let the Commandoes get even more thoroughly broken up, and out of hand than they are at present, the spirit of lassitude and longing for peace, which undoubtedly exists amongst them, would become irresistible, and that the war would be at an end more or less on our own terms.

People who do not know the Boers may think that they would not observe the armistice. I do not believe this.

They would observe it as well as we should.

The great difficulty would be with the Boers and rebels in Cape Colony. We may have to give them a safe conduct back into the Orange River Colony during the armistice.

But there would be no harm in this. If on the other hand we could avoid this necessity, we could employ the month in putting an overwhelming force into Cape Colony, and set that part of South Africa entirely in order.

To arrive at such an armistice as I have been describing, it might, of course, be necessary to consent to discuss certain points on which we are not prepared to give way, but on the other hand there is no harm in discussing anything, to any extent, provided you are quite firmly determined on the point at issue.

(4). Another point of a very different nature that I want to take up is the familiar one to us, and yet often so strangely ignored by others, of rifle-shooting.

You may say that our men have had no sort of practice now, for at least two years. To blaze away at a Boer galloping across the veldt, without knowing where your bullet goes, is no better practice than firing blank cartridges. You remember, just before we left South Africa, I got you to sanction a scheme for rifle-practice.

I am told, however, that this has never been acted on. Several recent actions seem to me to show that the Boers are learning that they can gallop in on our fellows, and their bad, unpractised shooting, without much risk to themselves. You will remember also how very strong I have always been on the point, that if they can gallop in to within 80 yards of our men, they are our masters, owing to their style of snap-shooting, like jack-in-the-boxes, without aligning their sights on the object.

But steady practice, which can be easily arranged for on the veldt will make our men just as good, and will also add to their morale and self-confidence.

I can think of a great many more minor points, but I think this will be enough for today.

I am rather sad I must say at having left England without having succeeded in impressing anyone in authority with what, I cannot help thinking, is the urgent necessity of making use of, and getting hold of, in some proportion at least, of our Boer prisoners. However this is an old story, and I will not bother you any more with it.

I am going to wire to you from Madeira, asking you if I can have one high-class senior clerk, of the stamp of Captain Bowers,[90] and one junior clerk who can do type-writing and shorthand.

I am going to make a great effort to get Lord K. to permit me to act as intermediary between him and the heads of his departments, and you will understand better than anyone else how such a clerk, of the superior sort to which I have referred, would assist me in carrying out this business. I may add that I do not think it at all likely that anyone will be disposed to surrender a first class man to me for this purpose.

P.S. We have about 500 passengers, none of whom I know – almost all Natalians going back, which seems to be a good sign as far as it goes.

The sea is perfectly smoothe, and I am very fit indeed.

LHCMA, Hamilton 2/3/1

88
Lieutenant-General Ian Hamilton to Lord Roberts
Cape Town. Nov 26th [1901]

[Typescript copy]

I arrived after a prosperous voyage this morning. I found a confidential letter from Hubert Hamilton awaiting me, which told me that Lord Kitchener was longing for me to arrive; that he had set a room apart for me in his own house, and that he wanted me to mess and live with him.

I was delighted, but I own just a little surprised, as I did not think that it was at all like Lord K. to long for anyone in this world. However, I gather, reading between the lines of the rest of the letter, and also from one or two things I have been confidentially told, that Lord K. is a bit down in his luck, thinking that he is not being appreciated by the press and public. Accordingly, perhaps for the first time in his life, he appears to feel the want of some senior officer to help him.

I suspect what he requires is rather moral support and assistance, than actual help, but if I am fortunate enough to be able to afford him the first, the second will come more easily, than would otherwise be possible.

On reading Hamilton's letter, I determined to make a push to clear my baggage, and make a start tonight, and it was most fortunate that I did so, as I shortly afterwards got the following clear-the-line message from Lord K.- "Most welcome, hope you will leave tonight with mail for the north. Has anyone come with you?"

I must say I have been very anxious, to the point of doubt, as to whether I would be allowed by Lord K. to help him, but this makes me feel more sanguine, and the more especially now that we are going to mess and live together, in the same house, as it seems to me that this will afford me a much better chance.

I have had talks with Sir Walter Hely Hutchinson, and Wynne. They both seem to think that it will be most difficult to clear out the Cape Colony, and that they will want more mounted men than they have now got to block up the rat-holes, and round up the rebels.

I have wired to French to meet me tomorrow at Matjesfontein. If he comes I will be able to have a talk with him, and get to know more about it all. I suppose I shall cross the next mail somewhere about Vereeinigen,[91] and I will write you in the train from there.

I have just seen Hickman, of whom you know I had no very great opinion as a column leader. I think he is at a loose end now and doing nothing, but he has been commanding a column down here, and told me an interesting story about Scheepers.

When Scheepers was so ill that he had to send in and ask for a doctor,[92] he also conveyed a message to Hickman, and said that he hoped he would write to Lord K. and recommend Grant for the V.C. as Grant was certainly out and away the bravest Khaki that he had ever seen. You will remember the case of Grant blundering on Scheepers with his convoy at night, and how Grant put a bold face on, and rode right into the laager with his revolver, with the result that the Boers began to shoot one another. I tell you this in case Lord K. did not pass Scheepers' message on.

Both Hely Hutchinson and Wynne seem to think that the coming of troops from India was a first class business, and that no better way could be desired of putting fresh vigour into operations, than by an extension of the principle of relieving African regiments by exchange with Indian battalions. I only mention this at second-hand, for your information, and do not yet venture to express any opinion of mine on the point.

LHCMA, Hamilton 2/3/3

89
Lieutenant-General Ian Hamilton to Lord Roberts

Head Quarters,

[Typescript copy]

Pretoria, Dec. 6th 1901.

I am established with my office in the very room in which I lay with my broken collar-bone, after the capture of Heidelburg. My bedroom is in Aileen's[93] old room, so you will understand exactly how I am located.

We get up very early in the morning, Lord Kitchener always being down by 6 a.m. and as a result the operations-telegrams are usually digested, and dealt with, by the time we breakfast at 8 o'clock.

Lord Kitchener has been extremely kind, and has taken me in every way into his confidence, and has already entrusted me with a fair amount of work. For one thing I have entirely relieved him of the work of seeing the heads of departments every morning. They now bring all their papers to me, and I find that, as a matter of fact, I can settle ¾ of the questions without troubling Lord Kitchener at all. It will be a long time, I fear, before I can be of sufficient use to him in the matter of operations, except of course by discussing general ideas, and by bringing a fresh mind to bear on many points, which he has at his fingers' ends. But the area is so enormous and the troops are distributed in such very small columns, that I feel it will take me several months before I can say with certainty where every corps, and every commander are located. Lord Kitchener himself has this knowledge in a truly remarkable degree. I have just been drafting a despatch, forwarding a letter from Mr Burger, on the subject of the refugee camps. It was an interesting job, and I think the reply will prove satisfactory. I hope you got my cipher telegrams all right. I felt a good deal of difficulty about sending them, as I felt, in a way as if I was discussing Lord Kitchener behind his back. I do not know if I sent the sort of news you expected or wished for, but I thought it most important that I should, if possible, give you a little insight into Lord Kitchener's views on the general situation, political as well as military.

Lord Kitchener has now come back from interviewing French, and starts again tomorrow for Natal, to see Lyttelton. I am thus having a really good dose of responsibility to start with, especially as this time he takes Hubert Hamilton with him, who during his last absence kept me on the right track.

As regards general operations, there is a concensus of opinion that the time for big drives is over. They were effective for clearing the country of cattle and of womens' laagers, but they are of no use for catching the present type of fighting Boer, who is an instance of the survival of the fittest, and a veteran soldier of a very high stamp. It seems certain that columns must be localized to deal with these local commandoes, for as Broadwood says in a letter on this subject, no one but a column-leader can realize the enormous importance of an intimate knowledge of the ground. By working thus in a definite district which is again more or less defined an [sic] extent by lines of blockhouses we shall, I really think, with luck, be able to do a great deal in the next month or two.

As regards what I may call military-secretary questions I have a few remarks to make. Wynne, at the Cape, will not work harmoniously with French. There is apparently a strain of obstinacy, and jealousy in his character, which makes him unsuitable for his present anomalous position, viz: to be working with, but not under the orders of a senior soldier. It is a great pity, for he is in many respects an excellent man, but Lord Kitchener had patched up differences too often, and there had to be an end of it.

I fear Rundle has been one of the great failures in a negative way. He has never had anything you could call a disaster, but his extreme caution in avoiding any risk of one has resulted in an inactivity, which is probably worse for the State, in the long run, than active work, checquered by occasional regrettable incidents, would have been. At present Lord K. intends to send him home, and give Bauer Campbell (who is no flyer, but much better than Rundle) the command, with Bully Oliphant to work under him, and inspire him with the energy, which it is hoped he will bring with him from Aldershot.

Thorneycroft is not being stellenbosched,[94] in being sent home on leave. Lord K. looks on him as an excellent man who has got a bit stale, and who will come round again very rapidly.

Campbell of the 60th, and Walter Kitchener are in the same category, and Lord K. looks forward to seeing them all out again.

Bethune is not in this class, and has been rather disappointing latterly, I am told. But as his regiment is out here, I suppose he will come back in due course, and will probably be given another try. I will not write any more personalities till I am more sure of my ground.

208

I advise you to get Henry Wilson to take in hand big maps of South Africa, and mark out on them the general system of lines of blockhouses completed, in hand, and in contemplation.[95]

You will thus get a far better idea, than you can from telegrams or despatches, of the actual situation, which you will find one of great scientific interests.

Having marked out your blockhouses area, you can get little flags made with the names of the 90 odd column commanders, and see how they fit into the general scheme.

I have begun my letter too late today, so must now bring it to a close.

LHCMA, Hamilton 2/3/6

90
Lord Roberts to Lord Kitchener

47. Portland Place – W.

[Manuscript copy]

13ᵗʰ December. 1901.

We are all delighted with the news of Bruce Hamilton's successes near Ermelo.[96] He seems to have done well and I hope that the captures he has made will seriously cripple Botha to whose commando they apparently belonged.

Your Blockhouse system is evidently having the desired effect, the only drawback to it is the number of Infantry required to hold the long lines, we are sending you some more Militia battalions in the hope that when they reach you, you will be able to let us have back some of the Militia that have been longest from home. The line of blockhouses from Kroonstad to Lindley, Bethlehem, and Harrismith will be very valuable, as will be the one from Standerton to Ermelo, and I am glad you have got the railway completed between Bloemfontein and Sannah's Post.

Majors Fraser[97] and Lloyd[98] of the Bedfordshire Regiment have both been retired, and I hope it will be possible now to get some good blood into that corps, for it has been singularly unfortunate in its Senior officers.

I see <you> recommend fairford [sic] to be transferred to the Bedfordshire, but is he a man likely to put life into a somewhat dull corps? He always struck me as being wanting in go himself, and I have a vivid remembrance of the trouble he gave over the casualty returns on the march to Bloemfontein.

I am sorry to learn from your telegram of the 8th instant[99] that you do not approve of Downe & Hotham being sent out for remount work, but I think you will find they will be of the greatest help. Birkbeck has had an extremely difficult task, a bigger business really than one man could carry out satisfactorily, but though I think he has done well the loss in horses has been tremendous, and, with senior officers able to move about the country, more supervision will be possible – a good Army battalion goes with Downe who will be useful, I hope, as he has been in South Africa during the war. You can assure Birkbeck that we have no fault to find with him, but it is not possible for him to be everywhere.

I have seen your brother. The death of his wife[100] was terribly sad, and I am glad you sent him away for a change. He has no wish to exceed his leave, and as soon as he has settled his children, he will be glad to return to South Africa.

Baden Powell starts tomorrow with Downe and Hotham. I cannot help thinking that Police would be more useful than soldiers now for settling South Africa. I found this to be the case in Burma, and after our fighting in the neighbourhood of Belfast I urged Milner to take up the question of Police. He talked first of all of 5000 men sufficing, and it was with difficulty I got him to agree to raising 10,000. I have just been talking to Ridley about the way in which the Police have been getting on. It has been uphill work for them, partly on account of their being too few, and because it has not been possible to meet their demands for horses, but where their posts have been firmly established, they seem to have got the country well in hand. I will try and see Baden Powell before he leaves London tomorrow, and I will bring the matter before the next meeting of the Defence Committee, Milner hesitates, I believe, to employ Police for fear that their cost would fall upon the revenues of South Africa. This would, no doubt, be the case eventually, but I shall be disappointed if the Government will not accept it as a war charge in the first instance.

When will you be able to spare Chesham? I am anxious for him to return to help me with the Imperial Yeomanry. They are gradually appreciating the fact that their role is Mounted Infantry not Cavalry, but it will not be easy to keep them up to this if their annual inspections are to be carried on by a Cavalry Soldier.

Good-bye and with every good wish for the season from us all.

NAM 7101–23–122–2–192

91
Lieutenant-General Ian Hamilton to Lord Roberts

Pretoria,

[Typescript copy]

Dec. 16th/01

Lord Kitchener has gone away inspecting along the Delagoa line, and I am left here to run the show in his absence. Everyone seems to agree that these constant and prolonged inspections by the Commander in Chief are a most valuable new feature, and do as much good to the army as to himself, which is saying a good deal.

The work here is steady and continuous. I get up as 5:30 a.m. every morning, and am down by six, at which time Lord Kitchener, Hubert Hamilton, and one A.D.C. also make their appearance. All the operation telegrams are then gone through, and the situation is discussed, and studied on the map, and with reference to the information received from the Intelligence.

Such telegrams as are at all pressing are also answered straight-away there, by Lord Kitchener or myself.

We breakfast at eight, and when all the officers of the Head Quarters come in to see me at 8 45, it is a great advantage to have considered and settled all strategical considerations, before dealing with the points they bring up, which usually hang a good deal on the general trend of particular operations. From this time on, we work steadily till 4 30 p.m. when we go out for a short ride, rarely more than one hour, as Lord K. is always anxious to be back to see

Colonel Henderson, his Intelligence Officer, who comes over for the second time, with whatever news he has, about 5 30 in the afternoon.

We dine at a quarter to eight, and sometimes do a little work after dinner, usually getting to bed by 10 30 p.m.

I have now got very clear information from Lord Kitchener, about some more of our senior officers. Mildmay Willson, Inigo Jones, Barton and Rundle, I know, he considers are very little use now, and will never be of any use to the army hereafter. Hart he places in a slightly superior category, saying that under certain exceptional circumstances, he might come out unexpectedly strong, and do a big thing, which none of the other four I have mentioned could ever, by any possibility, achieve. My own view about some of these officers is not so emphatic. Take General Barton, for instance. He is a fussy little man, who is inclined to devote all his attention to details, and to disregard, in doing so, more weighty matters. These are serious faults, but still he has a good deal of energy and keenness, and he certainly seems to have worked out the defences of Pretoria and neighbourhood in a very satisfactory style. Of course I have always understood that he is no leader of troops in the field, but this is mere hearsay. Nevertheless, to take a man of this calibre, and say that he will never be of any use at all to the army hereafter, is perhaps putting the case rather too strongly.

You will be surprised, and perhaps a little amused, to learn that the longer the war goes on, the more Lord Kitchener, and other people as well, think of old General Tucker, at Bloemfontein. All his faults, such as language, old fashioned manners, etc, etc, lie on the surface, whereas he really possesses many sterling good qualities, such as being an excellent disciplinarian, and full of energy and good commonsense. All his troops are very fond of him. In speaking of him, Lord Kitchener said to me "Frequent references are made to the fact that all our best officers are serving in South Africa". This may be so, but if so, the outlook inspires me with some anxiety, for I give you my word that, going carefully over the lists of officers, young and old, holding responsible independent commands, I can only total up about eight of them, whom I should describe as really first class men.

Under such conditions, is it not almost a pity to part with an excellent, and reliable old officer of the Tucker type?

No one would be more ready than I to see him go, if there were an abundance of first class young Generals coming on, as after all he is no Napoleon, but seeing that, on the contrary, there threatens to be a serious shortage in the way of really good generals, I must say I should like to see him get his Lieut. Generalship, so as to save him from retirement.

I think the tendency towards excessive centralization, which is the chief criticism levelled against Lord Kitchener, is tending steadily to decrease. You may take it from me that he leaves General French absolutely and entirely alone, except in so far as he does his very best to comply with all his requirements.

He gives General Tucker a considerable amount of power, and almost invariably approves of his action.

In the case of subordinate commanders in the Orange River Colony, I have noticed already that very much depends on the officer himself, whether or not, he is given a free hand. Thus Rimington is practically free from control and, subject to very general instructions, goes where he likes, and does what he likes. General Elliot might have much the same latitude, if he cared to take it, but he obviously does not, and prefers to be at the end of the wire. *I do not mean this as a reflection, but he is one of those men who prefer to refer important points.*[101]

In the Transvaal Lord Kitchener and staff <u>do</u> personally conduct the operations, in the East, but representations as to difficulties in carrying out orders, and suggestions for alternative movements, are always patiently considered. I dare say, however, there is some justification, in this instance, for the accusation of centralization, but, after all, the results have been pretty satisfactory.

In the Western Transvaal, Methuen does practically what he likes, coming in for two or three days, and starting off for a fortnight to work some line of country, which he himself has suggested, and all the details of dealing with which are arranged by himself.

On the other hand, and this furnishes a typical instance of what I mean by saying, that the individuality of generals is a leading factor in this matter, Mildmay Willson either does not, or cannot move fifty men without orders. The reason for this is, I take it in two words, that Lord Kitchener does not trust Willson, and that Willson does not trust himself.

General Oliphant has just arrived, and I have seen something of him during the last two days. I never in my life saw a man more changed. Instead of his usual bustling, rather self-assertive, cock-sure manner, he is as quiet and timid as a mouse.

In his conversation too he is most humbleminded, and altogether deprecates the idea of being able to accomplish anything with a column on "trek", saying he feels he will be much more suited, after a little time has elapsed, to take over something stationary, such as a town or a line of blockhouses.

This attitude of his is intensely amusing to anyone who knew him at all at home, in the role of an outside critic. Mr Broderick [sic], I am sure, will smile when he hears it. I am glad to say Lord Kitchener, to whom he told some of his amusing stories, has taken quite a liking to him, and thinks he will be able to get good value out of him. He is first to be sent, as a spectator, on trek with Lord Methuen, and then we shall try to find something suitable for him.

There is one point about General French, which you ought to know, and which I hesitate the less to tell you as you are aware of my great admiration for him, and how I prefer serving under him to almost anyone else. What I want you to know about him is his inclination to surround himself with personal friends, irrespective of their value as trained staff-officers. You will understand what I mean when I tell you that now, with thirty thousand men under him, and a variety of complicated operations in progress, his working staff consists of young Miller, of the Greys, and Milbanke,[102] 10th Hussars. This means that he has to do everything himself, and I feel certain that the operations and troops must suffer to some extent. He ought, of course, to have some men like Harry Rawlinson, Burney of the Gordons, or Murray of the Inniskilling Fusiliers. I mean, in fact, some trained experienced officer, and not young fellows like these, to help him to run the show. If this can be put right with his aquiescence, it will be, but in any case it is just as well that you should take note of this one little phase of his character.

Lord Kitchener is still away on the Delagoa Bay line, and I have just come up to Johannesburg, where we are going to stay in the old house for Christmas. I do not think we shall remain very long, although the climate makes a delightful change, and is more suited to good work being carried on than Pretoria, at this season of the year. But the prominence given to Johannesburg throughout South Africa, by Lord Milner's taking up his position here, has aroused such a strong feeling, amongst all colonists, who are not connected with gold-mining, that I think he is anxious not to give rise to any suspicion, that Army Head Quarters may be inclined to follow suit.

I am now dictating this to Victor Brooke in our old office room. Lord Kitchener, when he comes, is to have the drawing-room. Everyone is greatly pleased at the capture of Kritzinger.[103]

LHCMA, Hamilton 2/3/8

92
Lieutenant-General Ian Hamilton to Lord Roberts

Jeppe's House,
Johannesburg.

[Typescript copy]

Dec. 24th 1901.

Thank you so much, Sir, for your kind and interesting letter, dated 30th November.

I note what you say about giving the horses of the 7th Hussars a good rest. I spoke to Lord Kitchener about it, and have also written to Lawley,[104] their Commanding Officer. The horses will be given three or four days rest at Cape Town, until they are fit to travel by rail, and then will go to Craddock,[105] where I hope it will be found possible to give them a month.

As you are probably aware, it is one of Lord Kitchener's characteristics not to be able to endure the thought that any part of his forces is quiescent. The characteristic is in itself about the most valuable one any General Officer could have, at the present stage of a long and weary campaign like this, for it results in the

215

spur being constantly applied to counteract the slackness and languor, which are almost inevitably engendered by a protracted campaign. Of course, as in almost everything there is another side to the question. In this case the other side comes out in the fact that columns and horses practically never get a rest, and although we on the staff often try to hide away some detachments of cavalry or mounted infantry, in the hopes that he may forget their existence, and give the horses time to pull round a bit, nevertheless he has them so thoroughly well fixed in his mind that the device is rarely successful.

I am more glad than I can say that the tests of the shortened rifle continue to be satisfactory. I wish to goodness we could get a few thousand of them out here, and give them a fair and practical trial, but against that I must hope that the war will be over before the rifle is ready.[106]

Speaking of this reminds me that Lord K. had a long talk with me yesterday about the new field-gun. I told him that you had said to me that you thought we were in a fair way to get a very satisfactory weapon. It may interest you to hear his view on the subject, as it is a matter on which he has expended a great deal of thought. His idea is that our new gun should be an 18 pounder, firing shrapnel up to 6000 yards, and made to carry, when necessary, for short ranges, a double shell of about 24 pounds. He is very keen on fixed ammunition, holding that the greater the range the greater the necessity for accuracy, which he considers it is impossible to obtain when the charge is not fixed. He seemed to me to doubt the power of Woolwich, or of the Ordnance to work out the best possible gun by themselves. He maintained that the proper way to set about the business was to get hold of a committee with representatives from Woolwich, Armstrong, Vickers Maxim, and possibly one or two men from big continental firms in attendance. He spoke particularly highly of a man in Vickers Maxim, a Frenchman called Dadier, an expert in these matters, who gave him more help in working out his Egyptian mule-howitzers than anyone else. If you think of it, and have time, you might just tell me next time you write how the matter stands at present, with regard to our new field-gun. Also what the object is of our sending back all those worn out field-guns to be relined. Are they meant for the volunteers, or what is going to be done with them?

What with drafting despatches, and letters to the War Office, Lord Milner and Botha, and picking up all the routine work of Departments, I am uncommonly busy, but as that is what I came out here to be, I cannot grumble at it.

Methuen and Lady Mehuen[107] were here yesterday. The former looks wonderfully young and well. He spoke of leaving the service as soon as the war was over. I remonstrated with him, and I do not know if he will stick to his intention, but I think that whatever happens, he will stick out for a good long spell of leave when he gets home.

December 27th –

Harry Rawlinson arrived last night; he is looking extraordinarily well, too well indeed, for he threatens to become fat. He gives a very good account of matters down in the Eastern Transvaal, and says that the Boers are thoroughly alarmed by the excellent intelligence which Wools Sampson has been able to give to Bruce Hamilton. They are now all very scattered and restless, and it will be difficult to make a big bag of prisoners, but there are good hopes of a fair number of surrenders.

I do not write you anything about politics, as a rule, for you get that, I suppose, from the highest sources. I think, however, that now that I have been here a month, and got some grip of the general state of things, you might care to have a few words on the subject.

I can trace two distinctly different schools of thought in the matter of settlement with the Boers, as regards the war itself, and the political situation afterwards. On the one side stands Milner, with the Johannesburgers and some of the loyalists of Cape Colony and Natal, and on the other is Lord Kitchener, with nearly every soldier of any standing or experience, that I have spoken to on the subject up to date. The first party wish to crush the Boers utterly, just as we crushed the Burmese, or the Punjabis. The others think

217

it will strain the resources, even of England, to carry matters quite as far as this with a fine, hitherto independent white race like the Boers. The sharply dividing line between the two policies is shown by the views taken on the question of unconditional surrender, on the one hand, or a granting of some sort of terms on the other.

I will not, on this occasion, express any view on the subject myself, although, of course, I have my opinion.

It is a curious fact that Steyn and De Wet, who are, beyond all comparison, our two most inveterate enemies, should be adhered to, as any of the Johannesburg crowd. They know the extraordinary law-abiding nature of their Burghers, and they fear that if they subscribe to any terms at all, it will be very hard to make them disown the agreement, whereas if they surrender unconditionally, the bargain, although it allows us to treat them as we like, leaves them also with a free hand, as far as their conscience goes, to give us renewed trouble, at the first possible opportunity.

This attack on Firman's Column has been a very unfortunate business.[108] It is difficult to foretell how the tactical situation in these parts may ultimately work out, but I fear it throws them all back a month or six weeks.

We badly want some really good man to take the Orange [River] Colony in hand, but I do not see who we have, unless we take French from the Cape Colony, or unless Lord Kitchener himself takes the field.

In my telegram telling Proemial all about Firman's Column, I had to leave out a good deal, as Lord K. does not like long wires. For this reason, and also to simplify the story, I did not introduce Rundle's name, but he was within three miles with a small force of infantry, and of course he is the man primarily responsible for all the local arrangements, which may or may not turn out to have been the cause of this unfortunate affair.

Good-bye, Sir, for the present.

LHCMA, Hamilton 2/3/9

93
Lieutenant-General Ian Hamilton to Lord Roberts

Jeppe's House.

[Typescript copy]

January 1ˢᵗ 1902.

Thank-you so much for your kind letter of 6ᵗʰ December.[109] I am glad you were pleased with my telegram from Pretoria, as I felt bound to tell you exactly how matters stood with Lord K., both physically and mentally, and I was not quite sure that you might not be unhappy at hearing that he was a little sore on the question of the want of inducement given to the Boers to surrender. He is now in quite remarkable health and spirits, and I think the next move he contemplates is on to the Orange River Colony, where he may stay some time and exercise somewhat close supervision over the movements of columns, in those districts. Now that you have the beautiful maps I sent you, you will be able to follow these movements very much better than heretofore, and you will observe how restricted De Wet's area is becoming, owing to the blockhouse line, and how difficult it will be for him to evade our columns, for any length of time, once they get really to work at him.

Lord Kitchener will doubtless write you himself about his scheme for alternate columns, relieving one another, at intervals of eight days.

Lord Chesham has been appointed President of the Court of Inquiry, which will assemble to consider the successful attack made by De Wet on Firman's Column. I will not, therefore, anticipate their report by giving you my views, except in so far that I fear it was a case of complete surprise, and that I cannot but think that Rundle might have done something in their favor.

Rawlinson is still here, extremely well, and in the best of spirits. He is to have one of the four big columns, which are to commence harrying De Wet in about a week's time, and we have certainly given him the pick of South Africa for troops. Besides his own column, which has two of the best old M.I. regiments in it, he will have both regiments of I.L.H. under Mackenzie and Briggs[110] respectively, and Dawkins' Column, from the north. Dawkins is a very quiet unassuming fellow, but if I were asked to name our best commander of a small column, I am sure I am safe in saying that I could not name anyone better than Dawkins.

Lord Downe and Hotham have just arrived. Long has been sent down to Cape Town to meet them. Hotham will stay at Cape Town and look after fresh arrivals. Downe, accompanied by Long will make an exhaustive tour of inspection of all the Remount Depots, Veterinary Hospitals, etc, etc. Long has already been round, so he will be in a position to make himself very useful to Lord Downe, in this capacity.

I return you General Sladin's[111] note. The facts are well known to everyone here, and are briefly as follows:– De Lisle has had the 6th M.I. with him since I started from Bloemfontein in May, the year before last. He is extremely fond of the regiment. It was felt, at Head Quarters, that the 6th M.I. had earned a rest, and De Lisle was written to and told that, as his regiment must be rather played out, it would be relieved by another fresh corps. De Lisle strongly combated the idea that his corps was tired or fed up, and asked to be allowed to keep it. This request was acceded to. Meanwhile Sladin, who commanded the corps, had written in officially and unofficially to Alderson in altogether a different sense to De Lisle, and insisting that the men were so played out that it was wrong to keep them in the field any longer. About this time an official report was received from De Lisle, saying that Sladin was so wanting, even in the elementary knowledge of tactics, that he could not trust him out alone in command of the regiment. On this it became a question of the removement of De Lisle or Sladin, and accordingly Sladin was brought into Pretoria. There is necessarily a feeling that De Lisle's adverse report on Sladin may have been in consequence of his acute difference of opinion with him, on the subject already referred to. This, however, can only be suspected, although naturally it is Sladin's cue to emphasize this part of the business, and say that it is entirely on that account that De Lisle reported badly on him. Anyway, the view taken by Army Head Quarters is that Sladin is not, by any means, to be finally condemned on De Lisle's report. On the contrary he has been made A.A.G. under Kelly, where he has been doing very important and responsible work. Indeed I should say that up to date he has not suffered at all, either in the estimation of his superiors, or practically in regard to his position, by this unfortunate business. Only this morning, however, it was brought to my notice, that Sladin was corresponding somewhat freely with the 6th M.I., and with officers of the Army Head Quarters Staff, still harping on the subject of the 6th M.I. having been very badly treated, by not being brought in to rest, and I have thought it necessary to cause him to be warned privately, that if he perseveres in working at this question, now that he is no longer connected with the regiment, he may get into serious trouble.

I think you now have the whole story, and will be able to form your own opinion, as well as I can.

I enclose you a slip from Rawley,[112] regarding a certain Capt Tomlin,[113] whom he is very anxious to get into the Irish Guards, also a letter from Rimington, which will, I am sure, interest you, also a letter from Broadwood, which will show you, at the same time what a nice fellow he is, and how unfitted he has been for some time past for service in the field.

I also send you a copy of the telegram I sent to G.O.C. Cape Town, regarding a cable sent by him, which he had afterwards to contradict, and for which he was reprimanded by Mr Broderick [sic].

I have not yet written to Mr Broderick [sic] himself, although I promised him I would do so. Please give him my profound salaam, and tell him I will mend my ways, and let him know how we are getting on some time soon.

I dined last night with Lord Milner and Mr Rouliot, head of the Chamber of Mines. Lord Milner was in great form, and seemed very fit. It is impossible to talk to a man like that without being impressed by his views, and the brilliant way in which he puts them. At the same time one has one's own opinions, and thinking over the subjects of our conversation calmly this morning, I should say there was some danger of Lord Milner becoming too keen a Johannesburger, and acting as if Johannesburg were South Africa, whereas it has no more in common with the rest of South Africa, than Monte Carlo has with Peebleshire, in Scotland.

However, I will not moralize any more today, and, with kindest remembrances to Her Ladyship, and the girls,

LHCMA, Hamilton 2/3/10

94
Lieutenant-General Ian Hamilton to Lord Roberts

Jeppe's House.

[Typescript copy]

January 9th 1902.

Work seems to be increasing daily, and this week, for the first time, I have put off starting my letter to you until the last moment.

You must have had a very interesting dinner at Mr Brodrick's, and I hope that with Taylor and 11 doctors at the table you were very careful not to exceed.

I suppose Kitchener is sure to take Quetta, and I should think he would do very well for it.

I am particularly interested to hear of the talk you had with Ridley after dinner, for it has been very evident to me of late that Police are needed more than soldiers for the final pacification of the country.

The S.A.C. men are doing splendid work at present in clearing the country, and there is no doubt they are a very much finer type of man, and much better suited to act independently, and to cope with the difficulties of new surroundings, than the average soldier of the line. I wish to be very moderate and careful in making any such statement, but I do really think that at the present stage of affairs, one S.A.C. is worth three average soldiers. At first of course they were a bit raw, but drafts coming out to join them now, would have the advantage of the experience of the older hands, and would tumble to the business in no time.

You forgot to enclose the letters about Conan Doyle and Lionel James, so I do not know how I am expected to help them, but I do not think they are either of them very shy, and I dare say they will muster up courage to write to me direct, and tell me what they want.

I shall watch for the progress of the Buller question with very great interest. I should not wonder if it was not raised in the debate on the address. It will need delicate handling, of course, because, in exact measure as Buller is shown to have been an incapable General, so it will become difficult to justify his selection for the command of the First Army Corps. I hope myself the line taken will be to say that he was a soldier with a very fine record, who had deserved so well of his country, that you did not think that it was in the general interests of the service to emphasize too strongly the certain short-comings in his character as a leader in the field, which had forced themselves on your notice during the progress of the South African Campaign; that you had, therefore, recommemded the Cabinet to appoint him, in the full belief that he would grasp the situation, and that he would do satisfactorily; that however, just about this period, there were certain indications (about guns etc) that he was going to make difficulties, and quite apart from the South African War, or service qualifications, prove unsatisfactory, as head of our great practical military training ground. On the top of this came his speech, which needs no comment, and which, taken together with all the foregoing circumstances, forced you to the painful conclusion that, for the sake of the Service in general, and Aldershot in particular, he would have to be removed.[114] I expect the whole thing will be over long before you get this, but it may amuse you to see what I thought in anticipation.

I think that, as your Military Secretary, I must make out a list of all our column-commanders, and give you, in a few words, the position they occupy in the opinion of Lord Kitchener, and the army out here.

It will be a surprise to you, for instance, to find that C. Knox is hardly the man we thought him, when we left South Africa, that is to say that he is not altogether in the first flight. He is a good tactical leader in the field, and carries out his orders promptly, and without making any difficulties whatever; he is also popular, and a very pleasant fellow. These are pretty high qualifications, no doubt, but then unfortunately they say he is no use at all, when put in supreme charge of operations, in which case he seems to change his character altogether, and shows want of initi<ati>ve, and even of military instinct. I have once or twice heard his name coupled with that of Jimmy Spens, it being said that they are both very much alike, in all these particulars.

I have never seen Lord K. so much upset as he was by the telegram he received, telling him to hand over military farms to the civil power. He went, yesterday, to see Lord Milner about this, and found that the whole question had been raised on a misunderstanding; that is to say the Director of Supplies drafted, and got the Adjutant General to issue an order about these farms, for which he had generally received Lord Kitchener's sanction, but, in the stress of business, the Chief did not see, or initial, the actual order, which was worded in a manner he would never have approved of. Thus the heading of the order was "MILITARY STOCK AND AGRICULTURAL DEPARTMENT", which was divided into two branches:–

    (1)   STOCK DEPARTMENT
    (2)   AGRICULTURAL DEPARTMENT.

Naturally, when Lord Milner saw this, he thought we were really forming an Agricultural Department in the Orange River Colony, and Transvaal, and quite naturally he considered that this was rather a matter for civil than military administration.

Had he inquired of Lord K., the whole matter would have been cleared up, but, instead of this, he wrote straight home to Mr Chamberlain, with the result, I suppose, of Proemial's telegram. Now that it has been explained to him what these farms really are, he entirely accepts Lord Kitchener's view, and is writing, or telegraphing, home at once to have the matter set right.

In a case like this, all that the Army can expect is that it be supported, until it be proved to be in the wrong, or to have grasped something pertaining to someone else. But this it does hope for. I think, the more this matter is examined into, the more it will be seen that we are doing something purely for the good of the Army, which the civil administration could not possibly do for us. There are many reasons why civil administration would not be able to give the Army full benefit of these farms, however much they might wish to do so, but one of these reasons is, I think, conclusive. If the civil administration took these farms out of the hands of the military tomorrow, the day after tomorrow they might be served with a notice to quit, by the lawful owner, who would then quietly step into his farm, with or without, for this is not quite certain, paying compensation for the growing vegetables and forage.

I am keeping very fit and so, thank goodness, is Lord K.

All our minds are at present fixed upon De Wet. We have hitherto failed to score at all heavily in that region, but we are getting so many troops now to bear upon it,[115] that I think we shall either succeed in bringing off some important actions, with corresponding losses to the Boers, or else force De Wet to make a fresh bolt through a vast extent of practically barren country, to get to Cape Colony again.

I have this moment received your kind wire referring to Vallentin's death,[116] which I will send today to his poor widow.

LHCMA, Hamilton 2/3/11

95
Lord Roberts to Lieutenant-General Ian Hamilton

47 Portland Place. London W.

[Manuscript copy]

11th January. 1902.

Best thanks for yours of the 12th December. The steamer was late and I only received it a day or two ago. Since you wrote it affairs seem to have progressed favourably, and it cheered me to see your Chief name April as a possible date for the end of the war, for in a former letter he had hinted on its lasting until July. No doubt Leyds and Co are buoying up the leaders with hopes of the Opposition being able to put difficulties in the way of supplies being voted when Parliament meets, but they will find themselves disappointed, and they may perhaps then think it advisable to give in. If Steyn, or De Wet, could be caught, I believe the war would end at once, but so long as these two hold out, Botha and Delarey feel bound to continue fighting.

When the network of blockhouses is more complete, the capture of the two Orange Free Staters may become possible. I am sure it would be worthwhile to devote all your energies to that end.

I was very sorry to hear of Vallentin's death. I hope my telegram reached you, and that you were able to communicate with the poor widow.

What has become of Rawly, and how has he been getting on? And what has happened to Broadwood, who I see is on his way home? I was thinking of offering him the Cavalry Command at the Curragh, but I shall wait now until I get a reply to the telegram I am sending to Kitchener.

What made you tell Chesham that his appointment as Inspector General of Yeomanry could not be made, because it would interfere with Army Corps Commanders? That I know is Buller's and Wood's opinion, but it is not mine. The Yeomanry has to be formed and until that has been done, it seems to me essential that its control should be in the hands of a specialist. Hereafter possibly it may be considered advisable to place the Yeomanry more completely under Army Corps Commanders, but as regards the 1st Army Corps, the Commander would never have anything to say to them except for the few days a few regiments might be at Aldershot. There are no Yeomanry centres in the area of his command, and to make the Yeomanry efficient within any reasonable period, it seems to me essential that they should be in close communication with an Inspector General, who could personally see to all their wants and supervise their shortcomings. I am sure it is necessary to have a head to the Yeomanry, as it is to the Cavalry, and if there had been a head to the Artillery, we should not now be without Quick firing guns, nor would there have been no heavy guns sent with Buller's force in 1899. I was abusing the Ordnance Committee for our being behindhand in the matter of Artillery, when Brackenbury showed me in their proceedings, that after I had used the introduction of Q.F. guns at the dinner given by the Regiment to me on my return from India in 1893, the Ordnance Committee took the question up that year and the next, and on both occasions their proposals were vetoed by the Adjutant-General (Buller) and the Army Board. I hope we shall have a good gun now both for H<orse> A<rtillery> and F<ield> A<rtillery> but it will be a couple of years at least before a single Battery can be ready.

I have seen Wynne. He does not now want to go to India, so I have offered the vacant 1st ...... District to Kitchener's brother.

I have also seen Henry[117] and Campbell of the 60th.

226

I enclose a copy of a letter I wrote to a German lady, who referred to me about the atrocities our soldiers are said to have committed in South Africa. I hear the letter has been well received in America and on the Continent.

Your account of the way in which work is carried on at Pretoria is very interesting. Overlapping of duties is difficult to avoid in service. Things have to be done so rapidly that a General is apt to employ the man or men most frequently about him, and those who he finds respond most quickly to his wishes. We have changed the designation A-A-G.B. for A.Q-M-G and I would suggest you doing the same. You will see in the new Army List all Nicholson's assistants are now styled Q-M-Gs. He has one or two very able fellows in his Department, especially Altham.

For the present I think the railways must continue to be controlled by the military, but Kitchener will, no doubt, arrange so that they may be transferred to the civil administration at no distant date.

I don't think I have any news to give you. We shall be busier than ever when Parliament meets as the Buller business is to be one of the first matters brought forward. And, judging by the Duke of Bedford's address on the 9th instant, War Office reform is likely to come in for a good deal of attention. We are getting on by degrees. The change in uniform is practically settled, and henceforth officers will be put to less expense on that account. The alterations in the several drills are well advanced, and I hope to get Regimental Institutes placed on a more satisfactory footing than they are at present.

Of one thing I am quite clear and that is that officers must not be allowed to remain on the Staff for a length of time. I am going to send Wilson to command a provisional battalion, and I have refused Evelyn Wood's son[118] the berth. He says you promised him, as I find he has only done 5½ years regimental service, and will have been on the staff, one way and another, for five years next month. I am very sorry to lose Wilson, but he agrees with me that it is right for him to go to a regiment.

NAM 7101–23–122–3–211

96
Lieutenant-General Ian Hamilton to Lord Roberts

Jeppe's House.

[Typescript copy]

January 17th 1902.

You will be rather surprised to find me enclosing to you a lengthy letter to Mr Brodrick. The explanation is this.

I owed Mr Brodrick a letter, and I determined to write him just as frankly and freely regarding the political situation, as I write to you about military matters. Since the letter was dictated to Victor Brooke, Reuters have come in which seem to me to show that Roseberry's[119] speech has had no effect whatever, and that the Government are firmly set on the unconditional surrender and fight to the last man tack.

As this is so, I feel that in writing to Mr Brodrick as I have, I shall only be kicking against the pricks, and perhaps even displeasing him, without doing the slightest good to the interests I have so deeply at heart. But I do not like to waste a literary effort of this magnitude altogether, and that is the reason I send it on to you.

There is very little military news, for which, as far as the Orange River Colony is concerned, we are thankful, as we needed a couple of days yet to complete our arrangements for hustling De Wet properly, and it would be inconvenient, to say the least of it, if he assumed a vigorous in<it>iative meanwhile.

I have had several letters from French, and others in Cape Colony, from which I have been able to glean information regarding the commanders of small columns.

I understand that he thinks Crabbe is very good and reliable, especially in contact with the enemy, although otherwise a bit slow.

He thinks Kavanagh very good indeed.

Wyndham slow and not much use, although he and the 16th did very well the other day, on the occasion when their road with the convoy was intercepted by Smuts.[120]

Lund, although he was a brilliant squadron-leader, is absolutely no use in his present position:[121] indeed they say he drinks.

Callwell no use at all.

Walter Doran not much good.

Beauchamp Doran distinctly good.

Wormald good.

Capper very good.

I fear Scobell has got valvular disease of the heart, and will be little more use as a soldier in the field. This is a terrible pity, and is deeply regretted by all the cavalry branch of the Service.

I have a long letter from Nicholson, which I shall answer D.V. next mail.

People are finding me out, and the correspondence is getting quite beyond a joke, so I am very driven in the matter of trying to write home letters.

Lord Kitchener regularly goes away for three or four days now, as soon as he has got the English mail off his hands, but I do not know yet where he will start for tomorrow.

Goodbye for the present. Love to her Ladyship and the girls.

LHCMA, Hamilton 2/3/12

97
Lieutenant-General Ian Hamilton to Lord Roberts
Pretoria.

[Typescript copy with a few additions in longhand[122]]

Feb. 8th 1902.

Best thanks for your very kind letter of 18th January, which came in late last night, and was then briefly acknowledged by me, in a post-script.

As these are very busy times, I begin my answer to you next morning, so as to leave me lots of time.

Lord Kitchener went away early today to meet all his columns, who are just finishing their colossal drive, from East to West, along the parallelogram, Harrismith, Bethlehem, Lindley, Kroonstad, Honingspruit, Roodeval, Wolverhoek,[123] Heilbron, Frankfort, Vrede.[124]

I am afraid De Wet has got out, the night before last. A native was taken, who said De Wet had escaped, with about 50 men, through the Lindley blockhouse line, about half way between that town and Kroonstad. As no report had been rendered about any crossing, enquiries were instituted, and the wire-entanglement was found cut, at the place described, and the spoor of about 50 men, passing within very few yards of a post belonging to a regiment which had been specially interpolated between two blockhouses at that spot, and along the line to strengthen it.

The men all stoutly swore that they had neither heard nor seen anything, so I fear the only inference is that, in spite of the most earnest warnings to keep alert that night, they were sound asleep, or else, and this is more likely, they funked the Boers and did not dare to fire.

This is I confess rather a disappointment, as it means beginning it all over again, but still we hope there are a good many Boers left in the net, and that our columns, before nightfall to-day will report satisfactory hauls of prisoners, possibly including Steyn.

After Lord Kitchener has seen the columns, I think he means to go down and see French, and try to put more energy and method into the Cape Colony operations. I do not, therefore, really expect him back for about a week, during which time I shall be monarch of all I survey, that is to say, if things go right, it will be all right, and if they do not, I shall be written down an ass.

You ask me how to class men like Rimington, De Lisle, Alderson, Pilcher, Haig, Scobell, Campbell, Thorneycroft, Gough, Henry.

Before Lord Kitchener left this morning, I thought it would be much better if I ran over these names to him, and took his opinion, so that you would have the very best advice possible, and of course, if I differed, I could have given you my difference, for what it was worth.

I find that Lord K. rather shies at giving any comparative list of the merit of the officers you name, before the end of the war, as he says that, even after all this experience, his views on the merits, or otherwise, of an officer are still susceptible to modification. He had, however, no objection at all to giving a short character sketch of several of the officers, which I remember the better, as I entirely concur with his views.

With regard to your list, he said that it was incomplete, as it did not mention men like Allenby and Wing, who were quite as good, or better than some of those you have named. However, he will stick to your list, only cutting out Gough, who, though admirable in his way, comes, he thinks, in rather a different, because a very junior, category.

Rimington is, no doubt, a man of a soldiery turn of mind. He is an admirable partisan leader, has a good eye for country, can handle and manoeuvre his men under fire, or entering into action, and is full of energy and resource.

He has, however, serious faults of character. He is not a high class man, in any way. He is not trusted by the enemy, and his brother commanders do not trust him, where loyal co-operation is concerned. He is a bad subordinate, as he is always working for his own hand, and not a good superior, where commanding officers of detached columns are concerned as they say they are made to do more than their share of the work, and get less than their share of the credit. The foregoing, I think, fairly represents Lord K's views. I would only add that I, myself, always found Rimington a useful subordinate, but then

(1) He had no temptation to be otherwise.

(2) I think I see a deterioration since those days, judging by letters & talks alone, but this, of course, may be fancy on my part.

Regarding De Lisle, Lord K. said that he was a queer fellow, who impressed those under whom he was working immediately, more than those who stood altogether outside *or those who served immediately under him.*

He did not say much more than this, but I gather that several of the men who surround him have endeavoured *no doubt conscientiously and possibly correctly* to belittle De Lisle, with some success. In the earlier part of the war, I of course, knew him intimately, and I considered him quite the best man I had to work with. He is a strong character, and has always a clear and sensible opinion on any point. He has a good eye for country, and I personally think him, and I always shall continue to think him, unless I am convinced by ocular demonstration to the contrary, a determined and sagacious leader.

I must say, I do not think that anyone questions his determination.

He has, as you know a cavalry brigade under him, which is an unusual position for a young infantry officer, and one which has exposed him to some carping remarks, as he knows better than anybody else. The other day when orders came out, to cut down wheeled transport all round, De Lisle's cavalry regiments made some difficulty. They were warned that severe action would be taken, if they did not hand in their transport. The warning was disregarded and De Lisle burnt every stick of the transport then & there. This is no ordinary man.

Alderson is no use whatever, in the field. This is fully acepted by everyone. He becomes so excited under such conditions, that he really does no know what he is doing. On the other hand he is a first class Inspector General, *a sportsman popular, & with a good knowledge of men and horses.*

Pilcher is a very tough "cut and come again" customer. He is as full of energy and go now, as he was at the Dublin manoeuvres, or the first day he started on this campaign. He has not a very pleasant manner, and is not very popular, but all the same he is a good all round man, and valuable. *He is clever and educated as well as being keen and pushing.*

Douglas Haig, as you know, is one of the most thoughtful, educated, and large-minded of our staff officers. His reputation has lately been rather dwindling away, of inanition, as he does not seem to have been able to bring off any "coup", and, as far as fame goes, he might as well have been in winter quarters with his men, but I have heard nothing at all against him, or which would in any way lead me to think that he has actually fallen short of the high repute he had when you left South Africa.

Scobell is one of the very best leaders we have, but, alas, I fear there is very little use in my enlarging upon his merits, as his heart will never, I am told, enable him to take the field again.

With regard to Campbell, I think you know that I had always formed a very high opinion indeed of him, without, however, having had any opportunity of seeing him in the field. I gather that Lord K. whilst putting him far above the average, does not class him as high as you and I do. He has good sense, and energy, when roused, but is naturally rather self-indulgent and lazy, and is, to some extent, a bit of a humbug.

Mind you, Sir, I am giving you the weak points of everyone, and you must not lay too much stress on this part of my remarks.

Thorneycroft is an officer with a very good head upon him, most sensible and far-seeing. His men like him very much, and his personal gallantry is beyond all question.

The three or four months before he left, he was becoming *comparatively* useless, being worn out and lazy. I hope, to goodness, his leave will have put him all right again. I think a constitutional tendency to laziness is his chief drawback.

Henry is a curiously well marked instance of a man, who is a pushing good leader for a small attached column, while he is quite hopeless as a commander of anything larger, or acting on its own responsibility or initiative. The reason is an entire absence, not only of administrative ability, but of any power of grasping what administration means. If he took a force into the field entirely on his own arrangements, the first thing that would happen would be that horses and men would starve to death, it being much a matter of chance, which would come to the end of their supply first. *Such a statement sounds exaggerated but I think* you may rely upon it, for not only did I gather this, from Lord K., who, however, was rather more general, and contented himself with saying that he was useless for anything *independent* or important, but I have also heard it most emphatically, from men like Sclater, and the Ordnance, *who, like every one else are fond of the man personally.*

This ends your list, and I hope my victims are not altogether dead in your estimation. That is not my intention, for there is not one of them, who has not got excellent qualifications, if put to suitable work, and I think there are one or two of them, De Lisle, Haig, Scobell, and perhaps Thorneycroft, who would *do brilliant work anywhere.*

I enclose you a letter from Lord Methuen, to let you see what he says about B.P. I quite agree with him, and really I do not know what is going to become of the poor fellow. At times, he is as bright and clever as ever he was, and then he sinks suddenly into a vacant sort of a state, and with a look approaching imbecility on his face. I sincerely trust it is only physical, and that he will yet be able to pull himself together.

I do not trouble you with the more important matters, on which I know that you and Mr Brodrick are in direct correspondence with Lord Kitchener, as there is no use duplicating correspondence, but I must break my rule, just to make one remark about the Australian horses.

Before I left Johannesburg, I went, by special request, to see the shipment of Walers, that came in by the ship Norfolk, branded "J H." I never saw a more miserable lot of weeds. They were flat-sided, long-legged, split up to the tail, and absolutely the worst possible type you could imagine. I believe myself it would have saved the Government *a lot of money*, in the long run, to sell them for what they would have fetched in Johannesburg. There were hardly any of them you could expect to get fit before 3 months, and it was pretty obvious, that even then, at the end of that time, they would not do many marches, without getting sore backs. I think, whoever bought those horses ought to be *brought to book at once* and Birdwood tells me that the shipment, per the Fifeshire is even worse.

I like the look of the small Russian ponies extremely. It would not do to have all Russians, because they are very, very slow, and a regiment mounted on them would never be able to gallop down Boers, but they look as if they were very hardy. They eat anything, and I am told by column commanders, that when the better bred horses are stone cold, they are still able to raise a canter out of their Russians.

I have just sent you a wire telling you of Dunlop's success,[125] and also giving you rather fully the news from the Cape, of the capture of French's donkey-convoy,[126] with 160 men, and one or two other mishaps, in that part of the country. It is possible that Lord K. might think I had rather emphasized the disagreeable part of the news, at the expense of the good news. I do not think however, that I have done more than tell the exact truth, being anxious to convey to you an accurate impression of the real situation, for all my instincts warn me, that the danger just now is, that with things going as favo<u>rably as they are, *the press* and people of England may get into a state of exultation about South Africa, which would not be, in my opinion at least, warranted by the actual facts.

I may be wrong, but it seems to me that I see now a tendency amongst the people at home to harden their hearts, up to the point of refusing even to discuss a settlement, unless the Boers are first made to grovel for it. You know my views, as to what the result of such a policy will be, so I will not again enlarge upon them.

N.B. Finished by General (the day we went to Heidelberg).

LHCMA, Hamilton 2/3/16

98
Lieutenant-General Ian Hamilton to Lord Roberts
Feb 27th –/02

[Typescript copy]

Thank-you so much for your kind letter of February 1st. Victor Brooke is horrified to hear that my letter blew out of the window, owing to its being printed on tissue paper, and is taking steps to prevent the recurrence of this terrible misfortune.

I am now in the curious position of hearing a certain amount of outside gossip about the War Office, whilst I still, in a certain sense, am a member of that talented gang. Everyone seems to think that Kelly Kenny is doing remarkably well, and has thoroughly justified your choice. The only doubts ever expressed about him bear reference to his health, and as to whether that will enable him to stick it out very long.

I am delighted, beyond measure, to hear that you have really succeeded in decentralizing musketry from the War Office. I am sure that the War Office, itself, Hythe, and the Army generally, will all benefit by the changed conditions.

As regards canteens, and Army recreation rooms, I think Indian experience, not only shows that you are on the right lines, but also that with perseverance, you are bound to defeat the numerous hostile influences, with the greatest possible credit to yourself.

This capture of the Klerksdorp convoy[127] has stuck in my gizzard for the last two days, and filled me with melancholy, for as long as these sort of things go on, we can hardly expect the war to come to a close, and yet it is impossible to make such arrangements, as shall absolutely preclude the chance of such misfortunes.

We have very few details in yet, but it seems clear that the march of the empty convoy back to Klerksdorp was pretty accurately calculated, which is a matter, of course of A.B.C. and that a whip was then sent round to all the important commandoes, in the Western Transvaal, who were within a radius of some 60 or 70 miles, to meet at dawn on a particular day, and at a particular spot. The arrangement took some time, as is evident by the fact that the meeting place was perilously near (from the Boer point of view) to Klerksdorp. However it came off all right. Some of the Boers came 50 miles that night, just as our columns do now, when they wish to surprise a laager. Kekewich, who was out to the north, also made a night march to surprise a laager of the enemy, but naturally found the birds flown, they themselves being on the march to cut off our convoy.

As regards the actual fight, I do not myself see how 3 weak companies of infantry, a battalion of yeomanry, 2 guns and a pom-pom can hope to resist the determined attack of over a thousand men, if they are caught on the line of march. As you know a hundred waggons on bad roads take up, at least, a couple of miles, and this in [sic] an immense line to guard in a broken country.

I really think we shall come to having every tenth wagon a steel-lined blockhouse on wheels. That would do the trick absolutely, unless the Boers got hold of the guns, when the position of those in the ironclad wagon would become precarious. The C.R.E. has some admirable specimen wagons, ⅜ inch steel, entered by a trap-door from the bottom, and now the only thing is to persuade column commanders to take them, for use with their convoys. Lord Kitchener is away at Harrismith, so I do not know whether he will approve of my idea or not.

Garratt's New Zealanders, in Byng's column, made a proper mess of the Boers, the other day,[128] and a few more scrimmages of this description, will make them very shy of turning to break the line. It was fortunate that they happened on to the New Zealanders, who are about our best men, and who did not belie their reputation on this occasion. Any way, we all think that the big lot who did not succeed in forcing their way through, will find it harder than ever to screw up their courage to the sticking point, as the line draws on, and gets thicker and thicker, and so I think, with any decent luck, we ought to bring these fellows, whatever their numbers may be, into our bag.

Pretoria
Feb 28th

On coming in from my ride last night, I got the following personal wire from Lord K. "Harrismith. Feb 27th. 4 30 p.m. Majuba Day[129] so far produces 400 Stop Hope for many more as I have received few reports Stop Country seen from Platberg[130] is black with cattle being driven in." I was overjoyed, as you may imagine, at the splendid success of our scheme, and wired in reply:– "As an old Majuba man, pray accept my heart-felt congratulations on your felicitous master-stroke."[131]

I have had nothing more from Lord K. since, but I hear from the intelligence that there are over 600 prisoners, amongst them that nice old man, Commandant Truiter,[132] with whom I had that interesting conversation, when I was handing him over 23 dead bodies, from the point of Wagon Hill, at Ladysmith.[133] There are also, so the Intelligence say, 15,000 cattle, and 10,000 sheep. Altogether this is the biggest thing we have done for a long time.

What worries me most, I must say, is the way things seem to be going in Cape Colony. Of course I get down in my luck at a turn of bad fortune, like the capture of Von Donop's convoy,[134] but as I have tried to explain, it seems to me perfectly inevitable, that as long as the enemy have bands of 200, and upwards, within an area, wherein they can concentrate up to 700 or 800, by riding 50 miles, such accidents must inevitably happen, and are part of the game; – but in the Cape Colony there seems to be a certain slackness and want of efficiency all round.

Lord K. may ride rough-shod over people's feelings, and confiscate their cattle, horses, etc, with comparative impunity, because he makes up for this hardness of disposition, by a quite exceptional power of keeping everything, and everyone, bang up to the mark.

But, in the Cape Colony, whilst they seem just as inclined to ride rough-shod over private individuals, and their belongings and feelings, they do not, at least so it appears to me, compensate for it by working their own show properly, and thereby showing farmers that if they suffer, the Military, at any rate, are straining every nerve to put a period to the state of things, in which such disagreeable penalties are possible.

I sent you a wire this morning, in the name of Lord K. showing the exact position of the columns yesterday, which was the critical moment in the big drive.

You have never told me anything about my maps or my telegrams, whether you like them, or whether they have been sent to the House of Commons smoking-room. I hope, at any rate, someone benefits by being able to see, once a fortnight, how everyone really is placed.

Goodbye, Sir, for the present, I may be able to add a post script, after receipt of your letter, which I hope today's mail will bring.

LHCMA, Hamilton 2/3/18

99
Lord Roberts to Lord Kitchener

47 Portland Place. London. W.

[Holograph]

8th March. 1902.

Thanks for your two letters of the 7th February.[135] The "Quite Private" one I acted on without letting Brodrick know I had heard from you on the subject, and I don't think he will communicate with anyone again serving under you about matters which you should deal with. You were quite right to have all the replies about the stamp of horses, &c. sent to South Africa, submitted through you; in no other way could the Secretary of State get accurate and reliable information. I suppose it will be possible for us to continue sending you horses at the rate we have been doing lately but I observe that De Burgh, writing from New Orleans, does not seem hopeful of being able to get many more suitable animals in that part of the world. We have hardly tapped Russia yet, but I imagine that horses purchased in that country would have very long railway journeys before they could be shipped off – Montagu Gerard,[136] who has gone to Hungary, to enquire about the purchases of horses there, knows something of the resources of Russia, and he will be able to give us some information on the subject –

I hope you will think our proposals for increasing the pay of soldiers satisfactory and that you will approve of the altered conditions of service. I have long been an advocate for a 3 years' enlistment, provided sufficient inducements were held out for the required number of men for foreign service to re engage. And then we must have an ample reserve. This war has proved that 80,000 men are not enough to keep us going. Good conduct pay in its present form I have been averse to, I have always thought the extra pay should only be given to those who have proved themselves to be in all respects efficient soldiers. It will take some little time to ascertain whether the changes we have proposed will bring about the results we hope for – they are, however, in the right direction and have been generally well received.

I am looking forward with great interest to the next big "drive" you make. Though De Wet and Steyn both managed to escape, a good haul was made and I hope on the next occasion that the biggest fish will be landed. I have seen Scobell. He assures me he will be able to start in a month, and as he is most anxious to be transferred to his old regiment, I am telegraphing to you that this will be done, and suggesting you should make the command of the Greys over to Carr-Ellison[137] or anyone else you may think desirable as a temporary arrangement. I am asking also who you would recommend to succeed Scobell in the command at the 5th Lancers –

I am beginning to think we shall have to do without the four battalions of the Guards for the Coronation[138] and have warned the King this may be the case. It would never do to decrease your Infantry while the Blockhouse system is being extended, and I daresay we shall be able to manage with the scratch regiments we have at home.

239

I see Tucker and Rundle are both coming home. The latter will take up his own command at Dover, but what about the former? He will be 64 years of age next December, and must be retired unless he is promoted to Lieut. General's rank. Is he altogether good enough for employment as a Lieut. General? I wish you would send me a telegram as soon as you receive this and tell me exactly what you think of him.

NAM 7101–23–122–3–251

100
Lord Roberts to Lord Kitchener

47 Portland Place London W

[Manuscript copy]

14 March 1902.

I am afraid you have been a great deal worried since I last wrote to you – Methuens mishap occurred on the very day I was writing, it naturally caused a certain amount of excitement in this country – The mere fact of a General being captured made the public think that it was a bigger business than it really was – but on the whole people were fairly reasonable – I was glad to get your telegram yesterday saying that Methuen was expected to be at Klerksdorp during the day, and I hope soon to hear that his wound is progressing satisfactory, but a shattered thigh bone is not a pleasant thing while being jolted in a springless wagon over the rough Veldt[139] – I said a few words in the house about Methuen as I was afraid that the Press would refer to what happened in 1899,[140] and ask why he was not sent home then – My remarks were well received, and had a good effect I was told in the House of Commons, and the country generally – I have no doubt you are quite right not to move much from Cape Colony, and I should have hesitated even to suggest it, had you not in one of your letters said you were inclined to put French in charge of the operations in the N.E. of Orange River Colony, but you feared the change might be misunderstood and cause alarm in the Cape Colony – I feel sure you are wise not to give the Boers a chance South of the Orange River, and, as your brother is available to take Methuens place in the Western Transvaal, there is no reason to move French – I telegraphed to you about Paget, Pole Carew &c. because the King spoke to me about their being sent out, and I told His Majesty I did not wish to order any senior officer to South Africa without first consulting you –

Personally I am in favour of Paget being employed – He may be difficult with those above him, but I thought he did well when he had an independant command North of Pretoria – Pole Carew is of a different stamp, and has not sufficient self reliance or military acumen to be left to himself –

Your telegram (S.918) of the 12th instant[141] about Schalk Burgher [sic] making peace proposals is intensely interesting, and I long to hear that his visit to Steyn will bring about some satisfactory result – but I am almost afraid that they are not likely to propose any terms which you and Milner could accept. I am glad you have recommended Allenby for Command of the 5th Lancers – He will be gazetted shortly, and Scobell transferred back to the Greys – Sprott I never believed could be an efficient commander – who do you think should take his place?

I inspected the 3rd Lincoln and 3rd East York Militia yesterday on Salisbury plain – They leave for South Africa in a few days – They struck me as being rather a good lot of men, but both Battalions are weak, a little over 500 Each – I am glad you are arranging for the four Battalions of Guards which went out first to come home in time for the Coronation if the war is over – If it is not I have told the King you could not possibly spare them –

NAM 7101–23–122–3–254

101
Lieutenant-General Ian Hamilton to Lord Roberts

Pretoria.

[Typescript copy]

April 1st 1902.

The mail only left yesterday, so I am carrying out your precepts, and losing no time in beginning my weekly budget.

Clements has just been in here, looking extremely bright and efficient. He certainly is a most soldierly fellow, so much so, that I think it would pay you, even now, to overlook his curious little angles and defects of character, and regard him as a man with a possible future. He told me a really amusing story about Mrs Neville Lyttelton.[142]

You know, I think, how very bustling and managing she can be, and I think I have told you already how, when she was here, she discussed to any extent what she was going to do as Commander in Chief, and actually selected a site (and a very nice one too) for the Head Quarters of that official. But to return, however, to my story: she went down from Durban to Cape Town in the same ship as Ben Viljoen.[143] De Gex,[144] on Clement's Staff, was looking after Ben Viljoen, when she sent him a message to say she would like to have a talk with him. Viljoen said "All right, I do not mind, but I hope she will not be long, for I am feeling most desperately seasick." De Gex brought Mrs Neville up, and she talked to poor Ben for a solid two and a half hours.

At the end of the conversation, he was an awful sight, and the moment she went, he turned to De Gex and exclaimed:– "My God! Is she a political woman, or is she writing a book?" This is an absolute fact, and these absolute facts are always really more amusing than the best inventions.

I think your Remount Committee[145] ought to do very well, and for the reasons you have stated, except that poor old Tommy Cook[146] will, I expect, be a pure cipher.

I enclose you, privately, a letter I received from Harry Rawlinson. Although I suspect that you and I do not look at the political part of this South African question from quite the same stand-point, I think we would agree that Milner is trying to bite off more than he can chew, in planning to exercise despotic control over a vast continent, such as the two late republics, plus the Cape Colony, certainly is. I knew instinctively Lord Milner did hold the views, which he has now given expression to, but I hardly expected that he would go quite as far in declaring them. Anyway, if the Conference[147] breaks down, in about three weeks time from now, when you get this letter, you will have a very shrewd idea of one of the reasons. After all it seems to me that the points to be discussed at this Conference have narrowed themselves down to a very great extent, so much so that they are practically comprised in this:– Are we prepared to put down on paper all that we really intend giving them, and get their formal agreement to it, in the shape of regular terms of peace, or are we going to refuse to make any formal promises, and persist in what I have already described as the policy of inviting the most suspicious person on earth, to throw away his rifle, shut his eyes, open his mouth, and see the nice thing we shall put into it.

I feel fairly confident, from my many letters received from the officers in charge of these delegates, that there will be no break down of negotiations on any material point. That is to say, what we are already bound, as sensible proprietors of land, as well as by the requirements of our political constitution to give them, is really sufficient to satisfy them, but they want to know it first, and have it in black and white, of the strictest and most definite description. Personally, I think they are perfectly right, and if I was entering into an agreement with Mr Chamberlain, I would keep a sharp eye to see that there were no loopholes in the contract. I may be quite wrong, and perhaps you, for instance, or even Mr Brodrick, would unhesitatingly shut your eyes and open your mouths to Mr Chamberlain, but, if so, I fear I must be growing awfully suspicious in my old age, for I should await the result of such an experiment with many misgivings.

From all I can hear, we have nothing whatever to regret, except the sad but inevitable loss of life, in Lawley's sharp action East of Springs.[148] I believe the Bays under Fanshawe were very steady, under certainly difficult circumstances, and the 7th Hussars lost no time in coming to their assistance, and did so with an energy which has sometimes been wanting in recent operations. There is no doubt at all that the Boers have lost heavily, and I hope that during the next ten days or so we shall be able to arrange a proper round up for these gentlemen, who are distinctly "matter in the wrong place" in this cleared area, as they are too near the vitals of the country. The Boer prisoners taken by Lawley told him that they thought it a beastly "chouse" on the part of the Bays to attack them, as they had heard there was a peace conference on, and this was consequently no time for fighting. They added that, being in superior numbers, they had meant to attack Lawley on the Sunday, but they considered it a pity to lose life, when, politically speaking, peace appeared to be so imminent.

The latest from the Orange River Colony is that all the women are now most anxious for peace, and poor things, I dare say they well may be.

Our last drive there has not been much of a success, and the Boers in those parts are getting too knowledgeable about drives, although no amount of knowledge will render it less disagreeable to them to be hustled about for several days, and then to be forced to run the gauntlet in a thunderstorm at midnight, leaving most of their cattle and belongings behind them.[149]

This terrible "corvée" is greatly weighing me down, and must again account for my coming to a dead stop here.

I am praying very earnestly that things may go well for the next few weeks, and that the Boers will not be able to score anything, which they could by any possibility represent, either to themselves or to others, as a success. They are politically as sharp as needles, and fully appreciate the advantage it would be to them, in their negotiations, to make an opportune military score at our expense.

LHCMA, Hamilton 2/3/22

102
Lord Roberts to Lord Kitchener
47 Portland Place. London. W.

[Manuscript copy]

11th April, 1902.

We are all in anxiety, as you may imagine, to know what the result of the meeting between you and the Boer Chiefs will be. The Transvaalers, no doubt, are for peace, but I am almost afraid Steyn and De Wet will propose terms such as it would be impossible for you to accept. I see you anticipate something of the sort in your telegram No S.967. cipher despatched this morning.[150] It is an intensely interesting time, and I wish I were at Pretoria now.

I inspected 1000 Guardsmen this morning, who will embark to-morrow in the Canada. They are nearly all Reservists, and many of them have been in South Africa already. These will be followed by about 7000 ordinary Infantry drafts, some 6000 Yeomanry, and 1000 Artillery. The last named will be put through a course of musketry first, and 50 of them will be drivers as you desired.

"Ghazi" Hamilton[151] called this morning. He looks a little thin, but otherwise well. I will see if it is possible to employ him at home in training Yeomanry. It would be better for him to be here than in South Africa.

Ridley also called to-day. He sails in the Canada tomorrow. He complained that scarcely over half the South African Constabulary are mounted, and when I asked him why he did not represent this strongly when he was in command, he said he did not like to give his Corps away. I told him I could not agree with him and that it was his duty not to leave a stone unturned in endeavouring to get his corps efficient.

Plumer has not arrived yet.

I am so glad you recommended a second medal being given in commemoration of the Coronation, instead of Honours to officers – Only a certain number of the latter could be rewarded, whereas a medal would include every one who has been in South Africa since the Queen's death. I have constantly advocated a second medal, Brodrick does not object, and the King is anxious for it, but the Cabinet have opposed it. However, I hope it will be given now. The whole of the Spion Kop despatches will be published early next week,[152] and I fancy all the telegrams, &c from Buller to White, in fact everything that occurred before Colenso will have to be made public. The 2nd volume of "The Times" history of the war is, I hear, ready.[153] That I am told deals with Colenso business. Neither the despatches nor the History will be very pleasant reading for Buller, but he has only himself to thank for the former being published. We all wished to spare him as much as possible, but the demonstrations in Hyde Park, and the injudicious interference of his friends made this impossible.

Goodbye, I long for you to be able to bring the war to a close. What a welcome we will give you.

NAM 7101–23–122–3–263

103
Lord Roberts to Lord Kitchener

47 Portland Place, London, W.

[Manuscript copy]

18th April, 1902.

Affairs with you seem to be progressing satisfactorily, and your two telegrams S.982 cipher and S.983 cipher of yesterday[154] make me feel very hopeful that the Boer representatives will see the advisability of giving in to the terms you have been authorized to offer them. Their pressing to have time to consult "their burghers" does not, I fancy, mean much, for, unless we have been mistaken, it is the leaders and not the burghers who have been holding out. We must have patience now for the fortnight or three weeks you predict it will take before the representatives return to Pretoria, meanwhile I hope that Ian Hamilton will meet with further successes. His affair the other day when Potgieter was killed seems to have been well managed, and must have made Delarey feel sad.[155]

As peace really appears within the bounds of possibility in the near future, I should like to consult you about the military arrangements when you give over the command. As you will remember, I proposed that Lyttelton should succeed you – Milner wished this too – but at first and until the country settles down, I am inclined to think that it would be better to limit Lyttelton's command to the Transvaal and the Orange River Colony. To appoint another officer (with Lieut General's rank if you think proper) to command in the Cape Colony, and a Colonel on the Staff or a Major-General in Natal.

Who would you suggest for the Cape Colony and Natal? Methuen will, of course, come home as soon as he can travel.

French is required at home to take up the Aldershot command.

Tucker might be allowed to enjoy a long honeymoon, as I gather you do not require him again in South Africa. Barr Campbell showed me the telegram giving him leave, from which I imagine he is not wanted back

There remain Barton, Hart, C. Knox, Clements, Stephenson, W. Knox, Maxwell, Inigo Jones, Bruce Hamilton, Fetherstonhaugh, Settle, Willson, Oliphant and Brook.

Who of all these would you propose for Cape Colony and who for Natal? And who of the remainder do you think should be given commands at home?

Amongst the more junior officers I should like to employ here Plumer, Dixon (unless he is required for S.A.) Vyvyan (unless Do. Do.), Rawlinson and any others you may recommend.

Now, with regard to yourself, I would like you to come home as soon as possible after peace is made, and I fancy this would be your own wish, but I hope you will not hurry away. A great deal will have to be done before the country quiets down, and many important military matters will have to be settled [......?] the past year with Brodrick and the Cabinet on the matter of adopting drastic measures against officers for failures. I am now drawing up a memorandum on the subject, and I have arranged with Brodrick that all disciplinary telegrams are to be sent to you by me and not by him.

NAM 7101–23–122–3–267

104
Lord Roberts to Lord Kitchener

47 Portland Place W.

[Manuscript copy]

26th April 1902.

A good many things have happened in South Africa since you wrote your letter of the 30th March, and none more interesting than the interviews you had with the Boer representatives. I could not help wishing to be with you and see them all. Before this letter reaches you we shall probably know what their decision is, and I shall be greatly surprised if they do not give in. I think it is a good sign Schalk Burger going with Steyn and Delarey.

He will perhaps be able to convince them of the uselessness of continuing the war. Then there is a report that Mrs. Schalk

Burger and Mrs. Botha have both started back to the Cape, which looks as if they expected to be able to soon join their husbands.

Brodricks telegram of the 22nd instant No 706 Cipher – must have somewhat puzzled you giving the capitulation of Lee in the American Civil War as the example to follow in your dealings with the Boers. As soon as I saw the telegram I looked up the terms of Lee's surrender, and I cannot see how they could be in any way a guide to you.[156] I believe Chamberlain inspired the telegram, his nice American wife[157] may have told him something more of the terms than I can find in any book. I enclose a copy of the terms.

Brodrick is somewhat concerned at your thinking   he supported Chamberlain's and Milner's view about making the I.M.R. railways over to the civil government. He tells me he agreed to the proposal on condition that you concurred in it. I have explained to him that while war lasts you must have absolute control over these railways and I am glad you intend to resist any change being made should the matter be brought forward again, and if you want help send me a cipher telegram, I am sure I shall be able to prevent anything of the sort being carried out.

I enclose extracts from the D.M.T.'s diary which made me telegraph to you (No 703 cipher) on the 21st instant about Mr. Halse having informed Methuen on the 6th March that he would be attacked by the Boers in force the next morning.[158]

Your reply No S.991 Cipher reached me yesterday.[159]

We have had some difficulty with Sir Francis ...... in regard to General Courts-Martial on officers. I proposed that you should have the power of confirming the sentences as is the practise in India. He argued it would be unfair to the officers who like to think that their cases are submitted to the King before being finally decided. I brought up the Indian custom again, and with the result that the power was placed in your hands. Unfortunately the first General Court Martial sent home under the new rules somewhat supported ...... contention that officers officiating as Judge Advocate Generals are not sufficiently versed in Law to warrant the conduct of Courts-Martial being left altogether with them. I allude to the trial of 2nd Lieut. J.H. Cantloy 4/norfolk, for giving cheques which were dishonoured.

Pemberton, who acted as J.A. General summed up very weakly, and there was no evidence to show that the prisoner knew that he had not sufficient funds at Cox & Co's to meet his cheques.

...... has been told to return the proceedings to you for such action as you and your legal advisors may think necessary.

It would be as well to warn St. Clair[160] and his assistants that their work is being very carefully scrutinized by the J.A. General here.

You will, no doubt, make it very clear when coming to terms with the Boers that the prisoners can only be allowed to return to South Africa by degrees. I wanted this entered in the telegram to you but Brodrick thought we should be able to arrange this by not engaging the necessary transports. It would be better I think to lay it down clearly, for pressure will certainly be brought to bear on the government, when peace is made, to release all the prisoners at once. Tucker called upon me a day or two ago, and so did Plumer. Please telegraph on receipt of this whether you want Tucker back. He might do for the Cape Colony Command perhaps?

NAM 7101–23–122–3–270

105
Lord Roberts to Lord Kitchener

47 Portland Place W

[Manuscript copy]

9 May 1902.

Just after I had despatched my last letter, I received yours of 13th instant with your account of your meetings with the Boer delegates – Ten days hence I hope we shall hear the result of the conference at Vereeniging – if it is not for peace I shall be terribly disappointed, for I have made up my mind that they would never have consented to meet you unless they had felt that further opposition would be useless[161] – The successful drive you have just had <at> Vredefort Road, Heilbron and Lindley should leave a beneficial effect,[162] as should the destruction of crops which has been carried out by Ian Hamiltons Columns in the Western Transvaal –[163]

Then it seems to me that the sight of Johannesburg and Pretoria gradually settling down cannot but fail to impress the Delegates, as must the news of the reinforcements we keep sending out to you – Scobell was with me yesterday. He is to see the King on Monday, and sails for South Africa a few days later. He looks well and says he is quite sound again.

The question of clasps for the new medal was discussed the other day at the War Office Council, and it was thought for those who have the late Queens Medal, the only clasp on the Kings Medal should be "South Africa 1901–2" – but that those who only got the Kings Medal should have in addition, clasps for the Colonies in which they may have served – Will you approve of this –

The Coronation is approaching and stands are being erected in all direction<s> – the 26th 27th & 28th will be three trying days for some people – Coronation on the first, Procession on the 2nd and Naval review on the 3rd. It is to be hoped the weather will be propitious –

10.5.02. I hope that the announcement about Natal taking over a portion of South Eastern Transvaal[164] will not have the effect you anticipate, it would be very unfortunate if that were the case – I rather hoped it would help to convince Botha, whose property is in that part, it would be best for him to make terms –

This is a short letter but I have no news to give you today –

NAM 7101–23–122–3–277

106
Lieutenant-General Ian Hamilton to Lord Roberts[165]

In the Veldt
near the Groot Harts River

[Typescript copy]

May 18th 1902.

Thank-you so very much for your kind letter of April 12th only just received.

I have a very great deal to tell you, but as you know trekking with a large force does not give many opportunities for literary effort, and one portion of your letter appears to me to touch on a subject of such supreme importance to the future efficiency of our Army that I shall have to devote most of my time to its discussion. You tell me that there is a very strong feeling in the Cabinet, that officers in command of columns should be brought to book for failures, presumably by trial by Court Martial.[166]

I think it as [sic] possible Mr Brodrick might like to hear my views, as lately Chief of the Staff, and as Commander, at present, of some 10,000 men, embodied in 16 columns. I feel confident also that Lord Selbourne, with whom I have had the privilege of a considerable number of rides and interesting conversations, would be willing to give an ear to my views. But, in any case, the great thing is to put them clearly before you, although I do not feel there is likely to be any serious difference of opinion between us. You do not, however, give me your own ideas, except that you refer to the analogy of the navy. By using this analogy it may no doubt be possible to argue that army officers should not mind being tried by Court Martial – eels are said to become used to skinning – and perhaps it may be true that habit coupled with conscious innocence may allow a naval officer to think little of the Court Martial by which he is white-washed. The Army, however, is the most conservative body existing now on God's earth, and it will not be at any rate during your tenure of office, that this Army will accustom itself to treating Courts Martial as a matter of routine.

I shall therefore assume that it is considered a disgrace to be tried by Court Martial, whatever the verdict of that Court Martial may be. Now what will the effect be of suspending such a penalty, like the sword of Damocles, over the head of every Commander? I say positively that it will have the effect of determining him to take no chances and run no risks. As it is, there are only a select few, who will take their hardly earned reputation in both hands, and run the chance of a serious failure for the sake of what they think is the better chance of a big success.

If you march your Army about, like the Chinese do, with an executioner to punish mistakes, you will hang a log round the neck of every commander, except possibly the very, very few, who are perhaps born fatalists, and who will do their best, whatever

251

happens. The Chinese cut the General's head off if he fails; it is proposed by us to impose what, to put it as mildly as possible, must be described as an intensely painful ordeal, which would to many be a punishment worse than the first. During a war which lasts for nearly three years, only the supremely fortunate or culpably cautious (as distinguished from the most capable) can hope to escape occasional failures.

On this particular point I am not quite sure, Sir, that we are in complete agreement. You say, for instance that "nearly all the late mishaps have been caused by want of knowledge of the enemy's movements, and instead of our pouncing down on them, they have pounced down on us". This is no doubt true, and I will not enter now into any defence of the Commanders who have been surprised, although I think in several instances I might make out a very fair case for them. What I would urge, however, in defence of our Army, as a whole, is that, in making this statement, you do not give us our fair share of credit for the repeated occasions on which we have pounced down on the enemy, in their own country, instead of letting them pounce down upon us.

No army can expect, during a long campaign to be uniformly victorious; there must be failures, and there must be occasional reverses, if we are fighting that is to say with a foeman worthy of our steel. But I do think that if our successes, as a whole, more than compensate for our reverses we ought not to be too impatient.

Delarey surprised, at different times Clements,[167] Methuen[168] and Von Donop,[169] but how often has not Bruce Hamilton surprised Botha?[170] And I venture humbly to remind Your Lordship, that during the last month I have three times surprised the army of Delarey, and done him, I think I may say, as much damage as he has done us since the commencement of the war.[171] Surely, in the nature of things it is his turn now to score something! If I fight a man with my fists, I should be only too glad to get one hit from him for every three I gave him.

As to the information, General Cronje[172] tells me that Delarey removed every doubtful kaffir from the Western Transvaal a year ago, and if Woolls Sampson [sic] were here, instead of at Johannesburg, he would confirm this.

After all, Sir, are not the failures punished as severely as any Cabinet Minister could desire? The penalty may not be so prompt, or so widely advertised as in the case of trial by Court Martial, but real failure, as distinguished from the occasional unavoidable failure, has practically ended the careers of those who have met with it. Look at Buller,[173] Colville,[174] Talbot Coke,[175] Warren,[176] Brocklehurst,[177] Burn Murdock,[178] Gatacre,[179] Clery,[180] Carrington,[181] to name only the very big men who have hopelessly gone under. What additional satisfaction could have been gained by trying these men by Court Martial?

Then again, you have a large class of senior officers, whom perhaps it is wiser not to name, who may be lingering on in appointments, but will never go any further, entirely as a result of failure more or less pronounced during this war.

I really do think, Sir, South Africa has claimed sufficient victims, without bringing in the terrors of the law.

I have said enough about this now, perhaps too much; I would only reiterate my opinion, that if penalties are introduced for failure, especially trial by Court Martial, you will paralize [sic] some of your best men, who will let unrivaled opportunities slip because they contain in them the germ of a mishap, with its consequent immediate and pronounced disgrace. If a man *cannot manage to succeed with the inducements of patriotism*, honour, and "la gloire" do not let the Cabinet imagine that they can whip him into brilliancy by the fear of punishment. As it is, I am fully satisfied, that in 9 cases out of 10, column commanders who do nothing, month after month, with fine forces at their disposal, and who let opportunity after opportunity slip do so, not from any fear of the Boers, but simply from that fear of loss of reputation and disgrace, which you tell me it is now proposed actually to accentuate.

You may be surprised at my displaying so much earnestness on this point. One reason may be that the shoe pinches me personally. Let me give you a very recent instance.

When the right of my line was attacked the other day by Potgieter, the enemy were, as you know, driven off after a sharp and brilliant fight leaving 47 dead, including their Commander on the ground.[182] The mass of the enemy seemed to have retired South, but we knew that at least 300 had passed round our right flank, and were in the bush immediately behind our convoy. I ordered, as you know, Kekewich, and such of Rawlinson's men as were under my hand at the moment, to pursue, and Walter Kitchener, who was nearly 20 miles distant, to move rapidly so as to put himself across the enemy's line of retreat. Kekewich at once referred to his convoy, and to the risk of leaving it when we did not know precisely where the Boers had gone, or in what numbers they had moved in each direction. If I had chosen to play the safe game, I had already achieved a considerable success, and it was quite unnecessary, looked at from the point of view of my own reputation, to run any further risk. Feeling assured of Lord Kitchener's support, however, and being always inclined to back my own luck, I started in pursuit, first of all laagering up the convoy it is true, but by no means leaving it in a position which could be termed thoroughly satisfactory or safe.

We pursued 18 miles, took 2 guns and a pom-pom, found 4 more dead, and captured some 50 or 60 prisoners. All the time I was thinking of this blessed convoy, which I had left in a bad position, with an uncertain number of Boers in close proximity to it, and without any very strong guard; but I felt that, on the whole, taking the character of the enemy, and all other circumstances into consideration, the chances of success outweighed those of failure; moreover I felt pretty sure, that even if something did happen to the convoy, I should be able to satisfy Lord Kitchener that I had had justification for my action.

If, however, I had known that some outside power might force Lord K. to try me by Court Martial, if that convoy had been scuppered, I think it is quite possible that those two guns and the pom-pom might be still in Delarey's hands.

Our ancestors looked at these matters from a very different standpoint. They did not try men for attacking the enemy, and being beaten but, notoriously in the case of Admiral Byng, for not taking their risks, and *attacking*. If the Cabinet would insist on trying every Commander who, with a fine force at his command, and Boers within striking distance, had let the opportunity slip, simply because he thought there was just the off chance that he might get the worst of it: then I would cry bravo, set to work as soon as you like. There are a good number of such men, and it is they, and not the men who try and fail, who should be hauled before Courts Martial, if it is necessary to appease the British public. *On the other hand such negative crimes are hard to bring home to anyone only, in time, it gets to be understood that such & such commanders are "sticky".*[183]

One word more. If the Cabinet want to try people for failures, I presume they wish to do it because they think the public would like it; at least this is probably one of their reasons. If ever a man has to be tried on the failure principle, surely it is Lord Methuen; very well, then, try Lord Methuen, and I wish the Cabinet joy over the job, although I think they are more likely to get vexations and unpopularity.

Seventeenthly, and lastly, one final word with regard to the misleading analogy of the Navy; it seems to me hardly possible to compare the two things. If a man loses his ship in peace time, it is either an act of culpable negligence, or it is the act of God, but the ordinary cause of a military failure is the act of the enemy.

The only parallel I can think of in the Army, which would be equivalent to a man losing his ship in peace time, would be if a colonel took a cavalry regiment, at a gallop, over ground he ought to have known well, and landed them at the bottom of a chalk-pit, or if an Infantry Colonel, thinking to save time, marched his battalion through a tunnel, and met an express train in the middle of it.

Take it the other way, the only parallel I can think of in the Navy to a soldier suffering disaster in the field, would be if the Capt of a ship saw that he could destroy the enemy's fleet by passing through a certain channel, which might or might not be mined. Supposing he took his chances and got there, he would achieve a great success, supposing he lost his ship in the endeavour, would he be tried by Court Martial? I understand from you that he would. If so, all I can say is, more is the pity.

I have read your proposed modification of the Artillery Drill Book, and I think I need not tell you that I absolutely agree with

255

the amendment in question. I would put it even more strongly myself, and that is the only remark I have to make, except that, at the very end, instead of speaking of "other units of the same arm" I should say "with units of all arms". I am sending the paper on to Sclater, and I will ask him to write you direct about it.

I am enchanted to hear what you say about the chances of getting a second medal. It will be enormously appreciated by the troops, especially if it can be arranged that no-one shall wear the [sic], who has not put in a total of 18 months service in South Africa. Some people say a year, but this, I think, would be too short a time.

I have a sort of idea you asked me once before why Surtees[184] was given a D.S.O. instead of a C.B. The reason he did not get a C.B. is that he was notoriously incapable. The reason he got a D.S.O. is that he had just enough saving commonsense to let Granville Smith,[185] the 2nd in Command, and Marker, the Adjutant, run his battalion for him, which they did to everyone's satisfaction. No doubt Surtees may be able to get at some people to say he was a good commander, especially as he is really quite a nice fellow. If, however, you want to be quite sure about the matter, which was notorious out here, ask Kerry to take the opinion of any Capt or field officer in the Brigade of Guards on the subject, and I think you will find the D.S.O. is considered by them a very ample recognition.

I had tea two days ago with Mrs and Miss Delarey,[186] and found neither of them very attractive. They did not seem to me at all in the same class as the General himself.

P.S. [in longhand] *When we went West all the Boer women were breathing fire and flame. Now these same ladies are very nice and polite and say that as we have proved ourselves as good as their men they are willing to give our Govt. a fair trial.*

LHCMA, Hamilton 2/3/28

107
Lord Roberts to Lord Kitchener

47 Portland Place W

[Manuscript copy]

23 May 1902.

There is just a chance before this letter has to be posted I may hear that the Cabinet have agreed to approve of the proposals contained in your telegram of the 21st May (No. 1023 Cipher)[187] – As I told Brodrick yesterday they appear to me most reasonable, and certainly sufficiently liberal to satisfy anyone but an out-and-out irreconcilable – In the event of the Cabinet approval – I presume peace may be looked upon as certain, now that Botha and Delarey are prepared to break off with De Wet if he demurs to our terms (your S.1025 of yesterday)[188] – What a blessing it would be – I have longed for the war to be over and for you to have a good rest before taking up the command in India – Curzon named October as the month in which he would like you to join, but there is really no reason why you should hurry out, and, if you cannot manage to leave South Africa so as to admit of getting three or four clear months at home, you should put off your arrival in India until after October –

I have been going through your list of rewards, and think you have made a very good selection – There will probably be some difficulty about the C.M.G's for Chamberlain has refused to give any more to soldiers, however his heart may soften when he thinks of the peace, and is reminded what soldiers have done for him in South Africa –

I enclose his reply to your suggestion about one or two Boer leaders being sent home to take part in the Coronation Ceremony – Chamberlain evidently is not much in favour of it, and Lord Lansdowne thinks the same; Botha, Delarey, and one or two others would, I believe, be generally well received, but some ill conditioned people might make it uncomfortable for them – So on the whole we had better let the matter rest –

Tucker came to me yesterday, he starts for South Africa early next month in the Canada –

I am glad you have recommended H. Hamilton for an A.D.C ship to the King – A Military Secretary who has done well at such a time of difficulty deserves to be rewarded –

The only person I am doubtful about is M. Willson – He was not apparently a success in the field, and if made a K.C.B. he will expect a high command when he comes home – Making Settle a Major General seems to me all right, but I am telegraphing to you to ask whether E. Wood should not be made one also to protect his supersession – Nothing has come from Brodrick and I must close this, as I leave early tomorrow for Aldershot –

NAM 7101–23–122–3, p. 302

108
Lieutenant-General Ian Hamilton to Lord Roberts[189]

Pretoria.

[Typescript copy]

May 25th 1902.

I have just got here, having come up hurriedly in a truck, in order to be at Lord K's elbow throughout this crisis.

I have received your delightful letter of 2nd May, which seems an extraordinarily quick delivery to me now that I have been away so long from Head Quarters, and out on the veldt where mails are almost as irregular as they used to be long ago.

You are quite right, Sir, I am enchanted about the second medal, and I <u>do</u> value decorations, but may I humbly suggest that Your Lordship also is not so philosophical as to regard these pretty toys with complete indifference. Lord K. has made me President of a Committee, with the A.G. and M.S. as members, and we are to meet this afternoon and make our recommendation, which he may forward by to-night's mail to England.

It is a little difficult to speak without the book, but I think you are mistaken when you say that remarkably few gunners have come to the front. You say you can think of none except Keir, Butcher, Dawkins. Dawkins is very good and reliable, but distinctly slow; Keir and Butcher are all right, but cannot be placed much above fairly good – I mean of course in the capacity of Column Commanders. Aleck Rochfort is facile princeps amongst the gunners, so far as I have seen. He is a real good stirling commander; he is beloved by his men; he is willing to take any appointment which will enable him to see service, however humble it may be; he never makes the smallest difficulty about carrying out orders; he has no fear that I can see of responsibility, and when there are enemy about he is all for fighting; he is not what you would call a very clever man, but he has got good brains all the same.

Wing is also a very good and successful gunner, of the Rochfort type, but just a littl<e> behind him all round. I dare say if you look up my written characters, you may find that what I am writing now does not agree with them. If this is so, you must not take it as weakening my present statement, but only as showing how even the most carefully written characters must be incomplete, unless they are compiled by an individual who has been actually working in the field with the men on whom he is reporting. I have now been working with Keir, Dawkins, Rochfort and Scott, so I know them in a very different sense from what I did when I wrote you before. I was almost forgetting about Scott and Von Donop, both of whom have been under me. They are both excellent, but I think I shall have to write an appendix to my list of characters, to bring out their special points, for although they are both excellent they are very different types of men. Dunlop also has done right well. Dunlop and Von Donop are men of soldierly qualities, both a little rough and hard, and perhaps wanting in breadth of view and culture; in the field, however, I should call them thoroughly reliable good leaders, though not men of very great scope. I would like to go on, but I must stop this, as I literally have not got the time.

I thank you Sir 10,000 times for wiring me about Edwina.[190] It was the greatest relief to Rawlinson and myself.

Things are extremely exciting here just now, and, as far as our Government, Lord K., and the Boers are concerned, all looks very hopeful. The only danger is the one I have always anticipated. Lord K. has had an extraordinarily difficult task. Lord Milner says himself he is no diplomatist, and certainly it is always difficult to diplomatise in double harness. I must not discuss this further, but if ever the Minutes are published,[191] I think you will say that I have not misled you in my previous letters on the subject. It is curious to me to look back now on the Bloemfontein Conference,[192] and to realize that, under the circumstances, this bloody war was bound to be the result. So far, I believe that this result was little short of providential from an Imperial point of view, but the time has now come when we want quite another sort of wind up to the palaver.

I dined with Gen. Delarey last night – the occasion was the birthday of Smuts[193] – I sat between Botha and Delarey, on Botha's right was De Wet, on Delarey's left Smuts. I told Gen. Delarey that Tucker has got married. He said "Why he must be 60"[194]   I replied "Yes, but the lady also is no chicken" on which he rejoined:– "I hope, then, the clergyman may preach to them from the text:– Father forgive them, for they know not what they do –" I had the most enchanting evening, and never wish to meet better company. They told me a great many stories about the war, which it would give me much joy to repeat to you now, only I must go on with other business I fear. I may mention that the Boer losses at Colenso were 5 killed, 1 drowned, 23 wounded;[195] at Wagon Hill 77 killed (picked up), 30 missing, 200 to 250 wounded;[196] at Magersfontein, which I had thought their most severe knock, but which turns out to have been only second, 72 killed, and a proportionate number of wounded.[197]

Delarey and De Wet both told me exciting stories of their escapes, and it would interest you to know, on Botha's authority, that at Diamond Hill[198] a message from Delarey on his right, saying that he had got French in the hollow of his hand and could smash him as soon as the order was given, actually crossed a message from Tobias Smuts on the left of Botha's line, saying De Lisle had seized a position threatening their line of retreat, which latter message forced Botha to retire in a terrible hurry.

P.S. Later. My Committee with Kelly and Hubert Hamilton on the new Medal is just over. Our proceedings did not take the shape of a formally signed Report, but only of a rough draft for Lord Kitchener's guidance.

My position was very awkard, as it was impossible for me to make a fight for my own ideas without its seeming as if I was working for myself: possibly I was doing so unconsciously, but I think not. They wanted to make the service to reckon for the second medal continous service of 18 months. I felt I was not only speaking for myself, but for a large number of very deserving Officers and Men in the Army when I combatted this as likely to cause cruel injustice. Suppose a man serves with distinction for 17 months and then gets covered with veld sores and generally run down so that he has to take 3 months leave home. He comes out and does another 17 months when peace is signed. He will then have done 2 years and 10 months service in South Africa, and yet will not get the second medal, whereas another man who happens to have served 19 months straight on end will get the two medals. Even General Kelly saw this, and they both agreed that, after all, the main thing was the amount of good War service given out here in the aggregate, and not the mere accident that it was uninterrupted service. Whilst granting this however, they pressed that the term should be longer than has hitherto been named by anyone I have spoken to on the subject, viz: 18 months. They are very anxious indeed to limit the number of people to get the medal as much as possible, and it would have been rude of me to have suggested that possibly they were slightly influenced by the fact that they themselves had been out for a very long period. I therefore gave way on this point and let them put in 2 years, but I still hope that Lord Kitchener will recognise that this is too long. Even if I personally lose the Medal by it I shall feel consoled by feeling that I have put the matter right as regards continuous service being any sort of qualification as compared with aggregate service. Numbers of these people who would score by continous service over men who had put in much longer in the country have, as a matter of fact, had repeated spells of 2 or 3 weeks at Capetown, which, though thoroughly safe, enjoyable and remote from the perils and hardships of War, nevertheless does not break into the continuity of their service.

LHCMA, Hamilton 2/3/29

Epilogue
31 May 1902 and Beyond
Peace and Aftermath
Introduction

The Boer delegates had to accept the British proposals no later than midnight on 31 May 1902. The 'acts of peace', or rather the conditions under which the Boers would surrender, contained ten clauses, including the following: all burghers had to lay down their arms and recognise the British monarch as their legitimate sovereign; all Boer POWs could return on condition that they became British subjects (i.e. they had to sign a declaration that they accepted the terms of surrender); the burghers and repatriates would, as British subjects, retain their personal freedom and property; Dutch would be taught in Transvaal and ORC schools, and would if necessary be used in courts of law; licenced arms could be retained if necessary for protection; military administration would be replaced by civil administration, and representative government (followed by self-government) would be granted as soon as circumstances permitted; the question of whether black people should be given political rights would not be discussed before the introduction of representative government, and the British government would make available £3,000,000 for the reconstruction and development of the two former republics. On the afternoon of 31 May the peace proposals were accepted by 54 votes to six. Members of both republican governments then travelled by train to Pretoria where, at 23.05 in the dining-hall of Melrose House, Kitchener's headquarters, the conditions of surrender were signed by all parties [109].[1] While the Boers struggled to come to terms with the humiliation of defeat and the loss of their independence, the British could afford the luxury of congratulating themselves on the successful conclusion of hostilities [110, 111].

With the war over, it was time to count the cost. A total of 448,435 white soldiers had fought on the side of the British. According to official figures, at least 7,792 of these soldiers had been killed or had succumbed owing to wounds sustained in battle, while 14,658 had died of disease or in accidents. Furthermore, 75,430 soldiers were sent home either ill or wounded.[2] It is not known for certain how many black and coloured people, who had served on the British side, were killed or wounded. Not more than 78,000 Boers participated in action. At the cessation of hostilities, some 21,000 were still in the field; i.e. more than double the number estimated by the British. At least 3,997 Boers were killed on the battlefield, some 150 died in accidents, while those who had died owing to disease or wounds sustained in battle numbered between 1,800 and 2,200. Since no record was kept during the guerrilla phase of how many Boers were wounded, this number remains unknown.[3] Apart from white and black civilians who died in the concentration camps, an unknown number of black and coloured people died in the services of the Boer commandos. The war cost the British taxpayer more than £200 million.[4] It is impossible to determine the cost of the war to the Boer republics.

With the end of hostilities in South Africa, Roberts could now give all his attention to other matters concerning the British Army. However, his tenure as Commander-in-Chief was not particularly fruitful, his endeavours to reform the military system were ineffective, and came to a somewhat unhappy end when his post was finally abolished by the Balfour government on 8 February 1904. In the meantime, the British government appointed a Royal Commission to inquire into the military preparations and other matters connected with the war in South Africa. Lord Roberts spent some time giving evidence to the Commission, in the process answering no fewer than 930 questions.[5]

Roberts accepted a seat on the Committee of Imperial Defence, but his views on defence policy differed from those of the government and he resigned on 7 November 1905. He then became chairman of the National Service League, espousing a system of universal national service for home defence. When the First World War broke out on 4 August 1914, Roberts was appointed Colonel-in-Chief of Overseas Forces. While on an inspection visit to Indian troops in France, he died at St Omer on 14 November 1914. 'Bobs', as he was affectionately known, the most popular general of the Victorian age, was buried beside Wolseley in the crypt of London's St Paul's Cathedral.[6]

109
Lieutenant-General Ian Hamilton to Lord Roberts

Pretoria.

[Typescript copy]

June 1st 1902.

This is a great day, and I shall sign this letter with the same pen which was used last night by the Boer Delegates, for putting their names to the Declaration of Peace. It was a great and exciting moment.[1] The only one who made the smallest protest was Reitz, and that was quickly over.[2] We opened a bottle of champagne after they were gone, and drank to the health of our noble selves. Lord K. felt, I know, as if a mountain had rolled off his head. Milner, poor chap, must have realized that his difficulties were only just beginning. I do hope that he will back the man of Religion and rifles, rather than those, who I, perhaps rather pessimistically, consider to be chiefly actuated by motives of blather, and self-interest.

I hope, above all, that he will be large-minded enough to find some honourable and suitable employment for Botha, Delarey, and Smuts, who are, each in their own way, splendid fellows, and who, in this recent crisis, have worked literally night and day to pull this peace through to a happy conclusion. Anyway he is going to tackle his job with courage and zeal.

Lord K. came into my room early this morning, with an uncomfortable sort of look on his face, which, I knew not why, gave me a a shiver down my back-bone. My instincts, alas, were only too well justified, for he told me that he had been thinking during the night, that he could not afford to part with me just yet, and that even during the voyage he felt certain he would wish to make constant references to me. He therefore advised me to send the telegram to you which I duly despatched this morning.[3]

It is very sad, and Victor Brooke and I feel our joy in the peace just a little damped. However, his promise to recommend to you, that I should do a quick run over to Japan with Victor Brooke, after I have squared up the whole business in England, casts a slender gleam of hope over the future.

I enclose you, with this, my despatch to Lord K. on the big drive through the Western Transvaal, which the Intelligence fellows, who were down with the Boers at Vereeniging tell me completely changed the tone of Delarey, Kemp, and all his following, who would otherwise have stood out to the last against any terms, short of Independence.[4]

I usually take in hand Lord Kitchener's despatches but on this occasion I was so intimately concerned, that I preferred to hand the job elsewhere and not to look at them. I have been told, however, that Lord Kitchener has very freely used my report in question, in writing his own despatch.[5]

The reason I send you this copy of the despatch, and even ask you to read it very carefully, is that all the little subsidiary orders, as well as the attached map, bring out, I think, more clearly than has ever been done before the natures of a big drive, and the difficulties thereof. So many newspaper writers in England, and others, seem to imagine that it is merely a matter of making a line, and driving Boers like so many rabbits or partridges, which is far from being the case.

I enclose you a note I wrote for Lord K. to guide him in the selection of his I.C.[G?]C. in India. He has made up his own mind, so when you have read this please tear it up, as I do not send it you so much in this connection, as because it gives a series of those little character sketches you are so fond of, on the subject of our Cavalry Leaders.

I also enclose the last table concerning the balance of Boer artillery still unaccounted for.

Good-bye, for the present. Hubert Hamilton and Marker will give you the latest news. I should not wonder if we did not come home in the Canada this time also.

LHCMA, Hamilton 2/3/31

110
Lord Roberts to Lord Milner
[Holograph]
To Lord Milner
Johannesburg

London, 5th June 1902.

I congratulate you most heartily on the satisfactory terms in which peace has been concluded, and I wish you all possible success in the very difficult task before you. Roberts.

NAM 7101–23–122–4–289

111
Lord Roberts to Lord Kitchener
[Holograph?]
To General Viscount Kitchener, GA[?].
Pretoria

London,
5th June 1902.

None of your many friends are more delighted than we all are at your being made a Viscount and promoted to General's rank. May many more honours be in store for you.[6]

NAM 7101–23–122Y–288

Notes

Publication details of all works mentioned in the Notes are given in the Bibliography.

Introduction

1 T. Pakenham, *The Boer War*, pp. 547–8, 573; P. Warwick, *Black People and the South African War*, pp. 4–5; P. Warwick (ed.), *The South African War. The Anglo-Boer War 1899–1902*, pp. 62, 191, 196, 201. See also A. Wessels, *Die Militêre Rol van Swart Mense, Bruin Mense en Indiërs tydens die Anglo-Boereoorlog (1899–1902)*. Mohandas Gandhi organised a number of Indians to form an ambulance corps. At Mafikeng (Mafeking), and possibly at Vaalkrans, the Boers armed their black servants.

2 See J.F.C. Fuller, *The Last of the Gentlemen's Wars. A Subaltern's Journal of the War in South Africa, 1899–1902*.

3 See, for example, S.B. Spies, *Methods of Barbarism? Roberts and Kitchener and Civilians in the Boer Republics, January 1900 – May 1902*.

4 I.R. Smith, *The Origins of the South African War, 1899–1902*, p. 1.

5 B. Farwell, *Queen Victoria's Little Wars*, pp. 364–71.

6 A. Wessels, 'Die Britse Militêre Strategie tydens die Anglo-Boereoorlog tot en met die Buller-fase', pp. 213, 321.

7 *Dictionary of South African Biography* (henceforth referred to as *DSAB*), II, p. 598; *Dictionary of National Biography* (henceforth referred to as *DNB*), *1912–1921*, pp. 464–5.

8 As far as the Transvaal War of Independence is concerned see, for example, F.A. van Jaarsveld *et al.* (eds), *Die Eerste Vryheidsoorlog*; J.H. Lehmann, *The First Boer War*; J.H. Breytenbach and J. Ploeger, *Majuba Gedenkboek*; M.C. van Zyl, *Majuba. Die Onafhanklikheidsoorlog van die Transvaalse Afrikaners (1880–1881)*.

9 As far as Roberts' role in India is concerned, see B. Robson (ed.), *Roberts in India. The Military Papers of Field Marshal Lord Roberts 1876–1893*; F.S. Roberts, *Forty-One Years in India, from Subaltern to Commander-in-Chief*, I–II; D. James, *Lord Roberts*, pp. 13–233; G. Forrest, *The Life of Lord Roberts, K.G., V.C.*, pp. 16–39, 48–165.

10 See, for example, G. Cuthbertson and E-M. Cadell, *The Jameson Raid. A Centennial Retrospect*; W.J. du Plooy, 'Die Militêre Voorbereidings en Verloop van die Jameson-inval'.

11 See, for example, J. Ploeger, *Die Fortifikasie van Pretoria. Fort Klapperkop – Gister en Vandag.*

12 J.H. Breytenbach, *Die Geskiedenis van die Tweede Vryheidsoorlog in Suid-Afrika, 1899–1902*, I, pp. 22–4, 77–97.

13 As far as the causes of the war are concerned see, for example, I.R. Smith, *The Origins of the South African War, 1899–1902*; G.D. Scholtz, *Die Oorsake van die Tweede Vryheidsoorlog 1899–1902*, I–II; J.H. Breytenbach, 'Die Diplomatieke Voorspel tot die Tweede Vryheidsoorlog'; M.J. Hugo, 'Die Kruger-ultimatum. Vier Maande van Spanning'; M.J. Hugo, 'Die Stemregvraagstuk in die Zuid-Afrikaanse Republiek', *Archives Year Book for South African History*, X, 1947, pp. 1–196; J.C. Boltman, 'In how far was the Quarrel between Sir Alfred Milner and the Pretoria Government on the Franchise Question the Real Cause of the South African War of 1899 to 1902?'.

14 Breytenbach, *Die Geskiedenis van die Tweede Vryheidsoorlog ...* , I, pp. 136–9.

15 Wessels, 'Die Britse Militêre Strategie ...', pp. 204–16, 288–315.

16 Smuts' memorandum is published (original Dutch version, as well as an English translation) in W.K. Hancock and J. van der Poel (eds), *Selections from the Smuts Papers*, I, pp. 314–29.

17 *Report of His Majesty's Commissioners Appointed to Inquire into the Military Preparations and Other Matters Connected with the War in South Africa* (Cd. 1789), pp. 33–4.

18 Ibid, pp. 21, 34.

19 J.F. Maurice (ed.), *History of the War in South Africa 1899–1902*, I, p. 2.

20 Cd. 1789, p. 34.

21 Wessels, 'Die Britse Militêre Strategie ...', pp. 354–9.

22 Ibid, pp. 359–63; *Royal Commission on the War in South Africa. Appendices to the Minutes of Evidence taken before the Royal Commission on the War in South Africa* (Cd. 1792), pp. 103–4.

23 Cd. 1792, p. 105.

24 *Notulen der Verrichtingen van den Hed. Volksraad van den Oranje Vrijstaat in zijne Gewone Jaarlijkse Zitting aanvangende op Maandag, den 5den April 1897*, p. 35: Act No. 13 of 1897, articles 1 and 2.

25 Breytenbach, *Die Geskiedenis van die Tweede Vryheidsoorlog ...* , I, pp. 147–51, 153, 156–62.

26 After the official cessation of hostilities, at least three skirmishes took place: at Groenberg, south-east of Fraserburg, on 3 June (four British soldiers killed and two wounded); near Vereeniging (one British soldier killed and one wounded), and near Athole (one British soldier wounded) on 4 June 1902. J. Stirling, *The Colonials in South Africa, 1899–1902. Their Record, based on the Despatches*, p. 237; *List of Casualties in the Army in South Africa, from the 1st January, 1902, to the 31st May, 1902*, p. 95.

27 See A. Wessels, *The Phases of the Anglo-Boer War 1899–1902.*

Prologue
11 October 1899 to 10 January 1900
Introduction

1 *Dictionary of South African Biography* (henceforth referred to as *DSAB*), II, pp. 99, 599.

2 J.H. Breytenbach, *Die Geskiedenis van die Tweede Vryheidsoorlog in Suid-Afrika, 1899–1902*, I, pp. 387–90; L.S. Amery (ed.), *The Times History of the War in South Africa 1899–1902*, II, pp. 267–8.

3 As far as the 217-day siege of Mafikeng is concerned see, for example, J.P. Botha, 'Die Beleg van Mafeking tydens die Anglo-Boereoorlog', *passim*; A.P. Smit and L. Maré (eds), *Die Beleg van Mafeking. Dagboek van Abraham Stafleu*, *passim*; Amery (ed.), op cit, IV, pp. 568–97; B. Gardner, *Mafeking. A Victorian Legend*, *passim*.

4 As far as the four-month siege of Kimberley is concerned see, for example, H.G. Terblanche, 'Die Beleg van Kimberley', *passim*; Amery (ed.), op cit, IV, pp. 533–67; B. Gardner, *The Lion's Cage*, *passim*.

5 Amery (ed.), op cit, IV, pp. 226–36.

6 Ibid, II, pp. 141–74; J.F. Maurice (ed.), *History of the War in South Africa 1899–1902*, I, pp. 123–41; Breytenbach, op cit, I, pp. 214–36; G.S. Preller, *Talana. Die Driegeneraalslag by Dundee met Lewensskets van genl. Daniel Erasmus*, pp. 192–221.

7 Breytenbach, op cit, I, pp. 237–63; Amery (ed.), op cit, II, pp. 175–95; Maurice (ed.), op cit, I, pp. 157–71.

8 A. Wessels, 'Die Britse Militêre Strategie tydens die Anglo-Boereoorlog tot en met die Buller-fase', pp. 398–400.

9 Breytenbach, op cit, I, pp. 291–300; Amery (ed.), op cit, II, pp. 204–6; Maurice (ed.), op cit, I, pp. 151–6.

10 Breytenbach, op cit, I, pp. 172–95; Amery (ed.), op cit, II, pp. 212–60; Maurice (ed.), op cit, I, pp. 303–41.

11 *Royal Commission on the War in South Africa. Minutes of Evidence taken Before the Royal Commission on the War in South Africa*, I (Cd. 1790), p. 430: Roberts' answer to question 10183.

12 As far as the 119-day siege of Ladysmith is concerned see, for example, Maurice (ed.), op cit, II, pp. 531–85; Amery (ed.), op cit, III, pp. 145–205 and IV, pp. 515–32.

13 W.S. Churchill, *London to Ladysmith via Pretoria*, pp. 76–97; Breytenbach, op cit, I, pp. 364–71. Churchill was sent to Pretoria as a POW, escaped from a POW camp, and returned to the Natal front via Lourenço Marques and Durban, to take part in the attempts to relieve Ladysmith.

14 Breytenbach, op cit, I, pp. 372–85; Amery (ed.), op cit, II, pp. 308–17.

15 *South Africa. Further Correspondence Relating to Affairs in South Africa* (Cd. 43), p. 135: Steyn-Schreiner, 11 October 1899 (telegram).

16 Breytenbach, op cit, I, pp. 447–55; Amery (ed.), op cit, II, pp. 292–4; Maurice (ed.), op cit, I, p. 275; C.J.S. Strydom, *Kaapland en die Tweede Vryheidsoorlog*, pp. 42–3. As far as the role of and dilemma faced by the Dutch (Afrikaners) in the Cape Colony are concerned, see J.H. Snyman, 'Die Afrikaner in Kaapland 1899–1902'.

17 Wessels, op cit, 426–8.

18 Breytenbach, op cit, I, pp. 408–25; E. Broos, 'Die Noordelike Hooflaer in die Distrikte Zoutpansberg, Waterberg en Rustenburg, vanaf die Begin van die Tweede Vryheidsoorlog tot die Besetting van Pretoria', pp. 23–7; Amery (ed.), op cit, II, pp. 270–1.

19 Wessels, op cit, pp. 459–77.

20 South African National Museum of Military History, Johannesburg: J.D.P. French, Boer War Diary, 9th November 1899 – 17th March 1900 (manuscript), pp. 28–72; C.S. Goldmann, *With General French and the Cavalry in South Africa*, pp. 33–69; J.G. Maydon, *French's Cavalry Campaign*, pp. 100–8.

21 Breytenbach, op cit, II, pp. 196–225; Amery (ed.), op cit, II, pp. 362–82; Maurice (ed.), op cit, I, pp. 291–303; J. Meintjes, *Stormberg. A Lost Opportunity*, pp. 81–103.

22 Breytenbach, op cit, II, pp. 22–36; Amery (ed.), op cit, II, pp. 325–33; Maurice (ed.), op cit, I, pp. 218–28; W.B. Pemberton, *Battles of the Boer War*, pp. 43–54.

23 Breytenbach, op cit, II, pp. 37–95; Amery (ed.), op cit, II, pp. 333–61; Maurice (ed.), op cit, I, pp. 229–60; Pemberton, pp. 59–78.

24 G.R. Duxbury, *The Battle of Magersfontein 11th December 1899* (2nd ed.), *passim*; Breytenbach, op cit, I, pp. 96–183; Amery (ed.), op cit, II, pp. 383–420; Maurice (ed.), op cit, I, pp. 304–31; Pemberton, op cit, pp. 79–118.

25 H.A. Mocke, 'Die Slag van Colenso, 15 Desember 1899', *passim*; Breytenbach, op cit, II, pp. 226–332; Amery (ed.), op cit, II, pp. 421–67; Maurice (ed.), op cit, I, pp. 351–75; C.J. Barnard, *Generaal Louis Botha op die Natalse Front, 1899–1900*, pp. 46–71; National Archives of South Africa (Pretoria), LA, 77A: P.A. Nierstrasz, Der süd-afrikanische Krieg, 1899–1902 (typed manuscript), pp. 677–86.

26 Breytenbach, op cit, II, p. 339.

27 Ibid, p. 340; D. James, *Lord Roberts*, p. 265; D. de Watteville, *Lord Roberts*, p. 126.

28 Breytenbach, op cit, II, pp. 340–1; James, op cit, pp. 262–3; J. Symons, *Buller's Campaign*, pp. 171–3; NAM 7101–23–181: Lansdowne – Lord Roberts, 10 December 1899 (letter), and Lansdowne – Aileen Roberts, 11 May 1921 (letter); Churchill Archives Centre (Cambridge), Esher Papers, ESHR 2/10: journal entry for 18 December 1899.

29 Maurice (ed.), op cit, I, p. 381; *DSAB*, II, p. 599; T. Pakenham, *The Boer War*, pp. 242–5.

30 Breytenbach, op cit, II, p. 344; J.H. Lehmann, *All Sir Garnet. A Life of Field Marshal Lord Wolseley*, p. 387.

31 Breytenbach, op cit, II, pp. 344–5; *Royal Commission on the War in South Africa. Minutes of Evidence taken before the Royal Commission on the War in South Africa*, II (Cd. 1791), p. 206: Buller's answer to question 15374.

32 H.J. Botha, 'Die Moord op Derdepoort, 25 November 1899. Nie-blankes in Oorlogsdiens', *Militaria* 1(2), 1969, pp. 55–95; R.F. Morton, 'Linchwe I and the Kgatla Campaign in the South African War, 1899–1902', *The Journal of African History* 26(2 & 3), 1985, pp. 169–90.

11 October 1899 to 10 January 1900

1 The battle of Talana (also known as the battle of Dundee) took place on 20 October 1899 just east of the town of Dundee. At the outbreak of hostilities Major-General W. Penn Symons was stationed at Dundee with about 5,000 troops and eighteen field-guns. General Lukas Meyer's force of 1,500 burghers took up positions on Lennox and Talana Hill and his artillery bombarded Symons' camp. Symons led a frontal attack against the Boer positions, was mortally wounded, and Major-General J.H. Yule took over the command. The Boers withdrew, having lost at least 44 killed and 91 wounded. British losses amounted to at least 51 killed, 203 wounded and 246 POW. J.H. Breytenbach, *Die Geskiedenis van die Tweede Vryheidsoorlog in Suid-Afrika, 1899–1902*, I, pp. 214–36; J.F. Maurice (ed.), *History of the War in South Africa 1899–1902*, I, pp. 123–41; L.S. Amery (ed.), *The Times History of the War in South Africa 1899–1902*, II, pp. 141–74; G.S. Preller, *Talana. Die Driegeneraalslag by Dundee met Lewensskets van genl. Daniel Erasmus*, pp. 192–221.

2 The battle that took place at Elandslaagte on 21 October 1899. A Boer force of 800 men with two field-guns under General J.H.M. Kock occupied Elandslaagte Station, 16 km (10 miles) north-east of Ladysmith. White sent 3,500 men and eighteen field-guns under Major-General J.D.P. French to dislodge the Boers. The overconfident Boers were dealt a shattering blow, and apparently lost 38 killed, 113 wounded (including many taken POW) and 185 unwounded POWs. General Kock was mortally wounded. Many German and Dutch volunteers were among the casualties. The British lost 50 dead and 213 wounded. Breytenbach, op cit, I, pp. 237–63; Maurice (ed.), op cit, I, pp. 157–71; Amery (ed.), op cit, II, pp. 175–95.

3 When the war broke out, White had not more than about 16,500 soldiers in the whole of Natal under his command, and had to face a Boer invasion force of about 17,500 burghers. After the battle at Talana, Yule withdrew with his force from Dundee and Glencoe on the evening of 22 October, and reached Ladysmith unscathed on 26 October. Breytenbach, op cit, I, pp. 284–9.

4 See, for example, *South African War, 1899–1902. Confidential Telegrams. 12th October 1899 to 1st October 1902* (henceforth referred to as *Confidential Telegrams*), p. 34: Buller – Lansdowne, 1 December 1899.

5   Sir Redvers Buller arrived in Cape Town on board the *Dunottar Castle* on 31 October 1899 as Commander-in-Chief of all the British forces in South Africa.

6   About 250,000 of the Cape Colony's white population of about 400,000 were Afrikaners. The outbreak of war tested the loyalty of many of these people. The greatest majority stayed loyal to the British Crown (even though some had sympathy for the Boer cause), but at least 10,000 Cape Colony Afrikaners actively rebelled by taking up arms, most of them in the north-eastern region (after the Boer invasion of middle November 1899) and in the remote and sparsely populated Northern Cape. As far as the dilemmas faced by Cape Afrikaners are concerned, see J.H. Snyman, 'Die Afrikaner in Kaapland 1899–1902'. In Natal, only a few Afrikaners in the northern border areas rebelled.

7   As far as Basotholand and the war is concerned, see C.C. Eloff, *Oranje-Vrystaat en Basoetoland, 1884–1902. 'n Verhoudingstudie*, pp. 211–77.

8   Robert Arthur Talbot Gascoyne Cecil, 3rd Marquis of Salisbury – see Biographical Notes.

9   At the beginning of October 1899 it was envisaged that Buller would command approximately 67,000 soldiers in South Africa. See *Report of His Majesty's Commissioners Appointed to Inquire into the Military Preparations and Other Matters connected with the War in South Africa* (Cd. 1789), pp. 271–2: Appendix D, Lansdowne – British Cabinet, 3 October 1899 (memorandum). At the beginning of December 1899 there were approximately 70,000 British soldiers in South Africa. During the War of the Spanish Succession, 1701–14, John Churchill, later 1st Duke of Marlborough (1650–1722) at one stage (battle of Malplaquet, 1709) commanded about 110,000 soldiers. During the Peninsula War in Portugal and Spain, 1808–14, Arthur Wellesley, Duke of Wellington (1769–1852) at one stage (battle of Victoria, 1813) commanded about 75,000 British, Portuguese and Spanish troops. At the battle of Waterloo (1815) he commanded about 68,000 British, Dutch and Belgian troops. G. Bruce, *Harbottle's Dictionary of Battles*, pp. 156, 269, 273.

10 Cipher telegram, published in the *South African War, 1899–1902. Vol. I. Home and Oversea Correspondence by Field-Marshal Lord Roberts*, p. 1. In the BL there are two versions of this telegram: a typed ms, dated 15 December 1899, and a longhand ms, dated 16 December 1899. It is not clear why the typed ms was (apparently) completed a day before the longhand version. For this publication, the typed ms (which is identical to the published version) is used as basis. Where the longhand ms differs from the typed version, differences are indicated in square brackets.

11 On 15 December 1899 Buller, who at that stage had more than 21,000 soldiers with 46 guns and eighteen machine-guns under his command at Chieveley, launched an attack against General Louis Botha's force of about 3,000 burghers, a howitzer, three field-guns and a pom-pom which had

taken up positions along an extended front just north of the Thukela (Tugela) River. The attack, which was preceded by an artillery bombardment, was unsuccessful in all the sectors, and Buller ordered a withdrawal. He lost about 150 killed, 750 wounded and 250 missing (most of them became POW), as well as ten field-guns. Boer losses amounted to only seven killed, one drowned and 30 wounded, of whom one later died. C.J. Barnard, *Generaal Louis Botha op die Natalse front, 1899–1900*, pp. 46–71; H.A. Mocke, 'Die slag van Colenso, 15 Desember 1899', *passim*; Breytenbach, op cit, II, pp. 226–332; Maurice (ed.), op cit, I, pp. 351–75; Amery (ed.), op cit, II, pp. 421–67.

12 No signature in original ms.

13 Freddy Roberts (see Biographical Notes), only surviving son of Lord Roberts, was mortally wounded at Colenso.

14 Hilda Charters (died 1901), daughter of Lord Elcho (later 10th Earl of Wymess and March), first wife of W. St J.F. Brodrick. They had five children: one son and four daughters.

15 Lord Wolseley – see Biographical Notes.

16 I.e. at Windsor Castle.

17 See, for example, *Confidential Telegrams*, pp. 63 (No. 76: Buller – Lansdowne, 23 December 1899), 64 (No. 78: Lansdowne – Buller, 24 December 1899), 64–5 (No. 80: Buller – Lansdowne, 24 December 1899), 67 (No. 86: Lansdowne – Roberts, 26 December 1899).

18 A note in red (in a different handwriting) on the left-hand side of the ms reads as follows: I think the telegram was sent to the Commander in Chief.

19 I.e. machine-guns.

20 Evelyn Baring, 1st Earl Cromer (1841–1917). Agent and Consul-General in Egypt, 1883–1907. Created Baron, 1892; Viscount, 1898; Earl, 1901.

21 H. Maxwell, *The Life of Wellington. The Restoration of the Martial Power of Great Britain* (2 volumes, London, 1899; 2nd ed. late 1899; 3rd ed. beginning 1900). Vol. I, p. 126 refers, *inter alia*, to the fact that when a commanding officer does not have the confidence of his subordinates, he should be superseded, and that an officer should assist his commander in the mode in which the commander may deem his services most advantageous.

22 A Boer force of not more than 8,200 burghers, with five field-guns and five pom-poms, entrenched themselves at the foot of Magersfontein and adjoining hills over a front of about 7 km (nearly 5 miles). Lord Methuen, ordered to relieve the besieged Kimberley, had under his command about 15,000 troops, 33 guns and sixteen machine-guns. On 9 and 10 December 1899 he subjected the hills to the heaviest British bombardment since the siege of Sebastopol during the Crimean War (1854–6), but the shells flew over the entrenched Boers and only three were wounded. On 11 December the British frontal attack was repulsed. The British lost at least 288 killed,

700 wounded and 100 missing; the Boers 71 killed and 184 wounded. G.R. Duxbury, *The Battle of Magersfontein 11th December 1899* (2nd ed.), *passim*; Breytenbach, op cit, II, pp. 96–183; Maurice (ed.), op cit, I, pp. 304–31; Amery (ed.), op cit, II, pp. 383–420.

23 The Highland Brigade, under Major-General A.G. Wauchope, led the attack against the Boers and bore the brunt of the first volleys of Boer fire, which caught them by surprise. Wauchope was killed less than 200 yards from the Boer trenches; many soldiers fell even closer.

Part 1
11 January to 5 June 1900
Introduction

1 André Wessels Private Document Collection, Bloemfontein: G.F.R. Henderson (file). Henderson was promoted to the substantive rank of Lieutenant-Colonel on arrival in South Africa, 10 January 1900, and given the local rank of Colonel.

2 *DSAB*, II, p. 599, H. de Watteville, *Lord Roberts*, pp. 131–3.

3 *DSAB*, II, p. 599.

4 J. Symons, *Buller's Campaign*, pp. 194–5; J.H. Breytenbach, *Die Geskiedenis van die Tweede Vryheidsoorlog in Suid-Afrika, 1899–1902*, III, pp. 62–129.

5 As far as the battles at iNtabamnyama and Spioenkop are concerned see, for example, J.F. Maurice (ed.), *History of the War in South Africa 1899–1902*, II, pp. 366–402; L.S. Amery (ed.), *The Times History of the War in South Africa 1899–1902*, III, pp. 225–302; Breytenbach, op cit, III, pp. 130–236; O. Ransford, *The Battle of Spion Kop*, pp. 34, 42–3, 59–118; J.H. Cilliers, 'Die Slag van Spioenkop (24 January 1900)', *Archives Year Book for South African History* 23(2), 1960, pp. 1–7; E.B. Knox, *Buller's Campaign with the Natal Field Force 1900*, pp. 55–94; Symons, op cit, pp. 212–40; W.S. Churchill, *From London to Ladysmith via Pretoria*, pp. 293–313.

6 As far as the battle at Vaalkrans is concerned see, for example, C.J. Barnard, *Generaal Louis Botha op die Natalse Front, 1899–1900*, pp. 107–18; Symons, op cit, pp. 247–58; Knox, op cit, pp. 95–132; Breytenbach, op cit, III, pp. 288–330; Maurice (ed.), op cit, II, pp. 403–22; Amery (ed.), op cit, IV, pp. 303–30; Churchill, op cit, pp. 345–66.

7 A. Wessels, 'Die Britse Militêre Strategie tydens die Anglo-Boereoorlog tot en met die Buller-fase', pp. 724–7.

8 Ibid, pp. 730–1.

9 Breytenbach, op cit, IV, p. 27.

10 Ibid, III, p. 394.

11 D. James, *Lord Roberts*, pp. 280–1.

12 Breytenbach, op cit, IV, pp. 204–31; Amery (ed.), op cit, III, pp. 392–6; J.G. Maydon, *French's Cavalry Campaign*, pp. 140–8.

13 J.L. Basson, 'Die Slag van Paardeberg', *passim*; Breytenbach, op cit, IV, pp. 232–430; Amery (ed.), op cit, III, pp. 401–58, 473–87; Maurice (ed.), op cit, II, pp. 73–179.

14 Breytenbach, op cit, III, pp. 343, 398, 401–43; Amery (ed.), op cit, III, pp. 500–6; *History of the War in South Africa 1899–1902*, III, pp. 438–55; Churchill, op cit, pp. 380–96.

15 C.M. Bakkes, *Die Britse Deurbraak aan die Benede-Tugela op Majubadag 1900*, *passim*; Amery (ed.), op cit, III, pp. 513–46; Maurice (ed.), op cit, II, pp. 463–530; Breytenbach, op cit, III, pp. 476–567; Churchill, op cit, pp. 397–466.

16 Breytenbach, op cit, V, pp. 27–96; Amery (ed.), op cit, III, pp. 560–9, 573–86; Maurice (ed.), op cit, II, pp. 180–229.

17 As far as the role of the war correspondents in general are concerned, see R. Sibbald, *The War Correspondents. The Boer War*. It is interesting to note that two days after entering Bloemfontein, Roberts closed down the local anti-British *De Express* newspaper, and started in its place the bilingual *The Friend*, which was run by British war correspondents in their free time. T. Pakenham, *The Boer War*, p. 375.

18 André Wessels Private Document Collection, Bloemfontein: G.F.R. Henderson (file).

19 Amery (ed.), op cit, III, pp. 592–3; Breytenbach, op cit, IV, pp. 147–60, 439–51 and V, pp. 129–35; Maurice (ed.), op cit, II, pp. 250–6.

20 C.R. de Wet, *Three Years War*, pp. 79–80; Breytenbach, op cit, V, pp. 159–67.

21 J.E. Rabie, *Generaal C.R. de Wet se Krygsleiding by Sannaspos en Groenkop*, pp. 5–30; Breytenbach, op cit, V, pp. 196–225; Amery (ed.), op cit, IV, pp. 29–50; Maurice (ed.), op cit, II, pp. 274–99.

22 W.L. von R. Scholtz, 'Generaal Christiaan de Wet as Veldheer', pp. 120–7; Breytenbach, op cit, V, pp. 240–58, 269–81; Maurice (ed.), op cit, II, pp. 314–33; A. Wessels (ed.), *Anglo-Boer War Diary of Herbert Gwynne Howell*, pp. 37–46.

23 See, for example, BL MS Room, Lansdowne Papers: Roberts – Lansdowne, 29 February 1900. See also Roberts' evidence in this regard as published in the *Royal Commission on the War in South Africa. Minutes of Evidence Taken Before the Royal Commission on the War in South Africa*, II (Cd. 1791), pp. 466–7.

24 James, op cit, pp. 315–23; Amery (ed.), op cit, IV, pp. 77–141; *History of the War in South Africa 1899–1902*, III, pp. 40–77; Breytenbach, op cit, IV, p. 423 and V, pp. 413–529; Pakenham, op cit, p. 419.

25 Amery (ed.), op cit, IV, pp. 165–84; *History of the War in South Africa 1899–1902*, III, pp. 259–69.

26 Amery (ed.), op cit, IV, pp. 591–7; B. Gardner, *Mafeking. A Victorian Legend*, p. 191 *et seq*; A.P. Smit and L. Maré (eds), *Die Beleg van Mafeking. Dagboek van Abraham Stafleu*, pp. 219–71.

27 B.N. Reckitt, *The Lindley Affair. A Diary of the Boer War*, p. 9 *et seq*; Amery, op cit, IV, pp. 248–59; *History of the War in South Africa 1899–1902*, III, pp. 115–20, 122–3.

28 Breytenbach, op cit, V, pp. 529–49; Amery, op cit, IV, pp. 141–64; *History of the War in South Africa 1899–1902*, III, pp. 75–101.

11 January to 5 June 1900

1 I.e. the so-called Spioenkop campaign on the Upper Thukela (Tugela) River, which led to the battles at iNtabamnyama (20–23 January 1900), Spioenkop (24 January 1900) and Vaalkrans (5–7 February 1900).

2 Telegram No. 6 (not 7), cipher. See *Confidential Telegrams*, pp. 81–2. See also Roberts' despatch of 6 February 1900, published in *South Africa Despatches. Vol. I. From 1ˢᵗ November 1899 to 1ˢᵗ August 1900* (Cd. 457), pp. 50–2, in which he gave a concise account of the situation in South Africa on his arrival, 10 January 1900.

3 See *Confidential Telegrams*, p. 78, No. 95.

4 Roberts' Director of Military Intelligence, January–February 1900, was Colonel G.F.R. Henderson – see Biographical Notes.

5 There are two main types of horse-sickness in South Africa: glanders (brought to the country by horses imported from overseas), and (South) African horse-sickness (caused by gnats, usually during the rainy season). See also *Royal Commission on the War in South Africa. Appendices to the Minutes of Evidence taken before the Royal Commission on the War in South Africa* (Cd. 1792), pp. 101–2, Appendix 6: Report on the Army Veterinary Department in South Africa.

6 W. MacCormac (**not** MacCormac**k**) – see Biographical Notes.

7 The British force started their advance on the afternoon of 16 January 1900 and started to cross the Thukela River at Potgietersdrif, north of Springfield, that same evening.

8 It is unlikely that there were as many as 61,000 Boers in the field against the British at this stage. The highest number of burghers under arms and on commando ever was probably not more than 47,000 (about 35,000 Boers, 2,000 foreign volunteers and 10,000 rebels), and that was in the period December 1899 to February 1900. A. Wessels, *Die Anglo-Boereoorlog 1899–1902. 'n Oorsig van die Militêre Verloop van die Stryd*, p. 5.

9 Ralph Henry Knox (1836–1913) worked at the War Office since 1856, for example as Accountant-General, 1882–97; Permanent Under-Secretary of State for War, 1897–1901. The letter, however, was signed by Alfred Higgins, then Assistant Accountant-General at the War Office.

10 Probably Telegram No. 112B in *Confidential Telegrams*, p. 91: Buller – Lansdowne, 23 January 1900.

11 The battle at Spioenkop was in fact, after Colenso (15 December 1899) and iNtabamnyama (20–23 January 1900), Buller's *third* attempt to reach

Ladysmith. Lieutenant-General Sir Charles Warren, to whom Buller had given command of the Upper Thukela operation, ordered Major-General E.R.P. Woodgate to take control of the summit of Spioenkop. Woodgate's approximately 1,700 men succeeded in doing so without much opposition from the about 200 Boers who were driven off the summit on the night of 23–24 January. At dawn the British soldiers were subjected to an intense Boer artillery bombardment, while the Boers stormed the hill. Woodgate was mortally wounded, but reinforcements kept the Boers from overrunning the British positions. During the night of 24–25 January both opposing forces withdrew from Spioenkop, but early the next morning the Boers occupied the strategic position without any further opposition. After Paardeberg (18 February 1900 – see Note 39) this was the bloodiest battle of the war: approximately 225 British soldiers killed, 550 wounded and 300 missing or POW; 58 Boers killed and 140 wounded. J.H. Cilliers, 'Die Slag van Spioenkop (24 January 1900)', *Archives Year Book for South African History* 23(2), 1960, pp. 1–71; J.H. Breytenbach, *Die Geskiedenis van die Tweede Vryheidsoorlog in Suid-Afrika, 1899–1902*, III, pp. 168–236; J.F. Maurice (ed.), *History of the War in South Africa 1899–1902*, II, pp. 379–402; L.S. Amery (ed.), *The Times History of the War in South Africa 1899–1902*, III, pp. 245–302; E.B. Knox, *Buller's Campaign with the Natal Field Force of 1900*, pp. 55–94.

12 See *Confidential Telegrams*, pp. 93 (No. 113F: Buller – Lansdowne, 25 January 1900), pp. 101–2 (No. 131: Roberts – Lansdowne, 28 January 1900).

13 See *Confidential Telegrams*, pp. 101–2: Roberts – Lansdowne, 28 January 1900. According to notes on ibid, pp. xiv, 102, this telegram should have been sent to Buller, and repeated to the War Office, but the original and the repetition were accidentally interchanged.

14 There is a line in the ms where a word (?) has apparently been rubbed out.

15 George Henry Marshall (1843–1909), Major-General in command of Artillery, South Africa, 1899–1900.

16 Captain The Earl of Kerry, eldest son of Lord Lansdowne, and ADC to Lord Roberts in South Africa, 1900.

17 See *Confidential Telegrams*, pp. 105–6, No. 139: Roberts – Lansdowne, 31 January 1900.

18 Return re strength and distribution of troops not in Lansdowne Papers.

19 Once again, Roberts exaggerates the strength of the Boer forces – see also Note 8.

20 The number of infantry and cavalry are left out on the original ms.

21 See *Confidential Telegrams*, p. 110, No. 146A: Roberts – Lansdowne, 6 February 1900.

22 I.e. President M.T. Steyn (OFS) and President S.J.P. Kruger (South African/Transvaal Republic) – see Biographical Notes.

23 Original ms in Lansdowne Papers, BL MS Room. With one exception (see Note 20) the printed version only differs from the original in a few instances as far as punctuation is concerned.

24 See BL MS Room, Lansdowne Papers: Roberts – Lansdowne, 9 February 1900 (letter).

25 Colonel Ormelie Campbell Hannay (1848–1900). Previous service in Anglo-Zulu War, 1879. Saw action on Kimberley front, 1899–1900. Took part in Lord Roberts' advance to Paardeberg. Killed in action, Paardeberg, 18 February 1900, when he rode far ahead of his MI in an effort to spare his comrades and show Lord Kitchener the error of ordering the futile charge against the entrenched Boers.

26 On 11 February 1900 Colonel O.C. Hannay sent Captain H.B. de Lisle to attack a small Boer force that barred his way at Wolwekraal, some 25 km (15 miles) north of the Gariep (Orange) River. Although the British were unable to dislodge the Boers, Hannay's convoy was able to trek unscathed northwards. British losses amounted to at least four killed, 22 wounded and eleven POW. The Boers apparantly suffered no casualties. Breytenbach, op cit, IV, pp. 166–9; Amery (ed.), op cit, III, p. 381.

27 After a small skirmish with a few Boers, French's advance guard captured De Kielsdrif on the Riet River on 12 February 1900. Captain H.G. Majendie was mortally wounded and two soldiers wounded. (Breytenbach, op cit, IV, p. 176.) Henry Grylls Majendie (born 1865) previously saw service in Burma, 1888–9, and in the Sudan, 1898. He died on 13 February 1900, of wounds received the previous day at De Kielsdrif.

28 French and his cavalry rode into Kimberley on 15 February 1900, exactly four months after the siege began. See C.S. Goldmann, *With General French and the Cavalry in South Africa*, pp. 80–97; J.G. Maydon, *French's Cavalry Campaign*, pp. 140–9. As far as the siege in general is concerned see, for example, H.J. Terblanche, 'Die Beleg van Kimberley'.

29 Lieutenant-Colonel W. Ross commanded a small force that had to guard a huge British convoy at Watervalsdrif, about 20 km (12 miles) south of Jacobsdal on the Riet River. The wagons carried at least 180,000 rations for Roberts' force, as well as fodder and other supplies. The convoy as such was under the command of Colonel F.F. Johnson. Colonel C.P. Ridley was also present. A Boer force of about 550 burghers under General C.R. de Wet attacked the British camp on 15 February 1900. Roberts immediately sent reinforcements to save his provisions, but General J.B.M. Hertzog and his commando joined De Wet, and by the evening the convoy was in Boer hands. The British lost at least two killed, 22 wounded and 34 POW – as well as 180 wagons and the huge amount of supplies. The Boers lost three killed and two wounded. Breytenbach, op cit, IV, pp. 233–9; C.R. de Wet, *Three Years War*, pp. 47–9.

30 French operated on the Colesberg front from 20 November 1899 until 6 February 1900 when he and his cavalry secretly moved to the Kimberley front to support Roberts' flank march. Major-General R.A.P. Clements succeeded French as GOC at Rensburg. With his force considerably weakened with French's departure, Clements retired to Arundel on 14 February 1900. Breytenbach, op cit, IV, pp. 159–60.

31 From 1 January 1900 until 31 December 1901, Mr Henry Alfred Oliver (1854–1935) was the Mayor of Kimberley. He was re-elected in 1901 and in 1904.

32 Not in the Lansdowne Papers at the BL MS Room.

33 See, for example, Roberts – Lansdowne telegrams in *Confidential Telegrams*, pp. 129 (Nos 161A and 161B of 16 and 17 February 1900), 130–1 (No. 163: 18 February 1900), 131 (No. 164: 19 February 1900), 132 (No. 165: 20 February 1900), 134 (No. 170: 21 February 1900).

34 Lord Roberts was in fact not able to depart from Jacobsdal on 17 February 1900 because of a severe cold. Although this left Lieutenant-General T. Kelly-Kenny, as the most senior officer, technically in command of the British force at Paardeberg, Lord Kitchener in practise had the final say, for example, as far as the ill-fated British attack of 18 February was concerned (see Note 39). Roberts arrived at Paardeberg on 19 February. Amery (ed.), op cit, III, pp. 418–19, 453.

35 Several commandos, including that of General C.R. de Wet, raced to Cronjé's assistance. Breytenbach, op cit, IV, pp. 308–11.

36 It is not clear exactly how many women and children were in Cronjé's laager, but there were definitely not more than a hundred; probably only about 60. They included Mrs H.S. Cronjé, the General's wife. In the consulted sources there is no indication of any Boer women or children who became casualties. After the Boers surrendered, the women and children were set free. Mrs Cronjé chose to accompany her husband to St Helena. Breytenbach, op cit, IV, pp. 247–8, 424–7.

37 There was at least one doctor, a Dutchman, in Cronjé's laager. See Breytenbach, op cit, IV, p. 406.

38 The drinking of the polluted water led to an outbreak of typhoid (enteric fever) amongst the British soldiers, which resulted in the death of at least 500 of them in Bloemfontein, in the period 13 March to 3 May 1900, and forced Roberts to postpone his advance to Pretoria until 3 May 1900. A total of more than 1,800 British soldiers died in Bloemfontein during the war, most of them from typhoid. The least the British soldiers could have done at Paardeberg, is to have boiled the water before drinking it. See, for example, S.A. Watt, 'The Anglo-Boer War: The Medical Arrangements and Implications thereof during the British Occupation of Bloemfontein: March – April 1900', *Military History Journal* 9(2), 1992, pp. 44–54; *Royal Commission on South African Hospitals. Appendix to Minutes of Evidence taken before the Royal Commission Appointed to Consider and Report upon the Care and Treatment of the Sick and Wounded during the South African Campaign* (Cd. 455).

39 General P.A. Cronjé's force of about 4,000 men was surrounded by the British forces at Paardeberg on 17 February 1900. Early next morning, Kitchener, in the absence of Roberts, launched a series of unimaginative and unsuccessful frontal attacks against the entrenched defenders of the Boer

laager. The British suffered their heaviest casualties in terms of numbers killed (at least 303), and wounded (906) on a single day during the war, as well as 61 POWs. Total Boer casualties amounted to fewer than 70. Breytenbach, op cit, IV, pp. 286–323; Maurice (ed.), op cit, II, pp. 96–170; Amery (ed.), op cit, III, pp. 422–53.

40 General C.R. de Wet, who had rushed to Cronjé's assistance, occupied Oskoppies (Kitchener's Kopje), south-west of the laager, on 18 February 1900, in an effort to create an opportunity for Cronjé to break through the British cordon. On 19 February Roberts arrived at the scene of the investment and two days later he recaptured Oskoppies. During the clash of 21 February, De Wet lost at least ten killed, twenty wounded and twenty captured. British losses were apparently only six wounded. Breytenbach, op cit, IV, pp. 324–50; Amery (ed.), op cit, III, pp. 473–8.

41 Not in the Lansdowne Papers at the BL MS Room.

42 After Cronjé's surrender at Paardeberg (see Note 46), the Boer forces withdrew from the North-Eastern Cape Colony and the rebellion in that area collapsed, but continued in the Northern Cape. It was only suppressed towards the end of June of 1900. See, for example, Amery (ed.), op cit, III, pp. 593–4.

43 Shortly after entering the OFS in February, Lord Roberts issued his first proclamation to the burghers of that republic. See *Army. Proclamations issued by Field-Marshal Lord Roberts in South Africa* (Cd. 426), p. 2. See also Note 56.

44 See BL MS Room, Lansdowne Papers: Roberts – Lansdowne, 9 February 1900 (letter).

45 Moberly Bell (see Biographical Notes) of *The Times* wrote a letter to Sir Evelyn Wood, complaining about how long it sometimes took for news (for example telegrams) to reach his office, due to censorship.

46 After a ten-day siege and almost ceaseless bombardment, Cronjé and his force of about 4,000 men surrendered on 27 February 1900, the nineteenth anniversary of the British defeat at Amajuba during the Transvaal War of Independence, 1880–1. During the siege, at least 74 Boers were killed and 187 wounded. Breytenbach, op cit, IV, pp. 423–4.

47 See *Confidential Telegrams*, p. 138, No. 175A: Roberts – Lansdowne, 27 February 1900.

48 Amongst the senior Boer officers captured were Major R. Albrecht (OC, OFS Artillery), and Commandants M.J. Wolmarans and P. Schutte.

49 The conquest of Cingolo (17 February 1900) was largely due to Lord Dundonald's initiative, and his brigade also took part in the operations which led to the final break-through of the Boer positions and the relief of Ladysmith. Dundonald led the first British troops into a relieved Ladysmith, early evening, 28 February 1900. Amery (ed.), op cit, III, pp. 500–2, 545–6. See also the Major-General Dundonald Papers in the Scottish Record Office, General Register House (Edinburgh), for example volume GD233/128

50 Maude Petty-Fitzmaurice, née Hamilton (Lady Lansdowne), youngest daughter of the Duke of Abercorn. Married Lord Lansdowne in 1869. They had four children: two sons and two daughters.

51 Roberts occupied Bloemfontein unopposed on 13 March 1900.

52 As far as the Army Orders are concerned, see *South Africa. 1900. Field-Marshal Lord Roberts, K.P., &c. 1. – Proclamations. 2 – Army Orders and South Africa. Revised Reprint of the Principal Army Orders and Cape Colony District Orders from the Outbreak of Hostilities to the End of July, 1901 with the Principal Head Quarters' Circular Memo, for 1900 and 1901.*

53 Roberts visited Kimberley on 1 March 1900 to discuss matters with Lord Methuen. He returned to his HQ at Osfontein on 2 March. Maurice (ed.), op cit, II, pp. 182–3. See also postscript to document 19, p. 60, *supra*.

54 Address in RA VIC/P7/140.

55 Account in RA VIC/P7/141.

56 On 17 February and 15 March 1900 Roberts issued proclamations asking the Boers to lay down their arms under favourable conditions. As a result of the general demoralisation following the surrender of Cronjé and the capture of Bloemfontein, many Boers made use of this opportunity. See Cd. 426, pp. 2–3.

57 Original ms in RA VIC/P7/139. Punctuation has been altered to conform with the original ms.

58 As far as the role of war correspondents during the war is concerned, see R. Sibbald, *The War Correspondents. The Boer War.* There were haphazard attempts by the British government to manage news from the war front, but – notwithstanding the uneasy match between patriotism and a critical appreciation of events on the battlefield – the individualism of Victorian reporters generally triumphed.

59 The well-known author and poet, Joseph Rudyard Kipling (1865–1936) was an ardent exponent of an imperial ethic. The anti-imperial reaction to the war in South Africa made him less popular.

60 On 17 March 1900 a watershed meeting took place at Kroonstad when a Boer *krygsraad* (council of war) was convened. Presidents Kruger and Steyn, as well as most of the senior Boer officers were present. It was decided, among others, that the Boers would change their military tactics, and instead of trying to halt the British through the use of defensive positions, their efforts had to be aimed at destroying the enemy's lines of communication. Henceforth the Boer forces would also be organized into smaller, more mobile sections. This was in fact the theoretical start of the guerrilla phase of the war. Breytenbach, op cit, V, pp. 156–73.

61 Lord Roberts was joined in Bloemfontein by his wife (Nora Henrietta) and daughters (Aileen Mary and Ada Stewart Edwina) – see Biographical Notes – in the third week of April 1900. D. James, *Lord Roberts*, pp. 314–15.

62 Queen Victoria visited Ireland from 4–26 April 1900, staying at the viceregal lodge in Phoenix Park, Dublin. It was her fourth visit to Ireland, but the first since 1861. *DNB. From the Earliest Times to 1900*, XXII, pp. 1363–4.

63 On 4 April 1900, a fifteen-year old Belgian youth named Sipido, fired two shots at the Prince and Princess of Wales while they were sitting in their train at the Gare du Nord in Brussels, en route to Denmark. No-one was injured. The act was prompted by anti-British feeling in Belgium because of the war in South Africa. Sipido was found guilty and the court ordered that he be kept under supervision until the age of 21, but he soon escaped to France. *DNB 1901–1911*, p. 586.

64 Original ms in RA VIC/P8/65. Punctuation has been altered to conform with the original ms. The original ms includes the following postscript: 'The enclosed return showing the composition of the C.I.V. will, I think, interest your Majesty.' See RA VIC/P8/66 for the enclosure.

65 See BL MS Room, Lansdowne Papers: Lansdowne – Roberts, 6 April 1900 (letter).

66 The first guerrilla clash of the war took place on 31 March 1900 when General De Wet with about 1,500 men ambushed and defeated a British force of about 1,800 men under the command of Brigadier-General R.G. Broadwood at Sannaspos, about 30 km (20 miles) east of Bloemfontein. The British lost at least eighteen killed, 134 wounded and 426 taken POW, as well as seven guns and over 100 wagons and carts captured. On the Boer side at least three were killed and five wounded. (J.E. Rabie, *Generaal Christiaan de Wet se Krygsleiding by Sannaspos en Groenkop*, pp. 5–30.) It is interesting to note that Roberts rejected Broadwood's original despatch re the events at Sannaspos (in which Broadwood took the blame on himself), and that Kitchener subsequently assisted Broadwood in writing another despatch of a more 'favourable' nature. See PRO, WO105/7, as well as the Scottish Record Office (West Register House), Duke of Hamilton Papers (GD406), vol. 1819: Letter by Major Robert M. Poore to his father, 9 April 1901.

67 On 3 April 1900 De Wet surrounded and attacked a British force under the command of Captain W.J. McWinnie at Mostertshoek, east of the town of Reddersburg in the southern OFS. After ten British soldiers were killed, the whole British force (581 officers and men, including 35 wounded) surrendered on 4 April. The Boer casualties were apparently only three killed and three wounded. Breytenbach, op cit, V, pp. 240–58; W.L. von R. Scholtz, 'Generaal Christiaan de Wet as Veldheer', pp. 120–7.

68 From 9–25 April 1900 De Wet besieged the British garrison at Jammerbergdrif outside Wepener, without achieving any success. The British lost 34 killed and 146 wounded; the Boers ten or eleven killed and 25 wounded. Breytenbach, op cit, V, pp. 269–81; Maurice (ed.), op cit, II, pp. 314–33; A. Wessels (ed.), *Anglo-Boer War Diary of Herbert Gwynne Howell*, pp. 38–46.

69 While he invested Jammerbergdrif, General Christiaan de Wet sent his brother, General Piet de Wet, and General Andries Cronjé to defend Dewetsdorp. Lord Roberts ordered Lieutenant-General Leslie Rundle to Dewetsdorp, where on 20 April 1900 he attacked the Boers, but was unable

to dislodge them. Roberts sent reinforcements and fighting continued over the next few days. Dewetsdorp was occupied by the British on 24 April. Amery (ed.), op cit, IV, pp. 66–73.

70 Copy of Volksraad proceedings not in Lansdowne Papers, BL MS Room.

71 In the Cape Colony the British destroyed the farms of rebels in 1899. Farm-burning by the British also occurred from their first incursion into republican territory. On 9 January 1900 Major-General J.M. Babington entered the South-Eastern OFS on orders from Lord Methuen, destroyed several farmhouses and carried off the livestock. Houses were not destroyed in the town of Jacobsdal, but farmhouses in the district were burnt. Breytenbach, op cit, IV, pp. 85–6.

72 At Modderrivierspoort, near Poplar Grove Drift, De Wet took up position with about 5,000 burghers and seven guns over an extended front in an effort to stop Roberts' advance to Bloemfontein. The British launched an attack on 7 March 1900, and when French's cavalry threatened to outflank the Boer positions, they withdrew. British losses amounted to eight killed and 49 wounded; the Boers lost at least one killed and one wounded. Breytenbach, op cit, V, pp. 27–63; Maurice (ed.), op cit, II, pp. 180–207; Amery (ed.), op cit, III, pp. 560–9.

73 On 10 March 1900, in the vicinity of Abrahamskraal and Driefontein, De Wet, with not more than about 3,000 men and about twelve guns and pom-poms, staged a last attempt to stop Roberts' advance to Bloemfontein. The British attacked in several sectors at once, and after putting up fierce resistance, the Boers succumbed to the vastly superior numbers and fled eastwards. The British lost at least 60 killed and 361 wounded; the Boers at least 32 killed, nineteen taken POW (including a few wounded) as well as about 40 others wounded. Breytenbach, op cit, V, pp. 64–96; Maurice (ed.), op cit, II, pp. 208–29; Amery (ed.), op cit, III, pp. 573–86.

74 See Note 69.

75 Roberts' advance from Bloemfontein to Pretoria only started on 3 May 1900. Originally it was intended that the central column would start its advance on 2 May, but the 11th Division was delayed in arriving at Karee Siding, and the advance was postponed by 24 hours. Amery (ed.), op cit, IV, p. 102.

76 Colonel R.S.S. Baden-Powell, CO at Mafikeng (Mafeking) informed Roberts that he would not be able to hold out longer than 22 May 1900. Roberts then ordered Lieutenant-General Archibald Hunter to organize a relief force. On 4 May this force, consisting of about 1,150 men, four guns and two machine-guns, under the command of Colonel B.T. Mahon, left Barkly-West. On 15 May they met Colonel H.C.O. Plumer's force. Two days later Mafikeng was officially relieved. Amery (ed.), op cit, IV, pp. 596–7; A.P. Smit and L. Maré (eds), *Die Beleg van Mafeking. Dagboek van Abraham Stafleu*, pp. 258–70.

77 Komatipoort, on the Transvaal side of the border with Portuguese East Africa (Mozambique).

78 A regiment of Canadian rough-riders raised by D.A. Smith, 1st Baron Strathcona – see also Biographical Notes: D.A. Smith.

79 At 12.30 on 3 May 1900, the first British troops entered the town of Brandfort, about 50 km (30 miles) north of Bloemfontein. Only the Heidelberg commando and Colonel J.Y.F. Blake's Irish Brigade gave some resistance, but soon withdrew. The Boers lost one killed and seventeen wounded; the British six killed and 30 wounded. On 4 May Roberts halted at Brandfort with his infantry, so that the railway could be repaired and supplies forwarded. He continued his advance the next day. In the meantime, Lieutenant-General Leslie Rundle led the operations on Roberts' eastern flank. Amery (ed.), op cit, IV, pp. 102–5, 239; Breytenbach, op cit, V, pp. 420–6.

80 The first half of this letter is published in Amery (ed.), op cit, IV, p. 240. In the Amery version the punctuation and wording sometimes differ from the manuscript copy published here.

81 In practice the Boers opposed the British at the Vet River (5 May 1900) and Sand River (7 and 10 May), but on all three occasions the Boers yielded under pressure of the vastly superior British force. Not even the presence of Louis Botha, the hero of Colenso and new Transvaal Commandant-General after the death of Piet Joubert on 27 March 1900, could rally the Boers. On 12 May Roberts occupied Kroonstad. Breytenbach, op cit, V, pp. 437–83.

82 In practice the OFS seat of government was moved to Heilbron in the northern OFS, then to Lindley, and later to Bethlehem in the north-east of the country, before Steyn and his government-in-the-field accompanied De Wet's commando for most of the rest of the war.

83 Should be Drakensberg, i.e. Dragon's Mountain. See also Biggarsburg (which should read Biggarsberg) further on in this paragraph. Berg (mountain) is often mis-spelt in the documents.

84 Not in Lansdowne Papers at the BL MS Room. Buller eventually started his advance on 11 May 1900.

85 The First Irish Transvaal Brigade (initially consisting mainly of Irish Uitlanders who sympathised with the Boer cause, but later also including a group of about 50 Irish-Americans who arrived in March 1900) was officially formed on 1 October 1899 by Colonel J.Y.F. Blake (see also Biographical Notes), saw action in Natal, October 1899 – April 1900 (including the battle of Colenso, when they clashed with the Second Royal Dublin Fusiliers); then moved to the OFS to try to stem Roberts' advance, for example at Brandfort (3 May 1900). Breytenbach, op cit, V, pp. 420–4; A. Wessels (ed.), 'Irish Nationalists and South Africa, 1877–1902 (by J.L. McCracken)', *Christiaan de Wet Annals* 5, October 1978, pp. 171, 173, 176–80.

86 Mrs Râmèh Theodora Chamberlain was the wife of Joseph Chamberlain's (see Biographical Notes) brother, Richard. She visited South Africa from November 1899 to August 1900. As far as her submission to the Royal

Commission Appointed to Consider and Report upon the Care and Treatment of the Sick and Wounded during the South African Campaign (see Cd. 453) is concerned, see the *Royal Commission on South African Hospitals. Minutes of Evidence taken before the Royal Commission Appointed to Consider and Report upon the Care and Treatment of the Sick and Wounded during the South African Campaign* (Cd. 454), pp. 537–54.

87 See *South Africa Despatches. Vol. I. From 1st November 1899 to 1st August 1900* (Cd. 457), pp. 210–21: Roberts – Lansdowne, 26 March 1900.

88 Sir Godfrey Lagden – see Biographical Notes.

89 Charles Petty-Fitzmaurice, the younger of Lord Lansdowne's two sons. He was killed in action, 1914.

90 See document 28 for Roberts' reply.

91 I.e. the Witwatersrand; Johannesburg and surrounding gold-rich areas.

92 I.e. Cape Mounted Riflemen or Cape Mounted Police.

93 The Spioenkop despatches were eventually published in 1902 – see *South Africa. The Spion Kop Despatches* (Cd. 968).

94 Probably Colonel G.F.R. Henderson, Roberts' former Director of Military Intelligence – see Biographical Notes.

95 Alberta Frances Anne Hamilton, Marchioness of Blandford (1847–1932). Married the 8th Marquis of Blandford, 1869. He became the 8th Duke of Marlborough (died 1892).

96 See document 26.

97 The Reform Committee was established in 1895 by the Uitlander leaders in Johannesburg aiming at reforms in the ZAR so that they (the Uitlanders) might obtain more political rights. In collaboration with Cecil John Rhodes the Committee planned the uprising in Johannesburg which was to be supported by Dr L.S. Jameson's invasion force ('raiders'). The failure of the Jameson Raid brought an end to the Committee's activities. All except one of the 64 Committee members were arrested and tried for high treason. The leaders were sentenced to death but reprieved by President Paul Kruger. *Standard Encyclopaedia of Southern Africa (SESA)*, IX, p. 270.

98 Leander Starr Jameson (1853–1917) qualified as a medical doctor and in 1878 settled in Kimberley. He became Cecil John Rhodes' Private Secretary in 1886, Chief Magistrate of Moshonaland (in the present-day Zimbabwe) in 1891, and in 1895 also Resident Commissioner of that part of Bechuanaland bordering on the Transvaal. On 29 December 1895 Jameson led 510 policemen and volunteers (with three field-guns and eight maxims) into the Transvaal in an attempt to overthrow the government, but was defeated and forced to surrender at Doornkop, near Krugersdorp, on 2 January 1896. See, for example, G. Cuthbertson and E-M. Cadell, *The Jameson Raid. A Centennial Retrospect*, and W.J. du Plooy, 'Die Militêre Voorbereidings en Verloop van die Jameson-inval'.

99 See Note 81.

100 Even until shortly before the cessation of hostilities in May 1902, many Boers believed that countries like Germany, France, the Netherlands and Russia would intervene militarily on their behalf. The roots of this false hope can be traced back to, *inter alia*, the sympathy expressed towards the Transvaal by many European countries following the abortive Jameson Raid, 1895–6. What many Boers did not realize, was that the strength of the Royal Navy and the diplomatic situation in Europe, precluded any form of active support for the Boer cause by European governments.

101 Approximately 27,000 Boers were taken POW during the war. They were detained in camps in the Cape Colony, Bermuda, St Helena, and India (including in what is today Sri Lanka).

102 Rookes Evelyn Bell Crompton (1845–1940), an electrical engineer, served in South Africa in 1900.

103 Steam traction engines were used by the British in South Africa since March 1900, for example to take supplies to certain posts away from the railway lines. Amery (ed.), op cit, VI, pp. 348–50.

104 Reverend John Cox Edghill (died 1917). Ordained 1858, served at Aldershot, 1881–2; Portsmouth, 1882–5. Chaplain-General to Forces, 1885–1901.

105 Either Reverend Edward Henry Winnington-Ingram (1849–1930) or Reverend Arthur Foley Winnington-Ingram (1858–1946).

106 Not in Lansdowne Papers at the BL MS Room.

107 In March 1900 the governments of the two Boer republics decided to send a deputation overseas in an effort to procure foreign arbitration in the conflict. A. Fischer, C.H. Wessels and A.D.W. Wolmarans visited the Netherlands (April 1900), the USA (May–July 1900) and France, Germany and Russia (August 1900) without achieving any success.

108 See Note 76.

109 Driefontein. See Note 73.

110 Lieutenant-General I.S.M. Hamilton occupied Heilbron on 22 May. Amery (ed.), op cit, IV, p. 128.

111 The OFS was only formally annexed as the ORC on 28 May 1900, when Roberts reached the Vaal River, i.e. the northern border with the Transvaal, but the date was antedated to 24 May to coincide with Queen Victoria's 81st birthday.

112 Shortly afterwards Mackenzie was in fact appointed as Military Governor of Johannesburg – see also Biographical Notes.

113 Boers under the overall command of General Louis Botha took up positions on the Klipriviersberg, just south of Johannesburg. In the battle that took place there, and to the west, on 28 and 29 May 1900, the British lost 28 killed and 134 wounded. Boer losses were not recorded. The 1st Gordons, commanded by Colonel Forbes Macbean, took part in a gallant charge on 29 May and dislodged the Boers from a hill. The Gordons lost 21 killed and 85 wounded. Amery (ed.), op cit, IV, pp. 139–47; Breytenbach, op cit, V, pp. 524–35.

114 The Nederlandsche Zuid-Afrikaansche Spoorweg-Maatschappij (NZASM) was established on 31 June 1887, and built and owned most of the railway lines in the Transvaal. As war clouds gathered, the Transvaal government took over the NZASM's railways and workshop on 29 September 1899. On 12 September 1900 the British authorities confiscated all NZASM properties. The NZASM was dissolved on 13 October 1908. *SESA*, VIII, pp. 156–8.

115 On 29 (not 28) May 1900 Rundle launched an unsuccessful attack against a Boer force at Biddulphsberg, near Senekal in the ORC, suffering about 185 casualties. The Boers only lost one killed and three wounded, of whom one (General A.J. de Villiers) later died. *History of the War in South Africa 1899–1902*, III, pp. 122–3; Amery (ed.), op cit, IV, pp. 248–51; Breytenbach, op cit, VI, pp. 215–19.

116 On the eve of the British entry into Johannesburg, a number of Boers and foreign volunteers under Judge Anthonie Kock went to the Robinson Mine to blow it up, but were stopped by their fellow compatriots. D.W. Krüger, *Die Krugermiljoene*, pp. 18, 22–5. Sir Joseph Benjamin Robinson (1840–1929) was a pioneer mining magnate. For F.E.T. Krause – see Biographical Notes.

Part 2
6 June 1900 to 1 January 1901
Introduction

1 D. James, *Lord Roberts*, p. 354.

2 As far as the British military government in the Transvaal is concerned, see M.H. Buys, 'Militêre Regering in Transvaal, 1900–1902'.

3 L.S. Amery (ed.), *The Times History of the War in South Africa 1899–1902*, IV, pp. 264–5; W.L. von R. Scholtz, 'Generaal Christiaan de Wet as Veldheer', pp. 171–9.

4 T. Pakenham, *The Boer War*, p. 377.

5 A.E. Breytenbach, 'Die Slag by Donkerhoek, 11–12 Junie 1900', *passim*; H.F. Nel, 'Die Slag van Donkerhoek 11–12 Junie 1900', *Militaria* 15(1), 1985, pp. 52–8 and 15(2), 1985, pp. 17–30; *History of the War in South Africa 1899–1902*, III, pp. 204–25; Amery (ed.), op cit, IV, pp. 269–96; J.H. Breytenbach, *Die Geskiedenis van die Tweede Vryheidsoorlog in Suid-Afrika, 1899–1902*, VI, pp. 174–207.

6 Amery (ed.), op cit, IV, pp. 184–97, 398–400; *History of the War in South Africa 1899–1902*, III, pp. 273–83.

7 Amery (ed.), op cit, IV, pp. 349–54; *History of the War in South Africa 1899–1902*, III, pp. 236–48.

8 *Army. Proclamations Issued by Field-Marshal Lord Roberts in South Africa* (Cd. 426), pp. 10–11. See also Buys, op cit, pp. 102–5.

9   As far as the events in the Brandwater Basin and the first drive against
    De Wet is concerned see, for example, F. Pretorius, 'Die Eerste Dryfjag op
    hoofkmdt. C.R. de Wet', *Christiaan de Wet Annals* 4, October 1976.

10 B.G. Schultz, 'Die Slag van Bergendal (Dalmanutha)', *passim*; *History of the
    War in South Africa 1899–1902*, III, pp. 396–403; Amery (ed.), op cit, IV,
    pp. 380–413, 343–456; Breytenbach, op cit, VI, pp. 317–46.

11 Amery (ed.), op cit, II, pp. 460–3 and IV, pp. 436–50, 460–8, 479–80;
    DSAB, II, p. 101.

12 Amery (ed.), op cit, IV, pp. 474–83.

13 *DSAB*, II, p. 601; Pakenham, op cit, pp. 318–19, 384.

14 Scholtz, op cit, pp. 261–319; *History of the War in South Africa 1899–1902*,
    III, pp. 469–96; Amery (ed.), op cit, V, pp. 1–43.

15 M.H. Grant, *History of the War in South Africa 1899–1902*, IV, pp. 11–21;
    Amery (ed.), op cit, V, pp. 99–108. See also Document 60, Note 10.

16 As far as the Boer incursions into the Cape Colony are concerned see, for
    example, A. de Wet et al., *Die Buren in der Kapkolonie im Kriege mit England*,
    pp. 87–95; R.D. McDonald, *In die Skaduwee van die Dood*, p. 22 et seq.;
    N. Gomm, 'Commandant P.H. Kritzinger in the Cape, December 1900 –
    December 1901', *Military History Journal* 1(7), December 1970, pp. 30–2,
    34; J. Meinjes, *Sword in the Sand. The Life and Death of Gideon Scheepers*,
    p. 101 et seq.; G.S. Preller, *Scheepers se Dagboek en die Stryd in Kaapland
    (1 Okt. 1901 – 18 Jan. 1902)*, pp. 71–112; P.J. du Plessis, *Oomblikke van
    Spanning*, *passim*.

6 June to 1 January 1901

1   After occupying Johannesburg unopposed on 31 May 1900, Roberts
    continued his advance to Pretoria on 3 June. On 4 June British artillery fired
    a few shots at Fort Schanskop on a hill just south of Pretoria, and also at the
    station, but the fire was not returned and the Transvaal capital was occupied
    the following day. S. du Preez, 'Die Val van Pretoria', *Militaria* 5(3), 1975,
    pp. 22–39.

2   The Johannesburg Fort, and Fort Schanskop, Fort Wonderboompoort, Fort
    Klapperkop and Fort Daspoortrand on the outskirts of Pretoria, were built
    1896–8. See J. Ploeger, *Die Fortifikasie van Pretoria. Fort Klapperkop – Gister
    en Vandag.*

3   On 27 May 1900 the 13th Battalion Imperial Yeomanry under the command
    of Lieutenant-Colonel B.E. Spragge was surrounded by a Boer force 3 km
    (2 miles) north-west of Lindley in the OFS. As the Boers brought up more
    artillery, the British position became ever more untenable, and – after losing
    25 killed – the whole force of 443 officers and men (including 55 wounded)
    surrendered. Boer casualties amounted to about 70. B.N. Reckitt, *The
    Lindley Affair. A Diary of the Boer War*, p. 9 et seq.; *History of the War in
    South Africa 1899–1902*, III, pp. 115–20; L.S. Amery (ed.), *The Times*

History of the War in South Africa 1899–1902, IV, pp. 252–9; *Army. Findings of a Court of Enquiry held at Barberton on 25th September, 1900, to Investigate the Circumstances under which Lieutenant-Colonel B.E. Spragge, D.S.O., XIIIth Bn. Imperial Yeomanry, and Others, became Prisoners of War* (Cd. 470).

4 On 17 May 1900, Brigadier-General R.G. Broadwood, part of Lieutenant-General I.S.M. Hamilton's force, occupied Lindley, after a short skirmish. In the light of renewed Boer activities in the area, Hamilton withdrew from the town on 20 May, and the Boers, who had been waiting outside, re-occupied it. On 26 May Major-General H.E. Colvile entered the town without any opposition. Amery (ed.), op cit, IV, pp. 127–8, 246.

5 Roberts occupied Kroonstad on 12 May 1900 and resumed his advance on 22 May.

6 On 29 May 1900 Kruger left Pretoria by train and travelled to Machadodorp in the Eastern Transvaal, which became the temporary Transvaal seat of government (5 June – 27 August 1900), and where he in fact lived in a railway carriage. He left on 27 August when the advancing British forces shelled the town.

7 Petronella Meyer, née Burger (died 1961), second wife of General Lukas Meyer. They had no children.

8 The Nederduitse Gereformeerde Kerk (Dutch Reformed Church) building in Kroonstad. In places like Bloemfontein, Kroonstad and Pretoria, the British often used churches and public buildings as hospitals.

9 The Palace of Justice on Pretoria's Church Square was completed in 1900 and was used as a hospital by the British. Later the Transvaal Provincial Division of the Supreme Court of South Africa sat in the building. Many noteworthy trials have taken place in the building, including the Rivonia Trial, which led to Nelson Mandela and other senior members of the African National Congress being sentenced to life imprisonment in 1964.

10 See RA VIC/P10/102.

11 On 19 June 1900 General C.R. de Wet attacked Lord Methuen's convoy near Heilbron, but was driven off. On 23 June Major-General R.A.P. Clements' convoy of sick, en route from Senekal to Winburg, was attacked by General Paul Roux, but the Boers were driven off. On 26 June Lieutenant-Colonel H.M. Grenfell was attacked at Leliefontein between Senekal and Kroonstad, but he was able to extricate himself. Amery (ed.), op cit, IV, pp. 268, 300–1.

12 The Boxer Movement aimed to rid China of all foreigners. In May 1900 the Boxers marched on Peking (Beijing), assailed the foreign legations and caused a lot of damage. Britain and other foreign powers sent troops to China and in August 1900 the Boxer Rising was put down.

13 In January 1900 Roberts placed Major-General H.E. Colvile (see Biographical Notes) in command of the newly-formed 9th Division. He took part in Roberts' advance to Bloemfontein, but failed to give the necessary

assistance to Brigadier-General R.G. Broadwood at Sannaspos (see Part 1, Note 66) and Colonel B.E. Spragge at Lindley (see Note 3). Colvile was made the scapegoat for both reverses, and when the 9th Division was broken up at the end of June 1900, Roberts had him returned to his command at Gibraltar. When Colvile returned to England in November 1900, he gave his version of events to the press, fell in disfavour with the War Office, and was forced to retire in January 1901. *DSAB*, III, p. 170. See also H.E. Colvile, *The Work of the Ninth Division.*

14 William Flack Stevenson (1844–1922), Surgeon-General and PMO, Lines of Communication, South Africa, 1899; PMO, Lord Roberts' HQ Staff, 1900.

15 Buller occupied Standerton on 22 June 1900.

16 Foreign military attachés accompanied both the British and Boer forces during the semi-conventional phases of the war.

17 Colonel Viscount Downe. On Lord Roberts' staff, 1900; OC, Yeomanry Brigade.

18 I.e. the Roman Catholic nuns of the organization Sisters of Charity of Nazareth. They came to South Africa in 1884.

19 Also published in *South Africa. Further Correspondence Relating to Affairs in South Africa* (Cd. 420), p. 9. The version reproduced in document 38 is a transcription of the original document, and differs in a few instances as far as the use of capital letters and punctuation are concerned.

20 The Boers carried off about 1,000 British POWs with them, leaving over 3,000 behind at Waterval, just north of Pretoria. The Waterval prisoners were released on 6 June, after a force under the command of Colonel T.C. Porter put the Boers to flight. The other POWs were taken to Nooitgedacht in the Eastern Transvaal, where they were in due course joined by about 1,000 other POWs, and only released on 30 August 1900 when the Boers retreated further eastwards. Amery (ed.), op cit, IV, pp. 269–70, 457.

21 Should be spelt Middelburg. In most of the documents it is mis-spelt. Unless indicated otherwise in the Notes, the Middelburg referred to in the texts is always the (Eastern) Transvaal town; there is also a Middelburg in the Cape (Midlands).

22 Many Boer women and children went to Pretoria as refugees, placing additional pressure on the British food resources. Roberts held Botha responsible for looking after these civilians, and expelled several hundred of them to Botha's laager near Machadodorp. Buys, op cit, pp. 114–16; E. Hobhouse, *The Brunt of War and where it Fell*, pp. 33–4; T. Pakenham, *The Boer War*, pp. 449–50.

23 Lieutenant-General Archibald Hunter slowly but surely cornered a large Boer force, consisting of several commandos, in the Brandwater Basin, Eastern ORC. Slabbert's Nek was not guarded, and De Wet, Steyn, other members of the OFS government and about 2,600 burghers with five guns and more than 400 wagons and carts escaped via this route during the night

of 15–16 July 1900. The first drive against De Wet followed, but he successfully evaded the British columns that pursued him, escaped across the Vaal River and sought sanctuary north of the Magalies Mountains. F. Pretorius, 'Die Eerste Dryfjag op hoofkmdt. C.R. de Wet', *Christiaan de Wet Annals* 4, October 1976, p. 22 *et seq*. See also *Confidential Telegrams*, pp. 185–6, Nos 288 and 289: Roberts to Lansdowne, 16 July 1900 and 24 July 1900, as well as Note 27.

24 Lieutenant-Colonel Walter Philip Alexander (born 1849) had no previous war service.

25 The clash at Uitvalsnek (better known as Silkaatsnek), west of Pretoria, took place on 11 July 1900, and heralded the start of the guerrilla war in that region. Lieutenant-Colonel H.R. C-Roberts' force (see also Note 26) of about 250 men (Scots Greys and Lincolns) with two guns were attacked by about 300 Boers under General J.H. de la Rey. After holding out the whole day, the British surrendered shortly after sunset, having lost at least seventeen killed and 44 wounded. Roberts was amongst those wounded and taken prisoner. The 44 (or more) wounded plus at least 86 unwounded soldiers, were all taken prisoner. The Boers lost six killed and eight wounded. Lieutenant-Colonel W.P. Alexander did not give the necessary support to Roberts' force. Amery (ed.), op cit, IV, pp. 350–4; Breytenbach, op cit, VI, pp. 256–60; *History of the War in South Africa 1899–1902*, III, pp. 238–41.

26 Lieutenant-Colonel Henry Roger Crompton-Roberts (1863–1925). Operated in the Western Transvaal, 1900.

27 As Hunter's columns closed in on the Boer forces trapped in the Brandwater Basin, Marthinus Prinsloo was (under controvercial circumstances) elected Chief Commandant of the Boer forces in the Basin. He entered into negotiations with Hunter re conditions of a possible surrender, and on 29 July 1900 agreed to surrender all the forces in the Basin. Not all the senior Boer officers accepted Prinsloo's authority, and at least four Generals, five Commandants and about 1,500 burghers with eight guns, a pom-pom and two machine-guns broke out of the Basin to continue the struggle. However, by 9 August, three other Generals, nine Commandants, and 4,314 burghers had surrendered. The British also captured three guns, about 2,800 cattle, 4,000 sheep, nearly 6,000 horses, and approximately two million rounds of small-arms ammunition. Although Prinsloo's surrender dealt the OFS forces a serious blow (comparable to that of Cronjé's surrender at Paardeberg), it did not signal the end of Boer resistance in the ORC. *History of the War in South Africa 1899–1902*, III, pp. 293–306; Amery (ed.), op cit, IV, pp. 309–43.

28 Towards the middle of 1900 a six-man commission under the chairmanship of Sir Robert Romer (1840–1918), Lord Justice of Appeal, 1899–1906, was appointed to investigate the care of the wounded and the ill in South Africa. See *Royal Commission on South African Hospitals. Report of the Royal*

Commission Appointed to Consider and Report upon the Care and Treatment of the Sick and Wounded during the South African Campaign (Cd. 453), as well as the minutes (Cd. 454) and appendix to the minutes (Cd. 455) of the report.

29 Alfred Ernest Albert, Duke of Edinburgh and Duke of Saxe-Coburg and Gotha (1844–1900), 2nd son of Queen Victoria. Followed a naval career: Rear-Admiral, 1878; Vice-Admiral, 1882; Admiral, 1887. C-in-C, Mediterranean, 1886–9; C-in-C, Devonport, 1890–3; Admiral of the Fleet, 1893. Died suddenly at Rosenau, near Coburg, Germany, 30 July 1900.

30 King Umberto I (1844–1900) succeeded his father, Victor Emmanuel II, in 1878 as the united Italy's second king. On 29 July 1900 he was assassinated by an anarchist, Angelo Bresci, at Monza.

31 Original ms in RA VIC/P12/24. Punctuation and spelling have been altered to conform with the original ms. The original ms also has the following postscript: 'Hearing that Prince Christian Victor had no suitable appointment in Natal, I telegraphed and offered him an extra A.D.C. Ship on my staff. He has accepted and will, I hope, soon join me.'

32 At Brakfontein, on the Elands River, Lieutenant-Colonel Charles Owen Hore (1860–1916) and just more than 500 men, a muzzle-loading 7-pounder gun and two machine-guns, kept up the connection between Mafikeng and Zeerust. From 4–16 August 1900 the force was besieged by General J.H. de la Rey with at least 500 men, at least four guns, one pom-pom and two machine-guns. Several British columns were at some stage sent out to relieve Hore, but he was eventually only relieved by Lord Kitchener. During the siege the British lost at least twelve killed and 36 wounded. L. Wulfsohn, 'Elands River. A Siege which possibly Changed the Course of History in South Africa', *Military History Journal* 6(3), June 1984, pp. 106–8; Amery (ed.), op cit, IV, pp. 357–61, 428–9.

33 There were many Boer sympathizers in Pretoria and Johannesburg, and some of them kept on supplying the Boers with information, or even actively plotted against the British administration. In Pretoria, Hans Cordua, a German who served as a Lieutenant in the Transvaal State Artillery, and now on parole, plotted to kidnap Lord Roberts and other officers; and in Johannesburg a plot was afoot to celebrate Bastille Day (14 July) by overpowering British officers at a race-meeting planned for that day. Some 475 foreigners, some involved with the race-course plot, were arrested on 13 July, and Roberts had them deported. Cordua's plot was only discovered on 9 August. He was tried by a court-martial, sentenced to death, and shot. His grave can still be seen in the Old Cemetery, Pretoria. Amery (ed.), op cit, IV, pp. 392–3 and VI, pp. 593–4.

34 According to M.G. Dooner, *The "Last Post": being a Roll of all Officers (Naval, Military or Colonial) who gave their Lives for their Queen, King and Country, in the South African War, 1899–1902*, p. 169, Colonel Welman Hawker Helyar (born August 1844), OC of the 7th Battalion (Staffordshire) IY, was murdered by Boers on 26 July 1900.

35 The Spioenkop despatches were eventually published in 1902 – see *South Africa. The Spion Kop Despatches* (Cd. 968).

36 See *South Africa Despatches. Vol. II*, pp. 1–12: Roberts – Lansdowne, 14 August 1900.

37 See Note 12.

38 Lieutenant-Colonel Bernhard Drysdale Möller (born 1854), 18th Hussars, had no previous war service. He surrendered with more than 200 MI and Cavalry at Talana, 20 October 1899. See also Prologue, Note 1.

39 Probably Major William B. Peter, Volunteer Artillery Corps.

40 See Note 24.

41 Probably Commander Crowe (Royal Navy), the British Consul-General in Lourenço Marques, who organized an intelligence branch at Delagoa Bay.

42 Carrington reached Zeerust on 2 August 1900. Hampered by empty ox-wagons, he slowly moved towards Elands River. On 5 August he clashed with General H.L. Lemmer's force near Elands River, but rather than follow up his success, he decided to fall back to Zeerust. There he burned a great quantity of stores which he was unable to take away with him, and reached Mafikeng on 10 August. Amery (ed.), op cit, IV, pp. 358–60. See also Note 32.

43 Probably a letter dated 16 July 1900 is referred to, but there is no such letter in the BL MS Room. Roberts did, however, write to Lansdowne on 13 July and 19 July 1900, the latter published here as document 40. See also *South Africa Despatches. Vol. I. From 1st November 1899 to 1st August 1900*, pp. 362–73: Roberts – Lansdowne, 3 July 1900 (including Buller's account of his advance from Ladysmith to Newcastle, and telegraphic correspondence between Roberts and Buller).

44 According to James, op cit, pp. 314–15, there was some adverse comment re Lady Roberts' presence in South Africa, and that her being there perhaps even took Lord Roberts' mind off the campaign; but that in practice she and her daughters helped in looking after the material comforts of the elderly C-in-C, and took work off his hands by visiting the sick and wounded in hospital. According to Pakenham, op cit, p. 449, there were rumours that Roberts' gradual hardening policy towards the civilian Boer population had something to do with Lady Roberts' presence in Pretoria. See also document 45.

45 Not in the Lansdowne Papers at the BL MS Room.

46 See Note 12.

47 In the course of the war, about 30,000 white colonial troops from Canada, Australia, New Zealand and other oversea British colonies saw service in South Africa, as well as about 50,000 whites from what is today South Africa: colonials from the Cape Colony and Natal, and Uitlanders from the Transvaal. Especially amongst the Cape colonials, were several Afrikaans-speaking persons. In due course at least 5,500 former Transvaal or OFS republican burghers, who had laid down their arms, joined the British forces to fight against their former comrades. After the war these so-called 'joiners'

were to a large extent ostracized in the Afrikaner community. J. Stirling, *The Colonials in South Africa, 1899–1902. Their Record, based on the Despatches* and A.M. Grundlingh, *Die "Hendsoppers" en "Joiners". Die Rasionaal en Verskynsel van Verraad.*

48 See Note 23.

49 Original ms in RA VIC/P12/58. Punctuation has been altered to conform with the original ms.

50 See Part 1, Note 69.

51 See Part 1, Note 115.

52 At Paardeberg (see Part 1, Note 39) and at the battle of Abrahamskraal-Driefontein (see Part 1, Note 73) Kelly-Kenny commanded the 6th Division.

53 When Roberts advanced northwards from Bloemfontein, Kelly-Kenny was ordered to guard his line of communication. This he did so efficiently that Roberts placed him in overall command of the British forces in the ORC. The cutting of the railway line refers to De Wet's capture of Roodewal Station on 7 June 1900. In simultaneous attacks on Roodewal, Vredefort Road and Renoster River Bridge, De Wet's forces killed 45 British soldiers and captured 795 (including 125 wounded), and captured arms, ammunition and stores worth at least £100,000. Communication with Pretoria was restored on 14 June. Breytenbach, op cit, VI, pp. 222–8; Amery (ed.), op cit, IV, pp. 264–6.

54 I.e. the operations in the Brandwater Basin, Eastern ORC. See Notes 23 and 27.

55 In April 1900 he was given command of the 11th Division.

56 Brigadier-General John Baillie Ballantyne Dickson (born 1842). Previous service in Anglo-Zulu War, 1879; Sudan, 1884–5.

57 See Hutton's role at the clashes at Brandfort (3 May 1900), Vet River (5 May) and Doornkop (29 May), sallies in the direction of Rustenburg, and role in the Eastern Transvaal. See also Biographical Notes.

58 After the battle of Bergendal (Dalmanutha), 21–7 August 1900, the remaining commandos in Transvaal all had to resort to guerrilla warfare in an effort to survive, and it was impossible for the 75 year old Kruger to accompany the fast-moving commandos. The Transvaal government decided that he should go to Europe to promote the Boer cause. Accompanied by his private secretary and a few followers, he crossed the Portuguese border at Komatipoort on 11 September and departed from Lourenço Marques on 19 October on board the Dutch cruiser *De Gelderland*, which had been sent by Queen Wilhelmina of the Netherlands. *DSAB*, I, p. 453.

59 See *Confidential Telegrams*, p. 199, No. 326: Lansdowne – Roberts, 11 September 1900, and No. 327, Roberts – Lansdowne, 12 September, 1900.

60 See *Confidential Telegrams*, pp. 199–200, No. 327 (Roberts' No. 236, cipher, of 12 September 1900) and No. 328 (Lansdowne's No. 1161, cipher, of 13 September 1900).

61 On 14 September 1900 Lord Roberts issued his Proclamation No. 17 of 1900 re the resignation of President Kruger. Roberts sketched what he regarded as a hopeless situation for the remaining Boers, but warned that he would use every means in his power to end the guerrilla war. See Cd. 426, pp. 17–18.

62 See RA VIC/P13/68: H.D. Coutts – Lord Stanley.

63 See document 41.

64 Botha did not resign.

65 Helena Augusta Victoria (1846–1923) was the 5th child (and 3rd daughter) of Queen Victoria. She became Princess Christian of Schleswig-Holstein (Denmark) when she married Prince Frederick Christian Charles Augustus of Schleswig-Holstein in 1866. Nine private hospitals were sent to South Africa during the Anglo-Boer War. A 100-bed private hospital given by Mr Alfred Mosely opened at Pinetown in Natal (April 1900), and was called the Princess Christian Hospital. In July 1900 it was placed at the disposal of HRH Princess Christian, who presented it to the British Government. The hospital train 'Princess Christian' was constructed in Birmingham. In March 1900 it was assembled in Durban and was the first train to enter Ladysmith after the relief. It was presented to the military authorities in South Africa as a permanent hospital train in June 1901. Amery (ed.), op cit, VI, pp. 532–3, 536.

66 I.e. Roberts' appointment at the War Office as C-in-C of the British Army, a position he took up in January 1901 and held until it was abolished on 8 February 1904.

67 See document 47.

68 Richard John Seddon (1845–1906), Premier of New Zealand, 1893–1906.

69 Frederick Temple (1821–1902). Ordained, 1846; Examiner of Education Department, 1848–9; Principal, Kneller Hall, Twickenham, 1849–55; Inspector of Men's Training Colleges, 1855–7; Headmaster, Rugby School, 1857–69; Bishop of Exeter, 1869–84; Bampton Lecturer at Oxford, 1884; Bishop of London, 1884–96; Archbishop of Canterbury, 1896–1902.

70 In a letter to Lord Roberts dated 5 July 1900, the Archbishop of Canterbury expressed his concern re the form of welcome the soldiers would receive on their return to Britain from South Africa. The Archbishop suggested that Roberts should write to the papers and appeal to the people of England to welcome the soldiers in a responsible manner. Roberts reacted positively to the Archbishop's appeal. See Lambeth Palace Library: F. Temple Papers, Official Letters. 1900. Foreign C.1 – S.8. Vol. 41, ff. 415–16.

71 Dr Washbourne went to South Africa as a member of the Imperial Yeomanry Hospital Staff; locally appointed as a consulting physician.

72 Roberts annexed the ZAR on 1 September 1900 as the Transvaal Colony. See his proclamation (No. 15 of 1900), reproduced in Cd. 426, p. 16. On 25 October 1900 a parade was held in Pretoria to ceremonially inaugurate

the new British colony. More than 6,500 soldiers, led by Major-General C. Tucker, marched past Lord Roberts in Church Square. J.M. Cobban, *The Life and Deeds of Earl Roberts*, IV, pp. 157–60.

73 Prince Christian Victor lies buried in what is today known as the Old Cemetery in Pretoria, just west of the city centre. In the same cemetery are also the graves of more than 1,000 other British soldiers who died during the war, several burghers and Boer commanders, President and Mrs Kruger, Hans Cordua (executed for plotting to kidnap Roberts – see Note 33), as well as South African Prime Ministers J.G. Strijdom and H.F. Verwoerd. As far as the Prince's role in the war and his death is concerned see, for example, H. Warren, *Christian Victor. The Story of a Young Soldier*, pp. 300–97.

74 William Pitcairn Campbell (1856–1933). Previous service in Sudan, 1884–5. Saw action in South Africa, 1899–1902, for example in command of 1st Battalion KRR and a mobile column in the Eastern Transvaal. GOC, Southern Command, 1914–16; and Western Command, 1916–18.

75 Major Harry Francis Pakenham (born 1864). Previous service in Hazara Expedition, 1891; Miranzai Expedition, 1891.

76 Captain Herbert Richard Blore (1871–1955). Previous service in Chitral, 1895. Saw action in South Africa, 1899–1902. Later served in World War I, 1914–18. Lieutenant-Colonel, 1916.

77 Captain Louis Batie Cumberland (born 1870). Previous service in Isazai Expedition, 1892; operations in Chitral, 1895.

78 Captain Lord Robert William Orlando Manners (1870–1917). Previous service in Isazai Campaign, 1892. Saw action in South Africa, 1899–1902, and from 1914–17 in World War I (wounded).

79 Lieutenant Dermot Howard Blundell-Hollinshead-Blundell (born 1874) had no previous war record.

80 Lieutenant Hereward Wake (1876–1963) had no previous war record. Fought 1899–1902 (wounded). Also served in World War I, 1914–18. Brigadier-General, 1917; Major-General, 1932. GOC, Northern Home Guard, 1940–3.

81 Lieutenant Gerald Hamilton Martin (1879–1952) had no previous war service. Served in South Africa, 1899–1902, and later in World War I, 1914–18. Retired as a Colonel, 1932.

82 Lieutenant Henry Brewster Percy Lion Kennedy (born 1878) had no previous war record.

83 De Wet's attempt to invade the Cape Colony towards the end of November 1900 was thwarted by a full Gariep (Orange) River. On 10 February 1901 he succeeded in entering the Colony.

84 Brigadier-General T.E. Stephenson (see Biographical Notes) commanded the Barberton District. In the first week of December 1900 the Boers attacked several trains and fortified posts in the Eastern Transvaal. In the vicinity of Barberton the British lost two men killed and five wounded, and

one officer and thirteen men taken POW. M.H. Grant, *History of the War in South Africa 1899–1902*, IV, pp. 23–4.

85 On his way south in an effort to invade the Cape Colony, De Wet and his approximately 1,500 men besieged and defeated the British garrison at Dewetsdorp (named after his father), 21–23 November 1900. The British force of about 480 men was under the command of Major W.G. Massy, RA. Fourteen soldiers were killed; the rest (including 82 wounded) were taken prisoner. The two British guns were also captured. It is unknown how many Boers became casualties. W.L. von R. Scholtz, 'Generaal Christiaan de Wet as Veldheer', pp. 294–7; Amery (ed.), op cit, V, pp. 28–32.

86 Thomas Joseph O'Reilly was Mayor of Cape Town from 17 September 1900 to 12 September 1901.

87 After Major-General George Pomeroy Colley was killed at Amajuba in the Transvaal War of Independence (1880–1), Roberts was appointed as the new C-in-C of the British forces in South Africa, but by the time he reached Cape Town (29 March 1881), peace had been concluded and he left 24 hours later.

88 During the sieges of Ladysmith, Mafikeng and Kimberley the locally raised colonial troops played an important role in assisting regular British soldiers defending the respective centres. During the siege of Jammerbergdrif near Wepener, the Cape Mounted Riflemen played a prominent role, while other members of the Colonial Division took part in the relief – see also Part 1, Note 68.

89 The night of 15–16 December 1900 the commandos of General J.B.M. Hertzog and Commandant P.H. Kritzinger invaded the Cape Colony.

90 On 21 December 1900 Kitchener met with the Burgher Peace Committee, consisting of surrendered Boers who wanted to co-operate with the British in an effort to end the war. Kitchener supported their proposal to send emissaries to the Boer commandos to try and convince them to lay down their arms. Grundlingh, op cit, pp. 82–91. When these efforts failed, Kitchener had to rethink his anti-guerrilla strategy.

91 Lieutenant-Colonel Lewis Horace Phillips (born 1852). Previous service in Jowaki Expedition, 1877–8; Afghanistan, 1879–80.

92 Lieutenant-Colonel Arthur Edward Richards Curran (born 1853), OC of the 1st Battalion Manchester Regiment. Besieged in Ladysmith, 1899–1900.

93 Ernest Allardice Gardiner Gosset (born 1857). Previous service in Transvaal War of Independence, 1880–1; Egypt, 1882; Sikkim, 1888; North-Western Frontier, India, 1897–8.

94 Major William George Massy (1857–1941), RA. CRA, East Anglian Division, 1908–12. Served from 1914–17 in World War I. As far as his surrender at Dewetsdorp is concerned, see Note 85.

Part 3
2 January 1901 to 30 May 1902
Introduction

1 D. James, *Lord Roberts*, pp. 369–71; G. Forrest, *The Life of Lord Roberts, K.G., V.C.*, pp. 324–6.

2 W.L. van R. Scholtz, 'Generaal Christiaan de Wet as Veldheer', pp. 321–70; L.S. Amery (ed.), *The Times History of the War in South Africa 1899–1902*, V, pp. 131–57; H.C.J. Pieterse, *Oorlogsavonture van genl. Wynand Malan*, p. 125 *et seq.*; L.M. Fourie, 'Die Militêre Loopbaan van Manie Maritz tot aan die Einde van die Anglo-Boereoorlog', pp. 35–43; S.G. Maritz, *My Lewe en Strewe*, pp. 25–54.

3 S.J. du Preez, 'Vredespogings gedurende die Anglo-Boereoorlog tot Maart 1901'.

4 As far as the British blockhouse system is concerned see, for example, J. Hattingh and A. Wessels, *Britse Fortifikasies in die Anglo-Boereoorlog (1899–1902)*, p. 19 *et seq.*; Amery (ed.), op cit, V, pp. 396–412.

5 As far as the role of black people and coloureds are concerned, see Note 1 of the general introduction. As far as atrocities are concerned see, for example, B. Nasson, *Abraham Esau's War. A Black South African War in the Cape 1899–1902, passim*; K. Schoeman, 'Die Dood van Abraham Esau. Ooggetuieberigte uit die besette Calvinia, 1901', *Quarterly Bulletin of the South African Library* 40(2), December 1985, pp. 56–66; Fourie, op cit, pp. 118–20.

6 As far as the conviction and execution of rebels are concerned see, for example, J.H. Snyman, 'Rebelle-verhoor in Kaapland gedurende die Tweede Vryheidsoorlog met spesiale Verwysing na die Militêre Howe (1899–1902)', *Archives Year Book for South African History* 25, 1962, pp. 1–73; G. Jordaan, *Hoe zij stierven, passim*.

7 The most definitive study to date with regard to the role played by former republican burghers in the British ranks, is A.M. Grundlingh, *Die "Hendsoppers" en "Joiners". Die Rasionaal en Verskynsel van Verraad*. See also J.P. Brits (ed.), *Diary of a National Scout. P.J. du Toit 1900–1902*.

8 The most definitive study to date with regard to the effect the war had on South Africa's civilian population, is S.B. Spies, *Methods of Barbarism? Roberts and Kitchener and Civilians in the Boer Republics January 1900 – May 1902*.

9 P.A. Pyper, 'Generaal J.C. Smuts en die Tweede Vryheidsoorlog (1899–1902)', pp. 64–141; P. Burke, *The Siege of O'okiep (Guerrilla Campaign in the Anglo-Boer War), passim*.

10 D.M. Moore, *General Louis Botha's Second Expedition to Natal during the Anglo-Boer War September – October 1901*, pp. 14–102; Amery (ed.), op cit, V, pp. 334–59, 364–76; M.H. Grant, *History of the War in South Africa 1899–1902*, IV, pp. 305–15.

11 W.S. Churchill, *Ian Hamilton's March*, *passim*; *DSAB*, II, p. 285.

12 Scholtz, op cit, pp. 415–53; Amery (ed.), op cit, V, pp. 467–94.

13 J.F. Naudé, *Vechten en Vluchten van Beyers en Kemp "Bôkant" De Wet*, pp. 323–36, 345–9, 352–4; Grant, op cit, IV, pp. 410–21, 494–504; Amery (ed.), op cit, V, pp. 497–9, 501–8, 519–24, 531–7.

14 S.J. du Preez, 'Die Vrede van Vereeniging', pp. 170–232; *DSAB*, II, p. 712; J.D. Kestell and D.E. van Velden, *The Peace Negotiations between the Governments of the South African Republic and the Orange Free State, and the Representatives of the British Government, which Terminated in the Peace Concluded at Vereeniging on the 31st May, 1902*, pp. 1–45.

15 Du Preez, op cit, pp. 233–340; Kestell and Van Velden, op cit, pp. 46–201.

2 January 1901 to 30 May 1902

1 Probably Kitchener's letter to Roberts dated 28 December 1900 – see document 57.

2 See Prologue, Note 6.

3 Queen Victoria died at Osborne House on the Isle of Wight at 18.30, 22 January 1901.

4 Captain David Ramsay Sladen (1869–1923). Previous service in Suakim, 1888; Sudan, 1889; India, 1897–8. Served in South Africa, 1899–1902. Later served in World War I, 1914–18 (twice wounded): commanded 2nd KOS Borderers, 1915–17. Brigadier-General, 1917.

5 Lieutenant-Colonel Henry Vivian Cowan (1854–1918). Previous service in Afghanistan, 1878–80; Egypt, 1882 (wounded). Saw action in South Africa, 1899–1900, as Military Secretary to Lord Roberts.

6 From January–April 1901 Lieutenant-General J.D.P. French was in charge of a massive drive (initiated by Lord Kitchener) in the Eastern Transvaal, from Pretoria south-eastwards to the border of Swaziland and Natal. Major-General H.L. Smith-Dorrien commanded 3,300 of the total fighting strength of about 14,000. M.H. Grant, *History of the War in South Africa 1899–1902*, IV, pp. 111–23; L.S. Amery (ed.), *The Times History of the War in South Africa 1899–1902*, V, pp. 158–82.

7 On 10 February 1901 De Wet and about 2,000 men entered the Cape Colony via Sanddrif. Twelve British columns took part in the third drive against De Wet, with Kitchener rushing down from Pretoria and taking personal charge of the operation on 16 February. On the banks of an impassable Brak River and with the nearest British column only about 16 km (10 miles) behind him, De Wet decided on 19 February to try and return to the ORC. He side-stepped his pursuers, linked up with Hertzog's retreating commando on 27 February, and the next day both of them and their commandos crossed the Gariep River back to the ORC. De Wet's invasion attempt had lasted 43 days (i.e. since he started off for the Cape Colony), in the course of which he had travelled a distance of approximately 1,300 km

(800 miles). W.L. von R. Scholtz, 'Generaal Christiaan de Wet as Veldheer', pp. 321–70; Amery (ed.), op cit, V, pp. 131–57.

8 Field Marshal Donald Martin Stewart (born 1824) was C-in-C, India, 1881–5 and a Member of Council of India, from 1885 until his death on 28 March 1900.

9 Sir Guy Fleetwood Wilson, Assistant Under-Secretary of State for War.

10 On 13 December 1900 Generals C.F. Beyers, J.H. de la Rey and J.C. Smuts with about 1,700 burghers attacked the camp of Major-General R.A.P. Clements' force of about 2,000 soldiers (and ten guns) at Nooitgedacht at the foot of the Magalies Mountain in the Western Transvaal, as well as the entrenched positions on top of the mountain. The initial Boer assault against the camp was beaten off, but after the British positions on top of the hill were overrun, the British camp came under fire and the British fled. Against Boer casualties of 32 killed and 46 wounded, the British lost 109 killed, 186 wounded and at least 368 POWs. Grant, op cit, IV, pp. 11–21; Amery (ed.), op cit, V, pp. 99–108.

11 See *Confidential Telegrams*, p. 253, No. 479A: Kitchener – Brodrick, 22 February 1901.

12 As early as January 1900, British troops, under the command of Major-General J.M. Babington burned farms in the OFS. Sporadic farm-burning continued, and on 16 June 1900 Lord Roberts issued a proclamation warning the Boers that in cases where Boer guerrilla units destroyed the British lines of communication, they (the British) would retaliate by burning the houses in the vicinity. In due course blacks also burnt or dismantled farm-houses. S.B. Spies, *Methods of Barbarism? Roberts and Kitchener and Civilians in the Boer Republics January 1900 – May 1902*, pp. 29, 102, 176. See also *Army. Proclamations issued by Field-Marshal Lord Roberts in South Africa* (Cd. 426), p. 10: Roberts' Proclamation No. 5, 16 June 1900.

13 General Louis Botha ordered action against the burghers who surrendered; if necessary their farms had to be burnt down. In several cases the houses of burghers who surrendered or joined the British were in fact destroyed. *South Africa. Further Papers Relating to Negotiations Between Commandant Louis Botha and Lord Kitchener* (Cd. 663), p. 5: Botha – Commandant or Landdrost of Bethal, 6 October 1900; Spies, op cit, pp. 186–7; *South Africa. Returns of Farm Buildings, &c., in Cape Colony and Natal Destroyed by the Boers* (Cd. 979), *passim*.

14 The Middelburg peace negotiations lasted from 28 February (when Kitchener and Botha met for the first time) until 16 March 1901 (when Botha rejected the final terms put forward by the British government). S. du Preez, 'Vredespogings gedurende die Anglo-Boereoorlog tot Maart 1901', pp. 157–209; Amery (ed.), op cit, V, pp. 183–93; *South Africa. Papers Relating to Negotiations between Commandant Louis Botha and Lord Kitchener* (Cd. 528); *South Africa. Further Papers Relating to Negotiations between Commandant Louis Botha and Lord Kitchener* (Cd. 663).

15 The Order in Council of 21 November 1895 is reproduced in *Royal Commission on the War in South Africa. Appendices to the Minutes of Evidence taken before the Royal Commission on the War in South Africa* (Cd. 1792), pp. 272–3 (Appendix No. 41).

16 Captain Clement Yatman (1871–1940) had no previous war service. Served in South Africa in the 2nd Battalion Northumberland Fusiliers, 1899–1902. At the battle of Nooitgedacht, 13 December 1900, he was in charge of four companies on the summit of the hill. After losing nearly a third of his men killed or wounded, he surrendered. Later served in World War I, 1914–18. Colonel, 1916. Retired as a Brigadier-General, 1924.

17 See British defeat at Nooitgedacht (Note 10).

18 As far as the lack of proper strategic planning for the war in South Africa is concerned, as well as the initial decision to advance directly through the OFS (not via Natal) to Transvaal (a decision subsequently changed by Buller) see, for example, A. Wessels, 'Die Britse Militêre Strategie tydens die Anglo-Boereoorlog tot en met die Buller-fase', pp. 204–14, 288–300 and *Royal Commission on the War in South Africa. Minutes of Evidence taken before the Royal Commission on the War in South Africa*, I (Cd. 1790), pp. 376, 382–3, 395: Wolseley's answers to questions 8938, 9080, 9082, 9366.

19 See also Lord Roberts' minute of 11 May 1902 re officers who suffer defeat and who are then court-martialled. Cd. 1792, pp. 419–20.

20 The battle of Ladysmith, 30 October 1899 ('Mournful Monday') in practice consisted of two distinguishable battles, namely that at Modderspruit/Lombardskop and at Nicholsonsnek. The British attack against the Boer positions at Modderspruit failed and they were forced to evacuate their own positions on Lombardskop. In the meantime another British force of about 1,150 men with six mountain guns, under the command of Lieutenant-Colonel F.R.C. Carleton, moved northwards in an effort to capture Nicholsonsnek. This force fell behind schedule and Carleton decided to take up positions for the night on the summit of Cayingubo Hill. The Boers spotted the British on top of the hill, and Commandant L.P. Steenekamp and Acting Commandant (later General) C.R. de Wet stormed the hill with 300 burghers. The British were taken by surprise and after heavy fighting most of the defenders surrendered – at least 52 British soldiers died, 136 were wounded, and 927 (including the wounded) were taken prisoner. It is not clear what the Boer losses at Cayingubo/Nicholsonsnek were. J.H. Breytenbach, *Die Geskiedenis van die Tweede Vryheidsoorlog in Suid-Afrika, 1899–1902*, I, pp. 329–36; National Archives of South Africa (Pretoria), L.A. 7698: P.A. Nierstrasz, *Der süd-afrikanische Krieg, 1899–1902*, pp. 577–86; J.F. Maurice (ed.), *History of the War in South Africa 1899–1902*, I, pp. 186–95; Amery (ed.), op cit, II, pp. 237–55.

21 Captain Stuart Duncan (born 1865) had no previous war service.

22 Lieutenant-Colonel Frank Robert Crofton Carleton (1856–1924) had no

previous war service. Saw action in Natal, 1899 (taken POW) and 1900–2. Later Brigadier-General and Director of Organisation, War Office.

23 Captain Bertram Oliphant Fyfe (born 1864) had no previous war service.

24 A Court of Inquiry on Captain Duncan and eighteen other officers and men was held at Pretoria on 16 June 1900. With the exception of Duncan, all were exonerated. Cd. 1792, pp. 375, 403–8.

25 See Note 10.

26 See Part 2, Note 3.

27 Alfred William Robin (1860–1935). New Zealander. Served in South Africa, 1899–1901. OC, Otago Military District, New Zealand (NZ), 1902–7; CGS, NZ, 1907–12; IGS, War Office, 1912–14; GOC, NZ Military Forces, 1914–19.

28 Edward Frewen (1850–1919). Saw action as a Major (later Lieutenant-Colonel) in the Imperial Yeomanry in South Africa, 1900–1.

29 Frederick George Skipwith (1870–1964). Previous service in Sudan, 1898. Saw action in South Africa, and later in World War I, 1914–18.

30 The 10th (Prince of Wales's Own Royal) Hussars saw action on the Colesberg front, 1899–1900; then took part in Lord Roberts' advance to Bloemfontein; saw action in the OFS and Transvaal, 1900; and took part in anti-guerrilla operations in the Eastern Transvaal, ORC and Cape Colony, 1901–2. J. Stirling, *Our Regiments in South Africa 1899–1902. Their Record, based on the Despatches*, pp. 441–3.

31 Lieutenant-Colonel Ralph Bromfield Willington Fisher (born 1854). Previous service in Afghanistan, 1878–80; Mahsood Wuzeeree Expedition, 1881. Saw action on the Colesberg front, 1899–1900; took part in Lord Roberts' advance, 1900.

32 See NAM 7101–23–122–1–40 for a copy of the letter.

33 Colonel Robert Fulke Noel Clarke (born 1853). Previous service in Sudan, 1884–5. Principal Ordnance Officer, South Africa; invalided home, 1901.

34 E.E.A. Butcher. Major in the RA; OC, 4th Battery RFA, Cape Colony, 1899–1900.

35 Henry Walter Barrett (1857–1949), Lord Kitchener's Chief Ordnance Officer, 1900–1. Previous service in Anglo-Zulu War, 1879.

36 See *Confidential Telegrams*, pp. 271 (No. 516A: Kitchener – Brodrick, 4 April 1901) and 273 (No. 524: Kitchener – Brodrick, 12 April 1901, No. S.325, cipher).

37 Brigadier-General H.C.O. Plumer occupied Pietersburg in the Northern Transvaal on 8 April 1901, the town's importance as a source of supplies having been overlooked by the British so far. Amery (ed.), op cit, V, p. 203.

38 Milner arrived in London on 24 May 1901 (Empire Day), not only for ordinary leave, but to try and silence the growing criticism about the British waging of the war in South Africa. He was welcomed by the Cabinet and ennobled as Lord Milner of St James and of Cape Town. He returned to Cape Town on 27 August 1901. *DSAB*, III, p. 615.

39 Major George Duff Baker (born 1860) had no previous war service.

40 Lieutenant-Colonel Henry Pottinger Young. Previous service in Afghanistan, 1879. As censor at Kitchener's HQ he was criticized for the way in which he handled censorship. When Moberley Bell (see Biographical Notes) complained to the Secretary of State for War that private letters had been opened by Young, the latter was replaced.

41 See also Milner's letter of 24 June 1900 to Sir Edward Hamilton (Permanent Under-Secretary of the Treasury). C. Headlam (ed.), *The Milner Papers*, II: *South Africa 1899–1905*, p. 115.

42 See NAM 7101–23–33–23.

43 After the Jameson Raid the Transvaal bought four French 155 mm Creusot fortress guns ('Long Toms') to use in their forts. However, when the war broke out they were used during the sieges of Mafikeng, Kimberley and Ladysmith. After the Boers fell back to Transvaal, they took the guns with them, but when ammunition was expended, destroyed two of the guns in the second half of 1900, and the other two in 1901.

44 Raymond Roche Elles (1848–1934). Previous service in Looshai Expedition, 1871–2; Egypt, 1882; Hazara Expedition, 1888; India, 1897. GOC, Peshawur District, 1895–1900. Major-General, 1900. AG, 1900–1; Military Member of the Governor-General's Council, India, 1901–5. Lieutenant-General, 1907.

45 Sir Edwin Henry Hayter Collen (1843–1911). Previous service in Abyssinia, 1868; Afghanistan, 1880; Sudan, 1885. Major-General, 1900. Military Member of the Governor-General's Council, India, 1896–1901; Member, Regulations Committee, War Office, 1901–4. Lieutenant-General, 1905.

46 Prior to the Anglo-Boer War, Brigadier-General James Melville Babington (1854–1936) saw service in Bechuanaland, 1884–5. As GOC, 1st Cavalry Brigade, he was sent to South Africa in 1899, where he saw action under Lord Methuen on the Kimberley front, including at Magersfontein. In February, now under the command of Roberts, after the clash at Koedoesbergdrif where the British were unable to stop a Boer attack, Babington became over-cautious and was relieved of his command. From August 1900 he operated in the Transvaal, with varying degrees of success. C-in-C, New Zealand Defence Forces, 1902–7; GOC, 23rd Division, 1914–18; GOC, XIVth Corps, 1918–19. *DSAB*, III, p. 38. As far as Shekleton is concerned, see Biographical Notes.

47 Lieutenant-Colonel Edward Bleiddian Herbert (born 1858). Previous service in Anglo-Zulu War, 1879. Saw action in Natal, 1899–1900; anti-guerrilla operations, ORC and Cape Colony, 1900–1.

48 Harry William Ralph Ricardo (1860–1945). Previous service in Sudan, 1898. Saw action in South Africa, 1900–2, as 2nd in command of the 17th Lancers.

49 Mary Victoria Curzon (died 1906), daughter of American millionaire Levi Zeigler Leiler; first wife of Lord Curzon (married 1895). They had three daughters.

303

50 Lieutenant-General Sir George Luck (1840–1916), IG of Cavalry, India, 1887–93; IG of Cavalry, Great Britain and Ireland, 1895–8; GOC, Bengal Army, 1898–1903. General, 1905.

51 Edward Robert Bulwer Lytton, 1st Earl of Lytton (1831–1891), Viceroy of India, 1876–80; ambassador at Paris, 1887–91. Author of several volumes of verse (under the pseudonym Owen Meredith).

52 Lieutenant H.L. Borden, Canadian MI, killed in action at Rietvlei on 16 July 1900, was the only son of Frederick William Borden (1847–1917), Minister of Militia Defence, Canada, 1896–1911. M.G. Dooner, *The "Last Post": being a Roll of all Officers (Naval, Military or Colonial) who gave their Lives for their Queen, King and Country, in the South African War, 1899–1902*, p. 34.

53 I.e. the commandos of, for example, Commandant P.H. Kritzinger, Commandant Gideon Scheepers, Commandant W.D. Fouché and Commandant Manie Maritz.

54 See NAM 7101–23–122–1–75.

55 The long telegram was sent on 2 July, not 29 June 1901. See *Confidential Telegrams*, pp. 288–9: Roberts – Kitchener, 2 July 1901.

56 See NAM 7101–23–33–30.

57 See *Confidential Telegrams*, pp. 288–9 (No. 571: Roberts – Kitchener, 2 July 1901, No. 441, cipher), 291–2 (No. 579: Roberts – Kitchener, 5 July 1901, No. 445, cipher).

58 On 20–21 June 1901 the Boer leaders of the two republics met on the farm Waterval in the Standerton district to discuss the latest peace terms offered by Kitchener. They cabled to President Kruger (in exile in Europe) for his views, and he told them to hold out and continue their resistance. Amery (ed.), op cit, V, pp. 291, 297.

59 In an effort to defend the Cape Colony, a home guard consisting of the District Mounted Troops (or DMTs) and Town Guards was established. By May 1901 the home guard was about 20,000 strong, of whom about two thirds were DMTs.

60 Lord Kitchener's letter of 14 June 1901 is meant. See NAM 7107–23–33–32.

61 See *Confidential Telegrams*, p. 291, No. 578: Kitchener – Roberts, 4 July 1901, No. S.480.

62 See NAM 7101–23–33–33.

63 See Note 58.

64 On the night of 10–11 July 1901 Steyn and most members of the OFS government were sleeping in the town of Reitz (having occupied it when Colonel H. de B. de Lisle departed) when a British force under the command of Brigadier-General R.G. Broadwood entered. Steyn and seven others succeeded in escaping, thanks to his valet, a coloured man by the name of Ruiter. The other members of the OFS government, as well as senior officers (a total of 29 persons) were taken prisoner, and a large volume of documents captured, including correspondence between Steyn and the

Transvaal government, in which the latter's pessimistic view of affairs was reflected – the propaganda value of which was exploited to the full by the British. *DSAB*, II, p. 711; Amery (ed.), op cit, V, p. 301; Grant, op cit, IV, pp. 247–9; N.J. van der Merwe, *Marthinus Theunis Steyn. 'n Lewensbeskrywing*, II, pp. 20–4. For translations of some of the captured documents, see *South Africa. Further Correspondence Relating to Affairs in South Africa* (Cd. 903), pp. 54–7.

65 For more information on Reitz, see Epilogue, Note 2.

66 Field-Cornet P.J. Steyn.

67 Gordon A. Fraser, President Steyn's Private Secretary.

68 Telegram S 509, cipher is meant. See *Confidential Telegrams*, p. 299, No. 602: Kitchener – Brodrick, 19 July 1901.

69 In October 1900 Roberts ordered the formation of the South African Constabulary (SAC), with Major-General R.S.S. Baden-Powell as its GOC. The original purpose of the SAC was to operate as a police force in the former Boer republics to maintain law and order. Posts were erected for the SAC, and in due course these posts became part of the elaborate British blockhouse system. By January 1902 the SAC had about 10,000 members. G. Tylden, *The Armed Forces of South Africa*, p. 164; National Archives of South Africa (Pretoria), Microfilm M673: Report on the South African Constabulary.

70 See documents 81 and 97.

71 In March 1902 Kitchener said that there were 7,114 blacks and 2,939 coloureds in an armed capacity in British service. However, almost right from the start of hostilities, the British armed an ever increasing number of blacks and coloureds. By the cessation of hostilities approximately 25,000 of them were used as blockhouse guards, and as many as 25,000 others were employed as members of, for example, the flying columns. A further approximately 70,000 blacks and coloureds were employed in a non-combatant capacity, for example as servants and drivers. A. Wessels, *Die Militêre Rol van Swart Mense, Bruin Mense en Indiërs tydens die Anglo-Boereoorlog (1899–1902)*, pp. 9–20; P. Warwick, *Black People and the South African War, 1899–1902*, pp. 4–5.

72 See NAM 7101–23–122–1–90.

73 Should read Lichtenburg.

74 I.e. Bechuanaland, today Botswana.

75 Lieutenant-Colonel Cecil Foster Seymour Vandeleur (1869–1901). Previous service in Unyoro Expedition, 1895; Nandi Expedition, 1895–6; Niger-Sudan Campaign, 1897; Sudan, 1898. On special service in South Africa, 1899–1901. Shot and killed after the train in which he travelled was wrecked just north of Pretoria, 31 August 1901.

76 Brigadier-General Gilbert Henry Claude Hamilton (1853–1933). Previous service in Afghanistan, 1878–80; Transvaal War of Independence, 1880–1. Saw action in, for example, Transvaal, 1901–2.

77 Major-General Reginald Clare Hart (1848–1931) was GOC, Quetta District, India, 1899–1902. He served in Afghanistan, 1879; Ashanti Expedition, 1881; Egypt, 1882; Tirah Campaign, 1897–8. Lieutenant-General, 1908. C-in-C, South Africa, 1912–14. General 1914. For his brother, A.F. Hart, see Biographical Notes.

78 See Lord Kitchener's proclamation of 6 August 1901, in which he threatened to banish all Boers who did not surrender before 15 September 1901. *Correspondence relating to the Prolongation of Hostilities in South Africa* (Cd. 732), pp. 6–7.

79 John George, Marquis of Tullibardine (born 1871). Previous service in Sudan, 1898.

80 Probably Major-General Sir James Willcox.

81 Possibly Major-General Barrington Bulkley Douglas Campbell (born 1845).

82 See *Confidential Telegrams*, p. 306, No. 619: Kitchener – Brodrick, 18 August 1901.

83 The outbreak of the war led to serious political divisions in the Cape Colony, with one portion of the population and their political representatives giving unconditional support to the British war effort, while others in various degrees had sympathy with the Boers. W.P. Schreiner's ministry and their supporters tried to avert war and wanted the Cape to stay neutral; former premier Sir Gordon Sprigg and his followers supported the British policy. The first Boer invasion and subsequent rebellion, 1899–1900, aggravated circumstances. The question of how to deal with the rebels brought matters to a head; Schreiner's cabinet was split on the issue and he resigned on 13 June 1900. Milner requested Sprigg to form a new government. The second Boer invasion, 1900–2, led to renewed crises, mainly concerning martial law and the abolition of the Cape constitution. These problems continued after the cessation of hostilities. See, for example, C.J.S. Strydom, 'Die Kaapkolonie, 1899–1902: Skadevergoeding en die Rebelle in Ere herstel'.

84 On the eve of the outbreak of hostilities, President M.T. Steyn of the OFS promised W.P. Schreiner, Prime Minister of the Cape Colony, that as long as the Colony was not used as a springboard for operations against the OFS and Transvaal, the OFS would not invade the Colony. *South Africa. Further Correspondence relating to Affairs in South Africa* (Cd. 43), p. 135: Steyn – Schreiner, 11 October 1899 (telegram).

85 See *Confidential Telegrams*, pp. 314–15, No. 647: Kitchener – Brodrick, 18 September 1901.

86 Colonel Sir George Sydenham Clarke (born 1848). Previous service in Egypt, 1882; Sudan, 1885.

87 The published Spioenkop despatches reflected negatively on Buller's role in Natal, 1899–1900; however, it did not include his controversial telegram to Sir George White (16 December 1899) in which he suggested that he might not be able to relieve Ladysmith, and that White might have to surrender. Amidst rumours and allegations, Buller disclosed and tried to justify the

content of the above-mentioned telegram at a Queen's Westminster Volunteers luncheon, 10 October 1901. Subsequently, on 23 October 1901, Buller was relieved of his command and retired on half-pay. *DSAB*, II, p. 101; Amery (ed.), op cit, II, pp. 460–3; G. Powell, *Buller: A Scapegoat? A Life of General Sir Redvers Buller 1839–1908*, pp. 152–5. As far as Buller's controversial telegram is concerned, see *Confidential Telegrams*, p. 490, No. 26: Buller – White, 16 December 1899 (No. 88). See also the note following the published telegram that refers to Buller's telegram to White of 17 December 1899, in which he asked certain 'corrections' to be made re the telegram of 16 December.

88 Major Stapleton Lynch Cotton (born 1860). Previous service in Afghanistan, 1878–80; Burma, 1885–7.

89 Captain Victor Reginald Brooke (1873–1914). Served in South Africa, 1899–1900, and (as Lieutenant-General Ian Hamilton's staff officer) 1901–2 (wounded). Military Secretary to Viceroy, India, from 1907. Killed in action, World War I.

90 Probably Charles D'O.A.C. Bowers.

91 Should read Vereeniging.

92 Gideon Scheepers (see also Biographical Notes) fell ill (probably with pneumonia) on 28 September 1901. By 10 October he was no longer able to accompany his commando, was left on a farm in the Prince Albert district, where that same day he was found by a British column. *DSAB*, II, p. 627. See also G.S. Preller, *Scheepers se Dagboek en die Stryd in Kaapland (1 Okt. 1901 – 18 Jan. 1902)*.

93 I.e. Roberts' elder surviving daughter – see Biographical Notes.

94 I.e. side-lined; sent away to cool his heels; 'hidden', so that he can do no damage. From the name of Stellenbosch, a picturesque town just east of Cape Town. During the war it became customary to say that a failed commander had been stellenbosched.

95 The first blockhouses were erected at the beginning of 1901 in an effort to safeguard the railways and bridges. In due course approximately 8,000 blockhouses and other fortifications were erected across the length and breadth of South Africa, mostly in lines, dividing up the war zone in more manageable 'cages' in which drives would take place in an effort to corner the Boer commandos. J. Hattingh and A. Wessels, *Britse Fortifikasies in die Anglo-Boereoorlog (1899–1902)*, p. 21 *et seq.*; Amery (ed.), op cit, V, pp. 396–412 (including a fold-out map opposite p. 412 on which all the blockhouse lines, including dates of completion, are indicated).

96 Major-General Bruce Hamilton stationed eight columns on the Wilge River on 16 November 1901, from where they marched on Ermelo, reaching that town on 3 December, the same day that Louis Botha and his commando broke back through the British line. Amery (ed.), op cit, V, pp. 450–1.

97 Major Affleck Alexander Fraser (born 1855) had no previous war service; 2nd in command of the 1st Battalion Bedforshire Regiment.

98 Major Alfred Robert Lloyd (born 1854), 2nd Battalion Bedfordshire Regiment. Previous service in Chitral, 1895.

99 See *Confidential Telegrams*, p. 356, No. 787: Kitchener – Brodrick, 8 December 1901.

100 Kitchener's younger brother, Major-General F.W. Kitchener (see Biographical Notes), married Carolina Louisa Fenton in 1884. They had four children: one son and three daughters.

101 Portion in *italics* written in longhand.

102 John Peniston Milbanke (born 1872), 10th (Prince of Wales's Own Royal) Hussars, had no previous war service.

103 Commandant P.H. Kritzinger (see also Biographical Notes) crossed into the Cape Colony for a third time on 15 December 1901. He was immediately chased by more than one British column. In an effort to cross the central railway line on 16 December, Kritzinger was seriously wounded and captured. After spending some time in the British hospital at Noupoort, he was brought to trial in Graaff-Reinet on charges of murder and train-wrecking, but influential newspapers in Britain and the USA took up the cudgels on his behalf, and he was acquitted. *DSAB*, III, p. 484.

104 Colonel Richard Thompson Lawley (born 1856), who operated in the ORC and Transvaal, 1901–2. See also Note 148.

105 I.e. Cradock.

106 Since the commencement of hostilities, the British experienced problems with their Lee-Enfield rifles: undersighting occurred, as well as shooting to the right, and other inaccuracies. Lord Roberts was in favour of a rifle with a shortened barrel for use by both the Infantry and Cavalry. On 12 January 1901 approval was given for the manufacture of 1,000 Shortened Modified Enfield Rifles for troop trials. The trials that were conducted in the course of 1901 and 1902 were of the utmost importance and determined the future design of rifles of the British Army until after World War II. On 23 December 1902 the Short Magazine Lee-Enfield Rifle was introduced in the British Army as a weapon for the Infantry and Cavalry. E.G.B. Reynolds, *The Lee-Enfield Rifle*, pp. 61–89.

107 Mary Ethel Sanford (died 1941), cousin and second wife of Paul Sanford, 3rd Baron Methuen (married 1884). They had five children: three sons and two daughters.

108 On Christmas Day, 25 December 1901, De Wet attacked, surprised and overwhelmed a British force under the command of Lieutenant-Colonel R.B. Firman (see also Biographical Notes) on top of Groenkop, near the present-day Kestell in the Eastern ORC. At least 57 British soldiers were killed, 84 wounded and more than 200 (including several of the wounded) captured. The Boers, who also captured a large quantity of arms, ammunition and stores, lost fourteen killed and 30 wounded. J.E. Rabie, *Generaal C.R. de Wet se Krygsleiding by Sannaspos en Groenkop*, pp. 31–59; W.L. von R. Scholtz, 'Generaal Christiaan de Wet as Veldheer', pp. 407–15; Amery (ed.), op cit, V, pp. 431–44.

109 See NAM 7107–23–122–2, p. 298.

110 Colonel Charles James Briggs (born 1865) had no previous war service. He served on the Kimberley front, 1899–1900 (wounded at Magersfontein); in the ORC and Western Transvaal, 1900–2.

111 No General Sladin could be identified. If Slade was meant, it can refer to either Major-General F.G. Slade or Major-General J.R. Slade.

112 I.e. Colonel H.S. Rawlinson – see Biographical Notes.

113 Probably either Maurice Hilliard Tomlin (born 1868), or Morton J.B. Tomlin.

114 See Note 87.

115 A series of five so-called New Model Drives were launched in the Northern and North-Eastern ORC, February–May 1902, with De Wet's commando the main target. Blockhouses were used in conjunction with mobile columns in an effort to sweep the area clean of commandos. See also Notes 124, 131, 149 and 162.

116 Major John Maximilian Vallentin (1865–1902). Previous service in Burma, 1886–7. Saw action in Natal, 1899–1900 (besieged in Ladysmith); OFS and Transvaal, 1900–2. Killed in action at Onverwacht in the Ermelo district, Transvaal, 4 January 1902.

117 Possibly Major James J.C. Henry.

118 Probably Evelyn Fitzgerald Michell Wood (1869–1943), eldest of the three sons of General Henry Evelyn Wood (see Biographical Notes). All three H.E. Wood's sons followed successful military careers.

119 Archibald Philip Primrose, 5th Earl of Rosebery (1847–1929), Secretary of State for Foreign Affairs, 1886 and 1892–4; Prime Minister and Lord President of Council, 1894–5.

120 On 23 December 1901 the 16th Lancers (part of Lieutenant-Colonel P.G. Wyndham's force) attacked and put to flight a Boer force under General J.C. Smuts near Calvinia. P.A. Pyper, 'Generaal J.C. Smuts en die Tweede Vryheidsoorlog (1899–1902)', pp. 116–17; Grant, op cit, IV, p. 365.

121 Lieutenant-Colonel Frederick Thwaites Lund (born 1860) had no previous war service. Took part in Roberts' advance to Bloemfontein, and to Pretoria, 1900. One of French's column-commanders, Cape Colony, 1901–2.

122 Additions in longhand are printed in *italics*.

123 I.e. Wolwehoek.

124 The first New Model Drive lasted from 5–8 February 1902. A total of about 17,000 British troops took part, and about 300 blockhouses were also involved. A line of more than 88 km (55 miles) was formed by some 9,000 troops, with the Frankfort-Heilbron-Wolwehoek blockhouse line forming the northern flank, and the Bethlehem-Lindley-Kroonstad line the southern flank. The idea was to move westwards, sweeping the area clean of commandos, and pushing them against the Kroonstad railway line, which was also a blockhouse line, now manned by additional troops, and with four armoured trains patrolling the line. The drive, which was deemed to be

relatively successful by the British, led to about 285 Boers being killed, wounded or captured. However, De Wet and many others escaped, with De Wet and Steyn breaking unobserved through the Kroonstad-Lindley blockhouse line in the early hours of 7 February. Amery (ed.), op cit, V, pp. 475–81; J.W. Yardley, *With the Inniskilling Dragoons. The Record of a Cavalry Regiment during the Boer War, 1899–1902*, pp. 321–3; Grant, op cit, IV, pp. 401–4.

125 Probably a reference to the drive undertaken by Lieutenant-Colonel J.W. Dunlop's and other columns, from 20 January to 1 February 1902, between Liebenbergsvlei and the Wilge River in the ORC, which yielded 23 POWs. Grant, op cit, IV, p. 399.

126 At the beginning of February 1902 Lieutenant-Colonel W.R.B. Doran (see also Biographical Notes) escorted a convoy from Sutherland to Calvinia. The evening of 5 February the convoy was parked at Middelpos, while Doran and a portion of his force rode out to attack the laager of a group of rebels. In his absence, General J.L. van Deventer and 28 men attacked the British camp at Middelpos. The next morning the Boers were reinforced with the arrival of General J.C. Smuts and some men, and the British were defeated. Approximately 130 wagons were destroyed or captured, and the Boers also captured about 400 horses and mules. At least nine British soldiers were killed and 22 wounded. Four Boers were killed and ten wounded. A. de Wet *et al.*, *Die Buren in der Kapkolonie im Kriege mit England*, pp. 206–9; Amery (ed.), op cit, V, pp. 548–9; *List of Casualties in the Army in South Africa, from the 1ˢᵗ January, 1902, to the 31ˢᵗ May, 1902*, pp. 9, 13–14, 75.

127 In the Western Transvaal, Lieutenant-Colonel W.C. Anderson, OC of the 5ᵗʰ Battalion IY, escorted a convoy (sent by Lieutenant-Colonel S.B. von Donop from Wolmaransstad to Klerksdorp to get supplies) with about 700 men when, at 05.00 on 25 February 1902, it was attacked at Yzerspruit by about 1,000 Boers under the command of Generals De la Rey and Kemp. The British lost their convoy, a large amount of ammunition, two field-guns, a pom-pom, at least 33 killed, 129 wounded (most of them taken prisoner), and about 240 unwounded soldiers captured. The Boers lost at least twelve killed and 31 wounded, of whom three died later. Grant, op cit, IV, pp. 410–15; Amery (ed.), op cit, V, pp. 497–9; J.F. Naudé, *Vechten en Vluchten van Beyers en Kemp "Bôkant" De Wet*, pp. 323–6.

128 On the night of 23–24 February 1902, at Langverwacht, between the towns of Reitz and Vrede, Lieutenant-Colonel F.S. Garratt's New Zealanders, which formed part of Lieutenant-Colonel the Hon. J.H.G. Byng's column, were entrenched, when De Wet and his commando (accompanied by President Steyn) broke through the British lines. The Boers apparently lost fourteen killed and twenty wounded; the British at least twenty killed and 38 wounded. Amery (ed.), op cit, V, pp. 488–90; Grant, op cit, IV, pp. 426–7.

129 At the battle of Amajuba, 27 February 1881, the British suffered a severe defeat, and consequently the British government opted for a negotiated settlement with the Transvaalers, thus bringing the Transvaal War of Independence to a close. As a Lieutenant in the Gordon Highlanders, Ian Hamilton was wounded and captured at Amajuba. Amajuba Day became a public holiday in the Transvaal. On 27 February 1900, Cronjé surrendered at Paardeberg, and Buller broke through at Pietershoogte, relieving Ladysmith the next day. See Part 1, Notes 46 and 49.

130 Flat mountain, overlooking Harrismith in the North-Eastern ORC.

131 The second New Model Drive lasted from 13–27 February 1902. A total of about 30,000 British troops took part. The area to be swept stretched from the Frankfort-Heilbron-Wolwehoek blockhouse line in the north to the Bethlehem-Lindley-Kroonstad line in the south. Once again, blockhouses played an important role in the overall plan. De Wet and Steyn managed to escape, but the Boers lost about 50 killed, and the British took 778 POWs, and captured about 25,000 cattle, 2,000 horses and 200 wagons and carts. Amery (ed.), op cit, V, pp. 481–91; Yardley, op cit, pp. 324–7; J.D. Kestell, *Through Shot and Flame*, pp. 252–60; *South Africa Despatches. Despatch by General Lord Kitchener, dated 8th March, 1902, relative to Military Operations in South Africa* (Cd. 970), pp. 6–8.

132 Probably Commandant H.A. Truter of the Vrede Commando.

133 On 6 January 1900 the Boers launched attacks against the British positions at Wagon Hill and Caesar's Camp (together also known as Platrand) in an effort to capture Ladysmith. In one of the bloodiest battles of the war, the Boers were eventually beaten back. They lost at least 56 killed and 125 wounded; the British at least 150 killed and 250 wounded. The Platrand area fell under Hamilton's command. As far as the battle is concerned see, for example, J.H. Breytenbach, *Die Geskiedenis van die Tweede Vryheidsoorlog in Suid-Afrika, 1899–1902*, III, pp. 10–61; J.F. Maurice (ed.), *History of the War in South Africa 1899–1902*, II, pp. 555–70; Amery (ed.) op cit, III, pp. 176–205.

134 See Note 127. Lieutenant-Colonel Stanley Brenton von Donop (1860–1941) saw action in the Western Transvaal, 1901–2. Later Director of Artillery, 1911–13; MGO, 1913–16; Commander Humber Garrison, 1917–20. Knighted, 1914.

135 See NAM 7101–23–33–72 and NAM 7101–23–33–73.

136 Brigadier-General Montagu Gilbert Gerard (1843–1905). Previous service in Abyssinian Campaign, 1868; Afghanistan, 1878–80; Egypt, 1882. Military Attaché, St Petersburg, 1892–3; GOC, Hyderabad Contingent, 1896; Oudh District, 1899.

137 Probably Major Ralph Henry Carr-Ellison (born 1863).

138 26 May 1902. See also document 105.

139 At about 05.00 on 7 March 1902 De la Rey, assisted by Kemp and General J.G. Celliers, and about 750 men, attacked Methuen's column (about 1,300 strong)

near De Klipdrift in the Western Transvaal. Methuen was trekking from Tweebosch in the direction of Lichtenburg, co-operating with Colonel R.G. Kekewich and Lieutenant-Colonel H.M. Grenfell in an effort to corner De la Rey. British losses amounted to at least 68 killed, 121 wounded, and more than 800 POWs, as well as four field-guns, two pom-poms, and about 100 wagons and carts captured. The Boers lost at least eight killed and 26 wounded. Methuen was among those wounded and taken prisoner. Amid calls of protest from several Boers, De la Rey magnanimously decided to set Methuen free as soon as the latter's wound had been attended to. Accompanied by a doctor and a few others, Methuen was sent to Klerksdorp. Soon after his departure, pressure was exercised on De la Rey to reverse his decision. Messengers overtook Methuen's company, and they were taken to Gestoptefontein. At a meeting held on 9 March De la Rey more or less convinced the burghers that it would be in the interest of the Boer cause to set Methuen free. Methuen finally reached Klerksdorp on 13 March and fully recovered. Grant, op cit, IV, pp. 416–21; Amery (ed.), op cit, V, pp. 501–8; Naudé, op cit, pp. 327–36; *South Africa. Report from Lieut.-General Lord Methuen on the Action that took place near Tweebosh on 7th March, 1902* (Cd. 967).

140   I.e. at the battle of Magersfontein, 11 December 1899 – See Prologue, Note 24.

141   See *Confidential Telegrams*, p. 414, No. 1009A: Kitchener – Brodrick, 12 March 1902, No. S.918, cipher.

142   Katharine Sarah Stuart-Wortley married Neville Lyttelton (see Biographical Notes) in 1883. They had three daughters.

143   General Benjamin (Ben) Johannes Viljoen (1868–1917) saw action in several of the wars against black tribes in the Transvaal, and in the suppression of the Jameson Raid, 1896. As Commandant of the Johannesburg commando he fought in Natal, 1899–1900, and as Combat General in Transvaal, 1900–2. On 25 January 1902 he was ambushed and taken prisoner near Lydenburg in the Eastern Transvaal, taken to Durban, and then by ship via Cape Town to a POW camp on St Helena. After the war he went to Europe, then to Mexico (where, in 1911, he helped to overthrow Porfirio Díaz), and eventually settled in the USA, where he died. *DSAB*, IV, pp. 740–2. See also B. Viljoen, *My Reminiscences of the Anglo-Boer War.*

144   Francis J. de Gex (1861–1917) served in South Africa, 1899–1902. DAAG, South Africa, 1901–3. Colonel, 1913. AAG, Irish Command, 1914. Took part in World War I, 1914–18.

145   See *Proceedings of a Court of Inquiry i.e. Inquiry held at St. Stephen's House, Westminster, S.W., on the Administration of the Army Remount Department since January 1899, by Order of the Commander-in-Chief dated 20th February 1902* (Cd. 993) and H. Sessions, *Two Years with the Remount Commission.*

146   Probably Thomas N. Cook.

147   I.e. the discussions that took place at Klerksdorp, 9–11 April 1902, between members of the Transvaal and OFS governments re the possibility of entering into peace negotiations with the British.

148 Colonel the Hon. R.T. Lawley (see Note 104) operated from Springs. In the early hours of 1 April 1902, one of the units under him, the Bays (312 strong under Lieutenant-Colonel H.D. Fanshawe), together with 40 National Scouts under Major C.D. Vaughan, attacked a Boer laager at Enkeldebosch. A running fight ensued, ending at Boschman's Kop. British casualties amounted to twenty killed and 61 wounded; that of the Boers to about 35. Amery (ed.), op cit, V, pp. 559–61; Grant, op cit, IV, pp. 518–19.

149 The fourth New Model Drive lasted from 20 March – 5 April 1902. The area to be swept, stretched from the Heilbron-Frankfort-Bothaspas blockhouse line (northern flank) to the Lindley-Bethlehem-Harrismith line (southern flank), and the drive as such swept between these lines, from west to east. Only ten Boers were killed and 76 captured during this drive, and the commandos succeeded in breaking through the blockhouse lines and mobile columns. The British did, however, capture some 4,800 cattle and horses, 178 vehicles, and three Krupp field-guns. Amery (ed.), op cit, V, pp. 545–56; Yardley, op cit, pp. 332–3; Grant, op cit, IV, pp. 479–80.

150 See *Confidential Telegrams*, p. 431, Nos 1067 and 1068: Kitchener – Brodrick, 11 April 1902.

151 Could be Brigadier-General Edward O.F. Hamilton. 'Ghazi' is usually the name given to fanatics who sought death against the British forces in the 2nd Anglo-Afghan War (1878–80) as a means of going straight to paradise.

152 See *South Africa. The Spion Kop Despatches* (Cd. 968.)

153 L.S. Amery (ed.), *The Times History of the War in South Africa 1899–1902*, II (London, 1902) dealt with the military systems of the British and the Boers, the situation on the eve of the war, the limited Boer offensive (including the battles at Talana, Elandslaagte, Modderspruit and Nicholsonsnek), Buller's arrival, Methuen's advance to the Modder River, and the three British defeats during the so-called 'Black Week'.

154 See *Confidential Telegrams*, p. 440, Nos 1097 and 1098: Kitchener – Brodrick, 17 April 1902.

155 Ian Hamilton assumed command in the Western Transvaal on 8 April 1902. At about 07.15 on 11 April some 800 Boers under the command of Ferdinandus Jacobus Potgieter (1857–1902), Commandant of the Wolmaransstad commando, charged (across open veldt) the columns of Von Donop and Grenfell at Rooiwal. The British forces totalled about 3,000 men with six guns. The attack was beaten back, the Boers losing at least 43 killed (including Potgieter), more than 50 wounded (of whom 40 were taken prisoner), while 36 unwounded prisoners were taken. The British lost about twelve killed and 75 wounded. When Hamilton arrived on the scene of the attack he ordered a general pursuit. Later Rawlinson's columns also joined in the pursuit, but the Boers got away. The British recaptured two of their own field-guns and a pom-pom they lost at De Klipdrift/Tweebosch. Grant, op cit, IV, pp. 499–504; Amery (ed.), op cit, V, pp. 525, 531–7; Naudé, op cit, pp. 352–4.

156 See *Confidential Telegrams*, p. 443, No. 1109: Brodrick – Kitchener, 22 April 1902. Robert Edward Lee (1807–70), since 1864 C-in-C of all the Confederate forces during the American Civil War (1861–5), surrendered at Appomattox Court House on 9 April 1865.

157 Mary Endicott, third wife of Joseph Chamberlain. She was the only daughter of William Crowninshield Endicott, a distinguished USA judge and statesmen. Married 1888; childless. Chamberlain had two sons (including Neville – see Biographical Notes) and four daughters from his previous two marriages. *DSAB*, III, p. 142.

158 See *Confidential Telegrams*, p. 443, No. 1106. Mr Halse was, since the end of 1900, a member of Methuen's Intelligence Department – see *Confidential Telegrams*, p. 445, No. 1116: Kitchener – Roberts, 27 April 1902.

159 See *Confidential Telegrams*, p. 444, No. 1113.

160 Possibly Colonel J.L. St Clair, previously Deputy Judge Advocate to General Buller, 1899–1900.

161 Thirty delegates each for the Transvaal and OFS met at Vereeniging on 15 May 1902 to discuss whether or not to continue the struggle.

162 The fifth and final New Model Drive in the Northern ORC lasted from 2–9 May 1902. A total of 333 Boers were captured, and ten killed, but once again many more escaped the net. Amery (ed.), op cit, V, pp. 578–9; Yardley, op cit, p. 340; Grant, op cit, IV, pp. 485–7.

163 Ian Hamilton's last drive in the Western Transvaal lasted from 7–11 May 1902. See Note 171.

164 The former ZAR districts of Vryheid and Utrecht, as well as a portion of the Wakkerstroom district, were ceded to Natal in 1902.

165 Exactly the same letter was also, under cover of a letter dated 20 May 1902, sent to Winston Churchill. See Churchill Archives Centre, University of Cambridge: CHAR 1/34/48–57.

166 See also document 64, as well as Cd. 1792, pp. 419–20.

167 I.e. at Nooitgedacht, 13 December 1900 – see Note 10.

168 I.e. at De Klipdrift/Tweebosch, 7 March 1902 – see Note 139.

169 I.e. Anderson's column and convoy, sent out by Von Donop – see Note 127.

170 For example a portion of his convoy in October 1901. Amery (ed.), op cit, V, p. 357.

171 Hamilton defeated commandos under De la Rey's overall command at Rooiwal (see Note 155), and led 17,000 troops in the last drive in the Western Transvaal, 7–11 May. The idea was to drive the Boer commandos westward against the Vryburg-Mafikeng railway line and its blockhouses. The Boers lost only one man killed, but 363 taken prisoner, in addition to 326 horses, 95 mules, 20 donkeys, 3,600 cattle, 13,000 sheep, 175 wagons and 61 carts captured. (Grant, op cit, IV, pp. 506–9; Amery (ed.), op cit, V, pp. 579–81; National Archives of South Africa (Pretoria), microfilm M.672: Staff Diary, Colonel Rawlinson's force, entry of 12 May 1902.) Hamilton's view that in the course of April–May 1902 he had caused De la Rey as much

damage as he (De la Rey) had caused the British since the commencement of the war is, of course, in the light of De la Rey's role at the battles of Modder River and Magersfontein, 1899, Colesberg front, 1900, and guerrilla activities in the Western Transvaal, 1900–2, grossly exaggerated.

172 Andries Petrus Johannes Cronjé (1849–1923), brother of General P.A. Cronjé (see Biographical Notes), was Commandant of the Potchefstroom commando when the war broke out. Saw action on the Kimberley front, 1899–1900, and in the Western Transvaal, 1900. He surrendered voluntarily on 14 June 1900. He played a leading role in the National Scout movement, 1901–2, i.e. he joined forces with the British. *DSAB*, III, pp. 183–4.

173 See, for example, the battle at Colenso, 15 December 1899 – Prologue, Note 11.

174 Colvile, not Colville. See Part 2, Note 13.

175 Major-General J. Talbot Coke did not distinguish himself at Spioenkop (24 January 1900), Colenso Koppies (21 February 1900) or Pieter's Hill (27 February 1900). *DSAB*, III, p. 163.

176 See Part 1, Note 11.

177 Major-General John Fielden Brocklehurst, Baron Ranksborough (1852–1921) saw action in Natal as GOC, 2nd Cavalry Brigade, 1899–1900, including the siege of Ladysmith, and Buller's operations in Northern Natal; and in the Eastern Transvaal, 1900–1. He returned to England early in 1901. In general he lacked qualities of military leadership, and during the siege of Ladysmith his sorties were often unsuccessful. *DSAB*, III, p. 109.

178 In February 1901 Brigadier-General J.F. Burn-Murdoch (see Biographical Notes) commanded a convoy of 190 wagons, escorted by some 1,000 men and six guns, that had to take supplies from Newcastle to Luneburg. Although not attacked by the Boers, torrential rain and bad decisions by Burn-Murdoch turned the expedition into a nightmare. Amery (ed.), op cit, V, pp. 174–6.

179 Major-General W.F. Gatacre (see Biographical Notes) was defeated at Stormberg (10 December 1899), and the surrender of nearly 600 of his 3rd Division at Mostertshoek near Reddersburg (4 April 1900), under Captain W.J. McWhinnie, led to Gatacre being relieved of his command on 10 April 1900 and sent home. *DSAB*, II, p. 257.

180 Lieutenant-General C.F. Clery (see Biographical Notes) did not distinguish himself during the Spioenkop campaign or at Vaalkrans in Natal, 1900, being either inactive or hesitant. He was recalled to England in October 1900, and retired from the British Army in February 1901. *DSAB*, III, p. 160.

181 Major-General F. Carrington (see Biographical Notes) failed to relieve the besieged force at Elands River (see Part 2, Notes 32 and 42) and returned to Rhodesia in December 1900. *DSAB*, III, pp. 135–6.

182 See Note 155.

183 Portion in *italics* added in longhand. See also pp. 253 and 254.

184 Conyers Surtees (1858–1933). Previous service in Sudan, 1884–5. Served in South Africa, 1899–1901. Military Attaché, Constantinople and Athens, 1905–9. Served in World War I, 1914–18.

185 Major Granville Roland Francis Smith (1860–1917), Coldstream Guards. Saw action in, for example, Cape Colony, 1901–2. Later AAG and QMG, London District.

186 Jacoba Elizabeth Greeff (1856–1923) married J.H. de la Rey in 1876. They had twelve children: six sons and six daughters.

187 See *Confidential Telegrams*, pp. 458–9, No. 1164: Kitchener – Broderick, 21 May 1902.

188 See ibid, p. 460, No. 1166: Kitchener – Brodrick, 22 May 1902.

189 In Hamilton's letter of 24 May 1902 to Winston Churchill (see Churchill Archives Centre, University of Cambridge: CHAR 1/34/59–62) certain aspects of this letter of 25 May 1902 to Roberts is repeated. When Hamilton's letters to his wife, to Roberts and to Churchill are compared, it becomes clear that he sometimes wrote one basic letter per week, and sent somewhat adapted versions to the three persons.

190 Probably a reference to Roberts' second oldest daughter.

191 See J.D. Kestell and D.E. van Velden, *The Peace Negotiations between the Governments of the South African Republic and the Orange Free State, and the Representatives of the British Government, which Terminated in the Peace Concluded at Vereeniging on the 31st May, 1902* (London, 1902). English translation by D.E. van Velden.

192 At the Bloemfontein Conference, 31 May – 5 June 1899, which was arranged through the initiative of President M.T. Steyn (OFS) and W.P. Schreiner (premier, Cape Colony) in an effort to avert war between Britain and the Transvaal, Milner and Kruger met face to face, but no agreement could be reached.

193 I.e. General J.C. Smuts' 32nd birthday – see also Biographical Notes. According to Hamilton's letter of 24 May 1902 to Winston Churchill (Churchill Archives Centre, University of Cambridge: CHAR 1/34/59–62) the birthday celebration took place on the morning of 24 May 1902.

194 General Charles Tucker (see Biographical Notes) was 62 when he married Ellen (Nelly) O'Connell in 1902. From his previous marriage (1865), to Matilda Frederica Hayter (died 1897), he had two sons and a daughter. *DSAB*, V, p. 783.

195 See Prologue, Note 11.

196 See Note 133.

197 See Prologue, Note 22.

198 After the British captured Pretoria, General Louis Botha spread out his 6,000 burghers (and 23 guns) across the Delagoa Bay railway over a defensive line of some 40 km (25 miles) stretching from Doornfontein in the north, via Donkerhoek and Diamond Hill, to Kleinzonderhout in the south. On 11 and 12 June 1900 Roberts attacked the Boer positions at several

points, but could not outflank them. However, because of the superior British forces and artillery, the Boers evacuated their positions during the night of 12–13 June, and fell back eastwards. British casualties amounted to at least 28 killed and 145 wounded. Boer casualties amounted to about 30 (killed and taken prisoner). A.E. Breytenbach, 'Die Slag by Donkerhoek, 11–12 June 1900', *passim*; H.F. Nel, 'Die Slag van Donkerhoek 11–12 Junie 1900', *Militaria* 15(1), 1985, pp. 52–8 and 15(2), 1985, pp. 17–30; *History of the War in South Africa 1899–1902*, III, pp. 204–25; Amery (ed.), op cit, IV, pp. 269–96; J.H. Breytenbach, op cit, VI, pp. 173–203.

Epilogue
31 May 1902 and Beyond
Introduction

1 S.J. du Preez, 'Die Vrede van Vereeniging', pp. 341–401; J.D. Kestell and D.E. van Velden, *The Peace Negotiations between the Governments of the South African Republic and the Orange Free State, and the Representatives of the British Government, which Terminated in the Peace Concluded at Vereeniging on the 31ˢᵗ May, 1902*, pp. 201–8.

2 L.S. Amery (ed.), *The Times History of the War in South Africa 1899–1902*, VII, pp. 24–5.

3 T. van Rensburg (ed.), *Vir Vaderland, Vryheid en Eer. Oorlogsherinneringe van Wilhelm Mangold 1899–1902*, p. 356 (footnotes 17–19).

4 T. Pakenham, *The Boer War*, p. 572. The seventeen major wars in which Britain was involved since the end of the Crimean War in 1856, cost them £98.5 million. See V.G. Kiernan, *European Empires from Conquest to Collapse, 1815–1960*, pp. 140–1.

5 For Roberts' evidence, see *Royal Commission on the War in South Africa. Minutes of Evidence taken before the Royal Commission on the War in South Africa*, I (Cd. 1790), pp. 429–68 and II (Cd. 1791), pp. 46–71.

6 *DSAB*, II, p. 601; *DNB, 1912–1921*, p. 469; D. James, *Lord Roberts*, pp. 371–491; G. Forrest, *The Life of Lord Roberts, K.G., V.C.*, pp. 326–57.

31 May 1902 and Beyond

1 The conditions under which the Boers would surrender were signed at 23.05 on 31 May 1902 by representatives of the governments of Britain, the Transvaal and OFS in the dining-hall of Melrose House (Lord Kitchener's headquarters) in Pretoria.

2 Francis William Reitz (1844–1934), MP, Cape Colony, 1872–3; first Chief Justice of the OFS, 1875–88; President of the OFS, 1889–95 (resigned for reasons of health); Secretary of State of the Transvaal, 1898–1902, and as such signed the conditions of surrender, notwithstanding the fact that earlier that day (31 May 1902) he spoke out against accepting the British

terms. As a private citizen he declined to take the oath of allegiance to Great Britain, and went abroad as an exile. Union of South Africa Senator, 1910–20. Also known as a pioneer Afrikaans poet. *DSAB*, II, pp. 577–85.

3 In practice Lieutenant-General I.S.M. Hamilton returned to England with Lord Kitchener, but was re-appointed as Military Secretary at the War Office.

4 In 1899, General J.H. de la Rey did his utmost to avert war with the British, but once hostilities began he soon became a leading strategist and tactician in the field. At Vereeniging De la Rey said that he and his burghers could continue the struggle, but in the light of the fact that in most areas the commandos were in a terrible state, that the Boer civilians suffered terrible hardships and that the future of the Afrikaner people was at stake, the bitter end had come and the Boers had to accept the British peace proposals. At the eleventh hour, he and General Louis Botha persuaded General C.R. de Wet to give up his continued call for the continuation of the (now hopeless) struggle. General J.C.G. Kemp, on the other hand, was one of the minority who voted against accepting the peace proposals. *DSAB*, I, pp. 215, 217, 420.

5 See *South Africa Despatches. Despatch by General Lord Kitchener, dated 1st June, 1902, relative to Military Operations in South Africa* (Cd. 986), in particular pp. 5–8.

6 Kitchener was promoted to General in the first week of June 1902. He left South Africa for Britain on 23 June 1902, where he received a hero's welcome. Over and above being made a Viscount, Kitchener received £50,000, the Order of Merit, as well as several other honours, for services rendered during the war. *DSAB*, II, p. 368; G. Arthur, *Life of Lord Kitchener*, II, pp. 109–11; E.S. Grew, *Field-Marshal Lord Kitchener. His Life and Work for the Empire*, II, pp. 207–28.

Biographical Notes

Other persons mentioned in the transcripts are identified in the Notes.

Adye, Walter (1858–1915). Royal Irish Rifles. Previous service in Afghanistan, 1879–80; Transvaal War of Independence, 1880–1. DAAG, Army in Natal, 1899–1900. DAAG, Army, 1900–4.

Albrecht, Friedrich Wilhelm Richard (1848–1926). Previous service in Franco-Prussian War, 1870–1 (as NCO in Prussian artillery unit). Founder and commander of the State Artillery of the OFS, 1880–1900. Saw action on the Kimberley front, 1899–1900 (captured at Paardeberg, 27 February 1900).

Alderson, Edwin Alfred Hervey (1859–1927). Previous service in Transvaal War of Independence, 1880–1; Egypt, 1882 and 1884–5; Matabeleland, 1896. Saw action in North-West Cape Colony, 1899–1900; took part in Lord Roberts' advance to Bloemfontein, and to Pretoria, 1900; anti-guerrilla operations, Transvaal, 1900–1. GOC, Mounted Infantry, 1901–2; IG of Mounted Infantry, South Africa, 1900–2. Major-General, 1907; Lieutenant-General, 1914. GOC, Canadian Army Corps, France, 1915–16; IG, Canadian Forces, 1916–18.

Allenby, Edmund Henry Hyman (1861–1936). Previous service in Bechuanaland, 1884–5; Zululand, 1888. Saw action on Colesberg front, 1899–1900; took part in relief of Kimberley, advance to Bloemfontein, and to Pretoria, 1900; column commander, 1901–2. Major-General, 1909. GOC, 1st Cavalry Division, 1914; Cavalry Corps, 1914–15; 5th Army Corps, 1915; 3rd Army, 1915–17; C-in-C, Egyptian Expeditionary Corps, 1917–19; High Commissioner for Egypt and the Sudan, 1919–25. Knighted, 1915; Viscount, 1919; Field Marshal, 1919.

Altham, Edward Altham (1856–1943). Previous service in Bechuanaland, 1884–5. Served in South Africa, 1899–1900 as AAG for Intelligence. (Came to South Africa in April 1896 to do intelligence work. Served on Sir George White's Staff, September 1899–July 1900.) Later served in World War I: in charge of Administration, Southern Command, 1914; IGC, Dardanelles, 1915; IGC, Egyptian Expeditionary Force, 1916; QMG, India, 1917–19.

Ardagh, John Charles (1840–1907). Previous service in Egypt, 1882; Sudan, 1884–6. Private Secretary to Lord Lansdowne (Viceroy of India), 1888–94; Commandant, School of Military Engineering, Chatham, 1894–6; Director of Military Intelligence, War Office, 1896–1901; HMG Agent, South African Claims Commission, 1901; Member of Judicial Commission on Revision of Martial Law Sentences, 1902. Director of Suez Canal, 1903–7.

Baden-Powell, Robert Stephenson Smyth (1857–1941). Previous service in Zululand, 1888; Ashanti, 1895; Matabeleland, 1896. Defended Mafikeng for 217 days during Boer siege. Major-General, 1900. GOC a column in the Western Transvaal, 1900; raised and GOC, South African Constabulary, 1900–2. Lieutenant-General, 1907. GOC, Northumbrian Division of Territorials, 1908–10. Founder of the Boy Scouts, 1908; Sea Scouts, 1909; Girl Guides, 1910. 1st Baron Baden-Powell of Gillwell, 1929.

Balfour, Arthur James (1848–1930). Conservative MP for Hertford, 1874–85; Manchester East, 1885–1906; City of London, 1906–22. President Local Government Board, 1885–6; Secretary for Scotland, 1886–7; Chief Secretary for Ireland, 1887–91; First Lord of Treasury, 1891–2 and 1895–1905; Prime Minister, 1902–5. First Lord of Admiralty, 1915–16; Foreign Secretary, 1916–19; Lord President Council, 1919–22 and 1925–9. Earl, 1922.

Barton, Geoffry (1844–1922). Previous service in Ashanti, 1873–4; Anglo-Zulu War, 1879; Egypt, 1882; China, 1884–5; Suakim Expedition, 1885. Major-General, 1898. Saw action in Natal, 1899–1900; on Kimberley front, 1900; in the Western Transvaal, 1900–2.

Beatson, Stuart Brownlow (1854–1914). Previous service in Jowaki Expedition, 1878; Afghanistan, 1878–80; Egypt, 1882; India, 1897–8. OC of a mobile column, Transvaal and Cape Colony, 1901. Major-General, 1905.

Bedford, Duke of – see Russell, H.A.

Bell, Charles Frederic Moberly (1847–1911). Founder of the *Egyptian Gazette*, 1880; manager of *The Times* (London), 1890–1911; managing director of *The Times* Publishing Company, 1908–11. Published *The Times History of the War in South Africa 1899–1902* (7 vols, London, 1900–9).

Benson, George Elliot (1861–1901). Previous service in Sudan, 1884–5; Ashanti, 1895; Dongola, 1896. Lieutenant-Colonel, 1900; Colonel, 1901. Fought on Kimberley front, 1899–1900. Commanded a column in the Western Transvaal, and then in the Eastern Transvaal. Died of wounds sustained in clash with Louis Botha's commando at Bakenlaagte.

Bethune, Edward Cecil (1855–1930). Previous service in Aghanistan, 1879–80; Transvaal War of Independence, 1880–1. Raised a regiment of irregulars, Bethune's Mounted Infantry (better known as Bethune's Horse) in Natal, 1899. Saw action in Natal, 1899–1901; AAG, Field Force, 1900; Cape Colony and ORC, 1901–2. OC, Cavalry Brigade, 1901; OC, 16th Lancers, 1900–4. Brigadier-General, 1905; Major-General, 1908; Lieutenant-General, 1913. Director-General of the Territorial Force, 1912–17.

Bigge, Arthur John (1849–1931). Previous service in 9th Frontier War, Cape Colony, 1877–8; Anglo-Zulu War, 1879. Queen Victoria's Assistant Private Secretary, 1880–95; and Private Secretary, 1895–1901; Private Secretary to Prince (later King) George, 1901–31. Baron, 1911.

Birkbeck, William Henry (1863–1929). Previous service in Hazara Expedition, 1888; Chin-Lushai Expedition, 1889–90. Saw action in North-Western Cape Colony, 1901–2. Attached to Japanese 3rd Army, Manchuria, 1905;

Commandant of Cavalry School, Netheravon, 1906–11; Director of Remounts, Army HQ, 1912–20.

Blake, John Y. Filmore (1856–1907). Previous service in wars against Apaches in the USA. Arrived in Cape Town, 1895. Helped to quell the Matabele rising in Rhodesia (today Zimbabwe), 1896. Formed (a pro-Boer) Irish Brigade, mainly from Irish-Americans then resident in the Transvaal, 1899. Saw action in Natal, 1899–1900; Transvaal, 1900–2. Returned to the USA, 1902.

Blood, Bindon (1842–1940). Previous service in Jowaki Expedition, 1877–8; Anglo-Zulu War, 1879; Afghanistan, 1880; Egypt, 1882. Major-General, 1898. GOC, lines of communications, Eastern Transvaal, April–October 1901. General, 1906.

Botha, Annie Frances Bland (née Emmett) (1864–1937), an English-speaking woman of Irish descent; wife of General Louis Botha. Married 1886. They had five children: three sons and two daughters.

Botha, Louis (1862–1919). Boer General. C-in-C, Transvaal forces, 1900–2. Defeated Buller at Colenso, Spioenkop and Vaalkrans. Resorted to guerrilla warfare, 1900, operating mainly in the South-Eastern Transvaal. First Prime Minister of the Union of South Africa, 1910–19.

Brabant, Edward Yewd (1839–1914). Previous service in 9th Frontier War, Cape Colony, 1877–8; Moroosi Campaign, 1879; Basotholand, 1880–1. Brigadier-General, 1900. Raised Brabant's Horse, 1900; commanded the Colonial Division, 1900. Major-General, 1902. MP, Cape Colony, 1873–8, 1884–1902, 1905–7. Commandant-General of the Cape Colonial forces, 1902–5.

Brackenbury, Henry (1837–1914). Previous service in suppression of Indian Mutiny, 1857–8; Franco-Prussian War, 1870–1; Ashanti, 1873–4; Anglo-Zulu War, 1879; Sudan, 1884–5. Major-General, 1885. Director of Military Intelligence, War Office, 1886–91; Military Member of Viceroy's Council, 1891–6; President of Ordnance Board, 1896–9; Director General of Ordnance, 1899–1902.

Broadwood, Robert George (1862–1917). Previous service in Dongola, 1896; Sudan, 1897–8. GOC, 2nd Cavalry Brigade, 1900. Fought on Kimberley front. Defeated at Sannaspos, 31 March 1900. Fought until cessation of hostilities. C-in-C, Natal, 1903–4; ORC, 1904–6; China, 1906. Major-General, 1906. Killed in action, France.

Brodrick, William St John Fremantle (1856–1942). Conservative MP for Surrey (West), 1880–5 and Surrey (South West or Guildford), 1885–1906; Financial Secretary to the War Office, 1886–92; Under-Secretary of State for War, 1895–8; Under-Secretary of State for Foreign Affairs, 1898–1900; Secretary of State for War, 1900–3; Secretary of State for India, 1903–5. 9th Viscount Midleton, 1907; Earl of Midleton, 1920.

Buller, Redvers Henry (1839–1908). Previous service in China, 1860; Red River Expedition, Canada, 1870; Ashanti, 1873; 9th Frontier War, Cape Colony, 1877–8, Anglo-Zulu War (VC), 1879; Egypt, 1882; Sudan, 1884–5. QMG, 1887–90; AG, 1890–7. Major-General, 1881; Lieutenant-General, 1891; General, 1896. C-in-C, British forces in South Africa, 1899–1900.

Burdett-Coutts, William Lehman Ashmead Bartlett (1851–1921). Born in the USA. Special Commissioner, Russo-Turkish War, 1877. Married Angela, Baroness Burdett-Coutts, 1881, whose name he assumed. Correspondent of *The Times* in South Africa, 1900, concentrating on the plight of the sick and wounded; led to the appointment of a Royal Commission of Inquiry and a complete reform.

Burger, Schalk Willem (1852–1918). Previous service in Sekhukhuneland, 1876–7; campaign against Nyabêle, 1882–3; campaign against Mmalebôhô, 1893. Member of Transvaal Volksraad, 1886–1900; and of the Transvaal Executive Council, 1896–1902. General, 1899. Saw action in Natal, 1899–1900. Vice-President of the Transvaal, 1900; Acting State President of the Transvaal government-in-the-field, 1900–2. Senator of the Union of South Africa, 1913–18.

Burney, Herbert Henry (1858–1905). Previous service in Egypt, 1882–4; Sudan, 1884–5; Chitral, 1895; North-Western Frontier, India, 1897–8. As Lieutenant-Colonel, 2nd in command, 2nd Battalion Gordon Highlanders, took part in Roberts' advance to Pretoria, 1900 (wounded at Doornkop, 29 May 1900); anti-guerrilla operations, Transvaal, 1901–2.

Burn-Murdoch, John Francis (1859–1931). Previous service in Egypt, 1884–5; Dongola Expedition, 1896. OC, 1st Royal Dragoons, 1899–1901, for example in Natal; also OC, 1st Cavalry Brigade, 1900–1; OC, Newcastle Sub-district, 1901–2; Standerton, 1902–4; Potchefstroom, 1904–6. Temporary Major-General, 1916.

Callwell, Charles Edward (1859–1928). Previous service in Afghanistan, 1880; Transvaal War of Independence, 1880–1. Member of General Buller's staff, Natal, 1899–1900. OC of a mobile column, Western Transvaal and Cape Colony, 1900–2. Acquired reputation as military writer, for example *Small Wars. Their Principles and Practice*, 1896. Director of Military Operations and Intelligence, War Office, 1914–16. Major-General, 1917.

Campbell-Bannerman, Henry (1836–1908). Liberal MP for Stirling Burghs, 1868–1908; Financial Secretary to the War Office, 1871–4 and 1880–2; Parliamentary Secretary to the Admiralty, 1882–4; Chief Secretary for Ireland, 1884–5; Secretary of State for War, 1886 and 1892–5; Leader of the Liberal Party in the House of Commons, 1899–1908; Prime Minister, 1905–8.

Capper, Thompson (1863–1915). Previous service in Chitral, 1895; Sudan, 1898–9. Saw action in Natal and Transvaal, 1900; OC of a mobile column, Cape Colony, 1901–2. Commandant, Quetta Staff College, 1906–11; 13th Infantry Brigade, 1911–14; Inspector of Infantry, 1917; 7th Division, 1914–15. Major-General, 1914. Knighted, 1915. Mortally wounded, Western front.

Carrington, Frederick (1844–1913). Previous service in 9th Frontier War, Cape Colony, 1877–8; Griqualand West, 1878; Sekhukuneland, 1878–9; Basotholand, 1880–1; Bechuanaland, 1884–5, Zululand, 1888; Matabeleland, 1893 and 1896. Major-General, 1895. GOC, Rhodesian Field Force, Anglo-

Boer War, 1900: saw action in Transvaal. Returned to Rhodesia (today Zimbabwe), September 1900.

Cecil, Robert Arthur Talbot Gascoyne, 3rd Marquis of Salisbury (1830–1903). Conservative MP for Stamford, 1853–68; Secretary of State for India, 1866–7 and 1874–8; for Foreign Affairs, 1878–80; Prime Minister (and Secretary of State for Foreign Affairs), 1885–92; Prime Minister, 1895–1902 (and Secretary of State for Foreign Affairs, 1895–1900; Lord Privy Seal, 1900–2).

Chamberlain, Joseph (1836–1914). Liberal MP for Birmingham, 1876–86 (Birmingham West from 1886); Liberal Unionist for Birmingham (West), 1886–1914; President of the Board of Trade, 1880–5; President of the Local Government Board, 1886; Secretary of State for Colonies, 1895–1903.

Chamberlain, Neville Francis Fitzgerald (1856–1944). Previous service in Afghanistan, 1878–80 (wounded); Burma, 1886–7. Colonel, 1899. Private Secretary to Lord Roberts, 1899–1900. IG, Royal Irish Constabulary, 1900–16.

Chermside, Herbert Charles (1850–1929). Held various posts in Turkey and Crete, 1876–99, for example as military attaché. Major-General, 1898. Sent to South Africa as OC of the 14th Brigade, 1899; OC, 3rd Division, 1900. Protected the central railway line during Roberts' march from Bloemfontein to Pretoria. GOC, Curragh military home district, 1901; Governor of Queensland, 1902–4.

Chesham, Charles Compton William Cavendish, 3rd Baron (1850–1907). Member of Imperial Yeomanry Committee, 1899–1900. Saw action in OFS and Transvaal, 1900; in the Western Transvaal, as OC, 1st Yeomanry Brigade. IG, Imperial Yeomanry, South Africa, 1901–2.

Christian Victor, Prince – see Schleswig-Holstein, C.V.A.E.A.

Churchill, Winston Leonard Spencer (1874–1965). Previous service in Malakand, 1897; Tirah, 1898; Sudan, 1898. War correspondent of the *Morning Post* in South Africa, 1899–1900, and served in South African Light Horse, 1900. Conservative MP for Oldham, 1900–4; Liberal MP, 1904–6 for Oldham, for Manchester (North-West), 1906–8, for Dundee, 1908–22; Conservative MP for Essex (Epping), 1924–45, for Woodford, 1945–64. President of the Board of Trade, 1908–10; Secretary of State for Home Affairs, 1910–11; First Lord of the Admiralty, 1911–15 and 1939–40; Minister of Munitions, 1917–19; Secretary of State for War and Air, 1919–21; Secretary of State for the Colonies, 1921–2; Chancellor of the Exchequer, 1924–9; Prime Minister (and Minister of Defence), 1940–5 and 1951–5 (and Minister of Defence, 1951–2). Knighted, 1953.

Clements, Ralph Arthur Penrhyn (1855–1909). Previous service in Cape Colony, 1877–8; Anglo-Zulu War, 1879; Burma, 1885. ADC to Queen Victoria, 1896. GOC, 12th Infantry Brigade, 1899. Served on Colesberg front, in the OFS and in the Transvaal, 1899–1902. Major-General, 1904.

Clery, Cornelius Francis (1838–1926). Previous service in Anglo-Zulu War, 1879; Egypt, 1882; Suakim Expedition, 1884; Sudan, 1884–5. Chief of Staff, Egypt,

1886. Commandant of Staff College, 1888–93; GOC, 3rd Infantry Brigade, Aldershot, 1895–6; DAG, 1896–99. Major-General, 1894; Lieutenant-General, 1899. GOC, 2nd Division, Natal, 1899–1900; Transvaal, 1900. Returned to the UK, October 1900; retired 1901.

Cochrane, Douglas Mackinnon Baillie Hamilton, 12th Earl Dundonald (1852–1935). Previous service in Sudan, 1884–5. Saw action in Natal, 1899–1900; Transvaal, 1900. Major-General, 1900; Lieutenant-General, 1906.

Coke, John Talbot (1841–1912). Previous service in Canada, 1886; Sudan, 1889. Served in Natal, 1899–1900 (as OC, 10th Brigade of the 5th Division); Transvaal 1900.

Colvile, Henry Edward (1852–1907). Previous service in Sudan, 1884–5. Acting Commissioner in Uganda, 1893–5. Major-General, 1898. Served on Kimberley front, 1899–1900, commanding the 1st (Guards) Brigade of the 1st Division. GOC, 9th Division, 1900 (as part of Lord Roberts' force). Incurred the disfavour of Roberts and Kitchener, and had to return to the UK, end of 1900. Compelled to take his discharge from the Army, January 1901.

Connaught, Arthur William Patrick Albert, Duke of (1850–1942). Third son of Queen Victoria. Previous service in Egypt, 1882. Lieutenant-General, 1889; General, 1893; Field Marshal, 1902. GOC, Aldershot, 1893–8; Ireland, 1900–4; Mediterranean, 1907–9. Opened first Union of South Africa parliament, 1910. Governor-General, Canada, 1911–16.

Crabbe, Eyre Macdonnell Stewart (1852–1905). Previous service in Egypt, 1882; Sudan, 1884–5. Lieutenant-Colonel, Grenadier Guards, 1898. Saw action on Kimberley front, 1899–1900; in Cape Colony, 1901–2. Twice severely wounded during Anglo-Boer War.

Cronjé, Hester Susanna (née Visser) (1840–1903), wife of General Piet Cronjé. Married 1857. They had nine children: five sons and four daughters. She was taken prisoner with her husband at Paardeberg, 27 February 1900, and accompanied him to a St Helena POW camp.

Cronjé, Pieter (Piet) Arnoldus (1836–1911). Previous service in Transvaal civil strife, 1863; 2nd OFS-Basotho War, 1865; Transvaal War of Independence, 1880–1; suppression of Jameson Raid, 1896. C-in-C, Kimberley front, 1899–1900; outmanoeuvred, and forced to surrender at Paardeberg, 27 February 1900. POW on St Helena, 1900–2.

Cunningham, George Glencairn (1862–1943). Previous service in Egypt, 1882; Sudan, 1884–5 and 1887–9; OC, Unyoro Expedition, Uganda, 1895 (wounded); Niger-Sudan Campaign, 1897. Acting AAG, 3rd Division, South Africa, and in command of a Brigade, 1900–2, for example saw action in Eastern Transvaal, 1900; Western Transvaal, 1900–1; ORC, 1902. Brigadier-General, Plymouth General Reserve, 1914–16; special employment, BEF, France, 1917; Base Commandant, Brest, 1918.

Curzon, George Nathaniel (1859–1925). Conservative MP, 1886–98; Viceroy of India, 1898–1905; Lord Privy Seal, 1915–16; President of the Air Board, 1916; Lord President of the Council, 1916–19; Member of War Cabinet,

1916–19; Foreign Secretary, 1919–24. Baron, 1898; Earl, 1911; Marquis Curzon of Kedleston, 1921.

Dawkins, John Wyndham George (1861–1913). Previous service in Sudan, 1898. Saw action in Natal, 1899–1900; commanded a mobile column in the ORC and Western Transvaal, 1901 (wounded). Brevet Lieutenant-Colonel, 1900.

De la Rey, Jacobus (Koos) Hercules (1874–1914). Boer general who fought on the Kimberley and Colesberg fronts, 1899–1900, and as a guerrilla commander in the Western Transvaal, 1900–2. Opposed South Africa's participation in World War I, and was accidentally killed while involved in the planning of resistance against Louis Botha's government.

De Lisle, Henry de Beauvoir (1864–1955). Previous service in Egypt, 1885–6. Commanded the 2ⁿᵈ Corps Mounted Infantry, 1899–1902. Saw action on Colesberg front, 1899; took part in Lord Roberts' advance to Bloemfontein, and to Pretoria, 1900; took part in anti-guerrilla operations right across war zone, 1900–2. OC, 1ˢᵗ Royal Dragoons, 1906–10. Served in World War I, 1914–18. Major-General, 1915; Lieutenant-General, 1919; General, 1926.

De Wet, Christiaan Rudolph (1854–1922). Boer General who master-minded the guerrilla tactics. Previously fought against the British at Amajuba, 1881. Joined 1899 as an ordinary burgher. Acting Commandant, 1899; Combat General, 1899; C-in-C, OFS forces, 1900–2. Opposed South Africa's participations in World War I, took part in rebellion against Louis Botha's government, and was captured. Jailed for high treason, 1915. Freed after six months.

De Wet, Pieter Daniël (1861–1929). Younger brother of General C.R. de Wet. Previous service in the Transvaal War of Independence, 1880–1; campaign against Nyabêla, 1882. Saw action in Natal, 1899. General, 1899. Saw action in North-Eastern Cape Colony, 1899–1900; OFS, 1900. Surrendered voluntarily, July 1900. In British service as Chairman, Burgher Peace Committee in the ORC, 1900–1; OC, ORC Volunteers, 1901–2.

Dixon, Henry Grey (1850–1933). Previous service in Afghanistan, 1878–80; Egypt 1888–9. Saw action in South Africa, primarily in the Western Transvaal, 1901–2. Brigadier-General, 1901. GOC, Cyprus, 1916–18.

Doran, Beauchamp John Colclough (1860–1943). Previous service in Afghanistan, 1880; Egypt, 1884–5; Hazara Expedition, 1888; Miranzai Expedition, 1891; Tirah Expedition, 1897–8. Saw action in South Africa, 1899–1902: OC of a mobile column, Cape Colony, 1901–2 (severely wounded). Brigadier-General, 1912. GOC, 8ᵗʰ Infantry Brigade, 1912–15. Major-General, 1915. GOC, 25ᵗʰ Division, 1915–16; GOC, Southern District, Ireland, 1916–18; GOC, British Troops in France and Flanders, 1919.

Doran, Walter Robert Butler (1861–1945). Previous service in Egypt, 1882 and 1884–5; Hazara Expedition, 1888; Sudan, 1897–8. OC of a mobile column, Cape Colony, 1901–2; President of the Military Court at Graaff-Reinet. OC, 2ⁿᵈ Battalion Leinster Regiment, 1904–8; GSO1, 5ᵗʰ Division, 1909–12; GOC, 17ᵗʰ Infantry Brigade, 1912; GOC, Aldershot Command, 1915–19.

Douglas, Charles Whittingham Horsley (1850–1914). Previous service in Afghanistan, 1878–80; Transvaal War of Independence, 1880–1; Sudan, 1884–5. Chief of Staff to Lord Methuen, Kimberley front, 1899–1900. Major-General, 1900. GOC, 9th Infantry Brigade, OFS and Transvaal, 1900–1. AG, 1904–9; GOC, Southern Command, 1909–12; IG of Home Forces, 1912–14; CIGS, 1914.

Downe, Hugh Richard Dawnay, 8th Viscount (1844–1924). Previous service in Anglo-Zulu War, 1879. Served in South Africa as a Colonel, 1899–1902; for example as ADC to Lord Roberts. Brigadier-General, 1901.

Doyle, Arthur Conan (1859–1930). Worked (as a volunteer, without remuneration) as senior civilian medical doctor at the Langham Field Hospital, Bloemfontein, 1900. Well-known novelist (creator of the Sherlock Holmes character) and historian.

Dundonald, 12th Earl – see Cochrane, D.M.B.H.

Durand, Algernon George Arnold (1854–1923). Previous service in Afghanistan, 1878–80; Hunza-Nagar Expedition, 1891–2 (OC; severely wounded). Military Secretary to the Viceroy, India, 1894–9.

Edward VII (1841–1910). Field Marshal, 1875. King of the United Kingdom of Great Britain and Ireland, and Emperor of India, 1901–10.

Elliot, Edward Locke (1850–1938). Previous service in Afghanistan, 1878–9; Burma, 1887–9; Dongola Expedition, 1896. IG of Cavalry, India, 1898–1901. As Major-General commanded several units in the Northern ORC and Western Transvaal, 1901–2. GOC, 8th Division, Indian Army, 1905–10.

Elliot, Gilbert John Murray Kynynmond, 4th Earl of Minto, until 1891 known as Viscount Melguna (1845–1914). Previous service in Afghanistan, 1879–80; Egypt, 1882 (wounded); suppression of Riel Rebellion, Canada, 1885. Earl of Minto, 1891. Governor-General, Canada, 1898–1904; Viceroy, India, 1905–10.

Fanshawe, Hew Dalrymple (1860–1957). Previous service in Egypt, 1882–4; Sudan, 1884–5. Served in South Africa, 1899–1902, for example in North-Eastern ORC. Major-General, 1913. GOC, 1st Indian Cavalry Division, France, 1914–15; British Cavalry Corps, 1915; 5th Army Corps, 1915–16; 5th London Division, 1916–17; 18th Indian Division, Mesopotamia, 1917–19. Lieutenant-General, 1920.

Fetherstonhaugh, Richard Steele Rupert (1848–1932). Previous service in Anglo-Zulu War, 1879; Nile Expedition, 1888–9. GOC, 9th Brigade, Kimberley front, 1899–1900 (severely wounded). GOC, three columns in the Western Transvaal, 1901–2. Major-General, 1902.

Fiddes, George Vandeleur (1858–1936). Civil servant, 1881–1921, including Imperial Secretary and Accountant on the staff of the High Commissioner in South Africa and Governor of the Cape Colony, Alfred Milner, 1897–1900; Political Secretary (and adviser) to Lord Roberts, 1900; Secretary of the Transvaal Administration, 1900–2; Permanent Under-Secretary for the Colonies, 1916–21.

Firman, Robert Bertram (1859–1936). Previous service in Sudan, 1884–5; Burma, 1886–7. Saw action with the 11th Battalion Imperial Yeomanry in South Africa, 1899–1900, for example in ORC, 1901–2.

Forestier-Walker, Frederick William Edward (1844–1910). Previous service in Griqualand East, 1875; 9th Frontier War, Cape Colony, 1877–8; Anglo-Zulu War, 1879; Bechuanaland, 1884–5. Major-General, 1887. GOC, Egypt, 1890–95. Lieutenant-General, 1895. GOC, Western District, England, 1895–9; GOC, Cape Colony, 1899–1901. General, 1902. Governor and C-in-C, Gibraltar, 1905–10.

French, John Denton Pinkstone (1852–1925). Previous service in Sudan, 1884–5. Major-General, 1900. Fought in Natal, on Colesberg front, and in the OFS, Transvaal and Cape Colony, 1899–1902. CIGS, 1911–14; Field Marshal, 1913; C-in-C, BEF, 1914–15; C-in-C, Home Forces, 1916–18; Lord Lieutenant of Ireland, 1918–21. Knighted, 1900; Viscount, 1915; Earl of Ypres, 1921.

Garratt, Francis Sudlow (1859–1928). As a Lieutenant-Colonel, saw action on Colesberg front, 1899–1900; took part in relief of Kimberley and advance to Bloemfontein and Pretoria, 1900; Eastern Transvaal, 1900. Colonel, 1901. OC several columns; Transvaal and ORC, 1901–2. Saw action in World War I, 1914–18.

Gatacre, William Forbes (1843–1906). Previous service in Hazara Expedition, 1888; Chitral, 1895; Sudan, 1898. Major-General, 1898. GOC, 3rd Division, 1899–1900. Defeated at Stormberg (10 December 1899); relieved of his command, 10 April 1900, and returned to England. GOC, Eastern District, 1901–4.

Girouard, Eduard Percy Cranwill (1867–1932). Joined the Royal Engineers in 1888. Director of the Sudan Railways, 1896–8; President of the Egyptian Railway Board, 1898–9; Director of Military Railways, South Africa, 1899–1902; Commissioner of Railways for the Transvaal and ORC, 1902–4; High Commissioner in Northern Nigeria, 1907–8; Governor of East Africa, 1909–12; Director-General of Munition Supply, 1915–17.

Gordon, James Redmond Patrick (born 1860). Previous service in Afghanistan, 1880; Transvaal War of Independence, 1880–1; Bechuanaland Expedition, 1884–5; Burma, 1887; Expedition against the Jebus, Lagos, 1892; Ashanti, 1895–6. GOC, 3rd Cavalry Brigade, 1899–1900: took part in Lord Roberts' advance to Bloemfontein, to Pretoria, and eastwards along Delagoa Bay railway. GOC, 1st Cavalry Brigade, 1900–2: operations in Transvaal and ORC.

Gorringe, George F. (1868–1945). Previous service in Dongola Expedition, 1896; Sudan, 1897–8. ADC to Lord Kitchener, 1900; DAAG, HQ Staff, 1900; OC of a flying column, Cape Colony, 1901–2. Commanded operations, Southern Sennar, 1904; Brigadier-General Commanding 18th Infantry Brigade, 1909–11; Major-General, 1911; saw action in World War I, 1914–18 (severely wounded); GOC, 10th Division, Egypt, 1919–21; Lieutenant-General, 1921.

Gough, Hubert de la Poer (1870–1963). Previous service in Tirah, 1897–8. Saw action in Natal, 1899–1900; took part in anti-guerrilla operations, 1901–2, for example in Transvaal. OC, 16th Lancers, 1907–11; GOC, 3rd Cavalry Brigade, 1914; 2nd Cavalry and 7th Cavalry Division, 1915; I Corps, 1916; 5th Army, 1916–18. General, 1922.

Grierson, James Moncrieff (1859–1914). Previous service in Egypt, 1882; Sudan, 1885; Hazara Expedition, 1888. Took part, as Colonel, in Lord Roberts' advance to Bloemfontein, and Pretoria, 1900. DAG, China, 1900–1, on Count Waldersee's staff. Major-General, 1904. Director of Military Operations, War Office, 1904–6; GOC, 1st Division, Aldershot Command, 1906–10. As Lieutenant-General, and GOC, 2nd Army Corps, died on way to front, France, 1914.

Haig, Douglas (1861–1928). Previous service in Egypt, 1897; Sudan, 1898. Fought in Natal, on Colesberg and Kimberley front, in the OFS, Transvaal and Cape Colony, 1899–1902. Major-General, 1904; Lieutenant-General, 1910; General, 1914. GOC, Aldershot, 1912–14; 1st Army, 1914–15; C-in-C, BEF, 1915–19. Knighted, 1913; Field Marshal, 1917; Earl of Bemersyde, 1919.

Hamilton, Bruce Meade (1857–1936). Previous service in Afghanistan, 1880; Transvaal War of Independence,1880–1; Burma, 1885; Ashanti, 1895; Benin, 1897. Saw action in Natal, 1899–1900. GOC, 21st Infantry Brigade, OFS and Transvaal, 1900–1; GOC several columns, across whole war zone, 1901–2. GOC, 2nd Division, 1st Army Corps, 1904–7. Lieutenant-General, 1907; C-in-C, Scottish Command, 1909–13; General, Army Command Home Defence, 1914–18.

Hamilton, Hubert Ion Wetherall (1861–1914). Previous service in Burma, 1886–8; Sudan, 1897–9. Served in South Africa, 1899–1902, as a Lieutenant-Colonel, for example as DAAG and AAG, Army HQ, 1900, and as Military Secretary to Lord Kitchener, 1900–2; and later as his Military Secretary in India, 1902–5. OC, 7th Brigade, 1906–8; as Major-General on General Staff, Mediterranean Command, 1908–9; GOC, North Midland Division, 1911–14. Killed in action, World War I.

Hamilton, Ian Standish Monteith (1853–1947). Previous service in Afghanistan, 1878–80; Sudan, 1884–5; Burma, 1886–7; India, 1895. Major-General, 1899. Saw action in Natal (besieged in Ladysmith), 1899–1900; ORC and Transvaal, 1900. Lieutenant-General, 1900. Returned to UK, 1901, but back in South Africa as Kitchener's Chief of Staff, 1901–2 (and commanded four columns in the Western Transvaal, 1902). General, 1907. GOC, Southern Command, UK, 1905–9; AG, War Office, 1909–10; Mediterranean Command, 1910–15; Gallipoli Expedition, 1915. Knighted, 1900.

Hanbury-Williams, John (1859–1946). Major (later Major-General Sir). Previous service in Egypt, 1882. Lord Milner's Military Secretary in South Africa, 1897–1900; Secretary to Secretary of State for War, 1900–3; Governor-General's Secretary, and Military Secretary, Canada, 1904–9; Brigadier-General in charge of administration, Scotland, 1909–14; Chief of British Military Mission with HQ Russian Army in the Field, 1914–17; in charge of

British POW Department, the Hague, 1917–18, and Berne, 1918; Marshal of the Diplomatic Corps, 1920–34.

Hart, Arthur Fitzroy (1844–1910). Previous service in Ashanti, 1873–4; Anglo-Zulu War, 1879; Egypt, 1882. GOC, 5th Infantry Brigade, Natal, 1899–1900. Saw action in the Transvaal, ORC and Northern Cape, 1900–2.

Hely-Hutchinson, Walter Francis (1849–1913). Lieutenant-Governor of Malta, 1884–9; Governor of the Windward Islands, 1889–93; of Natal and Zululand, 1893–1901; of the Cape Colony, 1901–10.

Henderson, David (1862–1921). Previous service in Sudan, 1898. Saw action in Natal, 1899–1900 (wounded at Ladysmith); Lord Kitchener's Director of Military Intelligence, October 1900–September 1902. Director of Military Training, War Office, 1912–13; Director-General of Military Aeronautics, 1913; GOC, Royal Flying Corps, 1914–17. Lieutenant-General, 1917. Vice-President, Air Council, 1918; Area-Commandant, France, 1918. Military Counsellor, British Embassy, Paris, 1918–19; organized and directed the League of Red Cross societies, Geneva, 1919–21.

Henderson, George Francis Robert (1854–1903). Previous service in Egypt, 1882. Professor of Military Art and History, Staff College, Camberley, 1892–9. Director of Military Intelligence with local rank of Colonel on the staff of Lord Roberts, 1900. Returned to UK because of bad health. Author of several books and other publications.

Henry, St George Charles Henry (1860–1909). Previous service in Dongola, 1896; Sudan, 1897–8. Took part in Lord Roberts' advance to Bloemfontein, and Pretoria, 1900; took part in advance to Komatipoort, 1900; anti-guerrilla operations, Eastern Transvaal and ORC, 1901–2.

Hickman, Thomas Edgecumbe (1859–1930). Previous service in Sudan, 1884–5; Suakim, 1887–8; Egypt, 1889; Dongola Expedition, 1896; Sudan, 1897–8. Took part in anti-guerrilla operations across the war zone, 1900–2. GOC, Middelburg District, Cape Colony, 1902–8.

Hicks Beach, Michael Edward (1837–1916). Conservative MP for Gloucester (East), 1864–85 and for Bristol (West), 1885–1906; Parliamentary Secretary to the Poor Law Board, 1868; Under-Secretary of State for Home Affairs, 1868; Chief Secretary for Ireland, 1874–8 and 1886–7; Secretary of State for Colonies, 1878–80; Chancellor of the Exchequer, 1885–6 and 1895–1902; President of the Board of Trade, 1888–92. Viscount St Aldwyn, 1906; Earl St Aldwyn, 1915.

Hildyard, Henry John Thornton (1846–1916). Previous service in Egypt, 1882. Saw action in Natal, 1899–1900; Transvaal, 1900–1. Director-General of British Military Education, 1903–4; as Lieutenant-General, GOC-in-C, South Africa, 1905–8.

Hill, Augustus West (1858–1922). Previous service in Anglo-Zulu War, 1879. As Lieutenant-Colonel, OC, 10th Brigade, Natal, 1900, for example took part in Ladysmith relief operations; operations in ORC and Transvaal, 1900–1.

Hobbs, George Radley (1853–1907). Previous service in Anglo-Zulu War, 1879. Chief Ordnance Officer, Cape Colony line of communications, 1899–1901.

Hunter, Archibald (1856–1936). Previous service in Egypt, 1884–9; Sudan, 1896–8. Major-General, 1896. Besieged in Ladysmith, 1899–1900. Lieutenant-General, 1900. Forced Boers to surrender in Brandwater Basin, ORC, 1900. Invalided home, 1901. GOC, Scottish District, 1901–3; commanded the Western and later the Southern Army, India, 1903–8. General 1905. Governor of Gibraltar, 1910–13; at Aldershot, 1914–17. Conservative MP, Lancaster, 1918–22.

Hutton, Edward Thomas Henry (1848–1923). Previous service in Anglo-Zulu War, 1879; Transvaal War of Independence,1880–1; Egypt, 1882; Sudan, 1884–5. Took part in Lord Roberts' advance to Bloemfontein, and Pretoria, 1900; advance to Komatipoort, 1900. Returned to UK, October 1900. GOC, Australian forces, 1901–4; GOC, 21st Division of the 3rd Army, 1914–18.

James, Lionel (1871–1955). Reuters' special correspondent in the Chitral Campaign, 1894–5; Mohmund, Malakand, and Tirah Campaigns, 1897–8; Sudan 1898. Special correspondent of *The Times*, Egypt, 1899; South Africa, 1899–1901; America and Macedonia, 1903; Japan and Manchuria, 1904. Retired from journalism and *The Times*, 1913. As a Colonel, commanded a cavalry regiment, World War I, 1914–18. Author of several books, 1895–1929, including *On the Heels of De Wet* (1929).

Jones, Inigo Richmund (1848–1914). Previous service in Egypt, 1885. OC, 1st (Guards) Brigade, 1900–2: took part in Lord Roberts' advance from Bloemfontein to Pretoria; GOC, Midlands, Cape Colony, 1901–2. GOC, Scots Guards, 1903–5.

Kavanagh, Charles Toler McMurrough (1864–1950). One of French's column-commanders in the Cape Colony, 1901. OC, 1st Cavalry Brigade, 1909–13. Served in World War I, 1914–18 (wounded). Major-General, 1915; Lieutenant-General, 1915.

Keir, John Lindesay (1856–1937). Saw action in South Africa, 1899–1902, including as OC of a mobile column in the ORC and Western Transvaal, 1901–2. AAG, India, 1904. OC, Alahabad Brigade, 1907–11. Major-General, 1909. GOC, 6th Division, Ireland, 1914. Commanded in World War I, 1914–18. Lieutenant-General, 1916.

Kekewich, Robert George (1854–1914). Previous service in Malaysia, 1875–6; Sudan, 1884–5; Suakim, 1888. GOC, Kimberley, during siege, 1899–1900; commander of a mobile column, Western Transvaal, 1900–2. Major-General, 1902.

Kelly-Kenny, Thomas (1840–1914). Previous service in China, 1860; Abyssinia, 1867–8. Major-General, 1896. Took part in Lord Roberts' advance to Bloemfontein, 1900. GOC of all British forces in the ORC, 1900. Returned to UK with Lord Roberts. AG, 1901–4. General, 1905.

Kemp, Jan Christoffel Greyling (1872–1946). Previous service in Magato War, 1895; suppression of Jameson Raid, 1896. Saw action in Natal, 1899–1900; and then mainly in the Western Transvaal, 1900–2. Combat General, 1901. One of six delegates (out of 60) who voted against the peace terms, 1902.

Joined Union Defence Forces in 1912. Rebelled against Louis Botha's government and trekked to German South-West Africa (today Namibia), 1914; after initial successes surrendered, 1915; imprisoned, 1915, but released after serving just over a year, 1916. MP for Wolmaransstad, 1920–46; Minister of Agriculture, 1924–34; and of Lands, 1922–7.

Kitchener, Frederick Walter (1858–1912). Brother of Lord Kitchener. Previous service in Afghanistan, 1878–80; Dongola, 1896; Sudan, 1898. Fought in Natal, 1899–1900; Transvaal, 1900–2. Major-General, 1900; Lieutenant-General, 1906. C-in-C and Governor, Bermuda, 1908–10.

Kitchener, Horatio Herbert (1850–1916). Previous service in Franco-Prussian War, 1871 (as a volunteer with a French field ambulance); Egypt, 1882; Sudan, 1884–5. Governor-General of Eastern Sudan, 1886–8; AG of Egyptian Army, 1888–92; Sirdar of Egyptian Army, 1892–9. Defeated Khalifa's Army at Omdurman, 1898. Governor-General of Sudan, 1899. Roberts' Chief of Staff, South Africa, 1900; C-in-C, South Africa, 1900–2. C-in-C India, 1902–9. British Agent and Consul-General in Egypt, 1911–14. Secretary of State for War, 1914–16. Baron, 1898; Field Marshal, 1909; Earl, 1914. Went down with HMS *Hampshire* off Orkneys en route to Russia.

Knox, Charles Edmond (1847–1938). Previous service in Bechuanaland, 1884–5. Saw action under Lord Roberts, 1900. Wounded at Paardeberg. Anti-guerrilla operations, ORC, 1900–2. Major-General, 1902.

Knox, William George (1847–1916). Previous service in Abyssinia, 1867–8; Ashanti, 1873–4; Russo-Turkish War, 1877–8 (observer on Turkish side); Afghanistan, 1878–9; Anglo-Zulu War, 1879; war against Sekhukhune, Transvaal, 1879; Transvaal War of Independence,1880–1. Saw action in Natal, 1899–1900 (including siege of Ladysmith). Major-General, 1900. GOC, 23rd Brigade, ORC, 1900–2.

Krause, Frederick (Fritz) Edward Traugott (1868–1959). Chief Prosecutor in Johannesburg and Acting Attorney-General of the Transvaal, 1896–1900; Special Commandant of the Witwatersrand, 1900 (saved the goldmines from destruction, and surrendered Johannesburg to Lord Roberts, 31 May 1900). Represented Vrededorp in Transvaal Legislative Assembly, 1907–9. Transvaal judge, 1923–33; Judge-President of the OFS, 1933–8.

Kritzinger, Pieter Hendrik (1870–1935). Saw action in Cape Colony, 1899–1900; fought under C.R. de Wet in OFS, 1900; invaded the Cape Colony on three occasions, 1900–1. General, 1901. Wounded and captured, 16 December 1901.

Kruger, Gezina Susanna Frederika Wilhelmina (née Du Plessis) (1831–1901), second wife of President S.J.P. Kruger. Married 1847. They had sixteen children: nine sons and seven daughters, some of whom died young. She did not accompany her husband to Europe.

Kruger, Stephanus Johannes Paulus (Paul) (1825–1904). State President of the Transvaal, 1883–1902. Went to Europe in self-imposed exile, 1900. Died in Switzerland.

Lagden, Godfrey Yeatman (1851–1934). Previous service in Egypt, 1882–3 (war correspondent). Resident Commissioner in Basotholand, 1893–1901; Commissioner of Native Affairs in the Transvaal, 1901–7.

Lansdowne, Lord – see Petty-Fitzmaurice, H.C.K.

Lawrence, Herbert Alexander (1861–1943). Served in South Africa as Brevet Lieutenant-Colonel, for example as OC, 16th Lancers. Later served in World War I, 1914–18. Major-General, 1915; Lieutenant-General, 1918; General, 1919.

Lessard, François Louis (1860–1927). Canadian. Previous service in suppression of rebellion in North-West Canada, 1885. Saw action in South Africa, 1899–1901, for example took part in Lord Roberts' advance, 1900. AG, Canadian Militia, 1907–12; GOC, 2nd Division, 1912–15. Major-General, 1912. IG, Eastern Canada, 1915. GOC, MD No. 6 and OC Halifax Fortress Command, 1917–18.

Leyds, Wilhelm Johannes (1859–1940). Transvaal State Atttorney, 1884–8; State Secretary, 1888–98; Ambassador Extraordinary and Minister Plenipotentiary in Europe, 1898–1902.

Little, Malcolm Orme (1857–1931). Previous service in Afghanistan, 1878–80. Saw action on the Kimberley front, 1899–1900. OC, 9th Lancers, 1899–1900. Took part in Lord Roberts' advance to Bloemfontein, and Pretoria, 1900. GOC, 3rd Cavalry Brigade, 1900, South-Western Transvaal (wounded). Took part in anti-guerrilla operations, ORC and Transvaal, 1900–2. Served in World War I, 1914–18.

Lockhart, William Stephen Alexander (born 1841). Previous service in Bhootan Expedition, 1864–6; Abyssinia, 1867–8; Hazara Campaign, 1868; Dutch War in Acheen, 1875–7; Afghanistan, 1879–80; Burma, 1885–7; 1st and 2nd Miranzai Expeditions, 1891; Isazai Expedition, 1892; Waziristan Expedition, 1894–5; North-Western Frontier, India, 1897–8. Major-General, 1891; Lieutenant-General, 1894; General, 1896. Became C-in-C in India, 1898.

Long, Charles James (1849–1933). Previous service in Afghanistan, 1879–80; Sudan, 1897–8. Saw action in Natal, 1899–1900 (lost his guns and wounded at Colenso, 15 December 1899); took part in 2nd De Wet hunt, 1901. Inspector of Remounts, 1914.

Lyttelton, Neville Gerald (1845–1931). Previous service in suppression of Fenian Rebellion, Canada, 1866; Egypt, 1882; Sudan, 1898. Major-General, 1898. Saw action in Natal, 1899–1900; Transvaal and ORC, 1900–2. Lieutenant-General, 1901. GOC, Natal, 1901; C-in-C, South Africa, 1902–4; CGS, 1904–8. General, 1906. C-in-C, Ireland, 1908–12.

MacCormac, William (1836–1901). Qualified as medical doctor. Did voluntary medical service during Franco-Prussian War, 1870–1; Turko-Serbian War, 1876. Member of Central British Red Cross Committee, 1899–1901; government consulting surgeon to the field force, South Africa, 1899–1900: visited all the British hospitals in Natal and the Cape Colony, and went to the front on four occasions.

MacDonald, Hector Archibald (1853–1903). Previous service in Afghanistan, 1879–80; Transvaal War of Independence, 1880–1; Egypt, 1885 and 1896; Sudan, 1888–91 and 1898. Major-General, 1900. Commanded the Highland Brigade, 1900. Took part in the relief of Kimberley; Roberts' march to Bloemfontein (wounded at Paardeberg). Anti-guerrilla operations, Cape Colony, 1900–1. Commanded Belgaum District, India, 1901–2. Committed suicide before allegations of homosexuality could be investigated by a court of inquiry.

Mackenzie, Colin John (1861–1956). Previous service in Egypt, 1882; Burma, 1886–8; Hazara, 1888; Hunza-Nagar and Gilgit, 1891; Waziristan, 1894–5; Sudan, 1898. Lord Roberts' Director of Field Intelligence since February 1900 (after Colonel G.F.R. Henderson was invalided home); Military Governor of Johannesburg, 1900. Served in World War I, 1914–18, for example GOC, 61st Division, 1916–18 (wounded).

Mahon, Bryan Thomas (1862–1930). Previous service in Egypt, 1896–7. Commanded the column that relieved Mafikeng, 1900. Operated in Eastern Transvaal, 1900. Governor of Kordofan, Egypt, 1901–4; commanded Belgaum District, India, 1904–9; Lucknow Division, 1909–13; GOC, 10th (Irish) Division, 1914. Took part in Gallipoli Campaign, 1915. C-in-C, Salonika Army, 1915–16; C-in-C, Ireland, 1916–18; military commander, Lille, 1918–19.

Marker, Raymond John (1867–1914). ADC to Sir West Ridgeway, Governor of Ceylon, 1895–7; to Lord Curzon, India, 1899–1900; to Lord Kitchener during war, 1901–2, and in India, 1902–6. Decorated for capture of General De Wet's gun and pom-pom, Cape Colony, 1901. Died of wounds, World War I.

Marlborough, Charles Richard John Spencer-Churchill, 9th Duke of (1871–1934). Served with Yeomanry Cavalry in South Africa, 1900, and as ADC to Lieutenant-General Ian Hamilton. Paymaster-General, 1899–1902; Under-Secretary of State for Colonies, 1903–5; Parliamentary Secretary, Board of Agriculture, 1917–18.

Maxwell, John Grenfell (1859–1929). Previous service in Egypt, 1882; Egypt and Sudan, 1884–5 and 1886–9; Dongola, 1896; Sudan, 1898. Governor of Nubia, 1896–8; of Omdurman, 1898–9. Local Major-General, 1900. GOC, 14th Brigade, ORC and Transvaal, 1900. Military Governor, Pretoria, 1900–2. Substantive Major-General, 1906. GOC, Egypt, 1908–12 and 1914–15. Lieutenant-General, 1912. Served in World War I, 1914–18; GOC, Ireland, 1916; C-in-C, Northern Command, 1916–19. General, 1919.

Metcalfe, Charles Theophilus Evelyn (1856–1912). Previous service in Burma, 1886–7; North-Western Frontier, India, 1897–8. Served in South Africa as a Lieutenant-Colonel, 1899–1902, for example in Natal, 1899–1900 (including siege of Ladysmith) and in the Eastern Transvaal (severely wounded at Bergendal, 27 August 1900). Major-General, 1907.

Methuen, Lord – see Sanford, P.

Meyer (or Meijer), Lukas (or Lucas) Johannes (1846–1902). Previous service in the Transvaal War of Independence, 1880–1; Zululand, 1884. President of the New Republic, 1884–8, until it was incorporated into the Transvaal. Member of the Transvaal Volksraad, 1893–1900. Saw action in Natal, 1899–1900, but ill health prevented him from playing any further active role in the war. Died on 8 August 1902 in Brussels.

Milner, Alfred (1854–1925). Under-Secretary for Finance in Egypt, 1890–2; Chairman, Board of Inland Revenue, 1892–4. Governor of the Cape, 1897–1901; High Commissioner for South Africa, 1897–1905; Administrator of the Transvaal Colony and ORC, 1900–1; Governor of the Transvaal Colony and ORC, 1901–5; Member of War Cabinet, 1916–18; Secretary of State for War, 1918–19; Secretary of State for Colonies, 1919–21. Knighted, 1895; Baron, 1901; Viscount, 1902.

Minto, Earl of – see Elliot, G.J.M.K.

Murray, Archibald James (1860–1945). Previous service in Zululand, 1888. Served as a Major in Natal (including siege of Ladysmith), 1899–1900; as Lieutenant-Colonel on Staff of 10th Division, 1900; in the Northern Transvaal, 1902 (seriously wounded). Director of Military Training, HQ, 1907–12. Major-General, 1910; Inspector of Infantry, 1912–14. Lieutenant-General, 1915. Served in World War I, 1914–18: Deputy-Chief, IGS, then CIGS, 1915; GOC, Egypt, 1916–17; GOC, Aldershot, 1917–19. General, 1919.

Nicholson, William Gustavus (1845–1918). Previous service in Afghanistan, 1878–80; Egypt, 1882; Burma, 1886–7; Tirah Expedition, 1897–8. AG, India, 1898–9. Military Secretary to Lord Roberts, 1899–1900; Director of Transport at HQ, 1900. Lieutenant-General, 1901. Director-General of Mobilisation and Military Intelligence, War Office, 1901–4; Chief British Military Attaché, Japanese Army, 1904–5; QMG of the Forces, and 3rd Military Member of the Army Council, 1905–7. General, 1906; Field Marshal, 1911; Baron, 1912.

Oliphant, Laurence James (1846–1914). Previous service in Sudan, 1885. Major-General, 1898. Commanded mobile columns, 1901–2. GOC, Home District, 1903–6; Northern Command, 1907–11.

Paget, Arthur Henry Fitzroy (1851–1928). Previous service in Ashanti, 1873; Sudan, 1885 and 1888–9; Burma, 1887–8. Saw action on Kimberley front, 1899–1900. Major-General, 1900. GOC, 20th Infantry Brigade, 1900–1. Operated in OFS and Transvaal. GOC, 1st Division, Aldershot, 1902–6. Lieutenant-General, 1906. GOC, Eastern Command, 1908–11; C-in-C, Ireland, 1911–14. Knighted, 1906.

Palmer, Arthur Power (1840–1904). Previous service in suppression of Indian Mutiny, 1857–9; North-West Frontier, India, 1863–4; Abyssinian Expedition, 1868; Duffla Expedition, 1874–5; Achin, 1876–7 (with Dutch forces); Afghanistan, 1878–80; Suakim Expedition, 1885; raid on Thakul, 1885; Burma Expedition, 1892–3. Major-General, 1893; Lieutenant-General, 1897. Served in the Tirah Campaign, 1897–8. GOC, Punjab frontier force, 1898–1900. General, 1899. C-in-C, India, 1900–2. Succeeded by Lord Kitchener. Showed high administrative capacity in selecting regiments and commanders for the war in South Africa.

Parsons, Charles Sim Bremridge (1855–1923). Previous service in 9th Frontier War, Cape Colony, 1877–8; Anglo-Zulu War, 1879; Transvaal War of Independence,1880–1; Egypt, 1882; Dongola Expedition, 1896; Sudan, 1897–8. Saw action in Northern Cape Colony, 1900; ORC, 1900; Cape Colony, 1901. Deputy Military Governor of the Northern Cape (Griqualand West) and Commandant of the West Kimberley District, 1901–2. OC, British forces in Canada, 1902–6.

Petty-Fitzmaurice, Henry Charles Keith, 5th Marquis of Lansdowne (1845–1927). Under-Secretary of State for War, 1872–4, and of India Office, 1880; Governor-General of Canada, 1883–8; Viceroy of India, 1888–94; Secretary of State for War, 1895–1900, and for Foreign Affairs, 1900–5; Minister Without Portfolio, 1915–16.

Pilcher, Thomas David (1858–1928). Previous service in West Africa, 1897–8. Saw action on Kimberley front under Lord Methuen, 1899–1900; took part in Lord Roberts' advance to Bloemfontein, and to Pretoria, 1900; anti-guerrilla operations, Transvaal, ORC and Cape Colony, 1900–2. Major-General, 1907. GOC, 17th Division, BEF, England and France, 1915–16 (wounded).

Plumer, Herbert Charles Onslow (1857–1932). Previous service in Sudan, 1884. Relieved Mafikeng, 1900. Then operated primarily in the Eastern Transvaal. Major-General, 1902. QMG, 1904–5; GOC, 5th Division, Ireland, 1906–9. Lieutenant-General, 1911. GOC, Northern Command, 1911–14; 5th Corps, 1915; 2nd Army, 1915–17 and 1918; GOC, Italy, 1917–18. Baron Plumer, of Messines and Bilton, Yorkshire, 1919; Field Marshal, 1919. GOC, Army of the Rhine, 1918–19; Governor, Malta, 1919–24; High Commissioner, Palestine, 1925–28.

Pole-Carew, Reginald (1849–1924). Previous service in Afghanistan, 1879–80; Egypt, 1882; Burma, 1886–7. Major-General, 1899. On Buller's staff, Natal, 1899, but transferred to Kimberley front as GOC, 9th Brigade, 1899–1900; GOC 1st (Guards) Brigade under Roberts, 1900; Eastern Transvaal, 1900. Returned to UK. GOC, 8th Division, 3rd Army Corps, 1903–5. MP for the Bodmin electoral district, 1910–16.

Porter, Thomas Cole (1851–1938). Previous service in Afghanistan, 1879–80. Saw action on Colesberg front, 1899–1900. Took part in Lord Roberts' advance to Bloemfontein, and to Pretoria, 1900; Eastern Transvaal, 1900–1. OC, 1st Cavalry Brigade, 1900–1. Inspector of Yeomanry, Southern Division, 1904–6; GOC, Potchefstroom Sub-District, 1906–8.

Pretyman, George Tindal (1845–1917). Previous service in Afghanistan, 1878–80. Military Secretary, Madras, 1881–4. Major-General, 1897. Served in South Africa, 1899–1901: Military Governor and Administrator, OFS, 1900–1; GOC, Kimberley District, 1901. GOC, Secunderabad District, 1902–3; Commander of forces in Madras, 1904; Burma Division, 1906–7.

Rawlinson, Henry Seymour (1864–1925). Previous service in Burma, 1887–8; Sudan, 1898. Besieged in Ladysmith, 1899–1900; AAG on Roberts' Staff, 1900; operated against guerrillas, 1901–2. Major-General, 1909. Commanded

4th Division, 1914; 7th Division and 3rd Cavalry Division, 1914; GOC, IV Corps, 1914–15; 1st and 4th Armies, 1915–19. Knighted 1914; Lieutenant-General, 1916; General, 1917; Baron, 1919. GOC, Aldershot, 1919–20; C-in-C, India, 1920–5.

Rhodes, Cecil John (1853–1902). First came to South Africa in 1870. MP for Barkly West, Cape Colony, 1877–1902. Instrumental in the British occupation of Bechuanaland (today Botswana) and Southern Rhodesia (Zimbabwe). Made a fortune out of the diamond-fields of Kimberley and the Witwatersrand goldmines. Prime Minister, Cape Colony, 1890–6. Besieged in Kimberley, 1899–1900.

Richardson, Wodehouse Dillon (1854–1929). Previous service in Ashanti, 1873–4; 9th Frontier War, Cape Colony, 1877–8; Anglo-Zulu War, 1879; Transvaal War of Independence,1880–1; Bechuanaland, 1884–5. As Colonel, sent to South Africa in September 1899 as AAG to organize supplies and transport. Director of Supplies and Transport, January–February 1900; of Supplies only, February–November 1900. Director of Supplies in Britain, 1901–3.

Ridley, Charles Parker (1855–1937). Previous service in Egypt, 1884; Miranzai Expedition, 1891. As Brigadier-General saw action in South Africa, 1899–1900, for example as OC, 2nd Mounted Infantry Brigade, 1900: took part in Lord Roberts' advance to Bloemfontein, and to Pretoria, 1900; operated in Transvaal and ORC, 1900.

Rimington, Michael Frederic (1858–1928). Previous service in Bechuanaland, 1884–5; Zululand, 1888. Founder and commander of a volunteer intelligence unit called Rimington's Guides, or Scouts, 1899. Saw action on the Kimberley front, 1899–1900; in the OFS and Transvaal, 1900–2. Inspector of Cavalry, India, 1902.

Roberts, Ada Stewart Edwina (1875–1955). Fourth (and second surviving) daughter of Lord Roberts. Married Colonel (later Brigadier-General) Henry Frederick Elliot Lewen, 1913. One son, Frederick Roberts Alexander; killed in action, 1940.

Roberts, Aileen Mary (1870–1944). Elder surviving daughter of Lord Roberts. Never married.

Roberts, Frederick (Freddy) Sherston (1872–1899). Only surviving son of Lord Roberts. Previous service in Isazai Expedition, 1892; with Waziristan Field Force, 1894–5; Chitral Relief Force, 1895; Sudan, 1898. Mortally wounded, Colenso, 15 December 1899, while trying to save the guns. Died 17 December. Awarded the VC.

Roberts, Frederick (Fred) Sleigh, 1st Earl, of Kandahar, Pretoria, and Waterford (1832–1914). Previous service in suppression of Indian Mutiny (VC), 1857–8; Ambeyla Expedition, 1863; Abyssinia, 1867–8; Lushai Expedition, 1871–2; Afghanistan, 1878–80; Burma, 1886–7. Major-General, 1878; Lieutenant-General, 1883; General, 1885; Field Marshal, 1895. QMG, India, 1875–8; C-in-C, Madras Army, 1881–5; C-in-C, India, 1885–93; C-in-C, Ireland,

1895–9; C-in-C, South Africa, 1899–1900; C-in-C, British Army, 1901–4. Baron, of Kandahar, 1892; Earl, of Pretoria, and Waterford, 1901.

Roberts, Nora Henrietta (née Bews) (died 1920). Wife of Lord Roberts. Married 1859. They had six children, three of whom died in infancy. Those who reached adulthood were Aileen Mary, Frederick Sherston (mortally wounded, Colenso, 15 December 1899), and Ada Stewart Edwina.

Rochfort, Alexander Nelson (1850–1916). Previous service in Sudan, 1885. Saw action in South Africa, 1899–1902 (severely wounded), for example took part in Lord Roberts' advance; anti-guerrilla operations, ORC and Transvaal. Special service, Somaliland, 1902–4. Inspector, Horse and Field Artillery, 1904–10. Major-General, 1907.

Romney, Charles Marsham, 5th Earl of (1864–1933). Major, 4th Battalion Bedfordshire Regiment, since 1886.

Rosslyn, James Francis Harry St Clair-Erskine, 5th Earl of (1869–1939). Served with Thorneycroft's Horse at relief of Ladysmith, 1900; war correspondent, *Daily Mail*, South Africa, 1900.

Rouliot, Georges (1861–1917). Frenchman, who as General Manager of the Campagnie Générale des Mines de Diamants went to Kimberley in 1882. Appointed member of the Kimberley Mining Board, 1882; member of the Board for the Protection of Mining Rights, 1886–7; Du Toitspan Mining Board, 1886–92. President of the Transvaal Chamber of Mines, 1897–1902. Played a key role in re-opening the mines, 1901. Returned to France after the war.

Rundle, Henry Macleod Leslie (1856–1934). Previous service in Anglo-Zulu War, 1879; Transvaal War of Independence,1880–1; Egypt, 1882; Sudan, 1884–5, 1885–7 and 1889–1898. Major-General, 1896. AG, Egypt, 1896–8. GOC, 8th Division, 1900–2. Operated in OFS, 1900–2. GOC, 5th Division, 1902–3. Lieutenant-General, 1905. Governor and C-in-C, Malta, 1909–15; C-in-C, Central Force, 1915–16.

Russell, Herbrand Arthur, 11th Duke of Bedford (1858–1940). Previous service in Egypt, 1882. Later served in World War I, 1914–18. ADC to King Edward VII, 1908–10, and to King George V, 1910–20. Unionist.

Salisbury, Lord – see Cecil, R.A.T.G.

Sanford, Paul, 3rd Baron Methuen of Corsham (1845–1932). Previous service in Gold Coast, 1873; Ashanti, 1874; Egypt, 1882; Bechuanaland, 1884–8. GOC, Home District, 1892–7. GOC, 1st Division. Defeated at Magersfontein, 1899; captured at Tweebosch (De Klipdrift), 1902 (released soon afterwards). GOC, Eastern Command, 1903–8; GOC, South Africa, 1908–12, and Governor of Natal, 1910. Field Marshal, 1911. C-in-C and Governor, Malta, 1915–19.

Scheepers, Gideon Jacobus (1878–1902). Joined the Field-Telegraph Section of the Transvaal State Artillery, 1895. Saw action on the Kimberley front, 1899–1900; in the OFS under C.R. de Wet, 1900; invaded the Cape Colony, 15 December 1900; formed own commando and operated in the Cape Colony, 1901; fell seriously ill; captured by the British, 10 October 1901; convicted of murder, etc. and executed.

Schleswig-Holstein, Christian Victor Albert Ernst Anton, Prince of (1867–1900). Eldest son of Princess Helena (later also known as Princess Christian), Queen Victoria's third daughter. Previous service in Hazara Expedition, 1891; Miranzai Expedition, 1891; Isazai Expedition, 1892; Ashanti, 1895–6; Sudan, 1898. Major, 1896. Saw action in Natal, 1899–1900; Transvaal, 1900. Died of typhoid.

Schreiner, William Philip (1857–1919). Brother of novelist Olive Schreiner. Attorney-General, Cape Colony, 1893–6. Prime Minister, Cape Colony, 1898–1900. Campaigned to avert war with the Boer republics, 1899. Campaigned for political rights for blacks, coloureds and Indians, and against racial discrimination, 1908–14. South Africa's High Commissioner in London, 1914–19.

Sclater, Henry Crichton (1855–1923). Previous service in Sudan, 1884–6. Served in South Africa, 1899–1902, as AAG for RA, and Colonel on Staff for RA. Director of Artillery, War Office, 1903–4; QMG, India, 1904–8; OC, Quetta Division, 1908–12; AG, 1914–16; GOC-in-C, Southern Command, 1916–19. General, 1919.

Scobell, Henry Jenner (1859–1912). No previous war service. Took part in Lord Roberts' advance to Bloemfontein, and to Pretoria, 1900; operated in Transvaal, 1900; commanded a mobile column in the Cape Colony, 1901. Major-General, 1903. GOC, British troops in Cape Colony, and in charge of the Colony's administration, 1909–10.

Scott, Arthur Binney (1862–1944). Served in Anglo-Boer War, 1899–1902, for example as Lieutenant-Colonel in command of a mobile column, Western and Eastern Transvaal, 1901–2. Major-General, 1916. Served in World War I, 1914–18.

Seely, John Edward Bernhard (1868–1947). Saw action in South Africa as a member of the Imperial Yeomanry, 1900–1. Elected Conservative MP for the Isle of Wight (1900–4) while in South Africa. Liberal MP, Isle of Wight, 1904–6; Abercromby Division, Liverpool, 1906–10; Ilkeston Division, Derbyshire, 1910–22; Isle of Wight, 1923–4. Under-Secretary of State for Colonies, 1908–11; for War, 1911–12; Secretary of State for War, 1912–14. CO, Canadian Cavalry Brigade, 1914–18; Under-Secretary of State for Air, 1919; Chairman, National Savings Committee, 1926–43. Baron, 1933.

Settle, Henry Hamilton (1847–1923). Previous service in the Sudan, 1884–5 and 1888–9; at Takar, 1891. Co-ordinated anti-rebellion operations in the North-Western Cape Colony, 1900; anti-commando operations in the ORC and Transvaal, 1900; and Cape Colony, 1900–2. GOC, Cape Colony, 1902–3; Portsmouth Defences, 1905–8. Lieutenant-General, 1908.

Shekleton, Hugh Pentland (1860–1938). Previous service in Sudan, 1897–8. Lieutenant-Colonel commanding a column in the Western Transvaal, 1900–1. Later served in expedition to Dongola, 1906, and in World War I, 1914–18.

Smith, Donald Alexander, 1st Baron Strathcona and Mount Royal (1820–1914). Canadian financier. Conservative member of federal parliament, 1871–9;

played significant role in completion of Great Northern Railway, Canada, 1879, and Canadian Pacific Railway, 1885; Conservative MP for Montreal, 1887–96; Governor of Hudson's Bay Company since 1889; High Commissioner for Canada, 1896–1914. Baron, 1897. Raised at own expense Strathcona's Horse, a regiment of Canadian rough-riders, for service in South Africa, 1900.

Smith-Dorrien, Horace Lockwood (1858–1930). Previous service in Anglo-Zulu War, 1879; Egypt and Sudan, 1882 and 1884–5; Chitral, 1895; Tirah, 1897–8; Sudan, 1898. Commanded the 19th Brigade in South Africa, 1899–1900. Fought at Paardeberg; took part in advance to Bloemfontein, and to Pretoria, 1900; column commander, 1900–1. Major-General, 1901. AG, India, 1901–3; GOC, 4th Division, Quetta, 1903–7; GOC at Aldershot, 1907–12; Southern Command, 1912–14; II Corps and 2nd Army, 1914–15; East Africa, 1915–16; Governor of Gibraltar, 1918–23. Knighted, 1904.

Smuts, Jan Christiaan (or Christian) (1870–1950). Boer General. State Attorney of the Transvaal, 1898–1902. Saw action in Transvaal, 1900–1; Cape Colony, 1901–2. Colonial Secretary and Minister of Education in the Transvaal, 1907–10. Played key role in the formation of the Union of South Africa, 1910. MP, Union of South Africa, 1910–48; Minister of Defence, 1910–19 and 1939–48; of the Interior, 1910–12; of Finance, 1912–15; of Native Affairs, 1919–24; of Justice, 1933–9; of Foreign Affairs, 1939–48. Prime Minister, 1919–24 and 1939–48; Member of British War Cabinet, 1917–19. Created the Royal Air Force as an independent service, 1918. Field Marshal in the British Army, 1941.

Smuts, Sybella (Isie) Margaretha (née Krige) (1870–1954). Wife of General J.C. Smuts. Married 1897. They had six children that survived infancy: two sons and four daughters.

Smuts, Tobias (1861–1916). Previous service in war against Modjaj, 1890–1; against Mmalebôlô, 1894; against Magoeba, 1895; against Mphephu, 1897–8. Member of Transvaal Volksraad, 1899. Saw action in Natal, 1899–1900, first as Assistant-Commandant of the Ermelo commando, then (after the battle of Colenso, 15 December 1899) as Combat General; as Assistant Commandant-General commanding the Transvaal forces in the OFS, in an attempt to check Lord Roberts' advance, 1900; Transvaal, 1900–2. Deprived of his rank in August 1901 because, contrary to orders, he burned down Bremersdorp in Swaziland; fought to the end as an ordinary burgher. MP, 1910–16.

Spens, James (1853–1934). Previous service in Afghanistan, 1879–80. Commanded the 85th King's Light Infantry, 1899–1900; the 19th Brigade, 1900; and a mobile column, Transvaal, 1901–2. GOC, 12th (Eastern) Division, 1914–15; GOC, Australian Training Depot, 1915; GOC, Cairo District, 1915–16.

Spragge, Basil Edward (1852–1926). Previous service in Jowaki Expedition, 1877; Afghanistan, 1878–80; Burma, 1885–9. OC, 13th Battalion Imperial Yeomanry, OFS, 1900; surrendered at Lindley, 31 May 1900. Raised and commanded 2/1 Loyal Suffolk Hussars, 1914–16; on Staff of IV Corps, BEF, 1917–18.

Sprot, Alexander (1853–1929). Major; later Colonel. Previous service in Afghanistan, 1879–80. Took part in Lord Roberts' advance to Bloemfontein, and to Pretoria, 1900. Later served in World War I, 1914–18.

Stanley, Edward George Villiers, 17th Earl of Derby (1865–1948). Conservative MP for the West Houghton division of Lancashire, 1892–1906. Chief press censor, Cape Town, 1899–1900; Colonel, and Private Secretary to Lord Roberts, 1900. Financial Secretary, 1900–3; Postmaster-General, 1903–5; raised five battalions of King's Regiment, 1914; Director of Recruiting, 1915–16; Under-Secretary of State for War, 1916; Secretary of State for War, 1916–18 and 1922–4; Ambassador in Paris, 1918–20.

Stephenson, Theodore Edward (1856–1928). As Major-General GOC, 18th Brigade, South Africa, 1900 (for example took part in Lord Roberts' advance to Bloemfontein); GOC at Barberton, Eastern Transvaal, with charge of the Portuguese frontier, 1900–1; GOC, mobile columns, Cape Colony, 1901–2; GOC, Bloemfontein District and troops in ORC, 1902–4; GOC, Transvaal, 1904–6; acting C-in-C, South Africa, 1906; GOC, 6th Division, Colchester, 1906; GOC, 2nd Division, Aldershot, 1907–10; GOC, Straits Settlements and Malay Peninsula, 1910–14; GOC, 65th Division, 1916.

Steyn, Marthinus Theunis (1857–1916). Studied law in the Netherlands and in England (admitted to the Inner Temple, 1880; called to the bar, 1882). Attorney-General of the OFS, 1889; judge, 1889–96. President of the OFS, 1896–1902. Treated for ill health in Europe, 1902–5. Although still plagued by ill health, he played an important role in the reconstruction process after the war, and in the unification of South Africa.

Strathcona, Lord – see Smith, D.A.

Taylor, William (1843–1917). Surgeon-General. Previous service in Jowaki Expedition, 1877; Burma, 1885–6; Hazara Expedition, 1888; Burma, 1888–9; as Military-Medical Attaché in Japan-China War, 1894–5; Ashanti, 1895–6; Sudan, 1898. PMO, India, 1898–1901; Director-General, Army Medical Service, 1901–4.

Thorneycroft, Alexander Whitelaw (1859–1931). Previous service in Anglo-Zulu War, 1879; Sekhukhuneland, 1879; Transvaal War of Independence,1880–1. Raised two mounted corps of Natalians which became known as Thorneycroft's Mounted Infantry, 1899. Saw action in Natal, 1899–1900; anti-guerrilla operations in the OFS, Cape Colony and Transvaal, 1900–2.

Tucker, Charles (1838–1935). Previous service during Bhootan Expedition, 1865; at Perak, 1875; in Sekhukhuneland, 1878; Anglo-Zulu War, 1879. Major-General, 1893. Commanded the 7th Division in South Africa, 1900. Took part in relief of Kimberley and advance to Bloemfontein, and to Pretoria, 1900. Defended lines of communication in ORC, 1900–1; commanded several mobile columns, 1901–2. Lieutenant-General, 1902. C-in-C, Scottish District, 1903–5.

Victoria (1819–1901). Queen of the United Kingdom of Great Britain and Ireland, 1837–1901, and Empress of India, 1877–1901. Entirely approved of the policy of Lord Salisbury's government towards the Transvaal, especially as formulated and applied by Joseph Chamberlain. She keenly followed events in South Africa, and showed a sincere and constant interest in the welfare of her soldiers.

Vyvyan, Courtenay Bourchier (1858–1941). Previous service in Anglo-Zulu War, 1879. Saw action in South Africa, 1899–1902, first as a Major, then as Lieutenant-Colonel (for example siege of Mafikeng). Later served in World War I, 1914–18.

Waldersee, Alfred, Graf von (1832–1904). German Field Marshal. Chief of the Great General Staff, 1888–91. Commanded the Allied relief expedition to Peking (Beijing), 1900, but the Boxers had abandoned the siege before he arrived.

Ward, Edward Willis Duncan (1853–1928). Previous service in Sudan, 1885; Ashanti, 1895–6. Chief Supply Officer, Natal, 1899–1900 (besieged in Ladysmith). Director of Supplies to Lord Roberts, 1900. Under-Secretary of State for War, 1901–4; Secretary of the Army Council, 1904–14.

Warren, Charles (1840–1927). Previous service in 9th Frontier War, Cape Colony, 1877–8; Bechuanaland, 1884–5. Deputy C-in-C of British forces in South Africa and GOC, 5th Division, 1899–1900. Saw action in Natal, 1900; Military Governor, Griqualand West, Cape Colony, 1900. Returned to England, July 1900. General, 1904.

Wavell, Archibald Graham (1843–1935). Previous service in Anglo-Zulu War, 1879; Tembu and Basotho Campaigns,1880–1. OC, 15th Brigade, South Africa, 1900: took part in Lord Roberts' advance to Bloemfontein, and to Pretoria.

White, George Stuart (1835–1912). Previous service in suppression of Indian Mutiny, 1857–8; Afghanistan (VC), 1878–80; Egypt, 1884–5; Burma, 1885–9. Major-General, 1889; Lieutenant-General, 1895. C-in-C, India, 1893–7; QMG, War Office, 1897–9; GOC, Natal, 1899–1900. Defended Ladysmith during Boer siege, 1899–1900. Governor of Gibraltar, 1901–5. Field Marshal, 1902.

Willson, Mildmay Willson (1847–1912). Previous service in Sudan, 1884–5. As Major-General the GOC, military district to the west of Johannesburg, 1901–2; commanded mobile columns in that area, 1902.

Wilson, Henry Hughes (1864–1922). Previous service in Burma, 1886–7. OC, 4th Brigade Natal, 1899–1900, and took part in advance from Natal to the Transvaal, 1900. Served on Lord Roberts' Staff, 1900, with whom he returned to England. Commandant of Staff College, 1907–10; DMO, 1910–14; Assistant CGS to BEF, 1914–15; Liaison Officer with French Army, 1915; IV Corps, 1916; British Military Representative, Supreme War Council, 1917–18; Field Marshal; CIGS, 1918–22; Ulster Unionist MP, 1922. Assassinated.

Wilson, William Deane (1843–1921). Previous service in Afghanistan, 1878–80; Egypt, 1882–4; Sudan, 1884. Surgeon-General, 1898. Served in South Africa,

1899–1902: Kimberley front, 1899–1900; Lord Roberts' advance to Bloemfontein, and to Pretoria, 1900; anti-guerrilla operations, Transvaal and ORC, 1900–2.

Wing, Frederick Drummond Vincent (1860–1915). Saw action in Natal, 1899–1900 (besieged in Ladysmith); Transvaal and ORC, 1900–1; OC, mobile column, anti-guerrilla operations, Eastern Transvaal, 1901–2. Brevet Lieutenant-Colonel, 1900. ADC to C-in-C, 1903–4; Staff Officer, RA, 1907–10; AAG, War Office, 1910–13.

Wolmarans, Marthinus Johannes (1842–1920). Commandant of the Potchefstroom District commando. Saw action on the Kimberley front; wounded during siege of Mafikeng. Taken prisoner at Paardeberg, 27 February 1900, and sent to St Helena.

Wolseley, Garnet Joseph, 1st Viscount of Cairo and Wolseley (1833–1913). Previous service in 2nd Burma War, 1852–3; Crimean War, 1854–6; suppression of Indian Mutiny, 1857–8; China, 1860; Red River Expedition, Canada, 1870; Ashanti, 1873–4; Anglo-Zulu War, 1879; Egypt, 1882; Sudan, 1884–5. QMG, War Office, 1881–2; AG, 1882–90; C-in-C, Ireland, 1890–5; C-in-C, British Army, 1895–1901. Major-General, 1874; Lieutenant General, 1878; General, 1882; Viscount, 1885; Field Marshal, 1894.

Wood, Elliott (1844–1931). Previous service in Egypt, 1882–4; Sudan, 1885. Engineer-in-Chief, South Africa, 1899–1902, with local rank of Major-General.

Wood, Henry Evelyn (1838–1919). Previous service in the Crimean War, 1854–6; suppression of Indian Mutiny (VC), 1857–8; Ashanti, 1873; 9th Frontier War, Cape Colony, 1877–8; Anglo-Zulu War, 1879; Transvaal War of Independence,1880–1; Egypt, 1882. QMG, 1893–7; AG, 1897–1901. Major-General, 1882; Lieutenant-General, 1891; General, 1893; Field Marshal, 1905. GOC, 2nd Army Corps, Salisbury, 1901–5.

Wools-Sampson, Aubrey (1856–1924). Previous service in Sekhukhuneland, 1878; Anglo-Zulu War, 1879; Transvaal War of Independence,1880–1. A founder member of the Imperial Light Horse and an outstanding intelligence officer. Saw action in Natal, 1899–1900; Transvaal, 1900–2. Helped in suppressing the Bambatha Rebellion, Natal, 1906. Progressive MP for Parktown, Transvaal Legislative Assembly, 1907–10; Unionist MP for Braamfontein, Union of South Africa, 1910–15.

Wyndham, George (1863–1913). Conservative MP for Dover, 1889–1913; Under-Secretary of State for War, 1898–1900; Chief Secretary for Ireland, 1900–5.

Wynne, Arthur Singleton (1846–1936). Previous service in Jowaki Expedition, 1877; Afghanistan, 1878–9; Transvaal War of Independence,1880–1; Sudan, 1884–5. Saw action in South Africa, 1899–1901 (wounded): on Buller's Staff in Natal, 1899–1900; anti-guerrilla operations, Cape Colony, 1901.

Bibliography

A select list of the sources, manuscript and printed, used in this book. All books published in London unless otherwise stated.

Manuscript Sources

André Wessels Private Document Collection, Bloemfontein
G.F.R. Henderson (file)

Bodleian Library, Oxford
Milner Papers

British Library Manuscript Room, London
Airlie Papers
Arnold-Forster Papers
Balfour Papers
Campbell-Bannerman Papers
Hutton Papers
Lansdowne Papers
Wade Papers
War Office Papers
Weil Papers

Churchill Archives Centre, Cambridge
Esher Papers
Winston Churchill Papers

Devon Record Office, Exeter
Buller Papers, 2065

Gloucestershire Record Office, Gloucester
Sir Michael Hicks Beach Papers, D2455

House of Lords Record Office, London
Lloyd George Papers, A/9/2
Stanley Papers, ST/12/3

Hove Central Library
Wolseley Papers

Imperial War Museum, London
Esher Papers, 70/8
General Sir Horace Smith-Dorrien Papers, 87/47

Killie Campbell Africana Library, Durban
Various documents

Lambeth Palace Library, London
Archbishop Frederick Temple Papers – Official Letters, 1899–1902
Archbishop Randall Davidson Papers – Official Letters, 1899–1902

Liddell Hart Centre for Military Archives, London
Ian Hamilton Papers, 1/1, 2/1, 2/3–5, 3/1, 3/2/5, 4/2/8, 7/10/12, 17/6

National Archives of South Africa, Pretoria
K.G. 737–8, 743, 760–1, 854, 927
Microfilm Collection, M672–3, M722, M727, M812–16, M2939, M3140
P.A. Nierstrasz, Der süd-afrikanische Krieg, 1899–1902 (typed manuscript)
Photocopy Collection, FK 1894–1911
Roberts Papers, 60 volumes

National Army Museum, London
Hector Macdonald Papers, 7309–59
Hunter-Weston Papers, 6503–39
Lord Rawlinson Papers, 5201–33
Maxwell Papers, 7807–25
R.G. Broadwood Papers, 75–8–34
Roberts Papers, 7101–23
Spenser Wilkinson Papers, 9011–42

Public Record Office, Kew
Kitchener Papers, PRO 30/57/16–25
Roberts Papers, WO 105/5–40
St John Brodrick Papers, PRO 30/67/6

The Royal Archives, Windsor
King Edward VII Papers
Queen Victoria Papers

Scottish Record Office, Edinburgh
General Register House
Major-General Dundonald Papers, vols GD 233/124/1–4; 233/128–9;
233/130/1; 233/131; 233/135; 233/142/2; 233/143/1; 233/145–6;
233/162/2; 233/157/1–2; 233/177/111

West Register House
  Duke of Hamilton Papers (GD 406), vol. 1819
  Furgusson of Kilkerran Papers, (NRA(S) 3572) / 12/27

South African National Museum of Military History, Johannesburg
  J.D.P. French, Boer War Diary, 9ᵗʰ November 1899 – 17ᵗʰ March 1900 (manuscript)

The Sudan Archive, University of Durham
  Rundle Papers, 231/1, 231/3

Published Papers

Beckett, I.F.W. (ed.), *The Army and the Curragh Incident, 1914* (Army Records Society Vol. 2, 1986).

Guy, A.J. *et al.* (eds), *Military Miscellany I. Manuscripts from the Seven Years War, the First and Second Sikh Wars and the First World War* (Army Records Society Vol. 12, Stroud, 1996).

Hancock, W.K. and J. van der Poel (eds), *Selections from the Smuts Papers* (Vol. 1, Cambridge, 1966).

Headlam, C. (ed.), *The Milner Papers* (2 vols, 1931–33).

Robson, B. (ed.), *Roberts in India. The Military Papers of Field Marshal Lord Roberts 1876–1893* (Army Records Society Vol. 9, Stroud, 1993).

Official Publications

Army. Correspondence between Field-Marshal Lord Roberts, Commanding-in-Chief, South African Field Force, and Acting Commandant-General Louis Botha, dated 12ᵗʰ, 13ᵗʰ, 14ᵗʰ and 15ᵗʰ June, 1900 (Cd. 461, 1901).

—— *Findings of a Court of Enquiry held at Barberton on 25ᵗʰ September, 1900, to Investigate the Circumstances under which Lieutenant-Colonel B.E. Spragge, D.S.O., XIIIᵗʰ Bn. Imperial Yeomanry, and Others, became Prisoners of War* (Cd. 470, 1901).

—— *Proclamations Issued by Field-Marshal Lord Roberts in South Africa* (Cd. 426, 1900).

—— *Report by Lieut.-General Sir H.E. Colvile, K.C.M.G., C.B., on the Operations of the Ninth Division at Paardeberg* (Cd. 520, 1901).

—— *Return of Military Forces in South Africa 1899–1902* (Cd. 990, 1902).

Correspondence relating to the Prolongation of Hostilities in South Africa (Cd. 732, 1901).

Correspondence relative to the Treatment of Natives by the Boers (Cd. 821, 1901).

Correspondence with the Netherlands Government regarding the War in South Africa (Cd. 906, 1902).

Further Correspondence relative to the Treatment of Natives by the Boers (Cd. 822, 1901, Cd. 888, 1902).

Kestell, J.D. and D.E. van Velden, *The Peace Negotiations between the Governments of the South African Republic and the Orange Free State, and the Representatives of the British Government, which terminated in the Peace concluded at Vereeniging on the 31ˢᵗ May, 1902* (1912).

List of Casualties in the Army in South Africa, from 1ˢᵗ January, 1902, to the 31ˢᵗ May, 1902 (S.l., s.a.).

Notulen der Verrichtingen van den Hed. Volksraad van den Oranje Vrijstaat in zijne Gewone Jaarlijkse Zitting aanvangende op Maandag, den 5den April 1897 (Bloemfontein, 1897).

The Official Army List for the Quarter Ending 21ˢᵗ December 1899 (s.a.).

Papers relating to the Administration of Martial Law in South Africa (Cd. 981, 1902).

Proceedings of a Court of Enquiry i.e. Enquiry held at St. Stephen's House, Westminster, S.W., on the Administration of the Army Remount Department since January 1899, by Order of the Commander-in-Chief dated 20ᵗʰ February 1902 (Cd. 993, 1902).

Report of His Majesty's Commissioners Appointed to Inquire into the Military Preparations and other Matters connected with the War in South Africa (Cd. 1789, 1903).

Report on the Concentration Camps in South Africa by the Committee of Ladies appointed by the Secretary of State for War, containing Reports on the Camps in Natal, the Orange River Colony, and the Transvaal (Cd. 893, 1902).

Return of Buildings burnt in each Month from June, 1900, to January, 1901 including Farm Buildings, Mills, Cottages and Hovels (Cd. 524, 1901).

Return of Military Forces in South Africa, 1899–1902 (Cd. 892, 1902).

Royal Commission on South African Hospitals. Appendix to Minutes of Evidence taken before the Royal Commission Appointed to Consider and Report upon the Care and Treatment of the Sick and Wounded during the South African Campaign (Cd. 455, 1901).

—— *Minutes of Evidence taken before the Royal Commission Appointed to Consider and Report upon the Care and Treatment of the Sick and Wounded during the South African Campaign* (Cd. 454, 1901).

—— *Report of the Royal Commission Appointed to Consider and Report upon the Care and Treatment of the Sick and Wounded during the South African Campaign* (Cd. 453, 1901).

—— *Minutes of Evidence taken before the Royal Commission on the War in South Africa* (2 vols, Cd. 1790 and Cd. 1791, 1903).

—— *Appendices to the Minutes of Evidence taken before the Royal Commission on the War in South Africa* (Cd. 1792, 1903).

South Africa. Correspondence, &c. between the Commander-in-Chief in South Africa and the Boer Commanders so far as it Effects the Destruction of Property (Cd. 582, 1901).

South Africa. Correspondence respecting Terms of Surrender of the Boer Forces in the Field (Cd. 1096, 1902).

South Africa Despatches. Despatch by General Lord Kitchener, dated 8ᵗʰ March, 1901, relative to Military Operations in South Africa (Cd. 522, 1901).

—— *Despatch by General Lord Kitchener, dated 1ˢᵗ June, 1902, relative to Military Operations in South Africa* (Cd. 986, 1902).

—— *Despatches by General Lord Kitchener, dated 8ᵗʰ August, 8ᵗʰ September, and 8ᵗʰ October, 1901, relative to Military Operations in South Africa, including a Supplementary Despatch, dated 18ᵗʰ October, on the Actions at Itala Mount, Fort Prospect, and Moedwil* (Cd. 820, 1901).

—— *Despatch by General Lord Kitchener, 8ᵗʰ March, 1902, relative to Military Operations in South Africa* (Cd. 970, 1902).

—— *Despatch by General Lord Kitchener, 8ᵗʰ May, 1901, relative to Military Operations in South Africa* (Cd. 605, 1901).

—— *Vol. I* (Cd. 457, 1901).

—— *Vol. II. Natal Field Army* (Cd. 458, 1901).

—— *Vol. I. From 1ˢᵗ November 1899 to 1ˢᵗ August 1900* (*S.l.*, *s.a.*).

South Africa. Vols I. to VI. Telegrams and Letters sent by Field-Marshal Lord Roberts K.P., G.C.B., V.C. &c. From 23ʳᵈ December 1899 to 26ᵗʰ December 1900 (*S.l.*, *s.a.*).

—— *1900. Field-Marshal Lord Roberts, K.P., &c. 1. – Proclamations. 2. – Army Orders* (1901).

—— *Further Correspondence relating to Affairs in South Africa* (Cd. 43, 261, 420, 1900; Cd. 903, 1902).

—— *Further Papers relating to Negotiations between Commandant Louis Botha and Lord Kitchener* (Cd. 663, 1901).

—— *Papers relating to Negotiations between Commandant Louis Botha and Lord Kitchener* (Cd. 528, 1901).

—— *Report from Lieut.-General Lord Methuen on the Action that took place near Tweebosch on 7ᵗʰ March 1902* (Cd. 967, 1902).

—— *Returns of Farm Buildings, &c., in Cape Colony and Natal destroyed by the Boers* (Cd. 979, 1902).

—— *Revised Reprint of the Principal Army Orders and Cape Colony District Orders from the Outbreak of Hostilities to the End of July, 1901 with the Principal Head Quarters' Circular Memos, for 1900 and 1901 (for Reference)* (Cape Town, *s.a.*).

—— *The Spion Kop Despatches* (Cd. 968, 1902).

—— *Telegrams concerning the Siege of Ladysmith* (Cd. 987, 1902).

South African War, 1899–1902. Confidential Telegrams. 12ᵗʰ October 1899 to 1ˢᵗ October 1902 (*S.l.*, *s.a.*).

—— *1899–1900. Vol. I. Home and Oversea Correspondence by Field-Marshal Lord Roberts K.P., G.C.B., V.C., &c., &c., from 12ᵗʰ December, 1899, to 4ᵗʰ June, 1900* (*S.l.*, *s.a.*).

—— *1899–1900. Vol. II. Home and Oversea Correspondence of Field-Marshal Lord*

Roberts K.P., G.C.B., V.C., &c., &c., from 5ᵗʰ June to 5ᵗʰ September, 1900 (S.l., s.a.).

—— *1899–1901. Vol. III. Home and Oversea Correspondence of Field-Marshal Lord Roberts K.P., G.C.B., V.C., &c., &c., from 5ᵗʰ September, 1900, to 1ˢᵗ January, 1901 (S.l., s.a.).*

Staats-almanak voor de Zuid-Afrikaanse Republiek 1899 (Pretoria, 1898).

Statistics of the Refugee Camps (Cd. 1161, 1902).

Works of Reference

Bruce, G., *Harbottle's Dictionary of Battles* (2ⁿᵈ ed., 1979).

The Dictionary of National Biography (*DNB*, 29 vols, 1967–81).

Dictionary of South African Biography (*DSAB*, 5 vols, Cape Town, Durban and Pretoria, 1968–87).

Hazlehurst, C. and C. Woodland (compilers), *A Guide to the Papers of British Cabinet Ministers 1900–1951* (1974).

Hepworth, P., *Archives and Manuscripts in Libraries* (2ⁿᵈ ed., 1964).

Standard Encyclopaedia of Southern Africa (*SESA*, 12 vols, Cape Town, 1970–76).

Uys, I., *South African Military Who's Who 1452–1992* (Germiston, 1992).

Wessels, A., *Suid-Afrikaanse Verhandelinge en Proefskrifte oor die Geskiedenis van die Anglo-Boereoorlog. 'n Bronnestudie* (Pretoria, 1987).

Who was Who 1897–1960 (5 vols, 1935–67).

Biographies, Autobiographies, Published Diaries and Other Memoirs

Arthur, G., *Life of Lord Kitchener* (3 vols, 1920).

Brits, J.P. (ed.), *Diary of a National Scout. P.J. du Toit 1900–1902* (Pretoria, 1902).

Brodrick, W. St J.F., *Records and Reactions, 1856–1939* (1939).

Brooke-Hunt, V., *Lord Roberts. A Biography* (1900).

Butler, L., *Sir Redvers Buller* (1909).

Cairnes, W.E., *Lord Roberts as a Soldier in Peace and War. A Biography* (1901).

Churchill, W.S., *London to Ladysmith via Pretoria* (1900).

Cobban, J.M., *The Life and Deeds of Earl Roberts* (4 vols, Edinburgh and London, 1901).

Colvile, H.E., *The Work of the Ninth Division in South Africa 1900* (1901).

Comaroff, J.L. (ed.), *The Boer War Diary of Sol T. Plaatje, an African at Mafeking* (1973).

De Watteville, H., *Lord Roberts* (1938).

De Wet, C.R., *Three Years War (October 1899–June 1902)* (1902).

Dundonald, Earl of, *My Army Life* (1926).

Durand, M., *The Life of Field Marshal Sir George White* (2 vols, 1915).

Engelenburg, F.V., *General Louis Botha* (1929).

Forrest, G., *The Life of Lord Roberts, K.G., V.C.* (1914).

French, G., *The Life of Field Marshal Sir John French, First Earl of Ypres* (1931).

Grew, E.S., *Field Marshal Lord Kitchener. His Life and Work for the Empire* (vol. II, 1916).

Groser, H.G., *Field Marshal Lord Roberts* (1900).

Hamilton, I., *The Happy Warrior – A Life of General Sir Ian Hamilton* (1966).

Hancock, W.K., *Smuts* (vol. 1, Cambridge, 1962).

Hodges, A., *Lord Kitchener* (1936).

James, D., *Lord Roberts* (1954).

Kestell, J.D., *Through Shot and Flame* (Johannesburg, 1976).

Lehman, J.H., *All Sir Garnet. A Life of Field Marshal Lord Wolseley* (1964).

Lyttelton, N., *Eighty Years* (1927).

Magnus, P., *Kitchener. Portrait of an Imperialist* (1958).

Maritz, S.G., *My Lewe en Strewe* (Pretoria, 1939).

Maxwell, H., *The Life of Wellington. The Restoration of the Martial Power of Great Britain* (2 vols, 3rd ed., 1900).

Meintjes, J., *Sword in the Sand. The Life and Death of Gideon Scheepers* (Cape Town, 1969).

Melville, C.H., *Life of General the Right Hon. Sir Redvers Buller* (2 vols, 1923).

Newton, Lord, *Lord Lansdowne. A Biography* (1929).

Oberholster, A.G. (ed.), *Oorlogsdagboek van Jan F.E. Cilliers 1899–1902* (Pretoria, 1978).

Powell, G., *Buller: A Scapegoat? A Life of General Sir Redvers Henry Buller 1839–1908* (1994).

Preller, G.S., *Scheepers se Dagboek en die Stryd in Kaapland (1 Okt. 1901 – 18 Jan 1902)* (Cape Town, 1938).

Reckitt, B.N., *The Lindley Affair. A Diary of the Boer War* (Hull, 1972).

Reitz, D., *Commando. A Boer Journal of the Boer War* (1929).

Roberts, F.S., *Forty-One Years in India* (1897).

Smit, A.P. and Maré, L., (eds), *Die Beleg van Mafeking. Dagboek van Abraham Stafleu* (Pretoria, 1985).

Van der Merwe, N.J., *Marthinus Theunis Steyn. 'n Lewensbeskrywing* (2 vols, Cape Town, 1921).

Van Rensburg, T. (ed.), *Vir Vaderland, Vryheid en Eer. Oorlogsherinneringe van Wilhelm Mangold 1899–1902* (Pretoria, 1988).

Viljoen, B., *My Reminiscences of the Anglo-Boer War* (1902).

Warren, H., *Christian Victor. The Story of a Young Soldier* (2nd ed., 1903).

Wessels, A. (ed.), *Anglo-Boer War Diary of Herbert Gwynne Howell* (Pretoria, 1986).

——, 'Die Oorlogsherinneringe van kommandant Jacob Petrus Neser', *Christiaan de Wet Annals* 7 (March 1988).

Wheeler, H.F.B., *The Story of Lord Roberts* (1915).

Williams, W.W., *The Life of General Sir Charles Warren* (Oxford, 1941).

Secondary Works

Amery, L.S. (ed.), *The Times History of the War in South Africa 1899–1902* (7 vols, 1900–9).

Bakkes, C.M., *Die Britse Deurbraak aan die Benede-Tugela op Majubadag 1900* (Pretoria, 1973).

Barnard, C.J., *Generaal Louis Botha op die Natalse Front, 1899–1900* (Cape Town, 1970).

Bond, B., *The Victorian Army and the Staff College* (1972).

Breytenbach, J.H., *Die Geskiedenis van die Tweede Vryheidsoorlog in Suid-Afrika, 1899–1902* (6 vols, Pretoria, 1969–96).

——, *Gedenkalbum van die Tweede Vryheidsoorlog* (Cape Town, 1949).

—— and Ploeger, J., *Majuba Gedenkboek* (Roodepoort, 1980).

Burke, P., *The Siege of O'okiep (Guerrilla Campaign in the Anglo-Boer War)* (Bloemfontein, 1995).

Burleigh, B., *The Natal Campaign* (1900).

Churchill, W.S., *Ian Hamilton's March* (1900).

Curtis, L., *With Milner in South Africa* (Oxford, 1951).

Cuthbertson, G. and Cadell, E-M., *The Jameson Raid. A Centennial Retrospective* (Johannesburg, 1996).

Davitt, M., *The Boer Fight for Freedom, from the Beginning of Hostilities to the Peace of Pretoria* (3rd ed., New York, 1902).

De Villiers, O.T., *Met De Wet en Steyn in het Veld. Avonturen, Ervaringen en Indrukken* (Amsterdam, 1903).

De Wet, A. *et al.*, *Die Buren in der Kapkolonie im Kriege mit England* (Munich, *s.a.*).

Dooner, M.G., *The "Last Post": being a Roll of All Officers (Naval, Military or Colonial) who gave their Lives for their Queen, King and Country, in the South African War, 1899–1902 (s.a.)*.

Doyle, A.C., *The Great Boer War* (1902).

Du Plessis, P.J., *Oomblikke van Spanning* (Cape Town, 1938).

Duxbury, G.R., *The Battle of Magersfontein 11th December 1899* (2nd ed., Johannesburg, 1979).

Eloff, C.C., *Oranje-Vrystaat en Basoetoland, 1884–1902. 'n Verhoudingstudie* (Pretoria, 1984).

Farwell, B., *Queen Victoria's Little Wars* (1973).

Fortescue, J.W., *The Empire and the Army* (1928).

Fuller, J.F.C., *The Last of the Gentlemen's Wars* (1937).

Furgusson, T.G., *British Military Intelligence, 1870–1914. The Development of a Modern Intelligence Organization* (Frederick, 1984).

Gardner, B., *The Lion's Cage* (1969).

——, *Mafeking. A Victorian Legend* (1966).

The German Official Account of the War in South Africa (2 vols, 1904–6).

Girouard, P., *History of the Railways during the War in South Africa* (Chatham, 1904).

Goldmann, C.S., *With General French and the Cavalry in South Africa* (1902).

Gooch, J., *The Plans of War. The General Staff and British Military Strategy, c.1900–1916* (1974).

Grinnell-Milne, D.W., *Baden-Powell at Mafeking* (1957).

Grundlingh, A.M., *Die "Hendsoppers" en "Joiners". Die Rasionaal en Verskynsel van Verraad* (Pretoria, 1979).

Hattingh, J. and Wessels, A., *Britse Fortifikasies in die Anglo-Boereoorlog (1899–1902)* (Bloemfontein, 1997).

Hobhouse, E., *The Brunt of War and Where it Fell* (1902).

Iwan Müller, E.B., *Lord Milner and South Africa* (1902).

Jordaan, G., *Hoe zij Stierven. Mededelingen aangaande het Einde dergeven, aan wie gedurende de Oorlog 1899–1902, in de Kaap-Kolonie het Doodvonnis Voltrokken is* (Cape Town, 1917).

Kiernan, V.G., *European Armies from Conquest to Collapse, 1815–1960* (1982).

Knox, E.B., *Buller's Campaign with the Natal Field Force of 1900* (1900).

Krüger, D.W., *Die Krugermiljoene* (Johannesburg, 1979).

Kruger, R., *Good-bye Dolly Gray. A History of the Boer War* (1967).

Lehman, J.H., *The First Boer War* (1972).

Le May, G.H.L., *British Supremacy in South Africa 1899–1907* (Oxford, 1965).

Luvaas, J., *The Education of an Army. British Military Thought, 1815–1940* (1965).

Maurice, J.F. (ed.) and Grant, M.H., *History of the War in South Africa 1899–1902* (4 vols, 1906–10).

Maydon, J.G., *French's Cavalry Campaign* (1902).

McDonald, R.D., *In die Skaduwee van die Dood* (Cape Town, 1943).

Meintjes, J., *Stormberg. A Lost Opportunity* (Kaapstad, 1969).

Moore, D.M., *General Botha's Second Expedition to Natal during the Anglo-Boer War, September–October 1901* (Cape Town, 1979).

Nasson, B., *Abraham Esau's War. A Black South African War in the Cape 1899–1902* (African Studies Series 68, Cambridge, 1991).

Naudé, J.F., *Vechten en vluchten van Beyers en Kemp "Bôkant" De Wet* (Rotterdam, s.a.).

Pakenham, T., *The Boer War* (1979).

Pemberton, W.B., *Battles of the Boer War* (1964).

Pieterse, H.C.J., *Oorlogsavonture van genl. Wynand Malan* (Kaapstad, 1946).

Ploeger, J., *Die Fortifikasie van Pretoria. Fort Klapperkop – Gister en Vandag* (Pretoria, 1968).

Preller, G.S., *Talana. Die Driegeneraalslag by Dundee met Lewensskets van genl. Daniel Erasmus* (Kaapstad, 1942).

Rabie, J.E., *Generaal C.R. de Wet se Krygsleiding by Sannaspas en Groenkop* (Pretoria, 1980).

Ransford, O., *The Battle of Spion Kop* (1969).

Reynolds, E.G.B., *The Lee-Enfield Rifle* (1960).

Sampson, V. and Hamilton, I., *Anti-Commando* (1931).

Scholtz, G.D., *Die Oorsake van die Tweede Vryheidsoorlog 1899–1902* (2 vols, Johannesburg, 1948).

Sessions, H., *Two Years with the Remount Commission* (1903).

Sibbald, R., *The War Correspondents. The Boer War* (Dover (USA), 1993).

Sixsmith, E.K.G., *British Generalship in the Twentieth Century* (1970).

Smith, I.R., *The Origins of the South African War, 1899–1902* (1996).

Spies, S.B., *Methods of Barbarism? Roberts and Kitchener and Civilians in the Boer Republics, January 1900–May 1902* (Cape Town, 1977).

Stirling, J., *The Colonials in South Africa, 1899–1902. Their Record, based on the Despatches* (1907).

——, *Our Regiments in South Africa 1899–1902. Their Record, based on the Despatches* (1907).

Strydom, C.J.S., *Kaapland en die Tweede Vryheidsoorlog* (Kaapstad, 1943).

Symons, J., *Buller's Campaign* (1963).

Tylden, G., *The Armed Forces of South Africa with an Appendix on the Commandos* (Johannesburg, 1954).

Vallentin, W., *Der Burenkrieg* (Leipzig, 1903).

Van Jaarsveld, F.A. *et al.* (eds), *Die Eerste Vryheidsoorlog. Van Verset en Geweld tot Skikking deur Onderhandeling 1877–1884* (Pretoria, 1980).

Van Zyl, M.C., *Majuba. Die Onafhanklikheidsoorlog van die Transvaalse Afrikaners (1880–1881)* (Pretoria, 1980).

Warwick, P., *Black People and the South African War, 1899–1902* (Cambridge, 1983).

—— (ed.), *The South African War. The Anglo-Boer War, 1899–1902* (Harlow, 1980).

Wessels, A., *Die Anglo-Boereoorlog 1899–1902. 'n Oorsig van die Militêre Verloop van die Stryd* (Bloemfontein, 1991).

——, *Die Militêre Rol van Swart Mense, Bruin Mense en Indiërs tydens die Anglo-Boereoorlog (1899–1902)* (Bloemfontein, 1998).

——, *The Phases of the Anglo-Boer War 1899–1902* (Bloemfontein, 1998).

Wheeler, O., *The War Office Past and Present* (1914).

Yardley, J.W., *With the Inniskilling Dragoons. The Record of a Cavalry Regiment during the Boer War, 1899–1902* (1904).

Articles

Barnard, C.J., 'General Buller in the Spioenkop Campaign, January 1900', *Military History Journal* 2(1), June 1971, pp. 1–7, 14.

Botha, H.J., 'Die Moord op Derdepoort, 25 November 1899. Nie-Blankes in Oorlogsdiens', *Militaria* 1(2), 1969, pp. 3–98.

Du Preez, S., 'Die Val van Pretoria', *Militaria* 5(3), 1975, pp. 22–39.

Gomm, N., 'Commandant P.H. Kritzinger in the Cape, December 1900 – December 1901', *Military History Journal* 1(7), December 1970, pp. 30–2, 34.

Green, H., 'Spion Kop. The Nadir of British Generalship', *Army Quarterly* 94(2), 1970, pp. 242–50.

Morton, R.F., 'Linchwe I and the Kgatla Campaign in the South African War, 1899–1902', *The Journal of African History* 26(2 & 3), 1985, pp. 169–90.

Nel, H.F., 'Die Slag van Donkerhoek 11–12 Junie 1900', *Militaria* 15(1), 1985, pp. 52–8 and 15(2), 1985, pp. 17–30.

Pretorius, F., 'Die Eerste Dryfjag op hoofkmdt. C.R. de Wet', *Christiaan de Wet Annals* 4, October 1976.

Schoeman, K., 'Die Dood van Abraham Esau. Ooggetuieberigte uit die besette Calvinia, 1901', *Quarterly Bulletin of the South African Library* 40(2), December 1985, pp. 56–66.

Smith, I.R., 'The Origins of the South African War (1899–1902). A Reappraisal', *South African Historical Journal* 22, November 1990, pp. 24–60.

Watt, S.A., 'The Anglo-Boer War: The Medical Arrangements and Implications thereof during the British Occupation of Bloemfontein: March–August 1900', *Military History Journal* 9(2), 1992, pp. 44–54.

Wessels, A. (ed.), 'Irish Nationalists and South Africa, 1877–1902 (by J.L. McCracken)', *Christiaan de Wet Annals* 5, October 1978, pp. 157–84.

Wulfsohn, L., 'Elands River. A Siege which possibly Changed the Course of History in South Africa', *Military History Journal* 6(3), June 1984, pp. 106–8.

Theses

Bakkes, C.M., 'Die Militêre Situasie aan die Benede-Tugela op die Vooraand van die Britse Deurbraak by Pietershoogte (26 Februarie 1900)', M.A., University of Pretoria, 1966 (Published in *Archives Year Book for South African History* 30(1), 1967).

Basson, J.L., 'Die Slag van Paardeberg', unpublished M.A., University of Pretoria, 1972.

Boltman, J.C., 'In how far was the Quarrel between Sir Alfred Milner and the Pretoria Government on the Franchise Question the Real Cause of the South African War of 1899 to 1902?', unpublished M.A., University of Cape Town, 1943.

Botha, J.P., 'Die Beleg van Mafeking tydens die Anglo-Boereoorlog', unpublished D.Litt., University of South Africa, 1967.

Breytenbach, A.E., 'Die Slag by Donkerhoek, 11–12 Junie 1900', unpublished M.A., University of South Africa, 1980.

Breytenbach, J.H., 'Die Diplomatieke Voorspel tot die Tweede Vryheidsoorlog', unpublished D.Phil., University of Stellenbosch, 1944.

Broos, E., 'Die Noordelike Hooflaer in die Distrikte Zoutpansberg, Waterberg en Rustenburg, vanaf die Begin van die Tweede Vryheidsoorlog tot die Besetting van Pretoria', unpublished M.A., University of Pretoria, 1943.

Buys, M.H., 'Militêre Regering in Transvaal, 1900–1902', unpublished D.Phil., University of Pretoria, 1973.

Cilliers, J.H., 'Die Slag van Spioenkop (24 January 1900)', M.A., University of Pretoria, 1957 (Published in *Archives Year Book for South African History* 23(2), 1960).

Delport, P.J., 'Die Rol van genl. Marthinus Prinsloo gedurende die Tweede Vryheidsoorlog', unpublished M.A., University of the Orange Free State, 1973.

Du Plooy, W.J., 'Die Militêre Voorbereidings en Verloop van die Jameson-inval', unpublished M.A., University of Pretoria, 1959.

Du Preez, S.J., 'Vredespogings gedurende die Anglo-Boereoorlog tot Maart 1901', unpublished M.A., University of Pretoria, 1977.

——, 'Die Vrede van Vereeniging', unpublished D.Phil., University of Pretoria, 1986.

Fourie, L.M., 'Die Militêre Loopbaan van Manie Maritz tot aan die Einde van die Anglo-Boereoorlog', unpublished M.A., Potchefstroom University for Christian Higher Education, 1976.

Hugo, M.J. 'Die Kruger-ultimatum. Vier Maande van Spanning', unpublished M.A., University of Pretoria, 1943.

——, 'Die Stemregvraagstuk in die Zuid-Afrikaanse Republiek', D.Phil., University of Pretoria, 1946 (Published in *Archives Year Book for South African History*, 10, 1947).

Kruger, C.J.H., 'Militêre Bewind in die Oranje-Vrystaat, Maart, 1900–Januarie, 1901', unpublished M.A., University of Pretoria, 1958.

Maphalala, S.J., 'The participation of Zulus in the Anglo-Boer War', unpublished M.A., University of Zululand, 1979.

Mocke, H.A., 'Die Slag van Colenso. 15 Desember 1899', unpublished M.A., University of Pretoria, 1967.

Oosthuizen, J., 'Jacobus Hercules de la Rey en die Tweede Vryheidsoorlog', unpublished D.Litt., Potchefstroom University College, 1950.

Pienaar, A.J., 'Christiaan Roedolf de Wet in die Anglo-Boereoorlog', unpublished M.A., Potchefstroom University for Christian Higher Education, 1975.

Pyper, P.A., 'Generaal J.C. Smuts en die Tweede Vryheidsoorlog (1899–1902)', unpublished M.A., Potchefstroom University for Christian Higher Education, 1960.

Scholtz, W.L. von R., 'Generaal Christiaan de Wet as Veldheer', unpublished D.Litt., University of Leiden, 1978.

Schultz, B.G., 'Die Slag van Bergendal (Dalmanutha)', unpublished M.A., University of Pretoria, 1974.

Siwundhla, H.T., 'The participation of Non-Europeans in the Anglo-Boer War, 1899–1902', unpublished Ph.D., Claremont (USA), 1977.

Snyman, J.H., 'Die Afrikaner in Kaapland, 1899–1902', D.Litt., Potchefstroom University for Christian Higher Education, 1974 (Published in *Archives Year Book for South African History* 42(2), 1979).

——, 'Rebelle-verhoor in Kaapland gedurende die Tweede Vryheidsoorlog met spesiale Verwysing na die Militêre Howe, 1899–1902', M.A., University of

South Africa, 1961 (Published in *Archives Year Book for South African History* 25, 1962).

Strydom, C.J.S., 'Die Kaapkolonie, 1899–1902: Skadevergoeding en die Rebelle in Ere herstel', unpublished Ph.D., University of Cape Town, 1932.

Terblanche, H.J., 'Die Beleg van Kimberley', unpublished M.A., Potchefstroom University for Christian Higher Education, 1973.

Visser, G.R., 'Pres. M.T. Steyn in die Anglo-Boereoorlog', unpublished M.A., University of the Orange Free State, 1977.

Wessels, A., 'Die Britse Militêre Strategie tydens die Anglo-Boereoorlog tot en met die Buller-fase', unpublished D.Phil., University of the Orange Free State, 1986.

Index

ARMY RECORDS SOCIETY
(FOUNDED 1984)

Members of the Society are entitled to purchase back volumes
at reduced prices.
Orders should be sent to the Hon. Treasurer, Army Records Society,
c/o National Army Museum,
Royal Hospital Road,
London SW3 4HT

The Society has already issued:

Vol. I:
The Military Correspondence of
Field Marshal Sir Henry Wilson 1918–1922
Edited by Dr Keith Jeffery

Vol. II:
The Army and the
Curragh Incident, 1914
Edited by Dr Ian F.W. Beckett

Vol. III:
The Napoleonic War Journal of
Captain Thomas Henry Browne, 1807–1816
Edited by Roger Norman Buckley

Vol. IV:
An Eighteenth-Century Secretary at War
The Papers of William, Viscount Barrington
Edited by Dr Tony Hayter

Vol. V:
The Military Correspondence of
Field Marshal Sir William Robertson 1915–1918
Edited by David R. Woodward

Vol. VI:
Colonel Samuel Bagshawe and the
Army of George II, 1731–1762
Edited by Dr Alan J. Guy

Vol. VII:
Montgomery and the Eighth Army
Edited by Stephen Brooks

Vol. VIII:
The British Army and Signals Intelligence
during the First World War
Edited by John Ferris

Vol. IX:
Roberts in India
The Military Papers of Field Marshal Lord Roberts 1876–1893
Edited by Brian Robson

Vol. X:
Lord Chelmsford's Zululand Campaign 1878–1879
Edited by John P.C. Laband

Vol. XI:
Letters of a Victorian Army Officer:
Edward Wellesley 1840–1854
Edited by Michael Carver

Vol. XII:
Military Miscellany I
Papers from the Seven Years War,
the Second Sikh War and the First World War
Editors: Alan J. Guy, R.N.W. Thomas
and Gerard J. De Groot

Vol. XIII:
John Peebles' American War 1776–1782
Edited by Ira J. Gruber

Vol. XIV:
The Maratha War Papers of Arthur Wellesley
Edited by Anthony S. Bennell

Vol. XV:
The Letters of Lieutenant-Colonel Charles à Court Repington
1903–1918
Edited by A.J.A. Morris

Vol. XVI:
Sir Hugh Rose and the Central India Campaign 1858
Edited by Brian Robson